Healing A Nation

A Testimony

WAGING AND WINNING
A PEACEFUL REVOLUTION TO UNITE
AND HEAL A BROKEN RWANDA

Dr. Theogene Rudasingwa

ISBN: 1481857657
ISBN-13: 9781481857659

LCCN 2013901084
CreateSpace Independent Publishing Platform
North Charleston, South Carolina

We are never completely contemporaneous
with our present. History advances in disguise;
it appears on stage wearing the mask of the
preceding scene, and we tend to lose the meaning
of the play. Each time the curtain rises, continuity
has to be re-established. The blame, of course is
not history's, but lies in our vision, encumbered
with memory and images learned in the past. We
see the past superimposed on the present, even
when the present is a revolution.

Regis Debray, *Revolution in the Revolution*

Dedicated to my mother (Mama),
Coletta Bamususire

CONTENTS

PROLOGUE

It was very early in the morning. My mother (whom I call Mama in this book), Coletta Bamususire, had had a busy night contemplating what to do next. Mama, like many of tens of thousands of Rwandan refugees, had found herself in the Oruchinga refugee camp, Mbarara district, in southwest Uganda. Born in Rwanda probably in 1929, she was in her early thirties when my father, Gahigankwavu Hermenjilde, was killed during the early massacres that took place in Rwanda when the country witnessed a bloody revolution as it emerged from monarchical and colonial rule (1959-1962). She had been forced to flee Rwanda, and to seek refuge in neighboring Uganda. She had children to look after, and neither money nor other help.

Her life, and her children's, was extremely hard and harsh. She had given up and decided to take her own life and the lives of her own three children. Since death was so prevalent in the refugee camp, she was so fearful that one day she could die and leave her children behind as orphans. Worse still, she thought, her children would die and leave her heartbroken forever.

It was a cloudy morning. The refugee camp was situated near a small lake. She would pretend the whole family was going to fetch water, and would then drown her children first and herself last. She asked her children to come along, and we all walked together to the lake. Along the way, the oldest, Gahima, realizing this was an unusual routine, asked mama why we were all going to fetch water. Under the circumstances, as she contemplated a family suicide, she was evasive. If there was one particular dif-ficulty, she thought, it was drowning him. She thought about the order in which she could execute her plan. The children would be drowned, oldest first, and youngest last. Then she would drown herself. As she replayed the operation in her mind over and over again, she wondered what a misery it would be if she could drown one child and fail to complete the suicide plan. In the middle of this mental turmoil, as she later recounted the story to us, thun-der and lightning raged on. Mama says she heard a voice tell her, "why do you want to do such a terrible thing? I gave you life and entrusted you with the lives of these children. I promise you I will be their father and your husband. I will look after your family. Do not fear." The voice was so assuring and authoritative that mama, a devout Catholic, believed it was the voice of God.

Promptly she recited:

> Our Father in heaven,
> hallowed be your name,
> your kingdom come,
> your will be done,
> on earth as it is in heaven.
> Give us today our daily bread.
> And forgive us our debts,
> as we also have forgiven our debtors.
> And lead us not into temptation,
> but deliver us from the evil one.

And she continued:

Hail Mary, full of grace. The Lord is with thee.
Blessed art thou amongst women,
and blessed is the fruit of thy womb, Jesus.
Holy Mary, Mother of God,
pray for us sinners,
now and at the hour of our death.

Accepting God's promise, Mama was determined to work hard, pray relentlessly, and look after her children. After the abortive suicide plan, Mama fetched water, and, with her children, headed to the improvised structure that was home to the family. The two prayers would henceforth become part and parcel of the Bamususire family daily routine.

CHAPTER ONE

The Seven Year March

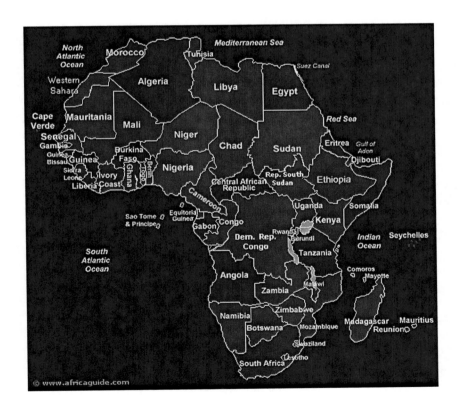

From the Oruchinga refugee camp, in Uganda, my mother had decided to head for Burundi, another small African country to the south of Rwanda. On a map of Africa, both Rwanda and Burundi are barely visible, compared to the other much larger immediate neighbors, Democratic Republic of Congo, Tanzania, and Uganda. From Rwanda, our family had first gone to Uganda, and we were now headed to Burundi. In a seven year interrupted journey, we had travelled, mainly on foot, through the jungles of east and central Africa. I cannot fully remember the long return journey to and from Burundi, back again to Uganda through Tanzania.

Faintly, I can recall some few childhood events during these journeys. During one of them, walking barefoot was especially painful. I was then the youngest among the children, probably four years old. The path was rough and full of stones. My feet were hurting. I had decided to pick the stones and get them out of the way before I could take the next step. Mama was amused and gently told me it could not work that way since we were going far away. In another memorable event, when we were so hungry and thirsty, we came by a well and wanted water to drink. It must have been somewhere in Tanzania. Mama drew some water from the well, and gave us to drink.

It was the sweetest water that I had ever taken. Later on I learnt that Mama's trick was to add some little sugar to the water. As we continued our journey, I kept on hoping that we would have another chance to drink sweet water. Occasionally we did, thanks to Mama's "miracles". On another round of travelling, we were so hungry and it was at the end of a long day somewhere in

Tanzania. All of a sudden we saw a row of ripe yellow bananas by the roadside. We feasted on the bananas and kept a few for the following day. This was like the Biblical manna from heaven.

Often as we walked through the jungles, the hazard of being close to wildlife became real. In one incident, during the night, my elder brother must have sleepwalked, and took a different path from the rest of the family groups that were walking in a single file. Not far from us we could hear hyenas laughing. Mama suddenly realized little Gahima was missing. There was panic as my mother and other adults in the group looked for him. Luckily, he had not strayed far from the main group. He was quickly rescued to the main group. In Kigamba refugee camp, in Burundi, we heard the wailing of men, women and children in the middle of the night. My mother told us the following morning that a man had been snatched from his hut and eaten by a lion.

In Burundi, as in Uganda, we were classified as refugees. The Oxford English dictionary online defines a refugee as "a person who has been forced to leave their country in order to escape war, persecution, or natural disaster." Established in 1951, the United Nations High Commission for Refugees (UNHCR) defines a refugee as a person.. "owing to a well-founded fear of being persecuted for reasons of race, religion, nationality, membership of a particular social group or political opinion, is outside the country of his nationality, and is unable to or, owing to such fear, is unwilling to avail himself of the protection of that country or return there because there is a fear of persecution..." Rwandan refugees were probably the earliest on the African continent, and our family found itself in this situation. In Uganda, the government of the day negotiated with the UNHCR to designate refugee camps in Oruchinga (current Mbarara district), Kahunge (Toro district) and Kyangware (Bunyoro district). Oruchinga was not much inhabited before this time due to infestation with Tsetse fly that carries the parasite that causes sleeping sickness, also called African Trypanosomiasis.

Our family returned to Oruchinga refugee camp some time in 1967. This refugee camp was to become home till 1994. The UNHCR provided initial emergency supplies of food rations for a period of six months, after which the refugees were expected to fend for themselves. Each family was given a few acres of land on which to cultivate their own food. Adjusting to this new life of living off the soil was not easy for some people who had lived a pastoral life before leaving their motherland. They were yet to learn to cultivate their own food.

Mama registered the lesson of self-help the hard way. At the expiration of the UNHCR support, many families survived by working as laborers among the local Ugandan population, the Banyankole, who had banana plantations. For a family of five like ours, this meant that Mama had to be accompanied by my elder brother, and spend a day working for bananas that would last for at least two days. Looking for food this way was not always assured. Sometimes, due to oversupply of labor, the work would not be available. Occasionally even when work was available one would be expected to bring one's own hoe. Such a critical asset was not easy to come by among locals and refugees as well.

At some point, absolute lack of food prompted my mother to change the family's survival strategies. One day, we were later told by Mama, that while she and my elder brother were looking for work, they experienced a discovery moment. Why were they working for other people when they could cultivate their own food? We had the land. What was lacking was the commitment to till it. Depending on matoke (plantains) which is mainly starch, without proteins, exposed one of us to protein-calorie malnutrition, otherwise known as kwashiorkor. She switched to cultivating her own food. She became successful at that, to the extent that she became a role model to others in our village of Rwekubo. She cultivated sweet potatoes, beans, peas and even had a small garden of bananas. Growing our own food stabilized the family, catered for our nutritional needs and, hence, reduced the risk of disease, and created space for us children to go to school, which was Mama's obsession.

Home was a simple round mud hut, thatched with grass, about 4-5 meters across. The whole family slept on an improvised bed, with reeds and grass forming the base on which a mat woven by Mama was placed. We had one blanket to cover ourselves with, occasionally supplemented by Mama's own cloth that was her dress during the day. Later my brother and I graduated to a small corner in the hut. One night, while my brother was away attending a boarding secondary school, I had the misfortune of sharing the corner with a huge snake. I was unharmed but it took the courage of one neighbor, by the name of Rugaju, to fight the snake in the early hours of the morning till he killed it. Behind the main hut was a smaller one that served as a kitchen, and behind it a small pit latrine that served as a toilet facility.

One of the commonest killer diseases in refugee camps are water borne diseases due to scarcity of water and poor hygiene. Having solved the problem of food, Mama enforced the discipline required to stay alive under such conditions. She not only had us children immunized against polio and tuberculosis, she insisted that we wash our hands and our bodies once in a while, even amidst the scarcity of water. We fetched water about 2 miles away and firewood from quite a distance. We were allowed to drink only boiled water, and mama enforced this rule with an iron discipline. In our hut's dusty floor, fleas were a common infestation. Since I was the most playful in the household, and the one least to pay attention to cleaning my bare dirty feet before going to bed, jiggers were indeed attracted to my feet. I received most spankings from my mother especially due to this partly self-inflicted neglect. We had probably the smartest compound in the village thanks to Mama's unrelenting attention to decoration and order.

Once mama had secured the basics of shelter, food, and health, her most urgent and important attention was focused on our education. Occasionally when we would ask Mama why we had to come to Uganda, go to Burundi, Tanzania, and then back to Uganda she answered that she was looking for the best opportunities for our education. When I first went to school in 1967, it was under a tree in Rwekubo village in Oruchinga. Children had neither exercise books nor pencils. The teacher himself, by the name of Sendarasi, was barely educated but portrayed enthusiasm and passion for teaching. He had neither blackboard, nor other teaching aids. We sat attentive as he read aloud A, B, C....and 1, 2, 3... He wrote in sand and we copied the amazing letters and numbers on hardened skins on our thighs. As it threatened to rain, he abruptly ended the day's lesson and asked us to go home. That first day at school is the most memorable, and has been the most transformative in my whole life.

There were two primary schools in our neighborhood. Rwekubo Primary School was initially supported by the Protestant Church, and Kahilimbi Primary School by the Catholic Church. Both schools competed for students, since a bigger school population attracted more support from the sponsors. Mama, a devout Catholic by faith, was very pragmatic and entrepreneurial in matters related to religion and our education. Whoever provided an opportunity she would seize it without thinking twice. Her preference was for us to attend a school affiliated to Catholics but when it was not possible she always found an alternative. Such was the case when we fell out of Kahilimbi Primary School due to lack of school fees. The headmaster of Kahilimbi Primary School was a young man by the name of Ernest Rutayisire. Around the time we fell out of Kahilimbi Primary School, an opportunity presented itself at Rwekubo Primary School, whose headmaster was a middleaged man by the name of Reuben Rwabuzisoni. Equally enthusiastic and passionate for educating refugee children, his school was one of the few that an English woman by the name of Penelope Carlyle supported. Mr. Rwabuzisoni knew little English. Nevertheless, he would venture into giving speeches in English whenever Ms. Carlyle visited the school.

One time, when Ms. Carlyle was visiting Rwekubo, Mama got introduced to her. As Mama narrated to her the problem of her inability to pay for our school fees, she also took the opportunity to include the problem of our aging hut. Ms. Carlyle sponsored our education at Rwekubo primary school, and had a new hut built for us. As part of the deal, Mama and ourselves converted to the Protestant church. During the day Mama was a Protestant but at night the same rituals that dominated our daily life remained. Her Rosary was always nearby, and recitals of Our Father and Hail Mary were bedtime and early morning constants.

We had spent one year at Rwekubo Primary School, when, unexpectedly, the headmaster of Kahilimbi Primary School delivered a letter from a "benefactor", as the foreign (usually a European white) sponsor was normally called. Her name was Catherine Sepulchre, a Belgian nun, and belonged to an organization called the Heart Open to the World. In the envelope was a picture of the nun and her sister. She promised to pay for our school fees till completion of primary school. Instantly we returned to Kahilimbi Primary School, and Mama "reconverted" to the Catholic Church.

Mama paid attention to matters of faith, and prayer was a daily routine that she enforced with rigor. When she realized we tended to fall asleep during prayer time after supper, she changed prayer time to before supper. A priest by the name of Bartholomew Kamugene once in a while came to conduct mass at Kahilimbi Primary School on Sundays. Riding an old motorcycle that sounded like a helicopter as it raced through the village, he always was an attraction to us young boys as we run after him all the way to church. The noisy machine was our interest, not his mass, which he occasionally but partly conducted in in the Latin language. After a while we learnt to memorize some bits and pieces of the liturgy. Another priest, Rubumbira, a Rwandese refugee himself, occasionally did come to conduct mass in our native language, Kinyarwanda.

In the world of peasants, refugees, displaced populations and poor people, seasons come and go by. Sometimes seasons are the only hope as you plant, expect rain, and patiently wait for the crops to grow. Other seasons are dry, rains fail and households grow hungry. Time moves slowly. For us children growing up, it was an opportunity for adventure.

After school, we fetched water within two to three miles and played soccer out of improvised balls made out of banana fibers. We walked long distances to look for firewood. While there we would eat wild fruits, sometimes coming very close to other wild competitors like snakes. This life colors the dreams of children brought up in these conditions.

When we first settled in Oruchinga, one of the remaining evidence of the earlier struggles with Tsetse fly was the big tractors that belonged to Uganda's Tsetse Fly Control Division. I was fascinated by this moving machine, and particularly by the man who drove it. There were two vehicles that passed close to the village. One was an aging bus, Lugaga Bus Service, owned by a local entrepreneur, Gordon Wavamuno, and a pick up. Both were in dangerous mechanical condition. The two were always a source of distraction and anticipation to me. Whether in school or at home, I always wanted to be by the roadside to witness this piece of action as the vehicles passed by at snail speed. My first dream in life was to become a tractor driver or at least a driver of a bus or pick up. My second dream was at least to ride a bicycle, which looked attainable, since I saw a good number of them around the refugee camp.

A few other things intrigued me. One day I was playing with a childhood friend of mine, the son of the headmaster Reuben Rwabuzisoni. His son, Bazatoha, was my age and playmate. Occasionally as we played around their hut, I could hear somebody talking, and later, someone singing. I stood and listened. I asked my friend what it was and he said it was a "radio". I asked him how big it was. Small, he answered. I wondered how a whole person, even a child, could fit within the size of what he described. Since that time, I kept on entertaining the dream that one day I would possess my own radio.

My other fascination that lingered in my dreams was a beverage by the name of Coca- Cola. The nearest town to Oruchinga was Mbarara. At a junction called "Mile 20", because it is 20 miles from Mbarara, was a shop/bar that had a juke box, and sold "coca cola". My cousin, Yubire, a little older than me, and a little street wiser than me, had bought a bottle of Coca-Cola and bread at this shop. He opened the bottle, drank from the bottle and allowed me to have my first sip of this drink. What a wonderful taste it was. I did pray many times after that for God to enable me buy my own Coca-Cola. What re-enforced my Coca-Cola dream was an encounter I had witnessed as a young boy later in life. One of my older relatives drank a whole of bottle of Coca-Cola and ate bread as I looked on, eyes almost popping, expecting that he would at least forego a sip and a few crumbs. He did not. I kept a grudge against him for a long time, and forgave him only when I could eventually buy my own Coca- Cola.

Life in the refugee camp was hard, but safe. Crime was very rare. We all spoke one language, Kinyarwanda. Prominent people in the refugee camp included the Headmasters and teachers, the village catholic catechist, the protestant preacher, the owners of the two shops in our neighborhood, the only medical assistant and nurse wife (Petronile and Alphonse Kabutura), and another "doctor on a bicycle", a private health worker, Kimonyo, whom I dreaded because he carried syringes and could administer injections. The most notable, however, were the Catholic priests, Kamugene and Rubumbira. Father Rubumbira smoked a pipe, and children spread a rumor that to receive the sacrament of confirmation, he would question you till his pipe was emptied of the tobacco. A few times in the year we attended mass at the Kyabirukwa convent, a very neat and elegant church that stood out in an otherwise dull peasant setting. It was here that I first received, and was intrigued by, the Eucharist, the white piece of bread that only the priest could dispense to you. Rumor among us children was that the Eucharist had to be swallowed as fast as possible, not chewed, and could not be taken outside the church. If you set your teeth on the Eucharist or took it outside, so the rumor went, you would drown in a sea of blood. One day, my cousin Yubire and I ventured and risked to test this hypothesis, saw no blood and never drowned, but had to confess our sins later.

Kyabirukwa convent had a thriving farm. Occasionally we went there to work as laborers in exchange for food. The very first day I worked as a child laborer, I got only one pumpkin in exchange for my day's labor. The nun in charge of the farm, the much feared Sister Nzera (I believe her real name was Angela), had probably estimated that one day's labor from a nine-year-old was not much, and had rightly and kindly decided to toss one big pumpkin to me. I was not amused, but at least I did not go home empty-handed.

In those early days in the refugee camp, all sorts of wild animals roamed the area. One day, my young sister, Kayitesi, and I were alone at home and saw a herd of buffaloes racing towards our compound. As neighbors sensed the danger, one older girl from a neighboring home came running as fast as she could and grabbed my younger sister, and we all sped to the neighboring home. The herd of buffaloes went past our small compound.

As a small boy I loved playing soccer. We had ways of improvising by weaving banana fibers into a soccer ball. Occasionally, my mother did help me in weaving such a ball for me, though she was aware that playing soccer with other boys was my main source of distraction.

As a child I was obsessed with music and singing. Being a single mom looking after four children did not leave much extra time for my mother. Nevertheless, she had time to narrate a few stories at night. One of the stories I still remember was about a tale of one old woman, Nyiragakecuru ko mu bisi bya Huye (the old woman from Huye), some place in central Rwanda. Nyiragakecuru had despaired from harsh conditions of life, and had cried out loud, seeking immediate death to end her suffering. Instantly, lightning struck, and, in panic, awed and fearful, Nyiragakecuru responded, "ego mana y'i Rwanda, ibyubu ntibigikinishwa!" (O, God of Rwanda, things of these days cannot be joked with?"). Later in life, I tended to think that my mother loved this story because it was analogous to her own life when she had despaired and wanted to take her own life and her children's.

Mama taught us a few Kinyarwanda songs, whose meaning I could not figure out then. In one, we sang:

> Yewe musare wari ku muvumumba, bangutsa ingashya n'ubwato musenyeri araje (fisherman on the river, bring the boat and the paddle, .the bishop is coming..)

And in another:
> Itora mwasabye ko ribakozeho nka loni y'indi izavahe? (The elections you asked for have left you disadvantaged, where will you get another United Nations?)

I later gathered that this was a common song among the Hutu after the 1959 revolution, the end of the centuries-old monarchy and the exile of the Tutsi.

In another sad Kinyankore (local language in Ankole, Uganda) song, my elder sister and I had picked from other kids, we sang about a person called Kennedy:

Aha kiro cyo kufa kwa Kennedy, akaba ari mu motoka no mu cyara we,
Akaba ari na dureva no muramuzi,

Konka owisire Kennedy aryayokibwa!
Chorus:
Konka, abantu ni babi
    Bakamugirira eitima bamwita
    Bakamutura busha ateine mushango
    Ai Kennedy omwana w'America!

      (My translation: On the day Kennedy died, he was in
the car with his wife, He was with his driver and a judge,
...but whoever killed Kennedy will be burned ......
....but, people are bad,
They were jealous and killed him
They killed him when he had done no wrong
O Kennedy, a child of America)

    It was sad, I thought. Who was this good American person
that was killed? What was America? The only thing I had seen
that had the word America written on it was the food rations
in cartons labeled "USAID: from the people and government of
the United States of America". Otherwise, I spent time trying to
sing lingala songs from Congo, picked from our neighbor's small
transistor radio that picked broadcasts from Rwanda. Much later,
when sons and daughters from refugee camps started going to
Ugandan secondary schools, during holidays they would return
with some elements of Western culture. They would return with
clean uniforms and shoes. Above all, they would sing songs by
Jim Reeves, which I tried to memorize and sing.

    The first such students in secondary school from our area
(they were known as abasiniya) included Alphonse Furuma,
Alfred Ndahiro, Rutsinga, Ngangure, the brothers Butamire and
Vatiri, Gapira and my own brother Gahima. Over Christmas, the
students would hold a dance party, and they would dance to what
they called "waltz", boys and girls holding each other. With other
small boys and girls we would run to Rwekubo Primary School to

watch these students dancing this strange dance and to English tunes. Rumor had it that these peasant sons and daughters, having been introduced to clean clothing, shoes and western dance, sometimes demanded that the household cater for new eating habits, using forks and setting small wooden suitcases as dining tables.

CHAPTER TWO

A Leap In Turmoil

I grew up during Uganda's difficult days when a military dictator by the name of Idi Amin ruled this former British colony. Uganda, famously described as the Pearl of Africa by Winston Churchill, gained independence from Britain in 1963, and had, by African standards, well-functioning institutions. Its experiment with democracy was rather tenuous and short-lived. In 1971, General Idi Amin, a semi-literate soldier, took over power in a military coup that was a harbinger of worse things to come for the next eight years of his bloody rule. The three leaders of the newly independent former British colonies of Uganda, Kenya and Tanzania, namely Milton Obote, Jomo Kenyatta and Julius Nyerere respectively had even established the East African Community in the hope of uniting the three countries. With the military coup in Uganda, and the deposed President Milton Obote fleeing to Tanzania, this African dream was shattered.

One evening during those Idi Amin days, calm routine of our village was broken by what the older people described as gunfire. I had never heard gunfire before. Though Idi Amin's soldiers were often deployed in such areas bordering the Uganda-Tanzania border, and once in a while we saw soldiers armed with guns, bayonets and grenades, I had never heard the sound we heard that night. It was the talk of the village for many days to come.

As a young boy, the sound intrigued me. One morning, as we ran to school through the valley that separated our camp from the school, a young man beckoned us to come and have a look at something. It was a horrible sight that I still vividly remember up to today. There were four decomposing skeletons, tied together at the arms and from behind. Idi Amin's soldiers had brought their victims to this remote village, and shot them. This was the nature of the killings perpetrated by the Amin regime. Idi Amin's dreaded State Research Bureau was behind many of these killings. People simply "disappeared", bodies dumped in undisclosed places, never to be seen or recovered by their relatives. Sooner, during that period of time, I again witnessed another dead body floating in water near our camp. Those were my first encounters with death. From then on, I always wondered why people would do such terrible things to other people.

Two other events further introduced to my young mind the hazards of life and conflict in general. In 1972, a group of Ugandan exiles in Tanzania, led by Yoweri Museveni, who is currently the President of Uganda, launched an abortive attack on Mbarara town in southwest Uganda. The axis of attack was through an area inhabited by Rwandan refugees. In subsequent days, as news of the rebel defeat swept through the camp, fleeing rebel soldiers were captured in the refugee camps and handed over to Idi Amin's soldiers to be killed. In my mind I wondered why these people could not be left alone to run to safety if they could not be hidden. I could hardly understand what was going on but in my heart I did not like it. The second event related to my own uncle by the name of Muyenzi. One evening I walked home with my mother from a neighboring village after a visit to my aunt. My mother looked sad and I could see she was crying. I had never seen her cry. She had probably learned how to hide her emotions since, to us, she was father and mother rolled into one. When I asked her what the problem was she told me Amin's people had killed her cousin Muyenzi. When I asked her why, she said she did not know. Muyenzi had recently married and his body was never recovered. Apparently, I was later to learn that some Rwandans in Uganda were at that time divided into two camps, *imburamajyo* and *ingangurarugo*, according to how they related to the former king of Rwanda, King Kigeli Ndahindurwa, who then lived in Kampala and was friends with Idi Amin. It was then dangerous to be *imburamajyo* in those days, since they were considered hostile to the king.

For a kid who grew up in a refugee camp no transition was as important as the leap from primary to secondary school. Having passed my Primary Leaving Examinations in 1974, almost miraculously with an average mark, I was placed in Makobore High School, in a small rural trading center called Rukungiri in southwest Uganda. I was excited to get my letter of admission, which, among other things, listed requirements that I had to report with on my first day at the secondary school. Among the requirements was a pair of shoes, underwear, a toothbrush, toothpaste, a mattress, pillow, and bed sheets. These were really novel in my life. I had never put on shoes or underwear before. I had never brushed my teeth with a toothbrush and toothpaste. I had never slept on a mattress or in bedsheets. The challenge remained where my mother would get money to buy these items that a whole family had never possessed. Full year tuition at Makobore High School, a public school, was six hundred and fifty Uganda Shillings. Even for Ugandan citizens, the 70's were extremely difficult economic times.

Idi Amin had expelled Indians in what he called economic war to empower Ugandans. Inflation was running high, all commodities were scarce, and the civil service was corrupted and broken. Under such conditions, the black market and smuggling were rampant. The new moneymen, often uneducated and called *mafutamingi*, would brag by saying, "look at all this wealth, where did I go to school?" It was impossible for my mother to raise the tuition, but, as she often said and prayed, God provided. I obtained a full tuition scholarship from Uganda's Catholic Secretariat.

When the day to leave for school approached, I was both excited and anxious. It was going to be the first time in my life I was leaving home, my mother and my sisters. My brother had taken the same leap much earlier in 1971. Would Mama get the money to buy me the requirements? How did a boarding school look like? I was excited about what I was going to learn and the new boys I would meet in the new school.

One morning, accompanied by my mother, I left the refugee camp on the Lugaga Bus Service to Mbarara. In Mbarara, Mama bought me a small wooden case, a pair of brown "Bata" shoes, a pair of white socks, a pair of used trousers and a used shirt, a toothbrush and toothpaste.

One requirement that needs further description was the mattress. The school expected students to come with foam mattresses. Most did. For a small number of students (mostly Rwandan refugees), we had to improvise. I came with a couple of meters of cloth (we called it "Jinja", the town in Uganda where the textile factory, Jinja Nytil, was located), and then sewed it into a sack. The school lawn grass was regularly cut and left to dry. It is this dry grass that I put into the sack, which was then sealed to function as a mattress on a spring bed.

Having given a farewell hug to mama, I boarded the bus from Mbarara to Rukungiri, The bus, called "Eliabu" from the Mbarara-based entrepreneur by the name of Eliabu, was an aging vehicle driven by an aging man. It took almost a whole day to reach the school, only about 100 km away from Mbarara. For the next four years of secondary education, this bus and its driver would always fascinate me. You never knew if or when you would arrive. In the hilly landscape that dots the beautiful scenery of Ankole and Kigezi, the driver frequently asked all passengers to get out and prop the bus with stones to prevent it from rolling back. He carried containers of water and fuel for the ever thirsty and overheating bus. I enjoyed this maiden journey, despite the mechanical condition of the bus that frequently demanded passengers to disembark and push the ailing machine even on very modest slopes.

Going to secondary school from refugee camps was indeed a promotion. Not only did I have breakfast, lunch, and tea after school and dinner, I also learned to eat with a fork and knife. I had regular showers and brushed my teeth. We had toilets that flushed with water and used toilet paper. On the first night at Makobore High School, as I lay on my improvised mattress on a spring bed, I looked at the wonder of the light bulb, and I was truly glad to be there.

Annual school tuition was heavily subsidized at 650 Uganda shillings, an amount that my mother could not afford. A Ugandan charity, the Catholic Secratariat, paid for my first year. I was excited about the new learning prospects, and I had a big appetite for books. Until then, the thirst for learning that had been aroused by my first day of schooling had been constrained by an environment of absolute lack of books, eager but constrained teachers, and a mother who could neither afford books nor tutor us in the ways of modern knowledge. Often, only one book changed hands in the village. In this type of environment my preference was often to be distracted by the usual stuff that young boys are attracted to. Playing soccer with my peers seemed to interest me more than routine chores or school. When I joined Makobore High School, I got so much absorbed in reading, class work, and had very little interest in sports. My teachers and peers respected me for being a serious and diligent student. I was interested in all subjects, and excelled in all except music and fine art. This serious attitude to academic work, and extra effort, paid handsomely. When I returned home for the holidays, evidently I had grown a few inches taller. Those were my years of adolescence, and, with better and assured nutrition in the boarding school, my growth spurt was understandable.

In second year, for reasons I have never understood, the school informed me and other Rwandese refugee students that our school fees had not been paid by the Catholic Secretariat, and that we were to be sent home. It was a sad day. Going to secondary school had been exciting academically and socially. Schooling was Mama's hope and my dream. Now we were headed back home. For the first time, I was being consciously reminded that I was not a citizen of Uganda, and that my life was dependent on the action and inaction of others. Around this time, I, and other Rwandese refugees, would be seen together on the school compound in groups. Sometimes naughty and mean boys would shout:"Ewaaya !" or draw emaciated images of refugees hanging onto power transmission lines, with mats and sauce pans on their outsized heads, as they were being "vomited"by Rwanda. I do not recall how I obtained money to transport me back to Mbarara, which was always the first stopover from Rukungiri on my way back home.

As the deadline for leaving the school premises approached we had decided we would make a petition to one Ms. Doreen Drake in Mbarara. Ms. Drake, a no-nonsense Catholic white missionary, resided in Nyamitanga, the location of a girls' secondary school, Mary Hill. It was always a dreaded moment to think of going to see Ms. Drake. Rumor had it that she would not hesitate to unleash her big dog if she got angry with you. For about a week, about eight of us camped in Mbarara, staying in a tiny room that belonged to some Rwandan who worked around town. Every morning, we would wake up and walk to a nearby market near the tiny river, Ruizi, which snakes around Mbarara, and buy sweet bananas for breakfast. For about a week our lunch, breakfast and supper were these sweet bananas as we struggled to get an appointment with Ms. Drake. Finally, she made it clear that she had no solution for us. After the bad news, we immediately disbanded. With my little wooden suitcase on my head, I headed home, about 20 miles away. All this time my mother did not know about this unhappy twist in our fortunes. When I appeared at home and explained to her what had happened, she was not thrilled at all.

My mother has always believed in the power of prayer, responding to problems as they came along. She suggested that I go to Kampala, the capital city of Uganda, where the Catholic Secretariat was based, and make a request that they re-instate the school fees.

It sounded radical and exciting to me. After all, I would travel in a bus for that long, and would be able to visit Uganda's capital city. While in Kampala I would stay with one of my older cousin who worked as a truck driver. The problem was that my mother had no money to pay for my public transport to Kampala. Always with an entrepreneurial mind, she had a thought. Those days there were local traders who would buy cattle from pastoralists in our area and transport them by truck to Kyetume in Mukono, near Kampala, for slaughter to provide meat to Kampala residents. Mama approached one of them and he accepted to take me to Kampala. My immediate companions in the truck were the long-horned cows of Ankole and Rwanda. On the day of departure, I witnessed the terrified cows being forced to embark the truck one by one. In my mind I was wondering where I would sit in this crowded truck. Behind, in the truck, was an aggressive young man who excelled in whipping the animals into submission. The agitated animals never stood still. It was not uncommon for animals to die along the way as they fell and got trampled by fellow animals.

The trader asked me to climb into the main body of the truck that was carrying 16 to 20 animals. I did, carefully trying to secure some less dangerous spot where I could position my little body. The aggressive boy did not talk to me much as he had a serious operation of keeping the animals in order. He was perched up on the truck main body, and I was on the truck floor, behind, in the left hand corner. I had to stand all the way, a journey of about 250 miles. For some time the journey went well, except for occasional cow movements that would shake the truck. Close to Kampala, pandemonium broke out in the truck. In my young mind, I was wondering whether the cows sensed they were close to the slaughterhouse.

As they pushed each other, they created a wave that started from the front and came crushing to the rear almost pressing me to the truck body. My instinct caused me to quickly climb the truck body, but not before one of the falling animals emptied its bowels on me, splashing its whole load of dung all over my body. I arrived in Kyetume a soiled young boy. It was a memorable first trip to Uganda's capital city, in search of education. I did not stay in Kampala for long. I did visit the Catholic Secretariat in Nsambya, Kampala, and my school fees were subsequently re-instated. My return to school was a big sigh of relief for my mother, my other siblings and myself.

CHAPTER THREE

Ploughing The Sea
Of Knowledge

The rest of my years at Makobore High School were eventful and full of hard work. Though Uganda was going through political turmoil and economic collapse, amazingly, we had the best teachers you could find anywhere. We had capable and committed teachers who sacrificed and gave their very best. Once in a while, each one of us comes across a teacher, who, like a mother or father, touches you in very profound and memorable ways. There are four teachers that I still recall, even now, with enthusiasm. The Headmaster, William Kiteywa, liked me and asked me to come back and work at the school after the required four years of study. My first job in life mainly involved beating the school drum to signal the change of class periods. I believe he just wanted to help me. He was a Geography teacher as well, and often insisted students had to be interested in the subject because human development influences, and has been influenced, by geography.

My physics and chemistry teacher, Odur, was an amazing instructor. He hailed from northern Uganda. He was tall, and had a beaming deep voice. You could read excitement and passion when he introduced concepts in physics and chemistry. In one demonstration of the Cathode Ray Oscilloscope, it was as if my brain had been switched on and I had experienced a eureka moment. If there was one person who got me into loving science, it was this humble and intelligent teacher. Whether he was teaching the periodic table or the laws of gravity, he always made it sound so simple and elegant.

During my high school years, I had two English literature teachers that influenced my interest in the English language and my thinking, especially on matters of social and political injustice. One was Mugabe, who taught me William Shakespeare's *Julius Caesar* and Chinua Achebe's *Things Fall Apart*. When he taught *Julius Caesar* you would think he was there during the times of the Roman Empire. Tall, haggard, and with a deep voice he would recite the opening lines from one Flavius to a carpenter, cobbler and other commoners:

> Hence! Home, you idle creatures get you home!
> Is this a holiday? What, know you not,
> Being mechanical, you ought not to walk
> Upon a laboring day without the sign
> Of your profession?—Speak, what trade art thou?

Whether he would echo the dying Caesar's words to Brutus, " Et tu Brute", or recite Mark Anthony's speech, "Friends, Romans, countrymen, lend me your ears..We come to bury Caesar, not to praise him.." Mugabe would occasionally burst into his native language, Rukiga, and ask us students, "mbwenu shi ngambe ki?" or translated in English, "what can I really say?" He described the rough and tumble of politics, the treachery, the backstabbing, and the betrayals in high places with such ease that he really fired my imagination.

In *Things Fall Apart*, now a classic, the story unfolds in a community in the African country of Nigeria. The community faces the advance of colonialism, Christianity and western culture. Okonkwo, the main character of the story, embodies the contradictions of the community. The tittle is taken from William Butler Yeats poem, *The Second Coming:*

TURNING and turning in the widening gyre
The falcon cannot hear the falconer;
Things fall apart; the center cannot hold;
Mere anarchy is loosed upon the world,
The blood-dimmed tide is loosed, and everywhere
The ceremony of innocence is drowned;
The best lack all conviction, while the worst
Are full of passionate intensity.

Okonkwo is an influential person in his community. He makes fateful decisions and ends up killing an adopted son, Ikemefuna, and commits suicide in order to assert his manhood and uncompromising stand towards the encroaching western influence. I was particularly saddened by the death of the young Ikemefuna, who pleads for life only to be struck by a guardian and protector, Okonkwo. By taking his own life, rather than face being parlayed in the white man's court for killing a white, Okonkwo was not able to read correctly the mood of his people, whose attitude was now to appease the white man and accept his religion and government.

Zabuloni Bakeiha was another memorable English teacher. Short, with a small build, and a no-nonsense attitude, he was a hard task master who taught us *Mine Boy* by Peter Abrahams, *A Grain of Wheat* by Ngugi wa Thiongo, and George Orwell's *Animal Farm*. His classes were often after lunch. In the tropical heat and after full-fledged carbohydrate-rich meals, students tended to be sleepy. Bakeiha would ask questions, and without much response, he would angrily say, "come on pen-pushers, come on passengers". Rumor had it that he had such a sharp tongue that got him into trouble with Ugandan government authorities while he worked with the government-owned Radio Uganda. It was rumored that, one time, then President Milton Obote had swallowed a fishbone that got stuck in his throat. He was taken to the national referral hospital, Mulago Hospital. The matter was supposed to be kept secret from the public eye. Bakeiha thought he had scoop and went on air to announce, " ..aho tukugambira aha, Peresidenti wi hanga Milton Obote, eigufa ry'engege nirimuzengerera omu maraka..". Translated in English, "….as we speak, a fish bone is moving around President Milton Obote's throat"

In *Mine Boy*, the story describes life in apartheid South Africa. The theme was human injustice and exploitation. Bakeiha introduced to us the two ideas that, "noblesse oblige", and that "to err is human and to forgive is divine". Paraphrased, "noblesse oblige" simply means that when you have been given much, much is expected from you. "To err is human and to forgive is divine" means that making mistakes is a universal human condition, and forgiving, a godly principle that we should try to cultivate. When he gave us a class assignment, I decided to use these two ideas in the *Mine Boy* context. When he returned our work, he distributed others except mine. A stern Bakeiha called me to the front of the class. He had given me an A+ for my essay, but remarked that it sounded too academic to have been done by me. I explained to him that I had done it myself. My essay became a "bestseller" to successive classes. I only wish I had kept a copy of the essay. Bakeiha introduced me, indirectly, to philosophy, and to being concerned with the human condition. George Orwell's *Animal Farm* was a perfect description of Uganda's Idi Amin, but Bakeiha treaded carefully. Many teachers and professors had lost their lives, and it was not uncommon to have informers in the classroom. The lessons *of Animal Farm* remain vivid in my memory.

I loved reading fiction. I combed through every other available novel by James Hardley Chase and Agatha Christie. It was a privilege to have very good and qualified teachers who introduced us to the world of ideas and knowledge. Although it was much later in life that I was to fully appreciate the impact of ideas and knowledge, there was something attractive in science, history and literature. Although we also read such books like Mark Twain's *Adventures of Tom Sawyer* and Adventures *of Huckleberry Finn*, as a young boy who grew up in a refugee camp I would often fail to relate to the contexts and characters in these classics. Through these readings, we were being introduced to the challenges that Africans faced during transition in which they came into contact with other foreign cultures through colonial conquest. We discussed apartheid, power and dictatorships, but in a simple and soft way that could not be misunderstood by the reigning regime in Uganda. I recall one day when our headmaster, William Kiteywa, told us that Luwum, the Archbishop of Uganda, had been killed. Even at a young age we had come to understand that every time a prominent Ugandan died under mysterious circumstances, Idi Amin was involved. In those days such bad news were treated like secrets, for no one dared discuss them in public.

I was an active member of the school's debating society. My literature classes were beginning to arouse my mind to questions of injustice. At this point I wasn't even thinking about my condition as a refugee. It was under these conditions that I sat for O-Level Exams. I passed with excellent grades, and was one of the two top students in the school that year, and among the best in the whole country. I enrolled at Ntare School, Mbarara, and opted to take advanced Biology, Physics and Chemistry in a two-year pre-medicine curriculum. By then, my brother, Gahima, had left Ntare School to study law at Makerere University, in Kampala. He influenced me into taking medicine. My natural inclination would probably have been literature, history and, or, economics. He had a point. He had suggested I consider studying Medicine at Makerere University. Now that he was studying law, adding a doctor to the family's portfolio would be something useful, and an achievement our mother would be proud of. Law and Medicine were supposed to put one in a special league of high achievers, the "cream of the cream".

I arrived at Ntare School in 1978, and enrolled into the biology, physics and chemistry class. For extra-curricular activities I enrolled into the drama society. I got the prize for the best actor, acting the role of a woman in the play, *Servant of Two Masters*, by Carlo Goldoni. In 1979, Uganda was then inching close to the throes of war against advancing Ugandan rebel groups backed by the Tanzanian army. Mbarara was to become the axis of the war. Early in 1979 as Tanzanian forces came close to Mbarara, the school asked all students to evacuate on their own. With a few students, I put my little suitcase full of books and a few other belongings on my head, and walked in the direction of Ibanda in south west Uganda. I did not know what my destination was. We were just fleeing the war. Earlier, my mother and young sister had managed to flee the Oruchinga refugee camp as well. I did not know their whereabouts. My elder sister, Toto, had completed her O-Levels and waiting for her results. Miraculously, our family re-united in Toro district, in a place called Kamwenge. In the evenings, I would join a few other people to listen to the progress of the war against Idi Amin on BBC and Voice of America. The government mouthpiece, Radio Uganda, kept assuring the population that everything was under control, and that General Idi Amin would defeat the invaders.

As usual, Mama was never the one to give up with regard to our education. Now three of us were out of school. She suggested that my elder sister and I go to Kampala to find avenues for going to school, however temporary. One day, my sister and I boarded the train from Kamwenge in Toro, and headed for Kampala. My second journey to Kampala was obviously better than the first one, where I shared space with cows. However, the train from Kamwenge to Kampala was overcrowded, dirty, and slow. Traders of chicken, eggs, roasted ground nuts, maize, sugarcane and meat were active at every station and while the train moved. My sister and I had little to spend on this journey except for a few mouthfuls of roasted groundnuts.

We arrived in Kampala when the city was already in turmoil, expecting the Tanzanian forces anytime. Fighting was already going on in Lukaya, in Masaka, not far from Kampala. We found ourselves joining thousands of people who were headed east for the Uganda/Kenya border. Soon, we were refugees in Kenya, being looked after by the UNHCR. My stay in this new camp was short-lived. Idi Amin lost the war and fled to Libya. Kampala fell to the Tanzanian forces in April 1979. A coalition of Ugandan political groups, the Uganda National Liberation Front (UNLF), under President Yusuf Lule, established a government of national unity. As the new government encouraged people to return, I took advantage and came back with the very first group of returnees. I left behind my sister, cousin and other relatives.

As soon as I returned to Kampala from Kenya, I went straight to our refugee camp home, still with my wooden case full of books. There I found Mama and my young sister Kayitesi. They had returned from Toro, only to find that Mama's black and white cat had kept vigil on the premises during her months of absence. Besides, the old hut which had been a gift from Ms. Carlyle had aged, and the effects of weather plus our absence had made it less habitable. The beautiful mango tree that my sister Toto had planted many years back had ripe juicy mangoes. As we settled down, we decided to build a new hut using our own efforts.

Soon, Mama was asking me to travel to Mbarara to find out whether we could resume at Ntare School. The school was in bad shape, and had been ransacked during the fall of Mbarara. Teachers and staff had been affected by the war. Since my class was scheduled to sit for exams at the end of 1979, the Ministry of Education distributed us to a number of schools that had been less affected by the war. Some students from my science class were assigned to Kigezi High School, in the town of Kabale, in south west Uganda, close to the Rwandan border. I was one of those assigned to Kigezi High School. We had very little time to prepare for the University entrance Advanced Level Exams. I thought of repeating the whole year to get enough time to prepare, but decided against it in favor of trying and repeating if I did not pass. I was not the only one affected by the disruptive effects of war. When the results finally came, to my pleasant surprise, I had obtained just enough marks to get me into Makerere University Medical School. It was a moment of joy for me and the whole family.

There was one hurdle to cross. To get into the University, and study Medicine, and on a government scholarship, I had to prove that I was a Ugandan citizen. Professions like law, medicine, and engineering were generally difficult to get into. It was even harder for refugees to have access to these professions. In a country that had seen its institutions at the central and local level collapse after years of conflict, war and mismanagement, there were loopholes that could be exploited. One citizen of Uganda introduced to me and my brother by a family friend, had signed off on the citizen verification form as my father. But then, a District Administrative Officer had to endorse the form.

My brother escorted me to the district office. During Idi Amin's regime, most district administrators were military men. I handed the form to the district officer. He looked at the form, raised his eyes and, in a stern voice, asked, "Are you a citizen of Uganda?" I answered sheepishly, with downcast eyes, "Yes." Frowning, he shifted his gaze to my brother, who he apparently knew from school days. If he knew him, he also knew his status. If I was his brother then it was a done deal that the district officer knew I was not a Ugandan citizen as I claimed. "Really?", he asked. "Yes.", I answered. "From where", he asked. " Isingiro", I responded. Isingiro was one of the counties in Mbarara district. He shook his head. At that moment I thought I was doomed. In the best case scenario he would reject my application. In the worst case my brother and I could end up in jail. For a brief moment there was an eerie silence. Then the district officer put on a mechanical half smile, signed the form, and said, "Congratulations and good luck, young man." We thanked him and left his office. One of my very first ethical dilemmas had been resolved in my favor.

CHAPTER FOUR

Makerere University Kampala

Established by British colonial authorities in 1922, Makerere University is one of the oldest institutions of higher learning on the African continent. For a person of my most lowly status and background, attending Makerere University was a dream beyond imagination. With a population of about five thousand in 1980, Makerere University, like many universities in the developing world, was an ivory tower to which very few would ever have access to. Joining the University was simultaneously an exit from the wretchedness of refugee camp life to and a pathway to a better life, one hoped. It was an entry into the world of ideas and knowledge.

In the 1980/81 Academic year, I was admitted to Makerere University Medical School. I stayed in Lumumba Hall on Makerere University main campus. My hall of residence was named after Patrice Lumumba, the Congolese nationalist who was murdered at the height of the Cold War to pave the way for then Colonel Mobutu to come to power in the Democratic Republic of Congo (DRC). Lumumba Hall was the largest hall on campus but lacked running water. We carried jerrycans to fetch water. Our one toilet facility, a pit latrine, was jokingly labelled "Kilometer 85" and was so bad that it would have qualified to be condemned as a public health hazard. Food was bad and comprised of maize meal, beans infested with weevils, black tea and occasional rice. Meal times were truly a case of the survival of the fittest, as hungry peasant students outmaneuvered each other to be the first in line. My first impression at Makerere was not a good one, but the overall situation in Uganda at this time was painful to everyone.

Our first lecture in human anatomy was given by Sebuwufu, a Professor of Human Anatomy. Bright, funny and exuding confidence, he told us we were there because we were the "cream of the cream". In teams, we were assigned a cadaver to dissect for the next two years. The first time my team's cadaver was uncovered for our maiden dissecting session, my mind quickly raced to the memory of the decomposing bodies I had seen during my primary school years, victims of Idi Amin's regime. As we dissected, I had moments of thinking about the fragility of the human condition. What kind of person was this while he lived? What did he do in life? What were his dreams? We were supposed to dissect the bodies of the dead so that we could ultimately save the lives of the living. Being in the company of the dead has a peculiar effect of both reminding you of your own mortality, and subsequently numbing your senses to the extent that you begin to view the cadaver as just another vessel that once housed a human soul, heart and mind. My first week at medical school was exciting except for the moments of sorrow about the ultimate fate of every human being.

The Medical School is located in Mulago Hospital, just across the main campus. Medical education is expensive, long and competitive. In the first two pre-clinical years you had to study the basic sciences: physiology, anatomy, biochemistry, pathology, and micro-biology. In most cases, learning was essentially by cramming most of this information in the shortest possible time and reproducing it during exams. This is not my particular strength. With time, my interest in medical studies was waning. My attention was also diverted by two new interests, namely, social life on campus and the world of radical ideas. Medical students, to succeed, have to deny themselves the luxury of social life. Their world is one fully occupied with books and reading. They were proud to be renowned for this. For me, I was discovering new things for the first time, and beginning to take a keen interest in the social life around campus, including the usual peer-induced indulgences like smoking and drinking.

Of more profound and enduring influence was my introduction to the world of radical ideas. Around this time, Uganda was going through political turmoil. After eight years under the brutal dictatorship of Idi Amin, a coalition of Ugandan political groups had obtained the support of the Tanzanian Government under President Nyerere, and dislodged Idi Amin from power. Under the umbrella of the Uganda National Liberation Front (UNLF), coalition forces established successive governments that were fractious, weak and short-lived. In quick succession, precipitated by internal squabbles and an overbearing Tanzania, Yusuf Lule was succeeded by Godfrey Binaisa, whose stay was even shorter. A Military Commission under Paul Muwanga overthrew him, preparing for the return of exiled former President Milton Obote. Milton Obote's Uganda People's Congress (UPC) came to power again in 1980 after what was considered a rigged election.

Yoweri Museveni, then in his thirties, had been in the coalition government heading a political-military organization called Front for National Salvation (FRONASA). Yoweri Museveni had been the mastermind of the abortive 1972 invasion of Uganda from Tanzania. He had survived, and established a liberation group, FRONASA, which was among the exiled groups that Tanzania helped to fight and defeat Idi Amin in 1979. He had been deliberately and progressively marginalized to pave the way for Milton Obote. He had formed a political party, Uganda Patriotic Movement (UPM) to contest the elections of 1980 that brought Milton Obote back to power.

During the political campaigns, I attended a few rallies addressed by him or his then good friend Eriya Kategaya. They talked about UPM's agenda for national and economic transformation. They threatened that if elections were rigged they would "go back to the bush" to fight. I came to learn that Museveni, Kategaya and their comrades had been influenced by Frantz Fanon and Walter Rodney. Frantz Fanon, born in the French territory of Martinique, was a French-Algerian and author of *The Wretched of the Earth*. Fanon was a physician, and his influential book was a reflection on the Algerian war of independence against French colonizers. Walter Rodney, a native of Guyana, was a historian and political activist who taught at Dar-es-salaam University in Tanzania in the 60's and early 70's. He authored the seminal work in a book, *How Europe Underdeveloped Africa*. I bought both books and began to read them. Hence began my journey on a radical path, and my slow separation from the world of medicine.

Rodney's central idea in *How Europe Underdeveloped Africa* was that Africa's poverty and underdevelopment could be explained. Africa had suffered from slavery for centuries, taking the most able-bodied and shipping them to plantations in the Americas and the Caribbean, thus disrupting African communities and nations. Africa had suffered from colonial conquest by European Imperial powers (British, French, German, Portuguese, etc.), further disrupting Africans by taking away their rights to self-rule and self- determination. As if slavery and colonial conquest were not enough, Africans had suffered and continue to suffer from what he called "unequal exchange'. Simply explained, Africa was exchanging its natural wealth (minerals, oil, timber, etc.) either for trivialities (mirrors, perfumes, etc..) or for expensive manufactured goods (machinery, clothing, medicines, etc.). His famous statement, "Africa produced what it did not consume, and consumed what it did not produce" summarizes the gist of his influential book. This triple assault on Africa, namely, slavery, colonial conquest and plunder, and unequal exchange by European powers had created the conditions for Africa's continuing underdevelopment. He attempted to show the pattern of social and economic development in pre-colonial Africa, and how this was disrupted by European intrusion.

On development he had this to say:

> Development in human society is a many-sided process. At the level of the individual, it implies increased skill and capacity, greater freedom, creativity, self-discipline, responsibility and material well-being. Some of these are virtually moral categories and are difficult to evaluate – depending as they do on the age in which one lives, one's class origins, and one's personal code of what is right and what is wrong. However, what is indisputable is that the achievement of any of those aspects of personal development is very much tied in with the state of the society as a whole. From earliest times, man found it convenient and necessary to come together in groups to hunt and for the sake of survival. The relations which develop within any given social group are crucial to an understanding of the society as a whole: Freedom, responsibility, skill, etc. have real meaning only in terms of the relations of men in society

Frantz Fanon's main idea in *The Wretched of the Earth* was that colonialism was inherently a violent phenomenon, and hence, decolonization had to be equally a violent process, but one on a higher moral ground because it sought to"liberate"both the colonizer and the colonized.

> Decolonization never takes place unnoticed, for it influences individuals and modifies them fundamentally. It transforms spectators crushed with their inessentiality into privileged actors, with the grandiose glare of history's floodlights upon them. It brings a natural rhythm into existence, introduced by new men, and with it a new

language and a new humanity. Decolonization is the veritable creation of new men. But this creation owes nothing of its legitimacy to any supernatural power; the 'thing' which has been colonized becomes man during the same process by which it frees itself. National liberation, national renaissance, the restoration of nationhood to the people, commonwealth: whatever may be the headings used or the new formulas introduced, decolonization is always a violent phenomenon.

In a preface to the book, the French existentialist philosopher, Jean Paul Sartre, had this to say to amplify Fanon's call for violence against the colonial regime:

It will not be without fearful losses; the colonial army becomes ferocious; the country is marked out, there are mopping-up operations, transfers of population, reprisal expeditions, and they massacre women and children. He knows this; this new man begins his life as a man at the end of it; he considers himself as a potential corpse. He will be killed; not only does he accept this risk, he's sure of it. This potential dead man has lost his wife and his children; he has seen so many dying men that he prefers victory to survival; others, not he, will have the fruits of victory; he is too weary of it all. But this weariness of the heart is the root of an unbelievable courage. We find our humanity on this side of death and despair; he finds it beyond torture and death. We have sown the wind; he is the whirlwind. The child of violence, at every moment he draws from it his humanity. We were men at his expense, he makes himself man at ours: a different man; of higher quality.

Fanon further critiqued the elite that now appeared at the head of the new independent nations; an elite that shared consumption habits with the Western middle class, but lacked the productive, creative and entrepreneurial abilities of the Western elite. Since he was a physician, he devoted a whole chapter on the psychological disorders prevalent during and after the wars of national liberation. With a couple of friends, including the late Wilson Rutayisire (Shaban), we spent time discussing these works at Charles Mutsinzi's small apartment in a suburb of Kampala called Wandegeya.

By the end of my first year at medical school, I had lost interest in my medical studies. Medical studies were now a secondary concern. I missed many lectures, and did last minute reading to catch up. I had just enough marks to proceed to second year. Second year was even more demanding, and my time for it was even less. I now started reading philosophy. On some days, when other students went to medical school, I would spend my time going through the main library, perusing through early and medieval philosophers, including advocates of anarchism like Proudhon, the French anarchist who had proclaimed that property was theft. I read books like *Deschooling Society* by Ivan Illich, sharply criticizing modern education as a tool for producing automatons, and not creative individuals. I read The *Pedagogy of the Oppressed* by Paul Freire, another sharp critic of traditional education, which treated a student as "an empty vessel that had to be filled with knowledge". Freire argued for an education that treated both teachers and students as co-creators of knowledge. My medical studies were not the only victims of this newly-found belief system. I divorced God and became an atheist. Internally, I developed deep anger, and was slowly recoiling into my own world, engulfed in the ideology of protest. Rwanda was not yet my target. I wanted to fight something, but the outline of this new enemy I could not properly define. At least, I thought, the Ugandan state, with its repression could be that target. Between my declining enthusiasm in learning by lot, my social life, and now time-consuming adventure in ideological pursuits, medicine had to wait. By the end of second year, I could not summon enough grades to proceed to third year. I had to repeat second year. My mother, and my siblings, were gravely disappointed. I did not care.

One thing that I was still debating in my mind in early 1983 was to figure out how to join the National Resistance Movement (NRM). In 1980, Museveni's Uganda Patriotic Movement (UPM) party and the larger Democratic Party (DP) of Kawanga Ssemogerere had lost the elections to Milton Obote's Uganda People's Congress (UPC). Museveni had honored his pledge to "go back to the bush", and, with 27 men, had launched the National Resistance Movement (NRM)/National Resistance Army(NRA) in the Luwero triangle of central Uganda. The Luwero triangle had among its inhabitants people of Rwandan and Burundian descent. Among his initial 27 men who started the insurrection were two Rwandese, Fred Rwigema and Paul Kagame. Obote's regime directed its reprisals against all its opposition, Rwandans, and people from Buganda and western Uganda.

In 1982, many Rwandans and Ugandans of Rwandan origin were massively uprooted from their homes, their property destroyed or confiscated, and driven to the Uganda-Rwanda border. Unwelcoming, the Rwandan Government could not accept the now stateless Rwandans and Ugandans to enter its territory. The policy of the Rwandan government had always been that Rwanda is small, and that a massive refugee return was not an option. Countries of asylum were being asked by Rwanda to naturalize the Rwandan refugees. Under pressure, the Rwandan government allowed some Rwandans to cross into Rwanda, but they were quarantined in a place called Nasho, in the eastern part of the country, like an unwanted or infectious breed of people. Many died in these harsh and humiliating conditions. In my mind, and to many Rwandese, this new development began to deepen a Rwandan consciousness. If before my enemy was a repressive Ugandan state, against whom I was determined to fight, now it dawned on me that the Rwandan state was the new enemy.

Many young Rwandan people were searching for avenues to join the ranks of Yoweri Museveni's National Resistance Movement/National Resistance Army, but with grievances against the Rwandan government. How could your own government disown you, and reduce you to permanent refugee status? The plight of Rwandans in Uganda and subsequently in Nasho in Rwanda crystallized into a deep longing for Rwanda especially among the youth. Being a refugee made you vulnerable. To end the refugee problem once and for all was the only just and sustainable solution. The path to this resolution of the refugee problem was through armed struggle, since the government in Rwanda was not willing to resolve it peacefully. Those days my own internal struggles meant that going to study medicine was now not my priority.

CHAPTER FIVE

Witnessing Death And
A Conversion

On the morning of April 17, 1983, I had a strange feeling of emptiness and sadness. I felt very unsettled. In the preceding weeks, my sister, Edith Abatesi (her childhood name was Toto) had left Kampala for Nairobi, Kenya, to explore education opportunities there after high school. My elder brother, Gerald Gahima, had been living in Kenya, after graduating in law at Makerere University. Like many Rwandese and Ugandans at that time, a teaching job in Kenya offered a more decent living that chaotic and insecure Uganda, rife with rebellion and economic hardships for more than a decade. My mother was living with him in Nairobi; so were Toto and our cousin, Jane. On April 17, I felt the urge to call and check on my mother. When I arrived at a friend's house in downtown Kampala, my friend's sister opened the door and, on seeing me, ran back crying. She composed herself and then asked me whether I had heard any news from Nairobi. Then she said, "Toto is dead." I did not say anything else. I walked out of the house, down the stairs, and onto the streets of Kampala. I did not cry. Alone and frightened, I felt the world crashing down on. The age of innocence was over. Death was real.

The death of Toto was a terrible tragedy to our entire family. My mother had lost a husband while she was a young woman. We had lost a father while we were babies. She had decided against suicide, thanks to divine intervention. She did not remarry, and singlehandedly sacrificed a lot to see her children grow and get an education thus far. Toto had completed high school. My youngest sister, Doreen Kaitesi, was close to joining secondary school. My elder brother was now working as a lawyer in Nairobi. Overall, despite being disappointed with me, which I am sure she kept to herself, she had everything to be proud of. Tragedy came unexpectedly and struck at a moment that could have been one of joy for my mother as she witnessed the fruits of her labor.

On that fateful day, Toto had stepped out of the house with a cousin, Jane, to buy a few household items. They were knocked down by a car. Both died instantly. A relative broke the news to my mother, who had seen the young girls just moments before. I was told she did not cry.

Like many African young girls, Toto was a very responsible girl from an early age. Though we were only two years apart, she was the one who did most chores. My mother had taught and expected her to do most of the household chores like cooking and sweeping. African girls start early to carry disproportionate burdens compared to their male siblings. As Mama spent almost every day out working, Toto was like the babysitter, looking after me and our youngest sister. She was entrepreneurial like my mother, and loved nature. She was the first one to appear home with a mango seed which she planted. It grew into a big mango tree that still stands where she planted it. She once obtained a chick which grew into a hen, which she named "Nyiramasibira". It gave us a few eggs, and produced a few other hens which we sold, boosting our family income.

She and I once ventured into working as laborers for unripe sweet bananas, which, once ripe, we attempted to sell. The problem was that they were sweet and enticing. Hanging in front of our hut as merchandise ready for sale, we could hardly resist the temptation or delay our gratification. Every time one of us passed by, we would secretly treat ourselves to the merchandise. As the merchandise progressively decreased, there was no corresponding increase in money to show. Knowing our weakness, our mother would tell us to finish them off and that he would pay us later. She never did, of course.

Toto and I shared a love for music, singing and dancing. Our knowledge of music in English had grown after joining secondary school and, together we used to recite a few of the songs by Jim Reeves, Dolly Parton, Bee Gees, Abba, and Boney M, Jimmy Cliff, and Bob Marley. My brother once came home with an old record player that had been given to him by a relative. Toto and I tried everything under the sun to get dry batteries to run the aging miniature machine. At first we were lucky since we were able to sell one of Toto's chickens. Once or twice our caring mother must have chipped in with a few coins to buy one or two batteries, just to make us happy. On such happier moments, we would place the recorder player on a clay pot to create a booming effect. I once walked the whole day, moving from village to village, to get a buyer for Toto's chicken so that we could buy batteries for the record player. I was unsuccessful, and returned home disappointed.

My mother occasionally offered us the sweet wine made out of fermented banana juice. Only Toto and I loved it. In fact, my mother once tried to boost her income by selling this local brew. She did not go very far with the trade because she realized it was overcrowding our small space, men were staying longer than necessary possibly wanting to make advances to her, and plus, as long as it was still sweet (as it ages it turns sour), Toto and I would have sips of this sweet wine. Toto and I took adventures together and often she led me into the naughty schemes. Those days mama smoked a pipe. One day Toto and I took turns with Mama's pipe, and the effect was horrible, as my head felt like spiralling out of control, almost making me vomit.

Toto was a fierce defendant of our family. She was also a serious girl who could tell it into your face. She often picked quarrels with my elder brother. Her last words to me were in my room, in Lumumba Hall, at Makerere University, shortly before she took her fateful journey to Kenya. She found me in my room, lying in bed. I had not gone for lectures that day, as I increasingly did during my period of descent into my own world of ideology and protest. She confronted me and asked why I had not gone to study. "Theo, whatever you are doing, do not turn into a fool." Those were her memorable and powerful parting words. We never spoke again.

As I walked the streets of Kampala, I remembered Toto's last words to me. I had to quickly figure out how my young sister and I could go to Nairobi to attend her burial. In Nairobi, I was able to see her embalmed body as we proceeded to bury her and Jane in Langata cemetery in Nairobi. Toto's death was Mama's, and our entire family's, worst loss. I did not know my father since he had died when I was a baby. We had grown and lived together as a very close family. Death had robbed us of one of us and it was a painful reminder that even young people could die. We had gone through more dangerous situations and survived; and here we were, agonizing over the loss of one of us from a car accident. That seemed to mark the passing of an age of innocence. We all remained composed and did not even grieve and mourn.

After Toto's burial, Mama, always a believer, spent most of her time reading the Books of Job, Lamentations, and Ecclesiastes in the *Holy Bible*. I took to drinking and smoking. I had become a grumpy angry young man who would spend days not talking to anybody. I decided not to go back to Uganda to resume my studies. My interest in medical studies had been dwindling. Toto's death created in me a total rebellion against all forms of schooling. If I had some hesitation about belief in God, now I stood denouncing as foolish any belief in God. My cousin Yubire and I would taunt my mother, a staunch Catholic, and my brother, who was a born again Christian, with such statements like, "if God lives, we dare him, let Him strike us with lightning!' We would lock ourselves in our small bedroom and let the cigarette smoke fill the room to ensure maximum inhalation.

In addition, my room was now adorned with photos of every known revolutionary: Karl Marx, Engels, Mao, Stalin, Kim IL Sung, Gadhaf, Sankara, Castro, Mugabe, Machel, Amilcar Cabral, and Mandela. Previously, my readings had been mainly *The Wretched of the Earth* and *How Europe Underdeveloped Africa*, now I began deep reading of works of Marx, Lenin, and Mao Ze Dong. I studied world socialist revolutions, national liberation movements in Africa, Latin America and Asia. I became conscious of the fact that Africans were not the only ones offended by imperialism and capitalism. The Soviet Union, communist eastern Europe, China, Vietnam, North Korea, Cuba, and Nicaragua were my friends. The United States and Western Europe, the capitalists and imperialists, were my enemies. I combed through the works on guerrilla warfare. My job became to read these works with a passion that I never had before or since.

Every new ideology comes with a new vocabulary. I was introduced to dialectical and historical materialism, classes and class struggle, capitalism, socialism and communism, the economic substructure, political and social superstructure, and how the world order was slowly moving to the fading away of the state, when the workers of the world would own the means of production, making "from each according to their abilities and to each according to their needs" would become a reality. Karl Marx's *Das Kapital* became my staple diet, even when, sometimes, I did not have any understanding of this deep and thorough work. I read *The Communist Manifesto* by Karl Marx and Frederick Engels, whose preamble began,

A spectre is haunting Europe – the spectre of communism. All the powers of old Europe have entered into a holy alliance to exorcise this spectre: Pope and Tsar, Metternich and Guizot, French Radicals and German police-spies.

Where is the party in opposition that has not been decried as communistic by its opponents in power? Where is the opposition that has not hurled back the branding reproach of communism, against the more advanced opposition parties, as well as against its reactionary adversaries?

According to Karl Marx, ""Religion is the sigh of the oppressed creature, the heart of a heartless world, and the soul of soulless conditions. It is the opium of the people". This resonated well with my new creed of Godless existence.

One of the earliest lessons that I gathered from these readings on revolutions and revolutionaries was that to succeed one had to be principled, disciplined and with a clear sense of purpose. To emulate these revolutionary giants whom I now adored, one day I quit drinking and smoking. With this first personal victory, I proceeded to the second challenge of a revolutionary. To succeed, Marxism taught, revolutionaries had to study both objective and subjective conditions that create the necessity and possibility for revolution. I had already created for myself an extensive reading list which included philosophy and western thought, geography, history, sociology, political economy and political science. Fortunately, in Nairobi there were many such books on sale by the street. It is in Nairobi that I was introduced to Che Guevara, the Latin American revolutionary, a standard bearer of revolutionary purity and self-sacrifice amongst young and prospective third world revolutionaries. Instantly, Che became my hero. I was also taught by this literature that modern struggles were class struggles. One had to take sides. A revolutionary intellectual had to "commit class suicide" to be alongside the peasants and working class.

One day, my new found love and devotion to Marxism and revolutionary literature landed me into an unexpected confrontation with my mother. As a child I was the most punished by my mother since I was the most prone to doing naughty things. Ever since my mother had served us with sweet water, I had remained with a thought of exploring these types of miracles. During the earlier years in the Oruchinga refugee camp, I once helped myself to half a pound of sugar, a rarity in our household, mixed it with cold water in a pot and and invited my playmates to come and enjoy the party. My mother discovered this after she noticed the tell-tale signs of a children's party that could not cover its tracks. I received several spankings as a well-deserved and just retribution. On another occasion, I committed an even more serious offence. With just one or two saucepans as the only cooking utensils in our poor household, there were a few artisans who could do the patchwork to seal the gaping holes at the bottom of overused old pans. I got hold of one of the pans that was still relatively intact, and with the help of a stone, hammered a nail into its bottom to "fix it". My attempt to seal the holes was unsuccessful. So were my attempts to conceal the crime. As usual, I received a spanking for this.

My offence as a young adult in Nairobi was of a different kind this time. Never before in memory had I seen my mother's temper explode with such fury. In 1984, my brother, who was the bread-winner, had obtained a scholarship to do graduate studies in law at the London School of Economics in the United Kingdom. He had left me with the responsibility to look after my mother and my sister. I had been thinking about joining the NRM struggle in Uganda through its networks in Nairobi. With this new and unexpected responsibility, I looked for a teaching job in one of the numerous commercial, Indian-owned secondary schools in Nairobi. My monthly salary was about 900 Kenya shillings. My first teaching experience itself was a nightmare, as unruly students went about their extra-curricular conversations as if I was not present. With such low income income, my mother and I relocated to a rural place, Kiambu, some few miles away from Nairobi. I realized soon that this was not a workable option due to mama's loneliness while I went to work, and the high transport costs. We returned to Nairobi and rented two rooms in Kawang-ware, where poor people of limited means lived. The one memorable thing about the place was the filthy and smelly common pit latrines that reminded me of those at Lumumba Hall, Makerere University, in Uganda.

At the end of the month, after I got my salary, I bought a copy of *Das Kapital* by Karl Marx, and a copy of the *Seven Military Essays* by Mao Zedong. I suspect my mother was aware that a substantial part of my monthly income was going into buying books, and yet we were barely surviving on a shoestring budget. I appeared at the front door with the books I had purchased from street vendors. She had just returned from the shops, carrying some bread and milk. As soon as she saw me with the books, she threw her food cargo onto the ground, and stepped on it several times to crush it. In my mind I wondered what I had done to deserve this. Was it because I had become a Marxist and an atheist? Was it a spontaneous outburst from her concealed grief due to Toto's death? Was it because I had become a failure and drpped out of school? Was it because I was failing to prioritize and making wrong choices? I kept quiet. She never uttered a word. I have never discussed this matter with her. Whatever the reason, it was strong and produced a scary moment.

Nairobi was home to many personalities whose names I had heard from my mother and later on read in books: the exiled King Kigeli Ndahindurwa, Michel Kayihura, Mungalurire, Sebyeza, and above all, Rucyeba, the selfless maverick and nationalist. Rwandese refugees in Kenya had not been resettled in rural camps as had been the case in Uganda, Burundi, and Tanzania. With refugee status, they were given monthly allowances. The lucky and hardworking among them had sought and obtained higher education, enabling them to live middle class life styles. A few drove cars and lived in decent homes. Increasingly they were joined by a new wave of Makerere University graduates who were seeking jobs and a better income. Many of these people got jobs as teachers. Here, in Kenya there was a heightened sense of being Rwandan, or to be more specific, being a Tutsi and a refugee. The cultural mood was upbeat, with a few associations that popularized Rwandan songs and dance. We listened to Kamaliza's and Cecil Kayirebwa's songs.

Post-colonial Kenya had generally enjoyed a stable political environment compared to her neighbors (Uganda, Rwanda, Burundi, Congo, Ethiopia, Sudan, and Eritrea). It was hence home to many refugee populations from all over Africa, including those from Apartheid South Africa, Mozambique and Angola. It is in this hot mix that Rwandese found themselves as probably the earliest refugees on the African continent. The Rwandese community was far from being a united community. Apart from the usual social status demarcations, there were also inter-generational squabbles between the old and young generation, as well as a lingering "cold war" within and among families loyal to the exiled king and those that claimed to be "leftist and modernizers". The radical young among this refugee population seemed to sympathize with the plight of Rucyeba, who was not a Tutsi, but had identified with the monarchists on a nationalist platform. He carried an old, almost threadbare bag that contained his political documents, to testify to what he called the treachery of Belgians, the United Nations and the Hutu regime. I met him once. His conversations were always on Rwanda. He always hoped that younger people would lead the people back home.

CHAPTER SIX

The Embers Of Revolution

The downfall of Uganda's Idi Amin in 1979, and the civil war in Uganda that followed from 1981, had rekindled hope among Rwandan refugees about the possibility of a new struggle to go back home to Rwanda. It is within this revolutionary fervor that some patriotic Rwandans established the Rwandese Alliance for National Unity (RANU) in 1979. Prominent among those who founded or led this organization over the years included Zeno Mutimura, Gabriel Sebyeza, Patrick Mazimpaka, Joseph Mudaheranwa, Peter Bayingana, James Butare, Geoffrey Byegeka, Rasana, Muzungu, to mention but a few. RANU was active in Nairobi. Later in the early 1980's, as the Museveni-led rebel war gained momentum in the Luwero triangle, many young Rwandans joined the ranks of the National Resistance Army. Already within the ranks of the NRM/NRA were young Rwandan officers, Fred Rwigyema and Paul Kagame. They were later joined by Rwandans from Nairobi. These included Dr. Peter Bayingana, Dr. Joseph Mudaheranwa, Geoffrey Byegeka, and many others. The story within Rwandan circles in Nairobi was that they had joined the Ugandan liberation struggle to acquire military skills that they would later use against the Rwandan regime.

In Nairobi, RANU members tried to recruit me and I declined. My elder brother was then a prominent member of this organization. At this point, I did not join the ranks of RANU partly out of sheer stubbornness, and partly due to my new found purist ideological position. For the first time, Rwanda became my major preoccupation. I had not succeeded in joining the NRM struggle in Uganda, but my own home country needed liberation. I sought other people who had Marxist leanings like me. Among them was Nzirimo, who became a very good friend of mine, Kabanda, and older Sebyeza to whom I related. My mother used to tease me saying I hang out with old people. I liked Nzirimo's calm and graceful demeanor. He was intelligent and intensely ideological, with a clear grasp of world history. He carried a strong and selfless passion for revolution. In him I saw some of the characteristics of the prized values of a good Rwandan that I had often heard being described by my mother and other older Rwandans. Though he was older than me, I could detect that he revered me and took me seriously. I started having deep discussion with him on what we could do together to orchestrate a people's revolution in Rwanda. Many other young people during this period were attracted to action, not theories. As a newly self-proclaimed and disciplined Marxist my pendulum had swung to the other extreme. I had completely ditched the study of medicine, and my social life. I had no time for less serious talk, and was less tolerant to other people's ideas. Mine, I thought, was a journey to revolutionary purity.

My brother's return from his graduate studies in London in 1985 meant I was relieved of looking after my mother and sister. It also coincided with the downfall of the Tito Okello military regime in Uganda and Yoweri Museveni's NRM coming to power.

In 1986, in a dramatic reversal of my earlier decision to abandon medical studies, I decided to go back to Uganda, this time with the determination to conclude my medical studies at Makerere University. Three things were on my mind as I returned to Uganda. First of all, I thought Uganda had become the vanguard in what I presumed to be a long term African revolution. The new players in Uganda, and the Rwandans who were associated with the changes there, would influence any revolutionary effort in Rwanda. Second, I felt a marginal and yet persistent inner voice that urged me to complete my university education. I felt that I owed it to my mother whose enormous sacrifices had taken me thus far. Third, I had also witnessed firsthand how difficult it was to live in the modern world without education to fall back to on a rainy day. By going back to medical school, I did not abandon my political agenda. I had matured and knew how to balance the requirements of medical school and those of a much wider and complex political agenda. However, I had scaled back on my high school ambitions to graduate at the top of my class and to proceed to become a distinguished pediatrician. Becoming a revolutionary doctor to deliver a sick society (Rwanda) seemed to me a more attractive and sufficient thing to do. Being a physician, and taking the Hippocratic Oath, was not contradictory to this other path. On the contrary, it would prepare me to become like Che Guevara at the right moment, so I thought.

Fortunately, I found the clinical years at Makerere University Medical School more interesting since they entailed less memorization of information as was the case in the preclinical years. In first and second year students go through a packed agenda of physiology, anatomy, biochemistry, microbiology, and pathology at breakneck speed. By the time you go to third, fourth and fifth year, most of this information crammed during the first two years has receded in memory. I particularly like the investigative and holistic approach of clinical practice. You look at a patient in his/her entire circumstances. You ask him/her about the history of their illness. You examine the patient. You may ask for further evidence from the laboratory. You make a diagnosis. You start the patient on treatment, and explain to him/her so that he/she becomes a partner in his/her own healing process. You follow up on the patient. I also loved public health, especially primary health care. You become attached to your patients, always eager and happy to know if the patient is making progress in the healing process.

I returned to medical school with the mind of a social scientist. Mulago Hospital, a teaching hospital, was a good laboratory of learning about the intersection between politics, social and economic conditions. Makerere Medical School was historically known in international circles. There were medical conditions that were first described here (Burkitt's lymphoma, Buruli Ulcer, etc.). Over the years, Makerere University faculty had become the victims of Idi Amin's tyrannical regime. Many fled. Economic collapse led to institutional decay. Mulago Hospital, the premier national referral hospital, was filthy and overcrowded. Patients came from all corners of the country, and ended up sleeping in corridors, under the beds, and anywhere there was space. Medicines and other essential supplies were scarce. As medical students or interns we carried our daily ration of specimen bottles, gloves, and intravenous giving sets in our clinical coats. Children often died due to lack of intravenous fluids or oxygen.

The fundamental question in my mind at that time was why a society could be governed in a way that such absurd conditions could exist, and for a long time. If rulers were not rectifying such conditions, what else were they thinking about and doing? How could people accept such conditions for that long without rebelling against such rulers? Many thought NRM's struggle, and now NRM rule, was premised in overcoming such conditions. Why is a country unable to have sterilizers? What does it take to produce basic intravenous fluids, oxygen, gloves, and syringes? What does it take to maintain basic cleanliness in a hospital environment? Why should one take so long to study medicine, even very rare conditions, only to find one literally besieged by mothers and their infants from afar, with preventable diseases like measles, whooping cough, diphtheria, tetanus, diarrhea, and respiratory conditions? Couldn't a society empower people in their communities to prevent such ailments, and train enough health workers as first responders to deal with these conditions at the primary, community level? I looked at the filthy conditions at the teaching hospital in Mulago, Kampala, and wondered why a society would be unable to get running water in its one and only national referral hospital. I would ask myself what it takes to manage sewage.

I could see the poverty which surrounded my patients, and how many of their conditions were related to poor livelihoods. We prescribed medicines which were not available, or which had to be bought expensively only by those who could afford them in downtown Kampala. Those were the early years of the HIV/AIDS pandemic and most patients on a medical ward were diagnosed with the disease. There was little that we could do at that time except to discharge the patient to die at home. It intrigued me that the virus itself was discovered in western organizations, by western scientists, and that many years later western pharmaceuticals would invent the treatment, to be supplied to African countries through the benevolence of western aid. Slowly it dawned on me that to be a good doctor required having a society that produces, a population that invests in disease prevention and health promotion, and good managers and leaders who fulfill promises.

In 1986, in a modest but poignant swearing-in ceremony for Yoweri Museveni as the new President of Uganda, the prevailing political mood in Uganda was one of triumph and hope. President Museveni told cheering crowds in Kampala that "this was not a mere change of guard, but a fundamental change". The NRM victory reinforced that struggles could be fought and won. The basic premise of revolutionary struggles, as I had read in Marxist theory and NRM seemed to confirm, was the *objective* conditions of the people. These included the social, economic, political, cultural, historical, regional and international factors. As objective conditions mature, there is need to mobilize, organize and lead. These later conditions are *subjective*. The confluence and maturity of objective and subjective factors challenge the status quo, subsequently producing revolutionary change. If Rwanda's objective conditions were ripe, how mature were the subjective factors?

Among the officers of Yoweri Museveni's National Resistance Army (NRA) were several Rwandan officers and men, among them Fred Rwigyema, Paul Kagame, Dr. Peter Bayingana, and Chris Bunyenyezi. These were to play a crucial role in the establishment of the Rwandese Patriotic Front (RPF) in 1987. The Rwandese Alliance for National Unity (RANU), established in 1979, now became RPF, given fresh impetus from NRM's victory and the presence of Rwandan officers and men in the new order of things in Uganda.

The presence of Rwandans in the military structures of Uganda was not new. During Idi Amin's regime some Rwandans were recruited in the military and intelligence and this had created resentment among Ugandans. This time the presence was massive and presented a significant dilemma to President Yoweri Museveni. On the one hand it was celebrated amongst Rwandans, who now became confident since they could no longer be persecuted in Uganda. On the other hand, it created some unease and animosity amongst many Ugandans, notably within the National Resistance Army itself, who began to question why "foreigners should rule Uganda". Fred Rwigyema, a charismatic soldier, had been promoted to the rank of General. Paul Kagame was a Major and director of administration within the Directorate of Military Intelligence. Dr. Peter Bayingana was a Major, and Director of Medical Services. There were Rwandan officers in the command and administration of the army, and they constituted a coherent group within Uganda's military. The officers knew that ultimately their loyalty was to General Fred Rwigyema. High expectations among Rwandans, and a sense of betrayal by former Ugandan comrades-in-arms, created tension within the leadership of NRM and the RPF. In the meantime RPF started mobilizing politically and militarily, developing cadres, often fresh graduates from Makerere University. Among the chief political mobilizers were Tito Rutaremara, Kabanda, Christine Umutoni, and the late Aloysea Inyumba. Young Rwandans enrolled into cadet military training schools in big numbers.

Tension within the RPF leadership at this point hinged on two crucial dynamics inherent in every transition. Peter Bayingana, Tito Rutaremara and other former RANU civilian leaders sought a speedy move towards the armed struggle in Rwanda. They were uneasy that General Fred Rwigyema, Major Paul Kagame and other officers in Uganda's National Resistance Army would become "comfortable" in their new positions, and fail to seize the momentum towards armed struggle in Rwanda. In addition, Dr.Bayingana and Tito Rutaremara felt that General Rwigyema and Major Kagame were soldiers who needed political guidance as well.

On his part, the charismatic General Rwigyema played a cautious approach, putting emphasis on the unity of purpose, and playing a delicate game with President Yoweri Museveni, as he prepared and considered options. At this juncture, many RPF leaders who are familiar with that period say Major Paul Kagame played a secondary, and yet very divisive role, in promoting the unity of refugees.

As I settled in the Medical School in 1986, I kept my political activities at a minimum. This was a time of heightened political activity within the Rwandan communities in Uganda and elsewhere among the diaspora. Having declined to join RANU in Nairobi, I kept a distance from RPF in Uganda. With some students at Makerere University, I formed a study group which regularly met to discuss the history, geography, economy, socio-economic conditions, culture, military and diplomatic relations of Rwanda. We discussed the Tutsi, Hutu, and Twa ethnic questions and gravitated towards Walter Rodney's explanation in *How Europe Underdeveloped Africa* that the difference in physical characteristics between the Hutu and Tutsi was based on diet. The Tutsi were pastoralists and had a high protein diet, and were hence taller. The Hutu depended on agriculture, and hence had a diet rich in carbohydrates. The Hutu, argued Rodney, were thus short and stocky. Since Marxism taught that all struggles hitherto had been class struggles, our outlook was to reduce all dividing lines to class, and pit the peasants against the state bureaucrats with their propertied allies. We wished we had a clean "working class versus capitalists" kind of revolution but Rwanda's conditions were different. Who were the national bourgeoise? Who were the petit bourgeoisie? Who were the proletariat? How did imperialism manifest itself in Rwanda at that time? Who were Rwanda's allies and why? In an armed struggle would Zaire's Mobutu, Belgium and France come to support Rwanda's military regime? Who could be our allies? We had the right revolutionary vocabulary, and we often wanted Rwanda's conditions to fit our Marxist analysis.

During my Nairobi days I had acquainted myself with protracted guerilla warfare. Mao ZeDong was an authority on the subject. For a few shillings you could obtain most of his works in English. Since my new found and recent heroes were Che Guevara and Fidel Castro of the Cuban revolution, Yoweri Museveni of the now victorious NRM struggle, Ugandan and Cuban experiences presented good case studies on how to wage and win a guerrilla war. Our minds wandered on the horizon to study Samora Machel's Frente de Libertação de Moçambique (FRELIMO) and the Mozambican war of independence, Augustinho Neto of Movimento Popular de Libertação de Angola – Partido do Trabalho (MPLA) and the Angolan war, Amilcar Cabral of Guinea Bissau and Cape Verde, Ho Chi Minh and the Vietnam War, the Sandinistas in Nicaragua, etc. This was still the era of the Soviet Union and the cold war, and clearly the east was "our friend" and the west "our enemy'. Ironically, even as protracted civil wars were going on in Ethiopia and Eritrea, President Mengistu was supposed to be our friend. Now that we had the "right ideology", we had to test it with practice.

With this revolutionary zeal and a quest for Marxist purity, I approached my older friend Nzirimo and my other friends in the Makerere University study group, and we established a liberation front, Front de Liberation National (FROLINA). My friend Nzirimo quit his teaching job in Kenya, and with a few of his savings joined me in Kampala towards the end of 1989. Early in 1990, when I was doing my internship at Mulago Hospital, he came to stay with me in my room. There, between my busy schedules as an intern, we discussed FROLINA's political military strategy. As a first step we needed to do a reconnaissance trip to the Uganda-Rwanda border. We planned to buy a farm in the vicinity of the border, recruit future freedom fighters from Uganda and Rwanda, and train them there. The next step would be to infiltrate the freedom fighters into Rwanda until we had a critical number in the nucleus to spark off an insurgency. The peasants, both Hutu and Tutsi, would begin to join FROLINA once we had mounted daring raids on the government's isolated military detachments, and begun the war to win their hearts and minds.

With this in mind, we bought a dilapidated typewriter off the streets of Kampala, to begin producing propaganda material. We bought a bicycle. One time we set off from the Oruchinga Refugee settlement to do the first of our reconnaissance missions, in search of a farm. Past Rwamurunga, Kajaho, we cycled till it was nightfall. These areas have undulating hills. After a while we were tired and walked most of the way, pushing the bicycles. Our meals comprised of sweet bananas bought alongside the road. We had miscalculated the distance involved. It was nightfall and we stood in danger of being questioned by suspicious local inhabitants. We called off the trip, and headed back. The reconnaissance would have to wait until we could afford a motorcycle at least. By the time we reached Kajaho on our way back, we had to pass by a relative of mine to look for food. The relative was very surprised to see us, but never suspected what kind of mission we were on.

My rigid ideological position in the meantime had alienated me from my own brother. Newly married to Anne Musominari in 1990, Gahima had abandoned his high paying job as a lawyer in a Nairobi law firm to work full time for RPF. He had been deployed in Bujumbura, Burundi. I could not see eye to eye with some fellow students who were RPF cadres. It was during my brother's pre-wedding functions that I met Major Paul Kagame for the first time. I was in such a rebellious and revolutionary mood that by the time of my graduation from the medical school, I did not even appear for the formal graduation ceremonies to take the formal Hippocratic Oath. Other than the busy routine of an intern, and the increasingly palpable mood of revolt, I had now started living with my mother who had returned to Uganda after my brother became a full-time volunteer with the RPF. It was a sweet time to live with my mother. I had delivered on the promise of completing my education. My sister, Doreen Kayitesi, had joined the National Resistance Army, and was now a second lieutenant. We stayed with our mother, and with meager earnings complemented each other to sustain the livelihood of the shared household.

Meanwhile the officers and men of the RPF in the NRA had become an army within an army. RPF was intensely involved in mobilization. It was no longer a question as to whether RPF would invade Rwanda but rather when. As for me, I was coming towards the end of my internship after which I would work full time for the revolution. The orderly life with my mother seemed to me to be a temporary calm before a fiery storm.

CHAPTER SEVEN

The Spark

One morning, on 1ˢᵗ October, 1990, as I walked to work, on the gates of Mulago Hospital in Kampala, I met a friend of mine who put me aside and whispered into my ear that "abahungu bambutse", (translated, " the boys have crossed"). He told me it was an invasion by RPF and consisted of several hundreds of Rwandan officers and men from the Ugandan army, the National Resistance Army (NRA). I asked him whether General Fred Rwigyema was part of the invasion. My friend confirmed to me that from what he had heard, General Rwigyema was leading the invasion. We did not discuss the subject any further. I got to the medical ward where I worked as an intern and conducted a ward round with my consultant, an American visiting physician. Shortly after 2 pm I left. As I drove back home that afternoon, I considered my options. This was the first defining moment in my young adult life. Would I join the RPF that had now launched an armed struggle or not? Would I abandon the medical career temporarily or for good? Would the RPF now accept me, having alienated myself from it for so long? Even if they accepted me would I be safe?

My first concern was an ordinary one. I now lived with my mother who had recently come back from Kenya after my brother had left his job to work full time for the Rwandese

Patriotic Front . Where and with whom could I leave her? As I got back home, I soon learnt that my sister, Doreen Kayitesi, then a Second Lieutenant in the NRA, had departed for Rwanda to join the Rwandese Patriotic Army (RPA), the armed wing of the Rwandese Patriotic Front (RPF). She just left behind a note for me, asking me to continue to look after our mother. My second consideration was more serious. Over the years, my intellectual and ideological development had somehow turned me into a very self-conscious being, with minimal tolerance for those who were less schooled than me in matters of ideology. I did not socialize and kept to myself, and had very few friends. The closest friends I had were Captain Enoch Nkunda of the NRA, and Nzirimo, a comrade- in-arms and co-founder of our infant politico-military organization, FROLINA. I did not belong to RPF , which I found militaristic, condescending and overbearing, expecting every Rwandese Tutsi refugee to belong to their organization. Despite efforts in Nairobi and Kampala to recruit me, I had declined. I was known among the leaders of the diaspora as an eccentric dissenter, and probably to few, as an "enemy". In my thought process I was wondering whether I should swallow my pride and join the struggle now that RPF had done what many Rwandans in the Diaspora were longing for. Whether RPF would accept me in their ranks and how safe I would be under the circumstances was a matter of speculation and not a priority at that moment.

My third concern was a bit moralistic and somewhat philosophical. Though I had not come to love the study of medicine in the early years, my clinical years had left me attached to the noble profession of saving lives. In the footsteps of Hippocrates, the Greek who lived in 5th Century B.C. and who is considered to be the father of modern medicine, I was beginning to like tending to the patients and looking forward to seeing their recovery after going through my hands. Such was the expectations of your revered teachers, and from the Hippocratic Oath.

As I contemplated the basic precepts on violence that Fanon popularized in the *Wretched of the Earth*, I also had the doctor in me that found taking other people's lives repulsive. The famous Prussian general and military strategist, Carl von Clausewitz, wrote in his seminal classic, *On War*, that "war is a continuation of policy by other means". The very idea of war run against my human and professional instincts. What was the greater ideal for which I was willing to die for, and to kill for? Revolutionary change was worth dying and killing for. Wasn't I being called upon to be a physician, to perform some midwifery, to deliver a new Rwandan society out of the old, as Karl Marx had taught? The revolution now had come and demanded my participation, even to sacrifice my life if required. Revolutionary ideology taught me to be open and flexible. The hour of decision had come. My decision was to join the revolution under the banner of RPF and shelve FROLINA.

I was very anxious to find a way of explaining my decision to my mother. Over supper with my mother, I thought I was breaking the news to her as to the day's historic developments. I found out that my sister had been at home earlier in the day and told her she was going. By the evening of that day I had already decided to go. Even before I announced my decision to my mother, she looked at me in the eye and said, "Theogene, I hope you are joining others". I said, "Yes." She understood the implications of having three children involved in war. But she also understood the need. Even with a very charged schedule she had, she always had time to talk about Rwanda, through tales and songs, and lullabies. Being in a refugee camp had kept our native language, *Kinyarwanda*, intact. She had always taught us hard work, being proud and respectful of Rwandan culture, and to love Rwanda. For somebody who never had any formal education, my mother has always amazed me. My Marxism and atheism did not impress her. She always argued with me that I was alive and educated because of her prayers and her rosary. She also had some skepticism about whether Rwandese refugees would ever summon enough wisdom to unite and go back home. Even if they did, she used to tell me, they would soon find cause to fight amongst each other like our Tutsi ancestors did. She would give numerous examples in ancient and modern Rwandan history of how divisions have always been the rule, rather than the exception. That night she was, like me, both upbeat and anxious about what would follow.

I had some time to look at some of the documents and revolutionary literature I had gathered over the years. Among them was the famous Che Guevara letter to Fidel Castro:

Fidel,

At this moment I remember many things; when I first met you in the (Mexico City) house of Maria Antonia, when you proposed I come along, all the tensions involved in the preparations. One day they came by and asked who should be notified in case of death, and the real possibility of that fact struck us all. Later we knew it was true, that in revolution one wins or dies (if it is a real one).

Today everything has a less dramatic tone, because we are more mature. But the event repeats itself. I feel that I have fulfilled the part of my duty that tied me to the Cuban revolution in its territory, and I say goodbye to you, to the comrades, to your people, who are now mine.

I formally resign my position in the leadership of the party, my post as minister, my rank of commander, and my Cuban leadership. Nothing legal binds me to Cuba.

Recalling my past life, I believe I have worked with sufficient integrity and dedication to consolidate the revolutionary triumph. My only serious failing was not having had more confidence in you from the first moments in the Sierra Maestra, and not having understood quickly enough your qualities as a leader and as a revolutionary.

I have lived magnificent days, and at your side I felt the pride of belonging to our people in the brilliant yet sad days of the Caribbean (missile) crisis. Seldom has a statesman been more brilliant than you in those days…

Other nations of the world call for my modest efforts. I can do that which is denied to you because of your responsibility at the head of Cuba, and the time has come for us to part.

I want it known that I do so with a mixture of joy and sorrow. I leave here the purest of my hopes as a builder and the dearest of my loved ones. And I leave a people who received me as a son. That wounds a part of my spirit. I carry to new battlefronts the faith that you taught me, the revolutionary spirit of my people, the feeling of fulfilling the most sacred of duties: to fight imperialism wherever one may be. This comforts and more than heals the deepest wounds.

I state once more that I free Cuba from any responsibility except that which stems from its example. If my final hour finds me under other skies, my last thought will be of the people and especially you. I am not sorry that I leave nothing material to my wife and children. I am happy it is that way. I ask nothing of them, as the state will provide them with enough to live on and to have an education.

Hasta la Victoria siempre! Patria o muerte!

Che

In a revolution one wins or dies if it is a real one. This was an uncomfortable truth. On 2nd October, 1990, my brother arrived in Kampala. His arrival was a great relief to me. Since he was one of the senior leaders of the RPF, I thought he would help me navigate what I had feared would be hostility towards me. Through contacts he knew in Kampala we organized to travel together to Kagitumba, the invasion point in North East Rwanda through which RPA forces had crossed the previous day. One more time, my brother and I had the opportunity to go back home to bid farewell to our mother. I had asked my very good friend, Captain Enoch Nkunda, an officer in the NRA, to do the best he could to help my mother. That night, my brother and I, together with a couple of other refugees boarded a small "Datsun 1200" pickup driven by a young man by the name of Roger Rutikanga. We were mostly quiet for most of the way, each man seemingly in a pensive and contemplative mood. We drove through Masaka, Mbarara, and Ntungamo in southwest Uganda, and finally to the entry point, Kagitumba, where the previous day an epic but brief battle had been fought. There, in the late hour of October 2, 1990, I set foot on Rwandan soil, beginning a journey that would be both dangerous and transforming in ways that I could never have imagined.

CHAPTER EIGHT

The Storm

In the early hours of the morning of 1st October, 1990, a group of soldiers under the command of General Fred Rwigyema deserted the Ugandan Army and crossed into north eastern Rwanda at a lightly defended border post of Kagitumba. A short skirmish ensued as the Rwandan army detachment was overpowered. With the opening shots, a spark of the second bloody revolution in modern Rwanda was ignited. Like all revolutions, RPF sought to change history by changing prevailing circumstances in Rwanda. What was the history that RPF wanted to change? What were the objective conditions that RPF sought to change? How would RPF change these conditions?

The history that RPF promised to change is a contested territory amongst Rwandans and foreigners who take interest in Rwanda. In history, Rwandans find justification for actions of the day's government or rebellion against it. In history Rwandans find evidence of their separateness or their unity. In history, Rwandans find their own distinctiveness and, they even argue, their greatness, in a region that over centuries saw the rise and fall of the centralized kingdom of Rwanda. Some see in Rwanda's history the story of great Tutsi kings while others would highlight the plight of the majority Hutu, and occasionally, the minority Twa. There is also the argument about who was there in the very beginning. Aren't the Twa and Hutu indigenous, and the Tutsi an alien conquering race that subjugated the rest? Even what we called objective conditions in Rwanda that needed to be changed were seen differently, depending on one's ethnicity.

Only 26,338 square kilometers (10,169 square miles) in land area, Rwanda is a landlocked country in central Africa that shares boundaries with the Democratic Republic of Congo, Uganda, Tanzania and Burundi. The longest distance across Rwanda is about 400 kilometers. Some writers have described it as a Lilliput (from Jonathan Swift's *Gulliver's Travels*) due to its small size, and the "Switzerland of Africa" due to its hilly nature and somewhat temperate climate, especially in the north. On a map of Africa, Rwanda is barely visible. It is a small country with a mystical and intriguing aura, complex problems and currently with oversized ambitions.

It is characteristically hilly, hence its description as "the land of a thousand hills". Rwanda is located in what is called the Great Lakes (the Interlacustrine) region because of the lakes Victoria, Kivu, Tanganyika, George, Edward and Kyoga among which developed the various centralized kingdoms of Buganda, Bunyoro, Ankole, Buhaya, Busubi, Buha, etc. Currently the population of Rwanda is about 11 million. There are three ethnic groups, Hutu, Tutsi, and Twa who all speak one Bantu language, Kinyarwanda. Rwanda is predominantly an agrarian society, with the majority of Rwandans living on subsistence agriculture. Many sources say Hutu are a majority , comprising about 85% of the population, Tutsi a minority (14%), and Twa (1%). The truth of the matter is that nobody really knows the precise percentages.

According to historians, early state formation in central Rwanda probably took place some time in the 14th Century, under Tutsi kings. Highly centralized, the kingdom was organized in social units called clans (ubwoko). Clans are defined by the Oxford English dictionary as a group of close-knit, inter-related families. Rwanda had 20 such clans , namely, Abanyiginya,

Abagesera, Abega, Ababanda, Abacyaba, Abasinga, Abashambo, Abahinda, Abazigaba, Abungura, Abashingwe, Abenengwe, Abasita, Abatsobe, Abakono, Abanyakarama, Abarihira, Abahondogo, Abashambo, and Abongera. It was also organized around lineages that traced descent from a common ancestor. The kings of Rwanda hailed from the Abanyiginya clan while the queen mothers hailed from the Abega clan. Like many African cultures, Rwandan culture, and history in general, is handed down from generation to generation orally.

These are the kings of Rwanda and their approximate periods of reign:

Ndahiro Ruyange	?
Ndoba	1386
Samembe	1410
Nsoro Samukondo	1434
Ruganzu Bwimbwa	1458
Cyilima Bugwe	1482
Kigeri Mukobanya	1506
Mibambwe Mutabazi	1528
Yuhi Gahima	1552
Ndahiro Cyaamatare	1576
Ruganzu Ndoori	1600
Mutara Semugeshi	1624
Kigeri Nyamuheshera	1648
Mibambwe Gisanura	1672
Yuhi Mazimpaka	1696
Karemeera Rwaaka	1720
Cyilima Rujugira	1744
Kigeli Ndabarasa	1768
Mibambwe Seentaabyo	1792

Yuhi Gahindiro	1797
Mutaara Rwogera	1830
Kigeri Rwabugiri	1860
Mibambwe Rutalindwa	1895
Yuhi Musinga	1896
Mutara Rudahigwa	1931
Kigeli Ndahindurwa	1959

Source: *Rwanda and Burundi*, Rene Lemarchand

As already mentioned, all kings were Tutsi, and from the Abanyiginya clan. The king's rule was absolute, with all other Rwandans, whether Hutu, Tutsi or Twa being his subjects. Under him were chiefs, most of whom, though not exclusively, were Tutsi. The production system in Rwanda was still simple, organized around cattle keeping, agriculture, pottery and handcrafting (including weaving and metal works). The population was still small, land productive, and the climate conducive, while there was voluntary exchange of products of labor. There was a client-patron system of *ubuhake* through which the socio-economic pyramid reproduced and sustained itself. Involving cows in the relationship, the patron afforded protection to the client, in exchange for services to the patron. Hence, the king was the patron-in-chief. Next to him in the hierarchy were the Tutsi chiefs, and all the way down the socio-economic ladder, with the ordinary Tutsi, Hutu and Twa at the bottom. This system existed for over six centuries through a combination of coercion (the king had an army), socio-economic means (*ubuhake*), and myths that exalted the king and the monarchy to almost godly status. Yet, in this pre-industrial, largely agrarian society, the demands of the monarchy on the day-to-day lives of ordinary Tutsi, Hutu or Twa could not have been too high as it happened later with the western colonial conquest. While the whole monarchical system was based on inequality, the social relationship between and among the Tutsi, Hutu and Twa was not sharply conflictual but rather symbiotic. The central kingdom was slow in extending its reach to all the corners of present day Rwanda, especially in the north and east.

Towards the end of the 19th Century, Rwanda became colonized by Germany, and later after the First World War, by Belgium. Germany's colonial rule was rather short, and did not have significant impact on the future of Rwanda. Belgian rule, which lasted until 1962, has had a deep, wide and enduring impact on the Rwandan society. Four parallel processes were introduced with the colonial administration.

First, colonial rule challenged the myth of the king as the top, almost godly, of the order of things in Rwandan society. For the first time since the establishment of the monarchy there was another authority above the king. The colonial authority worked through indirect rule, through the centralized structure of the monarchy.

Second, Christianity was introduced almost at the same time as colonial rule. Traditional Rwandan society believed in one god, *Imana y'i Rwanda* (the god of Rwanda). Christianity was a profound and disruptive idea. The religion established that there was only one God, and that Jesus Christ was His only Son, through whom humankind could receive salvation. Slow at adapting to this new religion, once the kings converted, the impact would soon be pervasive and of lasting consequences. In its message, religion was an equalizer, and ordinary Rwandans could receive salvation directly, bypassing the king and his chiefs. God was the King of kings. Some of the rituals that were part of the monarchy's mythology were banned as pagan, further undermining the authority of the king. King Musinga never warmed up to the colonizing power and their religion. He was banished into exile in Kamembe, southwest Rwanda, where he died.

Third, colonial rule and the Christian religion introduced western education, and with it, reading and writing. Colonial administration needed cadres to service it. The Christian church needed to produce local priests and catechists that would help in spreading the gospel. Education was at first a privilege for only the sons of Tutsi chiefs. Soon it would be extended to others as well. With time, especially among the Hutu, and generally in the whole society, education and Christian instruction created both a social group consciousness and expectations towards equal treatment under the colonial regime. This slowly created the opposition to the status quo.

Fourth, with colonial rule came the introduction of the rudiments of capitalism. Rwanda was now part of the global economy. As such, it was required to be part of the global market for finished goods originating from European industries. Rwanda was also supposed to be viewed as a source of raw materials for western industries. Eager to be self-sufficient within Rwanda, and probably produce a surplus, the colonial administration introduced forced labor (*uburetwa*), in addition to the existing *ubuhake*. This dual burden, especially on the shoulders of the Hutu, deepened the grievances against the Tutsi chiefs and the Tutsi king.

After the Second World War, as the quest for de-colonization in Africa gathered momentum, both the monarchy and the Belgian colonial administration tried some reforms to bring about representation of the Hutu in political and social spheres. King Mutara Rudahigwa, the reigning monarch since the deportation of Yuhi Musinga in 1933, might have sensed the dangers posed by the deepening and sharp inequalities that placed the majority Hutu at a disadvantage. He banned *uburetwa* and modified the *ubuhake* which now required of Tutsi patrons to share the cows with the Hutu clients. In the mid-fifties, a group of former seminarians, among them Gregoire Kayibanda, aided by the Catholic Church, was beginning to mobilize and organize around the idea of Hutu emancipation. For them, the priority was to be liberated from centuries of monarchical rule, and independence from Belgian colonial rule as a secondary demand. With their mouthpiece newspaper, *Kinyamateka,* and later through the *Bahutu Manifesto of 1957*, the political party Mouvement Démocratique Républicain Parmehutu (MDR-PARMEHUTU), popular support, colonial and church backing, the stakes were increasingly in their favor.

On the side of the monarchy the demands were of a different kind. First, King Mutara Rudahigwa's reforms, though limited, were unpopular among the Tutsi chiefs simply because they upset the power and privilege they had enjoyed for centuries. Second, to them the priority was to end colonial rule under a nationalist platform, Union Nationale Rwandaise (UNAR). It is under this contentious and acrimonious atmosphere that King Mutara Rudahigwa died abruptly in Bujumbura, Burundi, precipitating a dramatic succession to power of young King Kigeli Ndahindurwa in 1959.

The irreconcilable demands of this period, the just demands of the majority Hutu, the intransigence of the Tutsi monarchists, the ethnic bias of both the Catholic Church and the colonial administration in favor of the Hutu revolution, and the apparent helplessness of the United Nations to broker an equitable peaceful arrangement meant that the monarchy was historically in its last throes. When, on January 28, 1961, Hutu bourgmestres and local counselors gathered in the central Rwanda location of Gitarama under the guidance of the Belgian authorities to proclaim the end of the monarchy and the birth of the Republic, the 1959 Revolution had been consummated, leading to formal independence from Belgium on 1st July, 1962. Dominique Mbonyumutwa, a Hutu, became the first President of the Republic.

Subsequently, many Tutsi were massacred and others went into exile during and after the 1959 revolution. MDR-PARMEHUTU and UNAR were not the only political parties at the time of the 1959 revolution and its aftermath. Rassemblement Démocratique Rwandais (RADER) and Association pour la Promotion Sociale de la Masse (APROSOMA) were the other political parties that attempted to participate in the elections. However, soon the political space was closed, the leaders of the RADER and APROSOMA killed, and the political parties banned as Rwanda became one party state under MDR-PARMEHUTU, with Gregoire Kayibanda as the President. By then the king and UNAR were in exile. So were hundreds of thousands of Tutsi in neighboring Uganda, Burundi, Tanzania and Congo. Repeated attempts to launch an armed struggle by exiled Tutsi (known as *Inyenzi or* cockroaches) were futile, and prompted more reprisals in which more Tutsi were massacred in the 1960's. More massacres of Tutsi took place in 1972.

The center of gravity of the Kayibanda regime was southern Rwanda. With time his power base shrunk, as he consolidated more and more of the power into his hands and a narrow group of followers from his home commune. With Tutsi long subdued or out of sight in exile, the Hutu revolution was showing cracks, as President Kayibanda and his supporters from southern Rwanda sought to change the constitution and extend his rule.

In 1973, President Gregoire Kayibanda was overthrown by his own Defense Minister, General Juvenal Habyarimana, in a relatively bloodless coup that was more of a change of guard within the Hutu elite rather than a revolution. General Habyarimana hailed from the north of the country, and soon many politicians from the south, including former President Gregoire Kayibanda perished at the hands of the security organs of the new military regime. The new military regime later metamorphosed into Mouvement Républicain National pour la Démocratie et le Développement (MRND), and run on the promise of uniting the Rwandan people, peace and development. Rwanda remained a one party state, higly centralized under President Habyarimana.

As an individual, General Habyarimana was perceived by some Hutu and Tutsi as being soft on the ethnic question, meaning he was more tolerant to Tutsi than his predecessor, Gregoire Kayibanda. Some Tutsi were able to do business, and he brought some into government. Others, like Valens Kajeguhakwa were very close to him.

Still, the regime had a Hutu and northern bias, and institutions like the military and security services were, by and large, no-go areas for the Tutsi. Due to persecution, exile and discrimination in society, the Tutsi had more or less resigned to second-class citizen status. The powers of making laws, the judiciary, the executive, and the party were formally or informally vested in President Habyarimana and a narrowing circle of people, mainly from the northern part of Rwanda. Civil society was heavily under the influence of government, while independent media, till the late 1980's, did not exist.

On the eve of the RPF invasion in 1990, Rwanda still looked calm, and its chief executive, President Habyarimana exuded a calm demeanor. The regime had the right friends in Europe, notably France and Belgium. President Mobutu Sese Seko of Zaire (now Democratic Republic of Congo or DRC) was a close friend. Overall, President Habyarimana was respected in the region and internationally, notwithstanding the serious domestic problems. Aid money was flowing although the threats of declining prices of coffee and tea, and structural adjustment programmes from the International Monetary Fund and the World Bank were looming on the horizon. The wave of democratization was spreading across the world and, in Africa Rwanda was one of those countries that were still dragging their feet in the hope of delaying the re-introduction of multi-partyism. Still Rwanda scored high marks as a poor country that managed aid with results and impact. There was, evidently, tension within Rwanda, but President Habyarimana seemed to be managing. It was a deceptive calm before a violent storm.

It is this deceptive calm that the RPF invasion unmasked on the 1st of October. RPF sought to redress the past and the present problems through its political programme, namely,

- restoration of unity among Rwandans,
- defend the security of the people and their property,
- establish democracy,

- promote a mixed economy based on the country's natural resources,
- improve the socio-economic conditions of the people,
- end once and for all the problem of refugees,
- and promote regional co-operation and international peaceful relations based on mutual respect.

The most important and rallying cry for the 1990 RPF invasion was, however, the return of the Rwandan refugees. The invading force on the 1st October, 1990 comprised mainly of sons and daughters of exiled Tutsi. The charismatic General Fred Rwigyema, who led the invasion was himself barely three years old when his parents went into exile. He, like many in the invading force had either fled as babies or been born in exile. The majority were stepping on Rwandan soil for the first time in their lives.

CHAPTER NINE

Fred Rwigyema

On my first day at the Kagitumba border post, the scene was somewhat strange. Senior officers of the new army, the Rwandese Patriotic Army(RPA) seemed unusually relaxed. In my mind I thought it was evidence that things were under control. By the third day of October, there were many young Rwandans from Uganda who were joining the new revolutionary force in Rwanda. Many of them, like me, had never been in the military. We assembled in groups to be told what to do next. Major Peter Bunyenyezi, also dressed casually in sandals, briefly addressed the new recruits. He told us the war was progressing well, and that we had to be trained quickly to support the war effort. Once he had finished speaking and we had been dismissed, I saw my sister who was surprised to see me. We strolled to a nearby tree, and there under a shade she whispered to me that General Fred Rwigyema was dead and that he had been killed in action. I was silent. And soon, tears run down my cheeks but I quickly composed myself. I felt Fred's death personally.

Two days before, I had decided to join the revolution, and even die in it. I was assured in my mind that it was honorable to be led by Fred. I had never met him. He had built a reputation in Uganda and among Rwandese that he would never ask you to do what he himself could not do. He was a consensus-builder, cheerful, and large hearted. As my sister left, my mind was racing with so many questions. Was Fred a victim of friendly fire from within RPF, or was he the victim of his selfless charismatic style of leading from the front? What was the chance that the revolution would survive and succeed now that Fred was dead?

Fred Rwigyema was born in Rwanda and fled with his parents when he was a small child. As one of the victims of the 1959 violent revolution and the massacres of the Tutsi that followed it, Fred's parents fled to Uganda. He grew up in a refugee camp of Kahunge in the southwest region of Uganda, in the district of Toro. He later briefly attended secondary school at Mbarara High School, in Mbarara, in current Mbarara disctrict. Due to the tumultuous events of the early 1970's, Fred left school to join the then young revolutionary Yoweri Museveni in Tanzania to wage a people's protracted war against the regime of Idi Amin. During the 1979 Tanzania-Uganda war, Fred was one of the young military leaders in Yoweri Museveni's Front for National Salvation (FRONASA) that was part of the Tanzania-backed forces of Ugandan exiles. As the Uganda National Liberation Front (UNLF) governments unraveled rather quickly, and the political and security situation deteriorated in the run up to the elections of 1980, Yoweri Museveni had been relegated to a rather un-influential cabinet portfolio for regional cooperation. When Yoweri Museveni started the bush war in 1981, Fred was among the 27 men that fought alongside him.

By the time Yoweri Museveni's NRM/NRA captured state power on January 26, 1986, Fred had risen to be one of the most trusted, loved and charismatic officers.

The period from 1986 to 1990 saw Fred's political and military fortunes ebb and flow. Because he was a distinguished soldier and officer, he was always given demanding tasks. He was one of the commanders on the western front in Uganda in the run up to the fall of the Tito Okello regime. Before the RPF invasion in 1990, he had led the war effort in northern Uganda. Because he was a good officer, loyal to President Museveni, respected by his peers, and loved by those under his command, but a Rwandan, he was a subject of petty jealousies from other Ugandan officers, who felt he was a foreigner who was enjoying the limelight at their expense. At some point during this period, Fred essentially had become a jobless general. On the question of Fred and the Rwandans in general, a politically savvy Yoweri Museveni was navigating pressures from his military and from Ugandan political forces at large who demanded the resolution of the Rwandan citizenship question. His deployment to the northern war effort was seen by some Rwandans, and probably by Fred, as an opportunistic decision by President Museveni. "Fred and the Rwandans are his fighting machines", it used to be said. Still young, capable, but marginalized, Fred must have felt pushed by Ugandan factors to find a way of getting out of the situation.

On the eve of the RPF invasion, there were factors within Rwanda that were pulling General Rwigyema and the RPF to action. General Juvenal Habyamana was effectively in charge. He controlled a Hutu dominated army of about 5,000, security agencies, the party and the central and local administration. Rwanda was the darling of western donors, who sympathized with the small, landlocked and overpopulated country. They praised the general for a job well done, and occasionally gently prodded him to undertake democratic reforms. The Tutsi remained second-class citizens although the majority of the Hutu remained impoverished. Having registered some gains on the social and economic front, the pre-1990 years saw a decline in coffee and tea prices, an increase in soil erosion, and endemic famine in some areas of Rwanda. Structural adjustment policies of the World Bank and IMF had begun to bite. There was a mood of dissatisfaction within the ruling circles, and the Hutu intra-group solidarity was no longer taken for granted. The Hutu elite from the south of Rwanda were agitating for democratic reforms. Nevertheless, President Habyarimana still had good friends, notably France, Belgium, and Zaire. The internal situation in Rwanda could not have been the only worry that the late President Habyarimana had on the eve of 1990. His security apparatus must have appraised him of the threat from the north, from Uganda.

But first, a note on Rwandese refugees, because it is this particular endemic problem, more than anything else, that precipitated the 1990 civil war. A Jewish prophet, Prophet Jeremiah (NIV, Jeremiah 29:5-7) once advised his exiled fellow country men and women in exile in Babylon:

> Build houses and settle down, plant gardens and eat what they produce. Marry and have sons and daughters; find wives for your sons and give your daughters in marriage so that they too may have sons and daughters. Increase in number there, do not decrease.. Also, seek the peace and prosperity of the city to which I have carried you into exile. Pray to the Lord for it, because if it prospers, you too shall prosper.

The Psalmist (Psalms: 137), laments:

> By the rivers of Babylon we sat and wept
> when we remembered Zion.
> There on the poplars
> we hung our harps,
> for there our captors asked us for songs,
> our tormentors demanded songs of joy;
> they said, "Sing us one of the songs of Zion!"
> How can we sing the songs of the LORD
> while in a foreign land?
> If I forget you, Jerusalem,
> may my right hand forget its skill.
> May my tongue cling to the roof of my mouth
> if I do not remember you,
> if I do not consider Jerusalem
> my highest joy.

Prophet Jeremiah's words and the Psalmist's song highlight the dilemma that a conscious refugee perpetually faces. On the one hand, there is the urge to normalize life. Initially there is the self-denial that prompts you to refuse to accept that you have been uprooted. Given the politics of the refugee camps, expectation and anticipation are rife. Refugees always think they will be going back home soon. Month after month, year after year, it finally dawns on refugees that the sooner they begin to live "normal" lives, the better for them and their offspring. Seeking the "peace and prosperity" of the country of asylum, of the refugee camp, of the local community, is part of the refugee's survival instinct. This means seeking accommodation with the status quo, and moving the extra mile to be in the host's good books. In Burundi, Tanzania, DRC (then Zaire), Uganda, Kenya, and elsewhere a few Rwandese refugees sometimes succeeded in getting close to the powers of the day. Bisengimana was close to President Mobutu. Kigeli Ndahindurwa and a few Rwandan officers were close to Uganda's Idi Amin. Tribert Rujugiro was close to President Bagaza of Burundi. Fred Rwigyema was close to President Museveni. Occasionally, it was the Rwandese refugees' daughters and sons that became the relationship builders through marriage.

On the other hand, being a refugee concentrates your foreignness in ways that are hard to imagine or describe. Some of us had left Rwanda as babies. The majority of Rwandese had now been born and raised in exile. As you grow within the confines of the refugee camp, your separateness from the local community becomes a painful reality. As you navigate the world of education, employment, or business, you have to lie, beseech, appease, or simply work harder to impress. Being a refugee dehumanizes and therefore politicizes. As your consciousness increases no amount of "good life" would be sufficient to sacrifice the urge to go back home. The humiliation, death, destruction, and hardship were the constant reminders that the wretched condition was due to being refugees. Going back home is a hope that refugees entertain against all odds. Being a refugee also creates a deep longing, a somewhat romantic thirst for something one has lost, and which instantly attains a value which even money and power cannot buy.

Few countries, if any, made a policy choice to accord citizenship status to Rwandese refugees. The only exception was Tanzania during Mwalimu Nyerere's days. Where refugees obtained such status, it was through naturalization and manipulation of the weak systems in the countries of asylum. Uganda throughout the years of dictatorship and chaos, and DRC during Mobutu's corrupt reign, are examples where refugees took advantage of weak systems to acquire citizenship.

From the very beginning Rwandese refugees presented a special case to the Ugandan authorities. There are various Kinyarwanda-speaking citizens in Uganda. There are Bafumbira from Kisoro in southwest Uganda. There is an immigrant community who are the descendants of mainly Bahutu who had come to Uganda as laborers in coffee and tea plantations in Buganda, and copper mines in Kilembe. From 1959 onwards Rwandese refugees were the third wave. According to Uganda statistics, Banyarwanda are the sixth largest tribe in Uganda.

NRM's ascendancy to power had given some hope that: 1) the question of citizenship for Rwandese refugees would be resolved; and 2) that short of a peaceful negotiated settlement, Museveni's government would support an NRM-like struggle to liberate Rwanda. When the NRM was in the bush, the sacrifices of the Rwandese combatants, like sacrifices of Ugandans, were a factor for success. All combatants were supposed to be comrades-in-arms. But, even in the bush, the presence of Rwandese and the rise of some officers was not always a matter that non-Rwandese were happy about.

In power, NRM began to show reluctance and hesitation in dealing with the citizenship question. In Uganda, whenever the question of citizenship comes up, it is mainly in connection with Rwandese, and it tends to evoke strong passions. Initially, NRM's policy was very progressive. Probably too progressive for African standards. It stipulated that you could become a Ugandan citizen if you had been in Uganda for 10 years! Later, the problem of land, squatters, and landlords threatened to unravel NRM. Museveni compromised in favor of the landowners and citizenship was narrowly defined.

If General Rwigyema felt any sense of betrayal by his former Ugandan comrades in arms, he also felt pressure from his fellow Rwandan refugees to find a solution. RPF had mobilized and organized politically and within the NRA. With decades of refugee status behind them, disillusioned by the attitude of some Ugandans on the military and political front, the idea and possibility of going back home had become very attractive. Fred had to manage the promises and the very high expectations of young Rwandan officers and men, who once had attempted to invade Rwanda without him or the RPF. Being unfulfilled in Uganda, and beckoned by a new revolutionary need, innovative Fred seized the moment on the 1st of October. As I contemplate the death of Fred, I remember my high school years and the most often quoted verses in William Shakespeare's *Julius Caesar:*

> There is a tide in the affairs of men.
> Which, taken at the flood, leads on to fortune;
> Omitted, all the voyage of their life
> Is bound in shallows and in miseries.
> On such a full sea are we now afloat,
> and we must take the current when it serves,
> or lose our ventures.

Julius Caesar Act 4, scene 3, 218–224

Such was the historic, and yet fateful, decision that Fred had made on the 1st October, 1990. With it came his ultimate sacrifice, his life. He was in his early thirties when he died.

CHAPTER TEN

Chaos And Defeat

There has been a lot of speculation on Fred's death to this day. Many believe he was killed by a bullet from the government of Rwanda forces, FAR. The news of Fred's death was not announced by the RPF till sometime at the end of October, 1990. In the meantime, nobody really knew who was in charge. The unspoken word at the time was that Dr. Peter Bayingana, and Major Chris Bunyenyezi were the two most powerful personalities in the fluid situation. At that time, Major Paul Kagame was still at Fort Leavenworth, Kansas, in the United States, where he was attending a command and control course as a Ugandan officer. There are others who say he was killed by somebody within the ranks of RPF/RPA. If this is true, we are yet to find out.

At the beginning of the war effort, RPF/RPA had the challenge of regaining momentum quickly after the initial setback of Fred's death, while at the same time replenishing the high casualty rate from the battlefield. Training of the new recruits had to be quick (two weeks), and their deployment expeditious. There was massive training going on in the Akagera National Park in northeast Rwanda. This part of Rwanda is generally dry. Most parts have scanty vegetation. The Akagera River meanders around this region on its way to Lake Victoria. Some wild animals inhabit this ecosystem. Antelopes, zebras, hippos, elephants, and giraffes roam this generally dry area. Surprisingly, the area was also sparsely populated, and generally flat. In retrospect, one wonders why an experienced general like Fred would have chosen this particular area to launch a protracted people's war. With limited vegetation, there was no cover or concealment from the government forces. The flat terrain gave an advantage to the government forces, which could and did deploy its few motorized units against the RPA forces. In particular, from the stand-point of guerilla warfare, the sparse population, especially since it turned up hostile, was to be a serious problem on the RPA side. How could the population be aroused and organized? Where were their sympathies and co-operation? How could this military effort survive without the support of the local population?

In theory, I had read a lot about military strategy and tactics, but nothing comes close to a taste of reality. My two weeks of military training in the Akagera national park introduced me to the life of a soldier in war. I was a member of a company, a platoon and a section in which we were instructed on basic drills, handling the legendary AK-47, movement and manoeuvre skills. Our instructors were able, gifted, and toughened young men who sometimes took pleasure in ridiculing "intellectuals" like me to beat us into submission.

One of the aims of military drills is to break down your individualism and shape you into a cog in the military wheel, ready to obey commands and walk in step with your fellow men and women to achieve objectives.

Most post-colonial armies in Africa were established essentially as tools of domination of the new rulers. These armies were recruited from the ruler's tribe or ethnic group, and lacked a national outlook. In many countries, most of those recruited in the military were overwhelmingly uneducated. And in many such armies there is a subtle and sometimes covert hostility towards "intellectuals". The educated elite who have had the opportunity to preside over Africa's post-colonial regimes have often had a disappointing record. The elite are often removed from, and indifferent, to the needs of the majority. When a sergeant has a rare opportunity to be in charge in an inverted relationship where he is on top, he puts it to good use. In the drills, the ferocious no nonsense sergeant paid particular attention to me, often giving me as an example of an intellectual who was clumsy. My cap was not properly adorned, my salutes were pathetic, and occasionally in the rapid "left-right, left-right" drills, I would miss a step. After two weeks we graduated from the makeshift infantry academy. Most of my class went direct to battle. I was posted to a medical unit that looked after the casualties whose numbers were on the increase. The advantage of being a medic was that it quickly catapulted you into the ranks of the officers.

Food was very scarce during training and thereafter. When available, food comprised of boiled dry maize. Water in the Akagera Park was very scarce. Hungry and thirsty, our training routine was regularly interrupted by government reconnaissance aircraft, and occasional bombings. With surface to air missiles from Uganda, RPA was subsequently able to shoot down a couple of them and the menace eventually stopped. During the evenings we often had a compulsory *kipindi cya utamaduni* (cultural programme) in which we sang and danced to boost our morale. The songs were mainly those that officers and men of NRA had sung during the NRM revolutionary years: *Omwoto wawaka,* (fire burned) as well as those that spoke to the objective of the RPF war...*nta nikibazo cyambuza kujya iwacu mu Rwanda* (nothing shall prevent me from going back home), *Tusonge* (let us advance).

After graduating from the training I headed for the RPA medical headquarters at the Kagitumba border post. I had hoped to join the frontline, to put into practice what I had learned in the two weeks of training. RPA chose that I join the medical team that was already busy treating many wounded soldiers. As we parted, the mood was upbeat as young men from my section, platoon and company headed to the frontline as the war's tempo was gathering momentum.

The medical team was headed by Dr. Joseph Karemera, one of the senior leaders of the RPF. I quickly adjusted to serving as a medical doctor, a calling that I thought I had left behind two weeks earlier. Throughout the war effort, the medical team was very busy doing surgery with minimum surgical materials. I have come to call this medical practice "heroic medicine". Dedicated doctors, nurses, medical assistants, and other healthcare professionals did amazing things to save lives. In medical school you are taught all sorts of health conditions, some of which are so exotic that you may never encounter in life. You are taught that to do this type of surgery you must have that. For some of us who had worked in Ugandan hospitals, we were used to scarcity. However, nothing had prepared us to face emergency medical needs every day without the necessary supplies. I witnessed our teams do amputations and abdominal surgeries with a lot of improvisation. Sometime patients would be operated on lying on banana leaves, at night, with torches serving as the only source of light.

The number of casualties we received at the medical headquarters reflected the frontline activity. The third week of October was particularly busy. We received so many wounded officers and men, and our teams were working throughout the day and night. It was during the third week of October that Dr. Peter Bayingana and Major Chris Bunyenyezi died. We had barely recovered from the death of Fred, and now the next two senior leaders in the politico-military chain of command were dead. One of the lessons I had learned from my readings in history was that start up revolutionary organizations frequently die with the death of the founder leaders. That is why those fighting insurgents will do everything possible to decapitate the infant revolutionary organization by killing its leaders. It was an ominous sign of what was to follow in the days ahead. The deaths of these two leaders have been matters of speculation in RPF and Ugandan circles till now.

Like the death of Fred, the deaths of Dr. Bayingana and Major Bunyenyezi were at first held in secrecy, and released only later.

What seems to fuel speculation is that Major Paul Kagame had just returned from Fort Leavenworth in the United States around that time. Some people wondered who would be the supreme leader of the organization, and who among the three would be favorable to the authorities in Uganda, especially President Museveni and his young brother General Salim Saleh. Notwithstanding the sense of betrayal that Fred might have felt at times, there was at least a unique feeling of revolutionary kinship among Museveni, Saleh and Fred. Fred's death would leave many Ugandans, including President Museveni and his brother, disheartened. Secondly, from a purely opportunistic point of view, the death of Fred left a dangerous situation on Uganda's doorsteps. The RPF invasion took place when both President Museveni and President Habyarimana of Rwanda were in the United States. President Museveni had responded by saying the "boys" (some time he would say "my boys") had deserted the NRA without his knowledge.

It is possible that President Museveni might have been unhappy with RPF's conspiracy to invade Rwanda without his permission or foreknowledge. One would think that at least, with Fred at the helm, President Museveni would have imagined the possibility of an RPF success. Without Fred, the chances would be slim. Third, the most eligible contender to compete with, or succeed Fred, was Dr. Bayingana. Unfortunately he did not enjoy the level of revolutionary kinship with Museveni, Saleh (Museveni's young brother) and the rest of the NRA brethren. Dr. Bayingana was smart and independent minded. With him at the RPF helm, President Museveni could have pondered whether the final outcome, in the best case scenario, would be favorable to Uganda. Fourth, the next officer who would have been considered to be "one of us" from the Ugandan perspective was Major Paul Kagame. His formative years as a soldier had been in Uganda's National Resistance Army, NRA. He was one of the initial twenty seven men who launched the armed struggle in Uganda. He had risen to be one of the senior officers in NRA's military intelligence establishment. He might not have been one of President Museveni's best officers, but still he could be one of those with whom you could take measured risks with a venture like RPF's. Fifth, nobody knew how the Bayingana-Kagame-Bunyenyezi dynamic would have played out if the three had co-existed on the same frontline. This has led to speculation that Uganda eliminated Bayingana and Bunyenyezi to create an unchallenged pro-Museveni leadership position in RPF for Major Paul Kagame. Who killed these two officers remains a mystery.

After the three successive deaths of RPF's top leadership within one month, the organization was in deep crisis. By the end of 1990, the government of Rwanda declared victory over the RPF, having successfully dislodged the RPA from all positions within Rwanda. With defeat, confusion, and chaos in command, there were many deaths, desertions and wounded in the rank and file. Units just melted away into the Akagera National Park, with officers and men never to be seen again. The medical unit had just relocated to Uganda, across the Kagitumba bridge. There, just across the border, RPF established the sickbay for the wounded, sick and tired. The excitement of 1st October had fizzled away and was replaced by a mood of defeat and pessimism.

With the dramatic reversal of fortunes on the RPF side, the government side had every reason to be jubilant. The Rwandan composer and singer, Bikindi Simoni, had come up with upbeat songs that spoke to RPF's precarious condition of the moment:

> Nimwe mwariraye
> Ngabo z'u Rwanda
> Dore inyenzi zijya gutsindwa
> Zaratsinzwe no mu mutara....

The invasion of 1st October had taken the government by surprise. The Commander in Chief, President Juvenal Habyarimana, a general himself, had been at the United Nations in the United States. Son of a peasant from the northern part of Rwanda, Habyarimana became the Minister of Defence during the First Republic under President Gregoire Kayibanda. He deposed President Kayibanda on 5th July, 1973 in a bloodless military coup. Rwanda remained a one party state, with most of the power vested in the person of the President, and ruling through the tools of the single party, MRND, and the security institutions in which the Bahutu from the north dominated. People knew him as a devout Catholic.

On 1st October 1990, the Rwandan army, FAR, was still small, numbering about 5, 000. It had a few armored personnel careers, one or two reconnaissance aircraft, and a few helicopters. Except for a few encounters with the Tutsi rebels (Inyenzi) in the 1960's, the army had never fought in any war. It was a well-trained army, but its concept of the enemy was the Tutsi. This pre-occupation with Tutsi as the enemy caused Rwanda's army to always look south to Burundi as the possible source of a future war. The reason was no other than that the regime in Burundi was dominated by Tutsi at the political and military level.

However, President Habyarimana must have been worried about the northern front since President Museveni came to power in 1986. Before coming to power in 1986, President Habyarimana had helped the rebel leader Yoweri Museveni who was occasionally a secret guest to the government of Rwanda. With Museveni coming to power, and with a sizeable contingent of Rwandan Tutsi in his army, President Habyarimana must not have been comfortable. President Habyarimana received usual diplomatic assurances from President Museveni not to worry. During one of his visits to Uganda, the matter of Rwandan refugees was discussed. President Museveni had reportedly told President Habyarimana to "help me so that I can help you". President Museveni was selling the idea that if the Government of Rwanda could have a general policy to invite Rwandan refugees who wished to return, few would do so, and the rest would opt for naturalization from countries of asylum. President Habyarimana seemed to understand the idea and its urgency, but as he got home, the MRND government reiterated the same stance that Rwanda was small, and that countries of asylum should absorb the problem. President Habyarimana was also in Kampala, Uganda, during the ceremony of the official promotion of Fred Rwigyema to the rank of General.

President Habyarimana must have felt betrayed by President Museveni when the 1st October, 1990, RPF invasion took place. From the day of the invasion, the government of Rwanda consistently had one narrative to the effect that Rwanda had been attacked by Uganda, that the invaders were sons of *Inyenzi* whose agenda was to re-establish the Tutsi monarchy which the 1959 revolution had toppled to establish a republic, and that the Hutu should unite to prevent a return to Hutu serfdom. Quickly, some friendly governments came to aid the government side. France had airlifted a contingent of French legionnaires from their base in the Central African Republic. Belgium, Rwanda's former colonial master, sent in a handful of troops, only to be withdrawn due to public pressure in Belgium. President Mobutu of Zaire (now Democratic Republic of Congo) sent in a contingent from his army long known for its indiscipline.

There was a flurry of international and regional diplomatic initiatives to restore the situation to some normalcy. There were summits in Tanzania and DRC, and persistent calls for a negotiated peaceful settlement. Persistently, the government of Rwanda wanted it to be considered a case of aggression from Uganda. At this point it was not willing to consider direct talks with RPF. Now that RPF had been "defeated" on the battlefield, why would the government negotiate?

In retrospect, one may ask why RPF suffered major setbacks at the beginning of its 1990 campaign. It had some initial advantages. It had an experienced, able and charismatic leader. The core RPA fighters and men were seasoned fighters, probably some of the best that President Museveni's NRA had. Numbering 2,000-3,000 men, this was a sizeable force, especially since the government side had not many more than that. The RPA force had crossed with an assortment of weapons, including AK47s, all sorts of artillery pieces, and some heavy guns. Uganda was a friendly rear for logistics and supplies, and room for retreat if the worse came to the worst. Above all, it had a just cause on its side.

As the opening shots were fired in Kagitumba, the world awoke to the realization that the rebels were actually Rwandans and that they were demanding a right to return home. In Rwanda and internationally, there was a general attitude that seemed to accept that these refugees had a right to return.

First, the most costly strategic mistake had been the location and thrust of the invasion. Flat, under-populated and with little vegetation, Umutara region in north east Rwanda was not the ideal place for guerilla warfare, since it placed the advantage in the hands of the government forces. Since they outnumbered RPA, the government forces could use their artillery, aircraft, and armored personnel careers more effectively. RPA was fighting a conventional war on a terrain it was outnumbered and outgunned.

Second, with the initial number of experienced troops within the RPA, there was a general mindset that this was going to be a quick victory over an inexperienced enemy. RPF overestimated itself and underestimated its enemy. Officers took very risky decisions that exposed fighters to enemy fire, with the consequence of high casualty rates. They wanted to capture and hold territory at whatever cost. Third, it was assumed that Uganda was the friend who would chip in with men and materiel when things got tough. The spirit of self-reliance in a protracted military war that later developed in the RPF was absent in this early phase. Fourth, there was a very serious problem of indiscipline among the officers of the RPA that hampered co-ordination, command and control, leading to actions that were neither of strategic nor even tactical value. Most importantly, RPF/RPA had lost its leader, Fred Rwigyema, and its other senior leaders. Without command, the organization was at dangerous crossroads.

CHAPTER ELEVEN

Regrouping And Reorganization

After the initial setbacks of 1990, RPF had a new leadership in the wake of the deaths of its top leadership. Col. Alexis Kanyarengwe was made the Chairman, and Major Paul Kagame, the Vice-Chairman and Chairman of the High Command of the RPA. The executive committee of the RPF included Patrick Mazimpaka (Diplomacy), Pasteur Bizimungu (Information and Documentation), Emile Rwamasirabo (Logistics), Aloysea Inyumba (Finance), Jacques Bihozagara, Gerald Gahima, Christine Umutoni, Tito Rutaremara, Protais Musoni, and others. The RPA military command included senior officers like Sam Kaka, Ndungute, Muhire, Kayitare, Dodo, Kiza, Musitu, Bagire, and Ngoga. Frank Mugambage was the Chief Political Commissar, Kayumba Nyamwasa headed military intelligence and Wilson Rutayisire led the information campaign.

This new political-military line-up had the task to of regrouping and reorganizing RPF/ RPA which had suffered a major setback. Not only did it have so many casualties and desertions, the remaining troops were demoralized and scattered in bushes and banana plantations in Uganda near the border. There, with our small radio receivers we would listen to world news and to what the British Broadcasting Corporation (BBC) would say about the RPF. One Ugandan officer who had joined the RPA, Major Kabura, would ask in Runyankole, "Mbwenu shi BBC ebagambeho ki? Ngu muryo mu ntoke za Uganda?" Translated in English, it means "what would you like BBC to say about you? That you are in Ugandan banana plantations?"

The Chairman of RPF, Col. Alexis Kanyarengwe (now deceased) makes an interesting reading in the twists and turns of Rwandan history. A Hutu from the northern region of Ruhengeri, he had been one of the first officers in the post-colonial Rwandan army and one of the five "comrades of 5th July" (the military coup that toppled President Kayibanda and brought President Habyarimana to power in 1973). He had received his education in a Catholic seminary, and was an officer in the Rwandan army that battled the *Inyenzi* Tutsi guerrillas in the 1960's. Legend had it that he had been wounded on his head, leaving a scar. He had allegedly then sworn never to love any Tutsi until his scar grew hair.

When I first met him in 1991, I was curious to look for that scar. On lighter moments he would occasionally make fun of it and show us the scar and the story related to it. He had fallen out with President Habyarimana and gone into exile in Tanzania, from where General Fred Rwigyema made contacts with him. Many RPF members, especially Major Paul Kagame, were suspicious of him. He was suspicious of them too. Yet he had made a pragmatic and dramatic U-turn to embrace people whom he had previously considered his enemies. It must have been difficult for him to make that choice. General Rwigyema did not have the same baggage as Col. Kanyarengwe. Nevertheless, he had to make a similar choice to work with somebody that many Tutsi knew only in negative terms.

The new Vice-Chairman of the RPF and Chairman of the High Command, Major Paul Kagame, arrived on the scene at the most difficult moment. In the chaos and RPF losses that followed General Rwigyema's death, Paul Kagame arrived from the USA where he had been attending military studies at Fort Leavenworth, Kansas, as a Ugandan officer.

He had the task of leading and reorganizing a demoralized RPF/RPA into an effective fighting and political force. As the Vice Chairman of RPF and Chairman of the High Command of the RPA, he was effectively known to be the man in charge, first because the military drives politics in these types of revolutions, and secondly, because RPF never trusted its chairman, Col. Kanyarengwe. One of the first decisions that was made by the RPA leadership at this time was to relocate the main theater of operations to northern Rwanda, in the Virunga Volcanic Mountains, renowned for being the natural habitat of the mountain gorillas. The Akagera national park had been disastrous. The bamboo-covered mountains were a relatively secure environment that did not give undue advantage to the government troops. Regular armies love situations where they can deploy their lessons from military academies, their superior logistics, their transport and superior weaponry. The bamboo forest cover around Muhabura Volcano Mountains was a welcome hiding place and concealment from the regular bombardment. The problem was that it was too cold and wet, and, combined with hunger and disease; many of our fellow comrades succumbed to death.

Major Paul Kagame is a man with iron discipline when it comes to military and political matters. And he enforced it violently and unhesitatingly. He had built this reputation in Uganda during the NRM struggle. His inclination to violent measures had earned him the name of Pilato (after Pontius Pilate in the Bible). Initially. there was silent grumbling among officers of the RPA to the effect that he had never been a combatant in battle in contrast to General Rwigyema, Major Bunyenyezi, and others. With time, and working with the other military leaders of this period, he was able to restore a semblance of cohesion and discipline within the military and political wings of RPF.

I recall a meeting Major Kagame had with officers during those difficult moments. It had been a busy week in which the government troops were chasing units of RPA across hills. He first listened to officers as they listed reasons why RPA was losing, finding it difficult to stand any ground, and losing many young men and women on the battlefield. Almost all of the officers seemed to suggest that RPA's main problem was that we did not have enough artillery pieces, and they somehow expected Uganda would give us these weapons. There was an air of defeat. Some officers were even talking about taking entire RPA units somewhere in Uganda to "reorganize". When he spoke he challenged the officers to think of solutions from within. Why for example, he asked, weren't officers making it a must for soldiers to dig trenches to protect themselves from government artillery? Why were units leaving their dead and wounded on the battlefield? He insisted that the first step in fighting and winning a war is within one's mind. If you are resigned in your mind, he argued, no amount of weaponry will save you. I had met Kagame only once, but I liked his analysis of the situation.

In early 1991, two RPF military operations in the north close to the border with Uganda, one in Gatuna and another in Ruhengeri, rekindled hopes and raised the morale of RPF/RPA. Gatuna is a border post on the transport corridor that goes as far as Mombasa port in Kenya. Its strategic value is that most exports and imports from and to Rwanda are through this point. The operation essentially closed the border post and sent a signal to the government that RPF was still in existence. Insurgents who are still in a weak position are always desperate for battles that have political, military, or economic significance.

The Ruhengeri operation was even more important politically. Since 1973, the locus of power had shifted to the north. President Habyarimana hailed from Gisenyi, the province adjacent to Ruhengeri. Second, in the 1980's Habyarimana had fallen out with former ministers and officers like Kanyarengwe, Lizinde, Muvunanyambo , Biseruka, and others. Kanyarengwe had escaped to Tanzania where he sought political asylum. When

RPF sought a Hutu to put at the top of the organization, Colonel Kanyarengwe from Ruhengeri was the best candidate. Theoneste Lizinde, Muvunanyambo and Biseruka were in the Ruhengeri prison when RPA attacked and released all the prisoners. RPA came back with the three and a few others. It was a public blow to the regime and to President Habyarimana personally.

From then on, more soldiers came out of the sick bays, units were reorganized, command and control issues improved, discipline enforced, and joint RPF-RPA sessions were held to discuss politics, logistics, finance and diplomacy. With more methodical and carefully planned operations, RPA was able to slowly secure a small territory in northern Rwanda (Byumba) during the period 1991-1992.

CHAPTER TWELVE

A New Mission

One evening as I sat listening to my old and weather beaten portable Sony radio, I was told that I should report to the High Command the following day. I was surprised, and left wondering what business I could possibly have at the High Command. The following day I travelled to the High Command HQs on the Muhabura Mountains where Major Paul Kagame had his command post. That evening Major Kagame called me in. It was my first time to meet him in person. Kagame has an enigmatic presence that inspires fear. Way back then, even in the bushes, people had to talk in whispers to avoid him complaining of noise. He is tall, very thin, and wears thick glasses. In talking to him you learn to listen carefully because it seems he has a superb economy with words, which he uses sparingly.

In a few words he described my mission. I was to travel to Brussels, Belgium, with a Rwandan Hutu businessman, Silas Majyambere, to take advantage of his contacts and mobilize Hutu in Belgium. Majyambere was a prominent self-made, semi-literate, yet very entrepreneurial businessman who had been a close friend of President Habyarimana. Their friendship had expired, and Majyambere was now in exile. Majyambere had promised that he had contacts in Belgium, and would help mobilize them for RPF. When I was summoned to the High Command I found him around there. He struck me as an interesting character who talked too much. I overheard him promising soldiers that he would buy a plastic sheeting to cover the whole forest so that we could be protected from rain and cold. He also promised to build a bread-making machine in the Muhabura Mountains!

Kagame gave me a letter to take to his wife, Jeanette Kagame. Jeannette had recently had a baby, their first-born, and lived in Brussels with Kagame's sister and brother-in law, Kathie and Dr. Innocent Gakwaya. He also gave me a little pocket money for the trip. The following day I took a trip down the slopes of Muhabura into Kisoro, then Kabale and headed for Kampala. I had joined the struggle weighing 85 kgs. Now I was so thin and weighed 65 kgs. My body was dirty, and my clothes infested with lice. On the way down the slopes of Muhabura in Kisoro on the Ugandan side we shared the footpaths with donkeys. The haggard donkeys carried food rations up the slopes.

As we travelled to Kampala I reflected on how Rwanda, RPF, and myself had changed. Rwanda was never the same. RPF had to revise its own assumptions that underpinned the 1st October invasion. RPF was beginning to learn the importance of flexibility and adapting when strategy and tactics do no match realities on the ground.

Loaded with so much theory before the invasion, I was beginning to learn that theory and practice were two different things. The two inform each other, but clearly you could not win a war by going back to Marxism or even classical military theory. I was now learning, first-hand, how costly in human life armed struggles were. Most importantly, one realized the importance of organization, and within it, discipline and leadership.

In February 1991, I took a Sabena flight from Entebbe, Uganda, to Brussels, Belgium, where I joined Silas Majyambere. Flying in an aircraft for the first time was itself a fascinating experience. The only time I had ever come close to a flying machine was when I was a little boy in Idi Amin's era. One day a helicopter landed on our primary school's compound. It was chaos at school as we broke out of the classroom to witness a moment of a lifetime. Now, years later, I was in an aircraft bound for Belgium, the country that I considered to be historically at the heart of Rwanda's problems. Being in a commercial aircraft for the first time can tease a novice to the world of international travel. You have to be vigilant enough to know what to do with the small items that cabin crew distribute to passengers. Years laters, somebody told us a story of how one time a passenger attempted to eat a warm towel mistaking it for food! Besides, my imagination took me to wonder about the mechanics of keeping a heavily-loaded machine in the air. I remembered one of my high school lessons, Bernoulli's principle, and the American Wright Brothers. For most of the journey though, my intellectual encounter with Fanon's writings caused me to reflect on two things: Belgium and Majyambere.

How did Belgium, a small country, manage to colonize Congo, a country so many times its size? How it added Rwanda and Burundi to its vast territory of Congo was already familiar to me. To study Belgium's colonial history is to learn about King Leopold II. To learn about King Leopold II is to appreciate the greed, brutality, and sheer inhumanity that accompanied the West's scramble for Africa. Adam Hochschild's *King Leopold's Ghost*, and Thomas Pakenham's *The Scramble for Africa* are best-selling accounts on how Africa was partitioned, invaded, colonized, and annexed between 1881 and the start of World War I. Six European countries, namely the United Kingdom, France, Belgium, Spain, Portugal, and Italy had carved the entire African continent and its peoples among themselves.

Modern Belgium as an independent constitutional monarch is fairly recent (1831). History has it that the Catholic Church and French liberal intellectuals were instrumental in this process of liberation from the Netherlands. Its history is tied to the other two Low Countries: the Netherlands and Luxembourg. From

Rome, to the struggles between and within the Catholic and Protestant churches; from the rivalries and wars that were the lot of European powers, princes and kings in the 19th and 20th Centuries, Belgium is in a way a true European narrative. At different times, Belgium has been attacked and occupied by France and Germany (twice, in WW1 and WW11). But Belgium has also been saved by European and later American powers at its darkest hours. Internally, Belgium's political organization is amazing. Belgium has traditionally been divided between the French Speaking Wallonia, and the Dutch speaking Flanders, and is now constitutionally divided into ten provinces. As former Belgian colonies, we sometimes make fun saying that Belgium imported its internal rivalries into Rwanda and Burundi, with Walloons and Flanders as Tutsi and Hutu respectively.

Going to Brussels was an exciting encounter with a particular Belgian story, and a general European narrative. And there, in a small apartment on 5 Rue d'Observatoire, RPF had opened offices in the heart of Belgium, the only formal offices that our organization maintained from the beginning to the end of the civil war. An RPF cadre, Bosco Rwiyamirira, gallantly held the fort.

Brussels had a second message that would be profoundly disruptive to me in later years. For the first time I landed in a capitalist country, I was amazed at the beauty and orderliness of things. There was an airport teeming with so many planes. People were beautifully dressed. There were wide and paved roads, and so many cars. Buildings were so tall and elegant. Shops were full of stuff. Raised in a refugee camp in rural Uganda, I had had a glimpse of products of capitalism in Kampala, and Nairobi. I had learned about the capitalism-communism divide through readings of revolutionary and Marxist literature. I had taken sides: communists were my friends, capitalists were my enemies. In Brussels, my mind was being pushed to re-evaluate my beliefs and assumptions underlying them. Was capitalism all bad? Was communism all good?

While in Brussels, I was also able to encounter another challenge to my firmly-held belief in the struggle against capitalism
to establish a socialist order. If capitalism is irredeemably horrible,
I would ask myself, how does it create such an impressive array
of knowledgeable people, good infrastructure, first class services,
thriving businesses, and technology? Marxism taught that part
of the west's wealth was a product of primitive accumulation of
capital. Many argue that the wealth of Brussels, Antwerp , and
Belgium in general, is wealth stolen from Congo. To misappro-
priate the rich capitalist owners and put the means of production
in the hands of the workers was the socialist dream. Unresolved
until much later, this was the second time my theoretical con-
struct was beginning to be put to task. The first were the events
on the battlefield in the preceding months.

Majyambere was my first close contact with a "rich" African
businessman. For a person of my then leftist background, it was a
trial. In the *Wretched of the Earth*, Fanon had not only called for a
violent overthrow of the colonial regime. In the chapter entitled
"Pitfalls of National Consciousness" he poured venom on what
he called the "national bourgeoisie" that emerges in post-colonial
countries. He also vents his anger in a rather prescient estimate of
what becomes the victorious "ruling party" after the colonizers are
gone. He argues that the new business class is a trading, merchant
class rather than productive captains of industry. In comparison
to the Western middle class, which he recognizes as an inventive,
entrepreneurial and innovative class, the African bourgeoisie has
only inherited the west's consumption habits. He further argues
that the new government and party are hostage to the business
interests of this merchant class.

Majyambere's story, as I was told, highlighted this dual character of an African businessman. On the one had he was truly self-
made. With little western education he had risen from a humble
background, got involved in small trades, and finally became
nationally famous and rich in Rwanda. His rise symbolizes the

trials and tribulations small businesses have to undergo in African countries. When you become rich in a country whose citizens are generally impoverished you become noticed by all, including those at the pinnacle of the political establishment. Majyambere was essentially a trader. Once he had his money, he became close to the late President Habyarimana. This is the businessman that Fanon may have been talking about. Majyambere is flamboyant and maverick. In the 30 days or so we toured Europe together I soon realized he was on a business trip, and not on a political mobilization tour. There were no Hutu followers to recruit.

Travelling together, I came to know him better. I saw in him the ruthlessness and calculating mentality that made him survive and grow in a competitive business environment. He could be kind and emotional. There is some roughness that betrays his peasant origins, and his etiquette was so wanting. Though accomplished by Rwandan, and African standards, his manners could offend those who were not used to him. He could be funny and daring. In our first meeting in Brussels we went to see Bemba, a Congolese businessman who, I was told, had been a minister in Mobutu's regime in DRC (then Zaire). In a plush office in downtown Brussels, Bemba welcomed us. Majyambere was eager to show Bemba that he was now an important player in a rebel group in Rwanda, RPF. To show his clout Majyambere introduced me as a General in the rebel army, and now his escort. To which Bemba sarcastically replied, in French, "O, my dear Silas, you must really be important to have a general for an escort!"

In Belgium I stayed at Major Kagame's brother in-law's home in Nivelle, outside Brussels. Dr. Innocent Gakwaya and his wife Kathy were hospitable and very kind to me. There I found Mrs. Jeannette Kagame, who had recently given birth to their first baby boy, Ivan. On some occasions I would hang out at the RPF offices on 5 Rue de Observatoire. With Majyambere we would later briefly go to France, Germany, and the Netherlands.

Other than a small consignment of second-hand clothing he organized from the Netherlands, my trip with Majyambere accomplished nothing, as it turned out to be a chase for his business interests. I was beginning to feel like I was wasting my time in the capitalist world, being seduced intellectually by the wonderful things about capitalism, while my comrades in arms were suffering on the battlefield. When Major Paul Kagame asked me to return, I was greatly relieved.

CHAPTER THIRTEEN

A Rebel Diplomat

While on my European trip, RPF had signed the N'sele Ceasefire Agreement in Zaire, under the mediation efforts of Zairean President Mobutu. After the Ruhengeri attack, Habyarimana's government could no longer continue to make the claim that RPF had been defeated once and for all. Though it had been weakened from the earlier defeats and the leadership crisis that followed, RPF was now on the path to growth and recovery. Signed by Dr. Casmir Bizimungu, Rwanda's Foreign Minister, and Paul Kagame on behalf of RPF, the N'sele Ceasefire Agreement was a welcome development that imparted some degree of legitimacy to RPF. Neither side was convinced that this was the last word on the conflict. Both sides knew the agreement afforded them breathing space to build strength on the battlefield, from which a solution could be dictated by the stronger and victorious side. Internally, within Rwanda, pressure from an economic squeeze, displaced populations, and a resurgent political opposition to the regime were beginning to bite. As usual, the international community was also pressing both sides to find a peaceful settlement to the conflict. Nsele Ceasefire Agreement had brought in President Mobutu as a mediator.

When I returned from Belgium, I was given a new responsibility as Director for Africa in a reorganized Commission for

Diplomacy, headed by Patrick Mazimpaka. Jacques Bihozagara was made the Director in charge of Europe. It was time to intensify our diplomatic offensive. Because Addis Ababa was the Headquarters of the Organization of African Unity, it was the focus of my early work as the rebel diplomat in charge of the Africa region. The Organization of African Unity (OAU) which later became the African Union (AU), was established in 1963 in Addis Ababa, Ethiopia.

As the struggle for independence in former African colonies gathered momentum in the late fifties and early sixties, the leaders of the independence movements were equally asserting the need for African unity. They argued that African Unity was the realization of the pan-Africanist ideal of uniting all Africans on the continent and in the diaspora. They also thought that unity was necessary to speed up the process of decolonization, and more importantly, to pool efforts and resources together to achieve Africa's social and economic transformation. The founding fathers of the OAU were Ben Bella of Algeria, Hubert Maga of Niger, Maurice Yameogo of Burkina Fasso, King Mwambutsa of Burundi, President Ahamadu Ahidjo of Cameroon, President David Dacko of Central African Republic, President Francois Tombalbaye of Chad, President Fulbert Youlou of Congo (Brazzaville), President Gamal Abdel Nasser of Egypt, Emperor Haile Selassie I of Ethiopia, President Leon M'Ba of Gabon, President Kwame Nkrumah of Ghana, President Sekou Toure of Guinea,President Houphouet Boigny of Ivory Coast, President William Tubman of Liberia, King Idris of Libya, President Philbert Tsiranana of Madagascar, President Modibo Keita of Mali, Prime Minister Mokhtar Ould Daddah of Mauritania, King Hassan II of Morocco, President Hamani Diori of Niger, Governor General Nnamdi Azikiwe and Prime Minister Abubakar Tafawa Balewa of Nigeria, President Gregoire Kayibanda of Rwanda, President Leopold Sedar Senghor of Senegal, Prime Minister Milton Margai of Sierra Leone, President Abdella

Osman of Somalia, Presidend Farik Ibrahim Abboud of Sudan, President Julius Nyerere of Tanzania, President Habib Bourguiba of Tunisia, President Sylvanus Olympio of Togo and Prime Minister Milton Obote of Uganda.

Even before its founding, there were divisions within the ranks of the founding fathers. There were two factions, namely, the Casablanca and Monrovia groups, named after the capital cities of Morocco and Liberia where the drama had played out. The Casablanca group, comprising of Ghana, Algeria and Morocco were for an ambitious goal of African Unity there and then. They advocated for some kind of federated union like the current European Union. The Monrovia group, led by Nigeria, was for a slower process of building a united Africa. The cold war was at its peak and was reflected in the various shades of opinion and strategy, especially when it came to building even a semblance of African unity as the colonial edifice was crumbling. Nevertheless the founding fathers of the OAU were able to adopt a minimalist approach, and established the organization.

Principal among founding principles of the OAU were the notion of accepting the boundaries of the newly independent countries, their territorial integrity and national sovereignty, and above all, the principle of non-interference in each other's "internal matters". Over the next three decades the compromise and minimalist approach that seemed to protect "Africa as is" has witnessed moments when the OAU's survival has been at stake. The crises of the Congo, Angola, Morocco and Polisario, and others, tested the OAU. As the initial promise of Africa's post-colonial political, social and economic development gave way to violent tyrannies, military coups, economic collapse, and civil wars, the OAU was increasingly seen by Africans and non-Africans as an ineffectual club of African rulers, most of them dictators. A more realistic outlook was that even with the glaring weaknesses notwithstanding, the OAU was an essential undertaking to discuss and network on the common problems that Africa faces.

Once in a while the OAU has had shining moments. It established the Africa Liberation Committee, which supported decolonization and the anti-apartheid movement. It supported the Frontline States during the struggle against apartheid, and decolonization. In a refrain that was common among intellectuals and liberation movements across Africa, the OAU was just seen as a useless organization, hostage to foreign interests, and a club of tyrannical rulers. African people are better off without it, many would say. But once former rebels captured state power, they would recognize quickly that belonging to this club was important to confer some legitimacy to the new rulers.

As I arrived in Addis Ababa on my first trip to Ethiopia, I was thinking about both Ethiopia and the OAU. In Addis Ababa, I stayed with the family of Edith and Gideon Kayinamura. Kayinamura worked at the OAU. Like many Rwandese in the Diaspora, Kayinamura had worked through the international system as a citizen of a country of asylum, probably Uganda. In the United Nations, OAU, other international and regional bodies, you could find such "Ugandans", "Kenyans", "Burundians", "Tanzanians", and "Zaireans".

Ethiopia is an intriguing, unique story in African history. Stretching across millennia, Ethiopia was never colonized. Except for a brief occupation by Italians in 1935, Ethiopia has enjoyed its independence, and is home to some of the most impressive treasures in African civilization. Among them is Axum. On my mind those days were the more recent traumatic experiences and the struggles that were shaping this country. Ethiopia had seen the overthrow and eventual death of Emperor Haile Selasie in a military coup that brought Col. Mengistu to power. As rebel groups fought the communist and dictatorial regime of Mengistu, Ethiopia and its neighboring Somalia became hotbeds in the Cold War. As the Soviet Union collapsed, with the Cold War in its final days, Mengistu's regime collapsed, bringing to power the liberation movement, the Ethiopian People's Revolutionary Democratic Front (EPRDF), under the late Meles Zenawi. The collapse of the Mengistu regime also created new realities. A new state, Eritrea, was also born, carved out of Ethiopia. Isaias Afewerki was the leader of the new state, Eritrea.

My work in Addis Ababa was to talk to as many people in the OAU as possible and to many diplomatic missions represented here. At this time, Salim Ahmed Salim was the Secretary General of the OAU. Other than the Kayinamura family, there were a few other Rwandese who lived in Addis. Three ladies (Suzanne, Immaculee and Esther) were particularly very supportive of RPF. The embassies of Mozambique and Zimbabwe were helpful in helping me to navigate the bureaucratic hurdles within the OAU. One of the issues I was following up at the OAU was the Ceasefire Monitoring Team established in 1992, under the term of the ceasefire agreement. A Tanzanian officer, Brigadier Hashim Mbita, had been appointed the Head of the Neutral Monitoring Observer Group (NMOG). The small monitoring force numbered about 50, and had liason officers from the RPA headed by Karenzi Karake.

RPF's first encounter with the U.S. Government at senior leadership level was in Addis Ababa. A U.S. official, John Hicks, met RPF's top leadership. In the meeting was Chairman Alexis Kanyarengwe, Vice Chairman and Chairman of the High Command, Major Paul Kagame, Pasteur Bizimungu, Patrick Mazimpaka and myself. It was more of an introductory meeting to prove that we existed, we were a mixed group (Hutu and Tutsi), we were committed to a peaceful resolution of the conflict, that the Government of Rwanda was dragging its feet in the search for peace, and that we were seriously looking for partnership with the United States.

CHAPTER FOURTEEN

Going to America

I first came to the United States in 1991. My brief journey to Belgium early that year had opened my eyes to what else there was in the outside world. I had never been to the communist or socialist world, but I had taken a glimpse of capitalism in Belgium. The U.S. embassy in Kampala, Uganda, was aware of my travel and facilitated my visit by granting me a visa. I travelled on Ugandan passport. Johny Carson, currently Assistant Secretary of State for African Affairs, was then U.S. Ambassador to Uganda. My earliest encounter with America in thought was when, as a little boy in a refugee camp in Uganda, I had felt sad as I sang the Runyankole song lamenting the death of President John Kennedy. Later in my college years, infused with Marxism and revolution theory, I had taken an intellectual stand against the United States. As I read the story of Cuba, Fidel Castro and Che Guevara, I felt anger against the United States. The stories of CIA-inspired coups and assassinations in Latin America, Africa and Asia did not help. In Eduardo Galeano's *Open Veins of Latin America*, I had read the exploitation of Latin America by greedy capitalists from America. In Africa, US allies were the like of President Mobutu and Jonas Savimbi. In the epic battles that were fought in Angola's Cuito Cuanavale, pitting Cuban and Angolan troops against apartheid South Africa's troops in aid of

Savimbi's UNITA, wasn't the U.S. on the side of apartheid against the Cuban-supported Angola?

I stepped on U.S soil with a lot of ideological baggage. As in Brussels, an encounter with the United States, the mother of all capitalism, was bound to generate a lot of tension in my mind. It was a colossal and only remaining superpower, the Soviet Union having collapsed in 1989. Enormous size and superpower status are the kind of things that generate envy. Yet, there is something that is instantly awesome and charming, and inexplicable. Even before you get interested in its revolutionary history (it, too, fought a revolutionary war against a foreign oppressor), its civil war (pitting Americans against Americans), and the wonders of capitalism, the United States is a challenge to one's mind.

During my first trip to the United States I was received and accommodated by Dr. Charles Murigande and his wife Rosette in Arlington, Virginia. Murigande showed me around and accompanied me to the meetings he helped organize. When I visited the State Department for the first time, the Desk Officer for Rwanda was a lady by the name of Carol Fuller. I had been briefed that Ms Fuller was no friend of the RPF. Among Rwandans, this could easily be translated to mean that you are also anti-Tutsi. Every conversation I had with Carol Fuller seemed to confirm my belief that "she does not like us". Until much later, I did not appreciate that Ms. Fuller was just a civil servant who guarded a formal position of a government with respect to relationships with another government. In inter-state relations, stability rather than revolutionary change is frequently the preferred end goal. Hence, Ms. Fuller would tell me that the regime in Rwanda was supported by the majority Hutu, and would question how we, a minority, (RPF) hoped to impose our will on the majority.

In one encounter, when Major Paul Kagame and I were visiting the State Department to meet with then Assistant Secretary of State for Africa Affairs, Herman Cohen, Ms. Fuller developed a conversation with Major Kagame. Apparently, in 1992, an RPA operation had come close to the tea plantation in Kinihira, which was owned by an American. As we waited in the lobby to be escorted to meet Herman Cohen, Ms. Fuller warned us in strong terms that we should be aware that there are American interests in Kinihira. Irked by this, Major Kagame calmly but emphatically told Ms. Fuller that there are Rwandan interests in Kinihira, and that we represent Rwandan interests. Ms. Fuller fell silent. It was during this period, while in Washington DC, that the peace negotiations formally relocated to Arusha, with Tanzania as Facilitator and President Mobutu as Mediator. A U.S. military officer worked with us to draft amended terms of the ceasefire agreement. By then, it was evident that the U.S. military was beginning to have an interest in RPA.

In February 1993, the Arusha Peace talks had stalled and RPA launched a lightning attack that brought RPF the closest ever to Kigali. While the attack demonstrated the capacity of the RPA, it also caused massive displacement of the population, as thousands piled up in Nyakyonga on the outskirts of the capital city, Kigali. The attack coincided with my arrival in Washington D.C. I had the difficult duty of explaining the matter to State Department Officials. The Assistant Secretary of State for African Affairs was Ambassador George Moose, but I met his deputy. The message from State department was strong. RPF had to withdraw to its former positions. I argued that in the face of government stalling at the peace talks and continuing human rights abuses, we had a right to resume hostilities. I was running behind. Working through President Museveni, the Americans and the rest of the international community had pressurized Major Kagame to withdraw, and he had accepted. As Dr. Murigande and I were escorted down the elevator, I never spoke a single word to the Desk Officer and others who escorted us out.

Washington D.C. thrills any first visitor. With its monuments, museums, the White House, Capitol Hill, Embassies, the Pentagon nearby across the Potomac River and Corporate entities, it does exude an air that fits a superpower. New York City, New York, is an overwhelming story. I first studied New York City and its Manhattan district way back when I was studying geography in high school. Schools in Uganda expected students to memorize cities in the United States and former colonial countries. Hence, we would know the prairies, the Tennessee River Authority, the Great Lakes and the St. Lawrence Seaway, and the black-out that New York City experienced in 1977. New York City, especially Manhattan is overwhelming. It never goes to sleep, and is always buzzing with activity, with its yellow cabs, and many people.

It is in New York City that I encountered the United Nations, which has a long history in Rwanda. At the end of World War I, Belgium accepted the League of Nations Mandate of 1923 to govern Rwanda as part of Rwanda-Urundi and the adjacent territory of Congo. After World War II, Rwanda-Urundi became a United Nations Trustee Territory, with Belgium as the administrative authority. Apart from these historical facts, many Rwandese refugees had heard from their parents that the United Nations was not friendly to the Tutsi.

The United Nations has, however, been helpful to Rwandese refugees. The refugee camp that I grew up in was established under the auspices the United Nations High Commissioner for Refugees and the host country, Uganda. Established in 1951, the United Nations High Commissioner for Refugees (UNHCR) has given my family and millions of others emergency relief in the early days. As the possibility of voluntary resettlement receded each year, we had been resettled in the Oruchinga refugee camp in southwest Uganda. Though the Rwandan refugees were among the earliest on the African continent, their plight had essentially been forgotten. There was a feeling of betrayal among refugees that they had been abandoned.

Such was the thinking on my mind every time I visited the United Nations. Entry into the United Nations building without status was always difficult. Fortunately, RPF had its silent but active supporters in many international organizations. At the United Nations I met Manzi Bakuramutsa, who worked for the United Nations Development Programme (UNDP). I also met Ms. Clotilde Mbaranga, who also worked at the UNDP. These two individuals provided enormous help to me, Claude Dusaidi, Gerald Gahima, and other RPF visiting members. Not only did they accommodate us, but they also helped us navigate the strict security arrangements around the United Nations. Many times Dusaidi and I would hang around the lobby within the UN building, RPF documents in hand, ready to distribute them to delegations if they accepted them. In the UN lobby bar I would order sprite or coke, and Dusaidi, when he could afford it, would order some whisky. We would be served nachos with hot salsa on the side, and that would be our lunch.

On June 22, 1993, under the United Nations Security Council resolution 846/1993 was passed. The resolution established an observer mission, United Nations Observer Mission Uganda-Rwanda (UNOMUR), which was supposed to be deployed on the Uganda-Rwanda border, on the Ugandan side. The idea of this force, behind the RPF, was never a popular one with us. The government of Rwanda had always insisted, rightly so, that RPF was supported by Uganda. President Museveni was under pressure from Rwanda's friends abroad, notably France, to prove that this was not the case. This was mission impossible for UNOMUR, given the level of mastery of the terrain and co-operation with the local population, and with the Ugandan players at various official and unofficial levels who colluded with us. Headquartered in Kabale, southwest Uganda, the mission was supposed to monitor the movement across the border of lethal weapons and other materials for military use. The maximum strength of this mission rose to 81 and must have cost hundreds of millions before it was terminated in 1994.

The background to the Security Council resolution establishing UNOMUR provided an interesting opportunity for me to learn how the international system works. Before the Security Council voted on the resolution, the United Nations Secretary General, Boutros Boutros-Ghali had sent a fact-finding mission to Uganda and Rwanda. The head of the mission, a French General, had compiled a draft report that was not yet in the hands of the members of the Security Council. With good luck, Claude Dusaidi and I got the draft documents. Overnight, I wrote counter arguments to the draft documents, and dismissed it as a plot by the French and Rwanda to destroy RPF. Using a fax machine in a nearby kiosk, I distributed RPF's counter arguments to all UN Security Council members who had not even seen the draft document. It was a scandal to the UN establishment. I later learnt that an investigation was done and it was decided that I would never be allowed in the UN building unaccompanied. At the United Nations, then Ugandan Permanent Representative to the United Nations, Ambassador Perez Kamunanwire, was of enormous help to RPF, in personal and official terms. I, however, felt disappointed by Uganda when I later learnt that the Security Council had voted to establish UNOMUR. State and powerful interests had prevailed over any other considerations, especially for a rebel movement like RPF.

CHAPTER FIFTEEN

Negotiating for Peace

The start of the civil war in October, 1990 generated a lot of diplomatic initiatives in the search for peace. Most of the summits and meetings in the beginning involved regional Heads of State, and not RPF. There were high-level meetings in Mwanza, Tanzania (17th October, 1990); Gbadolite, DRC, (26th October, 1990); Goma, DRC, (20th November, 1990); Zanzibar, Tanzania, (17th February, 1991); and Dar-es-Salaam, Tanzania, (19th February, 1991). This diplomatic activity eventually provided the impetus for a ceasefire agreement that was signed at N'Sele in the Democratic Republic of Congo. The N'Sele Ceasefire Agreement of 29 March, 1991, was signed by Dr. Casmir Bizimungu and Major Paul Kagame on behalf of the Government of Rwanda and RPF respectively. President Mobutu of DRC was the mediator. Later, the N'Sele Ceasefire Agreement was amended in Gbadolite on 16th September, 1991, and in Arusha, Tanzania, on 12th July, 1992.

N'Sele Ceasefire Agreement took place at a difficult time for the RPF, which was at its weakest, as it had just started its re-grouping and re-organization. Anything that would enable it to buy time and build strength was good strategy. At the same time, the agreement for the first time put RPF at the negotiating table with the government of Rwanda which all along had resisted negotiating directly with the rebel movement. Through the agreement, RPF became a legitimate protagonist in the conflict. On the other side, The Rwandan Government was under pressure to negotiate. It was finding it difficult to deny that RPF had legitimate demands. Venue and mediation are important elements in a peace process. Within the Great Lakes region, DRC as a venue and President Mobutu as a mediator were more acceptable to the Government of Rwanda. France, close to both President Habyarimana and President Mobutu, felt the former was much safer with the latter being the mediator. RPF on its part was very suspicious of President Mobutu. He was very close to President Habyarimana and the French. President Mobutu and the French had sent troops to support the Rwandan regime. On ideological grounds, President Mobutu was seen by us as somebody who had betrayed Africa countless times, on behalf of western interests. Tanzania was a preferred alternative but regional and international power dynamics were such that President Mobutu had to be accommodated as a Mediator, while President Mwinyi of Tanzania became the Facilitator.

There were two most important challenges to the peace process, namely, a ceasefire that could hold, and sustained peace negotiations towards a settlement to end the civil war. The Government of Rwanda wanted the ceasefire more than anything else. RPF wanted the ceasefire as a stepping stone to negotiations, and to buy time as it considered any other options. The ceasefire and political negotiations created an opportunity for RPF to sell its agenda and gain acceptability among Rwandan players, especially the political parties in the opposition and Rwandan people in general, and the international community.

The Ceasefire Agreement of 12th July, 1992, brought a fresh impetus to the peace process. There was a neutral facilitator, under the auspices of the Tanzanian Government. There was a new venue, Arusha, in northern Tanzania, close to its border with Kenya. There were also fresh players in the negotiations. Under pressure to open up the political space, President Habyarimana had finally allowed the formation of a coalition government with three major opposition parties; namely, MDR, the Partci Sociale Democrate (PSD), and Parti Liberal (PL). RPF courted the internal political opposition, with the intention of distancing them from President Habyarimana and his party MRND, and getting them closer to itself. The internal political opposition on its part needed RPF as an armed group that would put pressure on President Habyarimana to accept genuine political negotiations and the reforms that would follow. Boniface Ngulinzira (deceased) who signed on agreement of 12th July, 1992, was a member of the political opposition (MDR) in a government that was headed by the opposition leader Dismas Nsengiyaremye, as Prime Minister.

The Ceasefire Agreement was ambitious enough to set the agenda and timetable for the negotiations, and made provisions on the structure for the monitoring and verification of the ceasefire, the Neutral Monitoring Observer Group (NMOG), and the Joint Political Military Commission (JPMC). I was a member of the JPMC.

The Organization of African Unity (OAU) was a new and vital player if the ceasefire was to succeed. With just a group of 50 monitors, NMOG reported to the OAU Secretary General, Salim Ahmed Salim, through its force commander, Brigadier General Hashim Mbita. Both Salim and Mbita are Tanzanian citizens. The continental organization had limited resources, and had to rely on international support to get the force up and running. Through NMOG, African countries contributing the troops were able to see for themselves the realities of Rwanda. RPA had its five officers, led by Karenzi Karake, as members of NMOG. RPF now had a formal presence in Kigali, which it put to very good use in terms of making contacts and collecting information on what we then called enemy territory. The Ceasefire Agreement also called on Burundi, DRC, Uganda, Belgium, France, the United States and Tanzania to be observers to the JPMC, in the hope that they would support the process all the way to implementation.

The Arusha peace negotiations had, as a starting point, the conversation on the rule of law. The Rwandan side was led by the Minister of Foreign Affairs, Boniface Ngulinzira. In his delegation was Ambassador Claver Kanyarushoki, whom everyone knew was the one who had the ear of President Habyarimana. Ambassador Kanyarushoki was Rwanda's ambassador to Uganda. Soft spoken, he was effective in conveying which lines were not to be crossed, depending on his instructions. The RPF side was led by Pasteur Bizimungu, who was assisted by Patrick Mazimpaka and a number of RPF cadres at different time. I was a member of the RPF negotiating delegation. Pasteur Bizimungu was our Rwanda expert, and he was a man of detail. He knew the Rwandan system, the key players, including President Habyarimana himself. He had served the system, at some point heading ELECTROGAZ, the national water and electricity utility. Like President Habyarimana himself, he was a Hutu who hailed from the north. Representing the Facilitator was Hassan Diria, Tanzania's Minister of Foreign Affairs. Ambassador Ami Mpungwe, a consummate networker, assisted the Minister.

The Protocol on the Rule of Law was not the most difficult to negotiate. Both sides went back and forth, but essentially we were dealing with ideas, albeit dangerous ones. Reading through the protocol you can see the whole history of western philosophy from the Greeks to the founding fathers of the United States of America written all over it. You can see the ideas of liberty, people's sovereignty, democracy and the consent of the governed, separation of powers, the rule of law itself, free and fair elections, pluralism and multi-party politics. Rwanda had gone through centuries of absolute rule under kings, colonialism, and one party state apparatus since independence. There were many among RPF, and Rwandans in general, who dreamt of a new order along the principles enunciated in the protocol. Many in the opposition shared the same ideals. There were moments in the negotiations on the rule of law when things seemed to stall. Benjamin Mkapa, who later became the President of Tanzania, chaired later sessions to get the negotiating parties out of deadlock; we stalled on the wording of the concluding article. The final wording was suggested by Gamaliel Ndaruzaniye, the Burundian Ambassador to Tanzania:

> The two parties concur that national unity; democracy and peace are invaluable and solemnly undertake to do everything possible so as to preserve these values in the interest of the present and future Rwandese generations.

The signing of the protocol rekindled hopes in Rwanda and the region that an end to the conflict was possible. The most difficult hurdles were yet to be crossed. Power sharing, creating a new national army and the return of the 1959 refugees were likely to make or break the peace process. Sharing power has, historically, been the most difficult thing to do in Rwanda. Throughout history the natural thing in human nature is to hoard, consolidate and monopolize power. That is what kings, emperors, and princes and presidents have done. Ceding absolute control of a key institution like the army is equally very difficult. The army is critical to maintaining the monopoly of power. The return of refugees, a key demand of the RPF, was certainly vexing.

The return of refugees, RPA's inclusion in a new national army, and RPF's inclusion in the Rwandan political structures would be a game changer, some of us imagined. Yet, in a country where the gains of one side are considered losses on the other, the Government of President Habyarimana was dragging its feet. So was RPF, because the purpose of revolutions, we taught cadres, was to capture state power, and to use this power for the common good. The question of sharing power among competing elites, creating a national army in which both Hutu and Tutsi were to be represented, and reversing the government policy on refugees were dangerous proposals to the status quo, and, ultimately to RPF as well.

Consider the following scenario that was envisaged with regard to power-sharing, creation of the new national army, new police (gendarmerie), and the return of Tutsi refugees:

In accordance with the provisions of Article 14 of the Protocol of Agreement signed on 30th October, 1992, the numerical distribution of the portfolios among political forces called upon to participate in the Broad-Based Transitional Government shall be as follows:

MRND: 5 portfolios
RPF: 5 portfolios
MDR: 4 portfolios (including the post of Prime Minister)
PSD: 3 portfolios
PL: 3 portfolios
PDC: 1 portfolio

Article 56

Nominative distribution of portfolios shall be as follows:

MRND

1. Ministry of Defense;
2. Ministry of Higher Education, Scientific Research and Culture;
3. Ministry of Public Service;
4. Ministry of Planning;
5. Ministry of Family Affairs and Promotion of the Status of Women.

RPF

1. Ministry of Interior and Communal Development;
2. Ministry of Transport and Communications;
3. Ministry of Health;
4. Ministry of Youth and Associative Movement;
5. Secretariat of State for Rehabilitation and Social Integration.

MDR

1. Prime Minister;
2. Ministry of Foreign Affairs and Cooperation;
3. Ministry of Primary and Secondary Education;
4. Ministry of Information.

PSD

1. Ministry of Finance;
2. Ministry of Public works and Energy;
3. Ministry of Agriculture and Livestock Development.

PL

1. Ministry of Justice;
2. Ministry of Commerce, Industry and Cottage Industry;
3. Ministry of Labor and Social Affairs;

PDC: Ministry of Environment and Tourism

Article 57

The two parties further agree that:

- With reference to Article 5 of the Protocols of Agreement signed on 30th October, 1992, the Presidency of the Republic shall go to the MRND party;
- one of the holders of the five (5) ministries allocated to the RPF shall bear the title of Deputy Prime Minister in accordance with Article 20, paragraph 3 of the Protocol of Agreement signed on 30th October, 1992.

In the Transitional National Assembly, the sharing of seats was as follows:

MRND: 11 seats
RPF: 11 seats
MDR: 11 seats
PSD: 11 seats
PL: 11 seats
PDC: 4 seats

And for the National Army

Article 74: Proportions and Distribution of Command Posts

During the establishment of the National Army, the proportions and distribution of Command posts between the two parties shall abide by the following principles:

1. The Government forces shall contribute 60% of the forces and the RPF 40% of the forces for all levels apart from the posts of Command described below.

2. In the chain of Command, from the Army Headquarters to the Battalion, each party shall have a 50% representation for the following posts:

Chief of Staff, Deputy Chief of Staff, Heads of Departments at the Army General Headquarters (G1, G2, G3, G4), Brigade Commanders, Seconds in Command of Brigades, Heads of Sections at Brigade Headquarters (S1, S2, 53, S4), Battalion Commanders and Seconds in Command of Battalions, Commanders and Seconds in Command of Specialized Units, namely: Para commando, Reconnaissance, Military Police Battalions, and of Support Units, Engineering Field Artillery, Anti-aircraft Artillery Battalions and the Logistics Center; Commanders and Seconds in Command of the Schools - ESM and ESO - and Commanders and Seconds in Command of the Training Centers in BIGOGWE and BUGESERA.

3. All top posts described above shall be distributed among the Officers of the Rwandese Government and those of the RPF in accordance with the principle of alternation.

Thus, the Rwandese Government forces and the RPF forces shall supply an equal number of Brigade and Battalion Commanders, of Seconds in Command of Brigade and Battalion, of Heads of Department at the Army Headquarters, of Heads of Section at Brigade Headquarters; of Commanders and Seconds in Command of Specialized and Support Units, of Schools and Training Centers described above.

However, neither force can hold at the same time the posts of Commander and Second in Command within the same Unit.

4. Without prejudice to Article 73, the proportions of the two forces in all the structures of the National Army shall be affected by no prerequisite condition in terms of

accessibility. Thus, adequate training shall be given to the servicemen retained without fulfilling all the necessary requirements in accordance with the modalities determined by the Army Command High Council.

5. The post of Chief of Staff of the National Army shall be held to the Government party and the one of Deputy Chief of Staff to the Rwandese Patriotic Front (RPF).

For the National Gendarmerie (Police), the sharing and distribution was supposed to be as follows:

Article 144: Proportions and Distribution of Posts of Command

During the establishment of the National Gendarmerie, the proportions and distribution of command posts between the two parties shall abide by the following principles:

1. The Government forces shall contribute 60% and the RPF 40% of the forces for all levels apart from the posts of command described below.

2. In the chain of Command, from the general headquarters of the National Gendarmerie to the level of Groupement, each party shall have a 50% representation for the following posts: Chief of Staff, Deputy Chief of Staff, Heads of Department at the General Headquarters (G1, G2, G3, G4); Commanders and Seconds in Command of Groupement; Heads of Sections at the Groupement Headquarters (S1, S2, S3,S4), Commanders and Seconds in command of Specialized and Support Units, namely: Republican Guard, Intervention Unit,

Logistic Services Group, Specialized Intelligence Service and Criminal

Investigation Service, and Commander and Second in Command of EGENA.

3. All top posts described above shall be equally shared between the officers of the Rwandese Government and those of the RPF in accordance with the principle of alternation. Thus, the Government forces and those of RPF shall provide respectively (6 and 5 or 5 and 6) Commanders of Groupement, (5 and 6 or 6 and 5) Seconds in Command of Groupement, and equal number of Heads of Sections at the Groupement Headquarters and Seconds in Command of Specialized Units as described above and of EGENA.

However, neither force shall hold at the same time the posts of Commander and Second in Command within the same Unit.

4. Without prejudice to Article 141 of this Protocol, the proportion of the two forces in all the structures of the National Gendarmerie shall be affected by no prerequisite condition in terms of accessibility. Thus, adequate training shall be given to the Gendarmes retained without fulfilling all the necessary requirements, in accordance with the modalities sped fled by the Command Council of the National Gendarmerie.

5. The post of Chief of Staff of the National Gendarmerie shall be held by the Rwandese Patriotic Front (RPF) and the one of Deputy Chief of Staff by the Government party.

And for Rwandan refugees, principles that reversed decades of a problem that had immensely contributed to the civil war:

Article 1
The return of Rwandese refugees to their country is an inalienable right and constitutes a factor of peace, national unity, and reconciliation.

Article 2
The return is an act of free will on the part of each refugee. Any Rwandese refugee who wants to go back to his country will do so without any precondition whatsoever. Each person who returns shall be free to settle down in any place of their choice inside the country, so long as they do not encroach upon the rights of other people

When, on the 4th August, 1993, delegations of the Government of Rwanda and the Rwandese Patriotic Front gathered in the small Tanzanian town of Arusha for the signing ceremony of the Arusha Peace Agreement, both parties were making achievable, yet exorbitant promises. Never before in the entire history of Rwanda had there been such sharing of power among Rwanda's elite and ethnic groups, and creation of an army that in great detail would be shared so as to protect everyone. The government side was represented by President Juvenal Habyarimana. The RPF was represented by the Chairman Alexis Kanyarengwe, and its Vice-Chairman, Major Paul Kagame. It was an irony that President Habyarimana and Colonel Alexis Kanyarengwe, both Hutu and architects of the 1959 revolution and the 1973 coup d'état, would sign on to pull down the pillars of the Hutu revolution. It was even more ironical that Chairman Kanyarengwe would sign on behalf of the RPF, predominantly Tutsi, while Major Paul Kagame, a Tutsi and the real power behind RPF, silently watched the drama of the day. Ambassador Ami Mpungwe of Tanzania and I did the protocol behind President Habyarimana and Chairman Kanyarengwe as they exchanged the signed copies of the agreement, and finally, reluctantly shook hands.

In its first article, the Arusha Peace Agreement boldly proclaimed:

Article 1

The war between the Government of the Republic of Rwanda and the Rwandese Patriotic Front is hereby brought to an end

There is a time for war and a time for peace. Amongst many Rwandans and the international community, it seemed like a time for peace had come and there was cause for celebration.

CHAPTER SIXTEEN

Escalation and Missed Opportunities

In the final provisions of the Arusha Peace Agreement, the Transitional Government was supposed to be established within thirty seven days. General elections would take place within 22 months. This was to be preceded by the establishment and deployment of a Neutral International Force that would be provided by the United Nations. UN Peacekeeping Operations are classified, under the United Nations Charter as CHAPTER VI, VII and VIII. The Neutral International Force would be a CHAPTER VI mandate.

- **Chapter VI** deals with the "Pacific Settlement of Disputes". UN peacekeeping operations have traditionally been associated with Chapter VI. However, the Security Council need not refer to a specific chapter of the Charter when passing a resolution authorizing the deployment of a UN peacekeeping operation and has never invoked Chapter VI.
- **Chapter VII** contains provisions related to "Action with Respect to the Peace, Breaches of the Peace and Acts of Aggression'. In recent years, the Council has adopted the

practice of invoking Chapter VII of the Charter when authorizing the deployment of UN peacekeeping operations into volatile post-conflict settings where the State is unable to maintain security and public order. The Security Council's invocation of Chapter VII in these situations, in addition to denoting the legal basis for its action, can also be seen as a statement of firm political resolve and a means of reminding the parties to a conflict and the wider UN membership of their obligation to give effect to Security Council decisions.

- **Chapter VIII** of the Charter provides for the involvement of regional arrangements and agencies in the maintenance of international peace and security provided such activities are consistent with the purposes and principles outlined in Chapter I of the Charter

Source: http://www.un.org/en/peacekeeping/operations/pkmandates.shtml

One of the very first undertakings between the Government of Rwanda and RPF was to send a joint delegation to the United Nations in New York. At that time, this gesture was significant in terms of confidence building. The government delegation included the Foreign Minister, Anastase Gasana and Ambassador Claver Kanyarushoki. The RPF delegation included Patrick Mazimpaka, James Butare and I. For the first time, RPF members received "ordre de mission", or travel authorization, signed by President Habyarimana himself, with an allowance of 3,000 U.S. dollars to each one of us. Our joint mission was to convince the United Nations to establish and deploy the Neutral International Force expeditiously so that the Transitional Government could be established within the 37 days. Our delegation met the UN Secretary General, Boutros Boutros Ghali, and we parted not very convinced that bureaucratic UN would act that quickly, but still with hope that something would work out.

There were a number of stakeholders and players in the Arusha peace process. These included the Government of Rwanda, which was a coalition between the MRND and the opposition political parties (MDR, PSD, PL and PDC), the Rwandese Patriotic Front (RPF), the Facilitator (President Mwinyi of Tanzania), the Mediator (President Mobutu of DRC), President Museveni of Uganda as the principal supporter of RPF, Rwanda's opposition political parties (MDR, PSD, PL, PDC and other small parties), the Organization of African Unity (OAU), the United Nations, France, the United States and Belgium.

Each of these players had a posture that in one way or another contributed first to the stalemate, and later to the tragic events of 1994. The primary responsibility, can however, be localized among the Rwandan players, notably the MRND Government and the RPF.

1. Government of Rwanda

Form the very beginning the Government of Rwanda had been a reluctant negotiator. The Second Republic under President Habyarimana was in essence a continuation of the First Republic under President Kayibanda, with some modification. The MRND government's outlook remained one based on Hutu power. Gradually, power gravitated from the south to the north of Rwanda (Ruhengeri and Gisenyi), and within the north, within the extended family of President Habyarimana. With time, the so-called comrades of the 5th July were marginalized, and fell out, as close and extended family members of President Habyarimana became the principal power brokers. The Arusha Peace Agreement reduced the powers of MRND, the Army and gendarmerie, the security organs, the power brokers and President Habyarimana himself. From having everything, they now had to share. This meant loss of power and privilege.

In anticipation of, and reaction to, the possible implementation of the accords, the MRND government intensified the efforts at least to shape the outcomes of the process. First, it courted factions within political parties that were supposed to participate in the transitional government. This way, MRND hoped, it would have a presence in the transitional government by other means. Hence were born the *pawa* factions of within the opposition parties. *Pawa* stood for Hutu power, born of Hutu fundamentalism or Hutu extremism. The rallying cry of these pawa factions was one centred on the idea that power belonged to the Hutu people, and that RPF is a Tutsi creation that must be contained by all means necessary. Second, MRND allowed or promoted the violent activities of satellite parties like the Coalition for the Defence of the Republic (CDR). CDR was proudly and unapologetically anti-Tutsi, and anti-Hutu (Hutu who were not MRND, not extremist, or not from the north) and openly called for their destruction. By promoting such MRND-friendly (and MRND-controlled) parties, MRND hoped to influence the course of events within the transitional government if ever it happened. Third, MRND allowed and promoted media like Radio Télévision Libre des Mille Collines (RTLM) and the newspaper *Kangura*, which preached hatred and extremist views against the political opposition and Tutsi in particular. CDR, RTLM, Kangura, pawa factions and many in the security establishment openly or silently amplified and popularized the spirit and practice of Hutu Ten Commandments.

THE HUTU TEN COMMANDMENTS
Source: *Kangura No.6, 1990*

1. Every Hutu must know that the Tutsi woman, wherever she may be, is working for the Tutsi ethnic cause. In consequence, any Hutu is a traitor who:acquires a Tutsi

wife;Acquires a Tutsi concubine; or acquires a Tutsi secretary or protégée.

2.Every Hutu must know that our Hutu daughters are more worthy and more conscientious as women, as wives and as mothers. Aren't they lovely, excellent secretaries, and more honest!

3.Hutu women, be vigilant and make sure that your husbands, brothers and sons see reason.

4. All Hutus must know that all Tutsis are dishonest in business. Their only goal is ethnic superiority. We have learned this by experience from experience. In consequence, any Hutu is a traitor who forms a business alliance with a Tutsi, invests his own funds or public funds in a Tutsi enterprise, borrows money from or loans money to a Tusti, grants favors to Tutsis (import licenses, bank loans, land for construction, public markets...)

5. Strategic positions such as politics, administration, economics, the military and security must be restricted to the Hutu.

6. A Hutu majority must prevail throughout the educational system (pupils, scholars, teachers).

7. The Rwandan Army must be exclusively Hutu. The war of October 1990 has taught us that. No soldier may marry a Tutsi woman.

8. Hutu must stop taking pity on the Tutsi.

9. Hutu wherever they be must stand united, in solidarity, and concerned with the fate of their Hutu brothers. Hutu within and without Rwanda must constantly search for friends and allies to the Hutu Cause, beginning with their Bantu brothers.

Hutu must constantly counter Tutsi propaganda. Hutu must stand firm and vigilant against their common enemy: the Tutsi.

10. The Social Revolution of 1959, the Referendum of 1961 and the Hutu Ideology must be taught to Hutu of every age. Every Hutu must spread the word wherever he goes. Any Hutu who persecutes his brother Hutu for spreading and teaching this ideology is a traitor.

This media particularly made vitriolic attacks on the Arusha peace agreement. Fourth, MRND expedited the training and arming of the militia, the notorious *Interahamwe*. Some factions within the security institutions (the army, intelligence, gendarmerie, Republican Guard) and MRND must have actively sought to put in place arrangements for Plan B. As part of this plan B, lists of Tutsi and Hutu were drawn, as the RTLM, Kangura and some officials relentlessly warned of an impending apocalypse.

2. The Rwandese Patriotic Front

RPF was a reluctant negotiator. Throughout the Arusha peace process, RPF projected an image of an interested party, yet the negotiations were never popular among RPF's supporters, most of them Tutsi. RPF's leadership tried to make an effort to explain to its members, especially the RPA combatants. It was during this period that RPF made key decisions, related to the Arusha Peace Agreement:

- The statutes and new structure of RPF as a political party, transitioning from a political-military organization. Colonel Alexis Kanyarengwe remained the Chairman, with three Vice-Chairmen (Paul Kagame, First Vice Chairman and Chairman of the RPA High Command; Patrick Mazimpaka, Second Vice Chairman; Denis Polisi, Third Vice-Chairman) and myself as the Secretary General.
- Determining RPF leaders who would represent the organization in the transitional government; as per Arusha Peace Agreement terms.
- The commissioning of formal military ranks. Only Paul Kagame had the rank of Major General. I received my rank of Major.
- The commissioning of the 600 men of RPA, under Charles Kayonga, to protect RPF's leaders in Kigali, starting with the CND building where they were supposed to reside.

Beyond these formal decisions that related to the Arusha Peace Agreement, it is important to note two backgrounds that made RPF an unlikely enthusiast in the kind of arrangements that the Arusha Peace Agreement provided. On the surface, RPF was the biggest winner in the agreement. It had started with nothing, and now had a significant portion of the state, at least on paper. RPF would have a deputy Prime minister, 5 cabinet positions, 40% of the new national army and 50% of its command positions, and 40% of the new gendarmerie and 50% of its command positions. Above all, the Tutsi refugees, RPF's natural constituency, were coming home. When you consider that the RPF-friendly political opposition had cabinet portfolios and that the new Prime Minister would be Faustin Twagiramungu, RPF had succeeded in making MRND and President Habyarimana a political minority.

However, RPF's recent and dominant background was the National Resistance Movement's revolutionary doctrine according to which the objective of a revolutionary movement is to capture state power by forceful or other means, and use the power for the benefit of the masses. If you have to share power after seizing the state, it has to be done on your terms. This is what the RPF leaders and RPA officers, while in Uganda's NRA, had seen, preached and experienced. Most importantly, Major Paul Kagame had worked under President Museveni both before and after capture of state power in Uganda. He had seen the inclination to centralize, monopolize and control power among revolutionary leaders. His personality also prepared him to play some cards close to his chest.

During this period, RPF infiltrated men and weapons to the CND and other parts of Rwanda, especially where communities of Tutsi could be found. It is estimated that by April 6, 1994, there were over and above 2,000 RPA men in and around the CND. Small arms were distributed to some Tutsi supporters. Small arms and heavy weapons were concealed in anticipation of disarmament and demobilization. RPF also intensified political work within Kigali, now that it had some significant access to RPF members in Kigali and beyond. It also worked very hard to court factions of the political parties, MDR, PSD, PL and PDC that were hostile to MRND and sympathetic to sharing power with RPF. RPF intensified its diplomatic effort to show that it was President Habyarimana and his MRND party that were stalling, asking the international community to bring pressure towards setting up the transitional institutions. RPF, MRND and CDR were involved in political assassinations, to eliminate potential competitors and to create a climate of fear. A climate of fear was important for RPF because it showed that the MRND system was ungovernable, and hence needed complete change rather than cosmetic change.

3. A Lukewarm Diplomacy

The international order, since 1990, had been dominated by major events in history. The Berlin wall had come down in 1989, the Soviet Union had disintegrated in 1990, Saddam Hussein's invasion had generated strong international action to reverse it, the Balkans were burning, and the short-lived international action in Somalia had left all, especially the United States, with a strong desire not to act militarily, especially in Africa. For this period August 4ᵗʰ,1993-April 6ᵗʰ, 1994, in the Great Lakes region, President Pierre Buyoya ruled Burundi; President Museveni, Uganda; President Arap Moi, Kenya; and President Al Hassan Mwinyi, Tanzania; and President Mobutu Sese Seko, DRC. At the OAU, the Secretary General was Salim Ahmed Salim, with Tunisia holding the rotating Chairmanship.

At the top of the international order was the President of the United States, Bill Clinton. His Secretary of State was Warren Christopher, and Permanent Representative to the United Nations was Ambassador Madeleine Albright. Anthony Lake was the National Security Adviser, James Woolsey was the Director of the Central Intelligence Agency (CIA), William Perry was the U.S. Secretary of Defense, and General Shalikashvili the Chairman, Joint Chiefs of Staff. In France, socialist President Francois Mitterrand reigned and had close relationships with President Habyarimana. Russia, Boris Yeltsin ruled. John Major was the Prime Minister in the United Kingdom. At the United Nations, Boutros Boutros-Ghali was the Secretary General, and Kofi Annan was head of U.N Peacekeeping.

Other than the Rwandese people themselves who should take the primary responsibility for the failure of the peace accords, all the above leaders and many more should share the blame for the failure. There was delay in deploying the UN Peacekeeping force of 2,700 far beyond the 37 day deadline. With Brigadier General Romeo Dallaire, a Canadian as its head, UNAMIR was "a Chapter VI mandate", lightly armed for self-defense, but unable to enforce peace as in a Chapter VII mandate. The Secretary-General's Special Representative to Rwanda, Jacques-Roger Boo-Booh, from Cameroon, was far leaning on the side of France and

President Habyarimana. RPF did not trust Roger Booh-Booh at all, possibly due to his French connections and especially because, due to his French connections, we considered him to be close to President Habyarimana. Both General Dallaire and Booh-Booh dealt with the various players in a shy and timid way. General Dallaire was aware of actions on both sides that constituted a breach of the accords.

He knew that the U.N. headquarters in New York was not about to order a full confrontation with the realities on the ground.

When the setting up of the transitional institutions delayed for seven consecutive months amidst rising tensions and possibility of escalation, at one point the bone of contention was the insistence of MRND to include the radically extremist party, CDR, in the transitional government. There was a continuing saga within political parties as to which list should be submitted for inclusion, with lines drawn along who is for MRND or RPF-sympathetic. Most diplomats in Kigali had bought into the idea that if the inclusion of CDR is the only sticking point, may be RPF should be flexible enough and allow that to happen so that the transitional government could be sworn in. RPF rejected the idea consistently.

At one point, Ms.Prudence Bushnell, then Deputy to U.S. Assistant Secretary of State for African Affairs Ambassador George Moose, came to RPF's Headquarters in Mulindi, Byumba, in northern Rwanda. I was in the meeting she had with General Paul Kagame. She insisted that RPF should accept MRND's demand to include CDR in the transitional government. Promptly, Kagame asked her whether the U.S ever considered including the KKK in the U.S. Congress`. Challenged, Ms. Bushnell just left the topic. As delegation after delegation visited Kigali and Mulindi, the two opposite poles of a contested domain, the stalemate deepened. No delegation ever put matters clearly to show the dangers and stakes involved in the escalation. In another meeting, General Paul Kagame met Gen. Romeo Dallaire and challenged him to having an ineffectual force that could not act amidst escalating crisis. The U.N. officer invoked the challenge of limited mandate. General Kagame hinted indirectly that if it were him he would pack his bags and go.

Belgium hand contributed troops to UNAMIR, as well as some logistical and financial contributions. France was in the background, essentially actively leaning towards the Habyarimana regime. The United Kingdom was unconcerned. China and Russia, as permanent members of the Security Council were far from being actively interested in the Rwandan saga.

4.   African Players

The Facilitator (President Mwinyi), the Mediator (President Mobutu), the Organization of African Unity (Secretary General Salim Ahmed Salim), and President Museveni of Uganda (leaning actively towards RPF) did not engage the players in a robust and candid manner. Part of the problem of the OAU then and the African Union now is that it operates on a minimalist agenda. The OAU rarely rebukes rulers of member states who misbehave. Heads of State in this body behave gently towards each other like members of a club. The principle seems to be "do not interfere in my internal matters, or else I will interfere in yours". Since some of them tend to have skeletons in their cupboards, they jealously uphold this principle.

The OAU had a small observer mission in Rwanda, to monitor and verify a ceasefire that was holding since 1992. The OAU did not have much influence on the RPF. The OAU has always had resource constraints. Even the small observer mission it led could only take off from the ground with donations of money and equipment from western powers. President Mobutu of DRC, supposedly a mediator in the conflict, was leaning on the side of France and President Habyarimana's regime. President Mwinyi of Tanzania was engaged, and Tanzania had invested much diplomatic capital towards the success of the Arusha negotiations. However, there were many in Tanzania's leadership who never trusted RPF. This led to a less than strong signal to the parties in the conflict, especially to the government side when it became evident that there were unnecessary delays in implementing the Arusha Accords.

With little trust and confidence in each other, a general pessimistic mood was developing in weeks immediately preceding April 6th , 1994. Each side was left to its own schemes.

Each was left to read and judge the situation in a self-fulfilling prophecy. During this period, the MRND Government and the RPF were working full throttle towards plan B, which in essence progressively became plan A. A spark any time would light the fire.

CHAPTER SEVENTEEN

Apocalypse

President Yoweri Museveni came to power in 1986 with an outlook that inspired many of us young Africans. As a devout student of Walter Rodney during his college days at the University of Dar es Salaam, he espoused a spirit of self-reliance and equal exchange in the south-south frame work. He even attempted batter trade with some communist countries like East Germany. He supported the Africa National Congress in the anti-apartheid struggle, and welcomed its freedom fighters to train in Uganda. He supported the late John Garang of Southern Sudan and his Sudanese People Liberation Movement/Sudanese People's Liberation Army (SPLM/SPLA). He was supporting the Rwandese Patriotic Front. He identified with the late Samora Machel, who was the President of Mozambique, and leader of FRELIMO, which fought for independence from Portugal. His allies included the late Muamar Gaddafi. His critics see in him a man who overestimates himself, with ambitions like those of the German Otto von Bismarck, determined to build larger political and economic entities through the barrel of the gun if necessary.

At the beginning of April 1994, the Pan African Movement was rekindled when it held an international conference in Kampala,Uganda. From its beginnings in the early 1900s, the Pan African Movement was dedicated to struggles for the independence of African colonized nations and towards the unity of Africans. Principal among its leaders in the early phase included luminaries like W.E.B. Du Bois (US), Kwame Nkrumah (Ghana), Jommo Kenyatta (Kenya), Patrice Lumumba (Congo), Julius Nyerere (Tanzania) and many others. Ultimately the Pan African Movement led to the establishment of the Organization of African Unity. The philosophy of the Pan African Movement was simple. An injury to one was an injury to all. Africa could not be free until the whole of Africa was socially, politically, and economically free. Africans included our dear brothers and sisters who had been enslaved for centuries and whose descendants were now scattered on the planet in North America, Latin America, and Europe. We had one struggle, and its objective was to overcome imperial domination. To do this we had to "unite, organize and not agonize."

The late Dr. Tajudeen Abdul Raheem was the Secretary General of the Pan African Movement in 1994. RPF was invited to attend the conference. RPF's delegation was led by Second Vice Chairman, Patrick Mazimpaka. I attended the conference. The late Wilson Rutayisire who headed our clandestine shortwave *Radio Muhabura,* and a good number of other senior cadres were in attendance. I remember sitting near General Aidid of Somalia in one afternoon session at the Nile Conference Center. He seemed to be a simple man, calm and spoke little when I enthusiastically tried to engage him in a conversation. The west called him a warlord. He received a standing ovation when he gave his speech. Pan Africanists preferred to call him an African freedom fighter who was standing up against imperialism in Mogadishu.

On April 6, I left the conference, had a couple of other meetings and retired at the home of my friend, Captain Enoch Nkunda. At 1 am on April 7, I tuned in to my small Sony radio receiver to listen to world news. As I was falling asleep, the BBC announced that a plane carrying President Juvenal Habyarimana of Rwanda and President Cyprien Ntaryamira of Burundi and their entourage from a summit in Dar es Salaam, Tanzania, had been shot down and all on board were dead. I woke my friend up to tell him the bad news. I wondered who had done it, what the motivation was, and what the likely consequences were. I knew for sure that Tutsi in Rwanda and Hutu in the opposition were in trouble. I worried about RPF's contingent at the CND (Parliament) building in the middle of enemy territory, encircled by government troops. I worried about the fate of the Arusha Peace Agreement. Rwanda was already on edge, and any trigger of this magnitude would derail the process for good.

Unable to sleep, I was restless for the rest of the night. I contemplated how dangerous it was to be Rwanda's ruler. A bloody succession, now known as the *coup of Rucuncu*, had left Rwanda's ruling Tutsi clans weak and divided towards the end of the 19th century. The winner in this coup was King Musinga who was himself banished by Belgian colonial authorities in the early 1930's. His body has never been recovered. In 1959, in another emotionally charged atmosphere at a time of transition, King Mutara Rudahigwa died abruptly in Bujumbura, Burundi, in mysterious circumstances. His successor, King Kigeli Ndahindurwa has been in exile since then, and now lives in the United States. President Gregoire Kayibanda was overthrown in 1973 and died a miserable death at the hands of the Habyarimana regime. Now another Rwandan leader, President Habyarimana had died violently, and was never buried in his motherland. It spoke volumes about power dynamics in Rwandan society, and the cut throat competition among the elite vying for this power. It is a matter of life and death. Winners take it all, and losers die or are banished.

Early in the morning I travelled back to RPF's headquarters in Mulindi in northern Rwanda. All the way on the road through Masaka, Mbarara, Kabale, and Gatuna I remembered the day in 1990 when I had travelled this road. The beginning of the civil war then had been flagged off with the death of a general, a Tutsi, Fred Rwigyema, who was the leader of RPF. Now, as Rwanda was beginning to think of an end to the civil war, another general, Juvenal Habyarimana, a Hutu, and President of the Republic, had died. In due course both Tutsi and Hutu would pay a price that never before Rwanda had witnessed in centuries of history.

I arrived at Mulindi in the late afternoon, and it looked like a ghost community. My military escorts and a few other people I found in Mulindi were in a state of excitement that President Habyarimana was dead. I gathered that General Paul Kagame had issued orders to the RPA senior officers to break the ceasefire on the night of April 6, 1994, immediately after the shooting down of the plane. The three pronged attack had the objective of capturing the capital city, Kigali, and ultimately the whole country.

I first met Chairman Alexis Kanyarengwe, and later General Paul Kagame, and we discussed the unfolding events, and how RPF could take advantage of the situation militarily, politically and diplomatically. I did not raise the matter of the shooting down of the plane with either of them. Neither of them raised the matter. In a briefing I received from General Kagame, RPF was to explain to the international community how the Hutu extremists opposed to the Arusha peace Agreement were responsible for the shooting down of the plane, and had already started killing Tutsi and Hutu opposition politicians. According to this narrative, the government side had broken the ceasefire, and the RPF was resuming hostilities 1) to stop the killings and 2) to restore law and order. As reports of killings spread to the outside world day by day, it was clear Rwanda was in the middle of a full-fledged *complex emergency*.

According to the United Nations Office for Humanitarian Affairs (OCHA);

> A complex emergency is "a humanitarian crisis in a country, region or society where there is total or considerable breakdown of authority resulting from internal or exter-

nal conflict and which requires an international response that goes beyond the mandate or capacity of any single agency and/ or the ongoing United Nations country program." (IASC, December 1994).

Such "complex emergencies" are typically characterized by:

- extensive violence and loss of life; massive displacements of people; widespread damage to societies and economies
- the need for large-scale, multi-faceted humanitarian assistance
- the hindrance or prevention of humanitarian assistance by political and military constraints
- significant security risks for humanitarian relief workers in some areas

It turned out that President Habyarimana and other regional Heads of State had been invited by the facilitator, President Mwinyi of Tanzania, to Dar es Salaam for a regional summit. The Dar es Salam meeting was intended to breathe fresh life into the stalled implementation of the Arusha Peace Agreement. Presidents Cyprien Ntaryamira of Burundi, Yoweri Museveni of Uganda, Ali Hassan Mwinyi of Tanzania as Facilitator, Daniel Arap Moi of Kenya had gathered in Dar es Salaam on April 6, 1994 to deliberate on the matter. President Habyarimana had taken with him his Army Chief of Staff, General Nsabimana. Reports from the summit indicated that President Habyarimana had pledged to his colleagues, the Heads of State, that the Transitional Government would be sworn in without further delay. In the evening of April 6, the President of Burundi, Cyprien Ntaryamira, decided to join President Habyarimana on the fateful flight from Dar es Salaam to Kigali International Airport. The Presidential plane, a Falcon 50 aircraft, was a gift from France to President Habyarimana. Its pilots were French. The plane was hit by two missiles as it approached Kigali International Airport at Kanombe, crashed just behind the Presidential mansion at Kanombe, and all on board were killed.

With President Habyarimana dead, together with his Army Chief of Staff, a moment of utmost national crisis presented itself without political and military leadership, and without a succession plan. The Hutu extremists in the military took over the reins of government and set up a Provisional Government under President Sindikubwabo and Prime Minister Kambanda. Convinced that the shooting down of the plane was the work of RPF and its Tutsi, the Hutu extremists descended on Tutsi and Hutu opposition politicians. In the next one hundred days, this factor, among others, would play out to the disadvantage of the government and to the advantage of RPF's quest for power. The hundred days would be the darkest in the entire history of Rwanda, in which genocide was committed against Tutsi, and war crimes and crimes against humanity committed against Hutu. Over one million lives would be lost, and the regime would collapse on July 4, as RPA captured the capital city, Kigali, and two weeks later set up a government on July 19, 1994.

Calls for Ceasefire

As the killings intensified, and the civil war gathered momentum, the international community exerted pressure on "both sides to exercise restraint and revert to ceasefire".

At this point, RPA had seized the military initiative and was absolutely single-minded on capturing state power. The killings discredited the regime in Kigali, and placed plenty of diplomatic capital in RPF's hands. Politically, the regime had lost any appeal as the country descended into mayhem. The pressure for ceasefire was best articulated through President Yoweri Museveni of Uganda.

Over a period of a week in April, 1994, President Museveni called for a meeting in Kampala in which a Rwanda embassy
official, Ambassador Claver Kanyarushoke, I, the Ambassadors
of the United States, United Kingdom, Tanzania, and France
were in attendance. A Ugandan officer, Kale Kayihura, currently
a General and Inspector General of Uganda Police, accompanied
me to these meetings. The ambassadors demanded a ceasefire. I
would tell them that the government of Rwanda was responsible
for killings and the breakdown of the ceasefire, and we could not
stop until the killings stopped. I would tell them how RPA combatants were discovering fresh massacres and mass graves as they
advanced. It was a very exhausting week. I would drive all the way
to northern Rwanda to report to General Kagame the proceedings of the meetings. I would return to Kampala the following
day.

After one of such sessions, President Museveni asked me and
Kale Kayihura to remain behind. I could sense he was visibly irri-
tated. He tongue-lashed me, saying, "You Rwandese are treacher-
ous". At one point he even asked me why I wasn't taking notes
as he spoke. I could not explain to him that as a doctor I had
learned how to memorize a lot of data. I had to take notes. When
he calmed down he told me RPF could not entirely ignore the
calls for ceasefire from the international community. Rwandans
had taken themselves into chaos that affected not only Rwandans
but the region and the international community as well. Hence,
RPF could not have the last word. We should have a ceasefire,
and if the Government breaks it, we can resume hostilities. It
was a game of diplomacy in support of military operations, he
explained. I quickly understood his message. He was RPF's sole
backer from the very beginning. He could not be ignored.

I returned to report the matter to General Kagame. RPF,
rather than negotiate a ceasefire with the Provisional Government, decided on a unilateral ceasefire. I travelled back to Kampala and, together with Kale Kayihura , met President Museveni

in his Nile Mansions offices. He was very happy that RPF had agreed to announce a ceasefire. I told him I would be proceeding to Arusha, Tanzania, where I would publicly announce the ceasefire. He immediately called President Mwinyi of Tanzania, and informed him about the good news about the ceasefire. I had just gone out of the office when I was called in again. President Museveni told me I could as well announce the ceasefire immediately, in Kampala. I understood that he had decided, rightly so, that it is through his relationship and pressure that RPF had agreed to the ceasefire. I presumed he wanted to take the credit. I immediately announced RPF's unilateral ceasefire.

I travelled to Nairobi that same day, and by road through Namanga border post in Kenya to Arusha, Tanzania. There, I announced again the unilateral ceasefire. In one of the meetings, Prime Minister Malecela castigated RPF for being a minority that was simply bent on capturing state power like Yoweri Museveni in 1986. Yoweri Museveni had negotiated with the regime of Tito Okello in 1985, only to overthrow it the following year. RPF had also negotiated the Arusha Peace Agreement, but now was bent on capturing state power by military conquest. I argued with him that the responsibility was the government's since it was killing citizens. I could detect some impatience on his face and I gently but forcefully defended the RPF position. Curiously, while in Arusha, I learnt that some ministers from the Rwandan Provisional Government were around. I had stern instructions that under no circumstances could I meet any one from the provisional government. Hurriedly, without notifying the Tanzanian authorities, I drove from Arusha to Nairobi, thus avoiding any contacts with the provisional government representatives.

Back in Rwanda, RPF was fighting on four fronts: 1) military; 2) political; 3) diplomatic; and 4) humanitarian. RPF decided to send Gerald Gahima and Claude Dusaidi to spearhead RPF's diplomatic offensive in Washington, D.C. and New York. We also sent Dr. Ben Rugangazi and Dr. Bosco Butera to be active in African capitals. On the humanitarian front, all RPF cadres were active in the footprints of a fast moving RPA, to deal with NGOs in the humanitarian catastrophe that was increasing daily. RPF also decided to encourage the 1959 Tutsi refugees to return and occupy the safe areas that had been liberated. On the political front, RPF was mainly involved in contacting any opposition politicians that survived the killings.

Rwandans Abandoned

The response of the United Nations, and its member states, especially the powerful ones, was a disaster without precedent. As killings intensified and the complex emergency gathered momentum, western embassies airlifted embassy personnel, even their pets, to safety. A cloud of darkness descended on Rwanda. The United Nations had been slow in sending the international peacekeeping force to Rwanda. Once it was assembled, and deployed, it was generally ineffectual. Its commander, General Romeo Dallaire, became frustrated as he had neither been able to protect Rwandan people who were dying day by day nor his own force. With the death of the 10 Belgian peacekeepers, and the decision by Belgium to pull out of the peacekeeping force, the United Nations Security Council decided to close down the peacekeeping operation, and leave behind a symbolic 270 men holed up in Kigali. The United States and France had a leading role to play in this decision.

At this point, RPF was not even interested in any international military presence in Rwanda that would stand in the way of its quest to seize power by military means. General Paul Kagame was saying that the departure of the UN force was actually a good thing. It was doing nothing, first of all, and would be a nuisance that would stand in the way of RPF's military advance. Once the United Nations and member states decided to quit, hurriedly leaving Rwandan people defenseless, it was a signal to the killers that they could proceed as they wished. RPF, on its part, had sufficient diplomatic ammunition to use against the international community. The departure of the UN force and diplomatic staff from Kigali essentially became a signal to the extremist Interahamwe and military to increase the tempo of the genocide. RPF forces, on their part, had a free hand to do as they pleased. Many Hutu were massacred by the advancing rebel troops.

During the month of May, as the situation in Rwanda deteriorated, there were fresh calls for a ceasefire, a return to the peace process, and for a new UN peacekeeping force, the so-called UNAMIR II. The position of the RPF was that it was rather too late since, as we always argued, all Tutsi who were supposed to be killed had been killed. Who would the UNAMIR be coming to save? There were no prospects for negotiations, and it was rather too late for a ceasefire. RPF could sense that an international peacekeeping force would freeze the situation and take away its military initiative. Gerald Gahima and Claude Dusaidi articulated this position in their Washington, D.C. and New York meetings. In RPF's media campaign, and on *Radio Muhabura*, our strategy was to attack the international community for abandoning Rwanda, and yet eager to stage a comeback at a time the genocide was more or less complete.

More Calls for Ceasefire, Negotiations and Peacekeeping

In May, Chairman Alexis Kanyarengwe led a delegation to Arusha, Tanzania for consultations with the Facilitator. One of the senior leaders of RPF, Simon Ntare, and I accompanied him to the consultations. Tanzania's Defense Minister, Colonel Kinana and the OAU Secretary-General Salim Ahmed Salim, were present. There was a big presence of the western diplomatic community. In all the meetings our delegation attended we were told to exercise restraint and go back to the negotiating table.

RPF's standard response was that there cannot be a ceasefire until the killings stop, and that we cannot negotiate with killers. The OAU Secretary-General, Salim Ahmed Salim, even proposed some indirect talks, but our delegation did not accept that proposal. Later in the night, one of the RPA security officers in our delegation came to wake me up and told me he had heard rumors that there was a document that RPF would be asked to sign separately from representatives of the provisional government. He told me Defense Minister Kinana knew something about it.

Disturbed by this development, I went down from my hotel room and confronted Col. Kinana. He denied it. Shortly after, around 1 or 2 am, I was told the diplomats were gathered in one of the hotel meeting rooms and wanted to see the RPF delegation. Chairman Alexis Kanyarengwe sent me and Simon Ntare to the meeting. The spokesperson for the whole group was the U.S. Ambassador, Peter Jon de Vos . He spoke in a very commanding and emphatic tone. In short, he said RPF was making a very big mistake. It was refusing ceasefire, negotiations, and pushing for capturing state power by military means. RPF would be held accountable. Irked by his remarks, I thanked him but reminded the whole audience that they should be more concerned about the plight of hundreds of thousands who had already died and were dying every day. I told them they should be demanding accountability from the Provisional Government, and not from RPF. I concluded by telling them that yes, when time for accounting comes, RPF will account. I reminded them politely that there will be a time when they too, the international community, will have to account for their own failures. The meeting ended shortly after and we headed home the following day.

On our way, in Kampala, Chairman Alexis Kanyarengwe and I had to go and brief President Museveni on the developments. He was in a casual mood, in sandals, and my eyes were fixed on his book shelf as he briefly talked to Chairman Kanyarengwe in

Kinyarwanda. He had inspired me to revolution, and I was curious to know what he read now that he was in power. I could see that social and economic development had remained a preoccupation. He reiterated to Chairman Kanyarengwe why we should still be interested in ceasefire because the international community demanded it. He was not emphatic this time, but explained why ceasefire remained an important diplomatic device in service of overall political and military objectives.

Meanwhile at the United Nations, plans were underway for launching another United Nations peacekeeping force in Rwanda, UNAMIR II. On May 17, the UN Security Council voted for a second peacekeeping operation, with approximately 5, 700 men. RPF's resistance to another force had been overruled. However, RPF was acquainted with the speed of United Nations operations. RPF hoped for, and worked towards, a scenario in which such an operation would soon be overtaken by events.

Operation Turquoise

As the United Nations was deliberating on UNAMIR II, another development on the diplomatic front was brewing. By June 1994, France was advancing the idea of a Chapter VII peacekeeping operation in Rwanda. The danger of the proposal was that it came from France, and there was bad blood between France and RPF way back from the first days of the civil war in 1990. Anything that France did, well intentioned or not was bound to be read as hostile by RPF. France probably read the situation in a similar way. RPF had campaigned since 1990 to show that France was leaning towards the Habyarimana regime. With genocide in progress, RPF always made sure that people understood that France was close to the Provisional Government. RPF campaigned internationally explaining that France was trying everything possible to support the Provisional Government and prevent it from what then seemed to be its inevitable defeat and collapse.

When France surfaced with an idea for a Chapter VII U.N mandate for a peace enforcement force in Rwanda in June, RPF raised a red flag.

As consultations at the U.N. were underway, RPF learnt that the French-led multinational force was to be called Operation Turquoise. Hurriedly, with encouragement from French contacts, RPF sent a delegation to Paris to dissuade the French from their well advanced idea. The delegation was headed by me, and included Dr. Jacques Bihozagara, who had been RPF's envoy to Europe throughout the civil war. Dr. Bihozagara, a natural diplomat in his manners, always tried to encourage RPF's leadership to be open minded in its dealings with the French. The overall mood within the RPF was always either hostile or skeptical towards anything French. Our view was that, like the Belgians, the French hated Tutsi. Translated, this meant that they hated the RPF, since the majority within RPF was Tutsi. How then, we would ask, could the French be coming to Rwanda to save Tutsi? RPF insisted that all Tutsi who were supposed to die had died, and it was unbelievable that the French were coming to save Tutsi. Of course not all Tutsi had died. In retrospect, this was a callous and cynical position that originated from General Kagame. It would have been worth the effort to save even one Tutsi. Every human being deserves to be saved.

Dr. Bihozagara and I arrived in Paris under conditions that showed RPF's fortunes had risen. Gone were the days when we were non-entities in western capitals. We were officially received by French government officials, driven in an official car, with a police car and security for protection. We were accommodated in a first class hotel, and told we were to meet France's Foreign Minister, Alain Juppe. When we arrived at the Quai d'Orsay, the French Foreign Ministry, we were received by Alain Juppe, the Foreign Minister, and settled for business immediately. Though

Dr. Bihozagara was French-speaking, as head of delegation I spoke in English. Mr. Juppe briefly mentioned how consultations were underway at the United Nations in New York for a resolution on a humanitarian peace enforcement multi-national force under the leadership of France. He hoped RPF would cooperate with the multi-national force.

In response, I told Mr. Juppe that RPF had had a strained relationship with France, but we were open to better relationships. It was RPF's view that there was no justification for a peace enforcement operation by France since genocide was more or less complete. Second, France could not be considered to be neutral in Rwanda, and RPF could interpret its intentions as hostile. I asked more questions about the nature of the force and Juppe said I could discuss the matter with the French generals. The meeting was not acrimonious and each side would stick to its plans. France was not about to change its plans. They even told us that our people on the ground were receptive to the idea of Operation Turquoise, which of course was not true. RPF was beginning to consider a long war with the French, in case the latter decided to support the Provisional Government openly and fully. As Juppe walked us to the door, he paused at the entrance of his office and told us that the U.N. Security Council had voted for the French-led "multinational force". The only other country that was in the multinational force was Senegal, France's closest ally in Africa.

In the afternoon, I had a meeting with senior French military officials. The head of the team was a General by the name of Le Mercier. They went to great lengths to allay RPF's fears, and repeated Juppe's statement that RPF should cooperate. I asked them for more details about Operation Turquoise and they handed me one page of scanty details, and jokingly I asked "Is this all?" They said it was early in the planning phase, and more details would be available as plans progressed. I asked for their concept of the operation-how many men, where will they be deployed, rules of engagement, weaponry, and exit strategy.

The one page included deployment of jaguar and mirage military jets, a hundred armored personnel careers, helicopters and several mortars. I asked again how such items were for peaceful purposes. We parted, having understood that it was a fait accompli, and RPF would have to deal with the new development. Madeleine Albright, President Clinton's Ambassador to the United Nations had gone along with, and supported, France's demands.

Operation Turquoise was immediately launched and deployed in the southwest of Rwanda, in the Cyangugu-Kibuye-Gikongoro axis, the route of escape of the Provisional Government, its army, militia, and the fleeing population. With their main base in Goma, eastern DRC, the French were now late in the game. Events were moving very fast. Within days, on July 4, 1994, the capital city, Kigali, fell to the RPA forces. Within two weeks after that, the whole country was in the hands of RPA forces as 2-3 millions of Rwandans poured into DRC and Tanzania. If, as RPF had charged, the French had intended to save the Hutu government, they did not show any sign of using their full force to do so. Many now testify to the fact that the French did save some Tutsi lives. In defeat, the provisional government just relocated with whatever remained of the machinery of government to eastern Congo in Goma.

In encouraging the mass exodus of Rwandan peasants, the Hutu extremists were making a statement that RPF may have scored a military victory, but it would govern an empty country. I received the news of the fall of Kigali when I was still in Europe. Like everyone else in the RPF, it was very exciting to be part of a winning team. Yet, it had come at an enormous cost. Over 800,000 Tutsi were dead. Unknown numbers, possibly hundreds of thousands of Hutu, were dead. Two to three million Rwandans were refugees in DRC and Tanzania. Thousands were holed up in camps of internally displaced people.

On my way back to Rwanda , I met General Paul Kagame in Kampala. He told me he had come to Kampala to meet President

Museveni. Among other things, they had consulted on the setting up of the new government in Kigali. I believe President Museveni did advise General Kagame to become the Vice President and Minister of Defense and give the post of President to a Hutu as a way of building the confidence of the Hutu. After all, General Kagame had been in the number two position below Chairman Kanyarengwe, and yet everyone knew he was effectively the number one decision-maker within the RPF and RPA. With a new Hutu President, still Vice President Kagame would control the most important institution, the military.

CHAPTER EIGHTEEN

Change of Guard

On July 19, 1994, Pasteur Bizimungu, a Hutu and the RPF's chief negotiator in the Arusha peace process was sworn in as the fifth President of Rwanda. It was approximately three and a half years since RPF's invasion in 1990, and almost three and a half decades since the 1959 revolution. The symbolism of the brief event was telling. With the military defeat of the MRND government, the 1959 revolution had come to a final abrupt end. With the military defeat alongside genocide, the entire state administrative machinery at the central and local level ground to a halt. Yet, as revolutionary history has revealed, ideas that generate revolutions do not die that easily. Nor do systems that are put in place to carry forward the revolutionary agenda. The irony of the moment was that one violent revolution had now superseded a previous one, but the symbols of the latter were still present.

At the swearing-in ceremony, the national anthem born with the First Republic, *Rwanda Rwacu*, was sung:

Rwanda rwacu Rwanda Gihugu cyambyaye
Ndakuratana ishyaka n'ubutwari
Iyo nibutse ibigwi wagize kugeza ubu
Nshimira Abarwanashyaka

Bazanye Repubulika idahinyuka
Bavandimwe, b'uru Rwanda rwacu twese
Nimuhaguruke
Turubumbatire mu mahoro, mu kuli
Mu bwigenge no mu bwumvikane

Impundu nizivuge mu Rwanda hose
Repuburika yakuye ubuhake
Ubukolonize bwagiye nk'ifuni iheze
Shinga umuzi Demokarasi
Waduhaye kwitorera Abategetsi
Banyarwanda: abakuru namwe abato
Mwizihiye u Rwanda
Turubumbatire mu mahoro, mu kuli
Mu bwigenge no mu bwumvikane

Bavuka Rwanda mwese muvuze impundu
Demokarasi yarwo iraganje
Twayiharaniye rwose twese uko tungana
Gatutsi, Gatwa na Gahutu
Namwe Banyarwana bandi mwabyiyemeje
Independansi twatsindiye twese hamwe
Tuyishyigikire
Tuyibumbatire mu mahoro, mu kuli
Mu bwigenge no mu bwumnvikane

Ni mucyo dusingize Ibendera ryacu
Arakabaho na Perezida wacu
Barakabaho abaturage b'iki Gihugu
Intego yacu Banyarwanda
Twishyire kandi twizane mu Rwanda rwacu
Twese hamwe, twunge ubumwe nta mususu
Dutere imbere ko
Turubumbatire mu mahoro, mu kuli

Mu bwigenge no mu bwumvikane.

English Translation

My Rwanda, land that gave me birth,
Fearlessly, tirelessly, I boast of you!
When I recall your achievements to this very day,
I praise the pioneers who have brought in our unshake-
able Republic.
Brothers all, sons of this Rwanda of ours,
Come, rise up all of you,
Let us cherish her in peace and in truth,
In freedom and in harmony!

Let the victory drums beat throughout all Rwanda!
The Republic has swept away feudal bondage.
Colonialism has faded away like a worn-out shoe.
Democracy, take root!
Through you we have chosen our own rulers.
People of Rwanda, old and young, citizens all,
Let us cherish her in peace and in truth,
In freedom and in harmony!

Home-born Rwandans all, beat the victory drums!
Democracy has triumphed in our land.
All of us together we have striven for it arduously.
Together we have decreed it- Tutsi, Twa, Hutu, with other
racial elements,
This hard-won Independence of ours,
Let us all join to build it up!
Let us cherish it in peace and in truth,
In freedom and in harmony!

Come let us extol our Flag!
Long live our President, long live the citizens of our land!
Let this be our aim, people of Rwanda:
To stand on our own feet, in our own right, by our own means.
Let us promote unity and banish fear.
Let us go forward together in Rwanda.
Let us cherish her in peace and in truth,
In freedom and in harmony!

Source: http://www.nationalanthems.info/rw-01.htm

Holding the old national flag, President Bizimungu took the oath of allegiance to the Republic, with the Arusha Peace Agreement as the fundamental law.

Old Rwandan flag (1962-2002)
Source: http://flagspot.net/images/r/rw-1962.gif

The old Rwandan court of arms (1962-2002)
Source: : http://flagspot.net/images/r/rw-1962.gif

Most of the members of the RPF, notably former Tutsi exiles, reluctantly sung the Rwandan National Anthem. The national hymn extolled the victory of the 1959 revolution, the triumph of the *rubanda nyamwinshi* (the Hutu majority), democracy, and the birth of a Republic after many centuries of monarchical (minority Tutsi) rule. Hence, to many of us in RPF, it was not *our* anthem, flag, and court of arms. These were *their* symbols, of Hutu power.

As RPF sung the *Intsinzi* (Victory) song that day, many Tutsi felt it was a bittersweet *Tutsi victory* against the Hutu. Yet, It was evident that it was a very difficult situation to manage. RPF inherited a failed state, which RPF itself had helped create. The human and physical devastation was overpowering. The country was almost empty. There had been genocide of the Tutsi. There had been war crimes, crimes against humanity and other serious human rights abuses against Hutu. There were about three million refugees in DRC and Tanzania. The remaining population in Rwanda consisted of internally displaced people. There were dead bodies and mass graves all over the country. There were hundreds of thousands of widows and orphans. There were no functioning schools. Most hospitals and clinics were either teeming with the sick and wounded, or had closed, staff having fled or died.

Economic activity had ground to a halt. There were no telephone links with the outside world. Only through RPF's satellite phone that General Paul Kagame kept could we access the outside world. There was no administration. The Hutu-Tutsi polarization was at its worst in its entire history of the Rwandan nation.

How had RPF finally achieved a military victory without attracting Hutu peasants and elite in its ranks? How could the MRND government, a remnant of the 1959 revolution, get defeated when it claimed to represent the Hutu majority? Could RPF translate its military victory into political victory by cooperating with what remained of the political parties, pacify the countryside and rally the population behind nation building? How could RPF tackle the grave emergency and the crushing humanitarian needs of the day, and slowly graduate to deal with medium to long term reconstruction and development? How could it deal with the problem of security, now that the defeated army and militia were just camped across the border in DRC, with refugees as their hostages, preparing a comeback by force? How could RPF reconcile a broken nation, on the one hand, and offer justice to the same nation that was bereaved and crying for justice? How could RPF deal with a discredited international community that had neither prevented, stopped nor mitigated the genocide, war crimes, and crimes against humanity during this period? How was RPF, a political military organization, going to transition to a political party that competed with other political parties? How would Paul Kagame, the victorious general, relate to President Bizimungu, Prime Minister Twagiramungu and other non-RPF members of the new transitional government?

RPF's Military Victory

How did RPF achieve this military victory in such a short time? By the end of 1990, RPF had lost its top leaders, suffered major setbacks, and was forced to retreat and reorganize. It had developed a coherent ideology or world outlook built around a just cause. Primarily, RPF's rallying call was the return of Tutsi refugees, and together with that, a demand for fundamental political, social and economic change. As a startup organization, RPF was then very entrepreneurial, with its political and military cadres motivated to exercise initiative. We all learned to do a lot with little material and financial resources. Sacrifice was a value to be cherished. RPF was even then a highly centralized organization, with a bare minimum of internal democracy. Its politico-military commanders, especially General Paul Kagame, enforced a disciplined code of conduct that punished dissenters with death. Although it had failed to attract many Hutu in its rank and file, RPF had used the platform of the Arusha peace process to sell its agenda, and by 1992/93, had attracted more sympathizers in Rwanda and abroad, particularly among the political opposition. It had utilized the ceasefire interlude to build its military capabilities as evidenced by the lightning attack of February 1993. Uganda remained a faithful supporter, and a supply corridor for both lethal and non-lethal materials required by the organization.

RPF was efficient in communicating its core message consistently to its members and to the outside world. Its propaganda machinery, especially *Radio Muhabura*, was effective. There was a collective ethic that encouraged people to work together, despite differences. The RPA officers and men had come a long way since the defeat, indiscipline, and disorganization of the early months of the invasion in 1990. There had emerged a unified command, good strategy and good operations if and when RPA fought. Finally, General Paul Kagame had determined that if President Habyarimana was killed, the whole Hutu enterprise would collapse. He would consequently be proved right. By effectively concealing its role in the death of President Habyarimana, war crimes and crimes against humanity against the Hutu, RPF seized the moral high ground, and turned the tables against the Provisional Government and the interahamwe as the genocide gathered momentum. RPF won the diplomatic, informational and political campaigns leading to the final military victory.

The fall of the MRND Government

Why, on the other hand, did the Government of Rwanda, under the MRND party fail? In highly centralized systems, the death of the top leader often means the dispensation built by him cannot hold for long. The death of President Habyarimana was a blow to the regime, which inevitably succumbed without him. He had been at the center of the system established by the 1959 revolution from the time of Rwanda's independence in 1962, and as the Head of State since 1973. Through the control of the security institutions and the party, MRND, he was able to play both soft and hard in sustaining some legacy of the Hutu revolution of 1959. Because such systems are born and sustained in secrecy, and suspicion, they do not have succession plans in case of a crisis. Rulers fear that contenders to power in a succession plan will want to precipitate crisis so that they take over. Once President Habyarimana died, Rwanda was like a ship, without a captain, adrift at sea.

For a country that was essentially still at war, the military and other security institutions had always been and were still vital to the survival of the MRND dispensation. Unfortunately, the Army Chief of Staff, General Nsabimana, died with the Commander in Chief, leaving the military without top command. General Nsabimana was reckoned to be an effective military leader, able to enforce orders down the echelons of command. Without both of them in a crisis situation, the center of the army could not hold. The army itself had progressively been seen to be an institution in which the northern Hutu influence (*abakiga*) dominated. The army was originally conceived and established to be the vanguard and guardian of the 1959 Hutu revolution. The decline of the southern influence (*abanyenduga*), removal of

President Kayibanda, his death along many of the southern leaders after the coup of 1973, meant that many Rwandans came to view the military as an instrument of domination by the north. The cohesiveness and solidarity among the Hutu that was a factor in the early success of the Hutu revolution had long dissipated. In the contention for power, the Hutu elite were deeply divided along the north-south divide. People who lived in Rwanda at this time say this divide was more prevalent than the usual Hutu-Tutsi divide. Exclusion, first of the Tutsi, and then of the southern Hutu, meant that the army could not exploit the full potential of all Rwandans, and could not count on their full support in times of crisis. With the progress of the RPF war against the government, there were many Hutu who saw it as a war between RPF's Tutsi and the northern Hutu.

It is under these conditions of declining cohesiveness and solidarity within the Hutu elite that RPF had invaded in 1990, and political opposition political parties were born. Both developments tested the MRND and the northern dominated security institutions. It had been long since the Rwandan military fought Tutsi insurgents (*Inyenzi*). In the 1960s, the 1959 revolution, with MDR-PARMEHUTU as its guardian, it was united and at its strongest. Now, in the 1990s, the military had to fight what they called the descendants of Tutsi insurgents at a time when Hutu were disunited. There is always an ethnic undercurrent in any political formation in Rwanda. The political opposition in Rwanda in the 1990s was predominantly a southern affair. It soon developed to be a counter effort against the north. For an army to fight, it must have the full backing of the government and the population. As the coalition government negotiated with RPF in Arusha, and on many issues sided with RPF, there were those in the army and MRND who considered Rwanda's political opposition (MDR, PSD and PL) to be less than supportive of the army. With an increasing number of displaced peasants in Byumba at the gates of Kigali in Nyakyonga, there was heightened tension that fueled the north-south divide, diminishing what should have been full support for the military.

There were additional economic, diplomatic and moral considerations that played into the demise of the MRND government. Rwanda is a poor and landlocked country that largely depends on foreign aid. Under normal circumstances, that is to say in peace time, foreign aid accounts for a big percentage of the development budget (education, health, infrastructure, etc.). That catered for, the government diverts a sizeable portion of the internal revenues to security purposes. The 1990s had begun with difficult social and economic challenges, notably the falling commodity prices of Rwanda's only exports, coffee and tea. The World Bank's and International Monetary Fund's increased surveillance and imposition of structural adjustment programs, constrained Rwanda's room for manoeuver. With the opposition controlling the Ministry of Finance, MRND and the military no longer had a free hand to move resources around as they wished to support war-related activities. With an elite that is used to distributing economic resources among themselves, a reduction in the resource envelope causes even deeper cleavages.

On the diplomatic front, the government of Rwanda did not have one coherent voice on strategy and policy. Every RPF cadre, whether in Rwanda or anywhere in the world, generally knew what the RPF was trying to achieve. RPF's diplomacy was advanced by ordinary members in RPF's structures all over the world, assisted by a small team of members of the executive who travelled to countries once in a while when situations demanded reinforcement. This was not the case with the government side. With a whole array of diplomatic missions and several people working for the government, there seemed to be as many voices as the political parties, the principal rift being that between MRND on one hand and the opposition on the other. And, like in Rwanda's security institutions, when recruitment and deployment of human resources is not based on merit, there is a reduction in efficiency, outputs, outcomes and impact. There were exceptionally able people in Rwanda's diplomatic service, but there were also missions that RPF's single agents were able to out-smart with limited resources and sheer resolve. In a contest that pitted RPF's motivated revolutionaries against government bureaucrats, the stage was set for progressive government losses leading to eventual defeat.

There was also a moral dimension. With the killing of President Habyarimana, Rwanda descended into chaos, and became a failed state. The so-called provisional government could not protect the citizens. Instead, its political leaders and security institutions were either helpless or got sucked into supporting genocidal activities, including those of the *interahamwe* militia, rogue elements, and media like radio *RTLM* and *Kangura*. With local and international media covering the progress of genocide almost live, day by day, and the culprits known to be MRND functionaries in the Provisional Government, the military and the interahamwe militia, what had remained of the Rwanda Government lost the moral authority to govern.

Finally, there was as usual, what historians have called the "imponderables of history", unintended consequences, and the decisions made by leaders at crucial junctions of history. The group of seminarians, notably Gregoire Kayibanda among them, had imagined a new order, and helped bring an end to a Tutsi monarchy that had lasted centuries, and with it, Belgian colonial rule that guided the violent revolution of 1959. Despite its success to liberate *rubanda nyamwinshi (*the majority Hutu) from the crutches of monarchist absolute rule, the 1959 revolution's vision never went far enough to embrace all Rwandans. The *Hutu* revolution never became a *Rwandan* revolution. President Gregoire Kayibanda and MDR PARMEHUTU ultimately became victims of their own creation.

President Habyarimana and his colleagues imagined the continuation of the Hutu revolution, with minimal modifications to obtain national and international acceptability, and minimal inclusion of the Tutsi elements, but ended up with a situation with a schism within the Hutu community along the north and south divide. President Habyarimana may have imagined a Rwanda for all, and may have thought reluctantly that the Arusha Peace Agreement would help him on that front, but MRND and its entire establishment finally fell due to primarily factors within itself and, secondarily, to factors outside it.

Setting up an administration

The aftermath of civil war and genocide had created a crisis in the minds of RPF cadres. We had always taught and preached that we are all Rwandans, and de-emphasized the problems of ethnicity. Whatever ethnic problem there was, we used to explain, it was a product of Belgian colonial history. Now, we realized that some Hutu had killed Tutsi on every Rwandan hill. Some Tutsi in the RPA had killed many Hutu, even if RPF was not about to admit this in public. We were not willing to acknowledge that our own Tutsi soldiers had committed serious human rights abuses against the Hutu population. How could we explain the mutual destruction without talking about ethnicity, which clearly defined who the victims and perpetrators were?

There was a lot of anger and frustration among all of us. I remember having a sharp conversation with one of our senior cadres about the notion that we now should partition Rwanda, with Tutsi in one part and the Hutu in their own part (the so-called Hutuland and Tutsiland solution). There were some in the international community that were selling this idea. Some even suggested there should be an internationally supervised swap of Hutu and Tutsi in Rwanda and Burundi, with each country exclusively Hutu and the other, exclusively Tutsi. I was ideologically opposed to both solutions. Most RPF leaders were equally firm against the partition idea. This anger and frustration among us, coupled with a still dangerous and fluid situation within and outside Rwanda, conditioned us to be in the suspicious and fighting mode. We also felt that we were perpetually under siege by Hutu.

In setting up the administration, RPA, and especially General Paul Kagame, had a final say in what happened next. Essentially, what we had was a military government, with civilians working under this authority. The President was a Hutu, the Prime Minister a Hutu, and a good number of Ministers were Hutu, but clearly the center of power was RPA, with General Kagame, now Vice-President and Minister of Defence, as the boss. Cabinet portfolios were given to the surviving leaders from the political parties MDR, PSD, PL, and PDC. I was the Secretary-General of RPF. Formally, I was supposed to report to the Chairman, Alexis Kanyarengwe. However, like every senior RPF cadre, we all knew that our boss was General Kagame. Even Chairman Kanyarengwe and President Bizimungu knew this was the unspoken and unwritten rule and always treaded carefully.

RPF had to jumpstart the administration with its own energetic, enthusiastic, hardworking and often overzealous cadres (military and civilian) deployed in both central and local government. I camped at the top floor of a tall building in Kigali that belonged to Felicien Kabuga, a rich businessman who had been very close to President Habyarimana. Most of the members of the RPF Executive had been deployed in government, and the RPF secretariat's human resource base was rather thin. The state is such an enticing place, and most cadres preferred to work for government. Chairman Kanyarengwe was also Minister for Public Service and Deputy Prime Minister. First Vice-Chairman Paul Kagame was Vice President and Minister of Defence. Second Vice-Chairman Patrick Mazimpaka was Minister of Rehabilitation. Third Vice-Chairman Denis Polisi was in the Transitional Parliament. Commissioners and other senior cadres were working hard in different departments of government to get things going.

We regularly held meetings of the expanded central committee in the Kanombe military barracks, with various members of RPF in government expected to attend. There were cabinet ministers, military officers, assistant ministers, and provincial governors. It had been decided by RPF that the Secretary-General should work full time for the party, supported by a few permanent staff.

In setting up the administration, RPF made sure it was in full control even when it included some Hutu in the administration. Where we had a Minister or any other official who was not RPF or a Tutsi, an assistant (almost in all cases, Tutsi) was deployed. It was another unwritten yet very much known rule about how RPF was to govern. The new administration was Tutsi-based and military-driven.

Responding to the Humanitarian Emergency

As the new administration was learning to take charge of Rwanda, it had to deal with a massive and unparalleled humanitarian emergency that climaxed in the 100 days of the genocide. A twin emergency later developed in Goma, DRC where thousands of Rwandan Hutu refugees were decimated by a cholera outbreak. The response of the international community to both emergencies would be a powerful public relations weapon in our hands for many years. We argued that the international community had double standards. The same international community that was unwilling to prevent or stop the genocide of the Tutsi was now in a stampede to save the Hutu, among them perpetrators of genocide. As the Rwandan refugees camped in Goma and its environs, hundreds of international relief agencies, supported by western governments and the United Nations, responded with humanitarian relief.

In July 1994, the United States launched *Operation Support Hope* to respond to the cholera epidemic in Goma, DRC, that was killing 3000 refugees per day.

President Clinton called the situation the "world's worst humanitarian crisis in a generation..." President Clinton announced on 22 July the US would aid the Rwandan refugees, dubbing the operation Support Hope. By July 24th, American military personnel had been deployed to Goma (Zaire), Kigali (Rwanda), and Entebbe (Uganda), setting up the necessary infrastructure to complement and support the humanitarian response community. A joint task force deployed to the region, its peak strength 2,592 (USAFE peak deployed strength, at locations in Africa and Europe: 325). C-5s and C-141s flew 381 sorties during the operation, supported by USAFE-controlled aerial tankers, C-130s flew 996 sorties. Two USAFE C-130s deployed and flew their last mission in central Africa on 27 September. The Army contributed to the US government's desperately needed humanitarian relief operations in Rwanda by providing clean water to combat outbreaks of cholera, helping to bury the dead and integrating the transport and distribution of relief supplies.

Source: http://www.globalsecurity.org/military/ops/support_hope.htm

The United Kingdom, France, Japan, Israel, and almost every who is who in the international community and relief agencies were there. Among us RPF cadres the thinking was that the so called international community is in love with the Hutu, despite the fact that among the refugees was an entire government with its army and militia. The presence of international NGOs and relief agencies would later become a serious problem within Rwanda.

Within Rwanda, the RPF government approached the humanitarian emergency with a four-pronged pathway. The first was to rely as much as possible on our own efforts. The second was to insist that the matter had to be driven by ourselves. The third was to push a minimum of co-ordination among the key players, phasing out those we considered not to be friends with the RPF. We discovered that western NGOs, on the other hand, were not easily willing to submit to our authority. Those in the aid industry, western governments and NGOs alike, do not like the idea of coordination. Each bilateral donor agency (like USAID, British DFID, Swedish SIDA, German GTZ, etc) knows that aid is an element in the donor country's foreign policy tools. Each multilateral agency like the World Bank, International Monetary Fund, European Union and United Nations Agencies has its own agenda and rules of engagement and is reluctant to forego their way of doing things. The fourth strategy was to constantly speak to the failure of the international community in preventing and stopping genocide.

Humanitarian relief is very attractive to NGOs and relief agencies. For a number of them, that is only what they do, and that is where the money is. At the height of the humanitarian situation, there were no less than 250 NGOs working in Rwanda. We felt that most were useless and that some had an evil agenda to spy on us. The RPF government insisted that the NGOs had to submit to the demand that they account and fully disclose where they get resources from, and how the resources are used in Rwanda. A good number resisted the call for accountability and were asked to leave. Those that remained gradually learned how to cooperate on the terms that were written and acceptable to RPF.

The approach to UNDP, World Bank, IMF, and the bilateral agencies was that Rwanda would like to move from emergency to rehabilitation and development as soon as possible. One of the early eye-opening discoveries on how international finance institutions work involved the World Bank and the IMF. When the government approached the World Bank for help, it was told Rwanda owed about 3 million US $ in arrears to the bank. Before there could be negotiations on opening new or restarting old programmes, this money had to be paid first. Rwanda's treasury was empty. The Provisional Government had had enough time to ransack even the Central Bank. Where could the government get the money? To some of us newcomers in the world of international finance it seemed to confirm what our revolutionary ideology had taught us. The international finance institutions were tools of imperialism to suck the blood out of the poor. Rwanda was bleeding and the World Bank was, like Shylock in Shakespeare's *Merchant of Venice*, "demanding his pound of flesh". In the end, a few countries, including the Netherlands, paid Rwanda's arrears so that it could access the World Bank's financing.

Coordination among the donor agencies also proved to be a difficult challenge. The United Nations agency, United Nations Development Programme (UNDP), wanted to preside over the roundtables in which financial resources were pledged. Bilateral agencies and multilateral institutions were reluctant to submit to UNDP's self-declared role. Slowly by slowly, the RPF government persuaded or coerced these agencies and institutions into doing business in the RPF way or leaving it. RPF also almost perfected the art of approaching each of these institutions individually while playing the matter of coordination pragmatically.

Relationship between RPF and other political parties

With the RPF now firmly in the driver's seat, the political parties that were part of the transitional government were soon to learn a brutal lesson. They too, had to do things the RPF way or leave it. Civil war, genocide, war crimes and crimes against humanity against Tutsi and Hutu had left the Hutu elite and political parties MDR, PSD, PL and PDC seriously weakened. MRND had first weakened them through divisions and creation of *pawa* factions. Now most of their members and leaders had fled or been killed. The surviving leaders had survived because they were saved by RPF or simply because RPF had won the war.

RPF felt they owed a lot to it, and were expected to follow its own script.

Two of the members of the Transitional Government, namely, Prime Minister Faustin Twagiramungu (from MDR), and Seth Sendashonga, Minister of Interior (from RPF), exemplified the tension that emerged early on during the RPF rule. Both Hutu, Twagiramungu and Sendashonga were insisting that RPF needed to respond to human rights abuses by RPA soldiers across the country. Twagiramungu insisted that political parties cohabiting with RPF had to have some real power, as envisaged in the Arusha Peace Agreement. He pointed out that for RPF to appoint 117 Tutsi out of 145 bourgmestres (local administrators) was not justifiable on any grounds.

This continued for a while. Word went around RPF cadres that Seth Sendashonga and Twagiramungu *barapinze* (Sendashonga and Twagiramungu have rebelled). Amongst RPF cadres, it was often said that Sendashonga was the most dangerous among the Hutu. It was rumored that he carried with him a long list of Hutu who had been killed by the RPA soldiers. It was even reported to us by General Kagame that Minister Sendashonga had asked to register the old monarchist party, UNAR, using the late Rukeba's son. He said he thought Sendashonga's aim was to divide the Tutsi and undermine the RPF.

Most importantly though, General Kagame said, Twagiramungu and Sendashonga were disrespectful and defiant towards him.

Over a couple of weeks, Minister Sendashonga refused to attend RPF meetings. Vice- President Kagame asked me to write to Sendashonga reminding him that attending RPF meetings was not optional. By then events were moving fast. General Kagame came head-on collision with both Twagiramungu and Sendashonga in one cabinet meeting over the matter of RPA's human rights abuses, especially over the *Kibeho Massacres* and the *Gersony Report*. In Kibeho, southwest Rwanda, a camp of about 100,000 internally displaced Hutu people was attacked by RPA soldiers, and an estimated 5,000 of them killed and many wounded on 22nd April, 1995. Seth Sendashonga tried to intervene, but was prevented by the RPA on the orders of Vice-President Kagame.

The Gersony Report is named after Robert Gersony, an American consultant who was hired by the United Nations High Commissioner for Refugees (UNHCR). His team concluded that between April and August 1994, RPA had systematically killed between 25,000-45,000 people. The die was cast. In August 1995, after a cabinet meeting, I heard from one RPF Minister, Dr. Joseph Mudaheranwa, cursing and swearing that both Twagiramungu and Sendashonga had to go because *bubahutse afande* (they dared General Kagame). Apparently, confronted, Vice President Kagame defiantly stormed out of the cabinet meeting. Twagiramungu, Sendashonga and other cabinet ministers were fired before they resigned, closing a short chapter of cohabitation with RPF. From then on, RPF dropped any pretense of trying to organize Rwanda's government and society along Arusha Peace Agreement principles. Whispers within the RPF were that we were being too lenient towards Hutu. RPF was now working on individual members of the parties who were sympathetic to our line of thinking and work. This is how the likes of Dr. Biruta, Celestin Rwigyema, and Bernard Makuza emerged. From then onwards, RPF would work towards weakening and marginalizing Hutu who wanted to play independent.

Justice and Reconciliation

Civil war, genocide, war crimes and crimes against humanity left Rwanda more polarized than ever before. The civil war had been won by the Tutsi RPF. The victims of genocide were Tutsi. Tutsi had been subject to all sorts of injustice since the 1959 revolution in which the Hutu were the victors. During the civil war there were massacres of Tusti in Bigogwe, Kibilira and

Bugesera. The killing of President Habyarimana that triggered the genocide, the killing of the Bishops and priests in Kabgayi, and the war crimes and crimes against humanity perpetrated by RPA against the Hutu were matters that RPF was not interested in addressing. Rwanda's cyclic story had come full circle. The victors of the 1959 revolution were the vanquished of the 1994 revolution. Trust and confidence between the two communities were at their lowest. Tutsi demanded justice, even revenge against the Hutu. The voices of the Hutu were subdued, since many of them had run away from the country, and those inside Rwanda were not permitted to articulate their interests and grievances. At the height of the problem, there were close to 140,000 genocide suspects in Rwanda's overcrowded prisons. This was a testimony to the coercive powers of the state, the popular participation of the Hutu in the crimes, as well as to the arbitrariness of arrests that took place after RPF captured state power in 1994. Justice for the Tutsi was RPF's main, if not sole concern in the aftermath of the civil war and genocide of 1994. Reconciliation would have to be based on accepting RPF's account of events. Tutsi were the victims. Hutu were the perpetrators.

Another complicating factor in dispensing justice was that Rwanda's justice system had been weak even before the civil war and genocide. The impact of civil war and genocide was devastating to Rwanda's human resources. The justice sector was equally affected. Rwanda lacked investigators, prosecutors, judges, lawyers, administrators, policemen, and prison staff to deal with so big a problem. Many of them had fled or died. It was clear in our minds that it was going to be victor's justice. This required an ambitious training programme to create the necessary critical mass to handle the large caseload of genocide suspects. As for reconciliation, it was imperative for RPF to remain on message despite the genocide. Our narrative remained that a Hutu clique had taken a huge risk by coercing or enticing the ordinary Hutu to participate in the crime of genocide. This Hutu clique had also killed their own President because he (President Habyarimana) was about to compromise with RPF, which would have led to the formation of the Transitional Government. In public we would say ordinary Hutu are fine, in private we would denounce all Hutu as criminals, greedy, cowards and unreliable. Mentioning ethnic identity was banished. A Unity and Reconciliation Commission was established to help promote reconciliation along the RPF's version of the story. There were seminars and workshops, and every donor was interested in supporting this effort.

Meanwhile there were also efforts to respond to the problem of genocide at the international level. Ultimately the International Criminal Tribunal for Rwanda (ICTR) was established to investigate, prosecute and punish those responsible for committing the crime of genocide. The United States was instrumental in the setting up of the ICTR, and not the Government of Rwanda as is commonly believed. The U.S. Ambassador in Kigali at this time, David Rawson, and then Assistant Secretary (Bureau of Democracy, Human Rights and Labor) John Shattuck, were very active on this front. The Government of Rwanda was represented at the United Nations by our new Permanent Representative, Ambassador Manzi Bakuramutsa. Negotiations had been taking place on the matter of the International Criminal Tribunal for Rwanda (ICTR), and Rwanda had presented a number of concerns but the U.N. Security Council went ahead and passed the resolution 977 of 22nd Frebruary, 1995, setting up the tribunal to be based in Arusha, Tanzania.

Even at this early stage, some in the international community, especially human rights organizations were beginning to insist that RPA had also committed war crimes, crimes against humanity and other serious human rights abuses against the Hutu community. Nothing evoked strong reaction from us like this matter. We always reacted by listing the sins of the international community since 1959: Where were you when we were refugees? What did you do when Tutsi were marginalized and killed for decades?

You did nothing to prevent or stop the genocide. We would insist that RPA was a disciplined army, and that there were no systematic and widespread human rights abuses by the RPA. The voices were relentless to such an extent that when the ICTR was established, investigating, prosecuting and punishing war crimes and crimes against humanity committed by the RPA was part of its mandate.

Security

Matters of security were priority number one in RPF. Everything else was subordinated to security considerations. The major challenge was that we never trusted the Hutu we were working with within the country. Yet, just across the border in DRC, the entire MRND military-militia establishment was camped, training, arming and waiting for an opportune moment to launch a counter-attack. We were a country on edge in those days. We were in crisis mode. Three issues were consistently brought to the attention of the international community: 1) the question of refugee camps at the border; 2) the problems posed by the presence of political and military leaders of the former government who were responsible for genocide and who had taken the population hostage; and 3) the problem posed by international relief agencies, whose material and financial assistance was being converted into capabilities to attack Rwanda. As 1994 drew to a close and we entered 1995, it was evident that the status quo would not be sustainable. The international community procrastinated as usual, there were international meetings and regional gatherings to consider the matter, but little came out of it. In mid-May, 1994, the United Nations Security Council established UNAMIR II, against RPF wishes. The United Nations had been discredited due to its failures, and RPF did not see any use whatsoever in the new circumstances when RPF was in charge. The international community wanted a UN presence to deal with its own failure to prevent, stop or mitigate the genocide. UNAMIR II was supposed to help in the emergency and rehabilitation work but did little. Unable and unwilling to help on the security front, and marginalized by the RPF, it finally had to wind up in 1996.

With security institutions in the country firmly in the hands of the Tutsi officers of the RPA, it was a question of time before the security situation in eastern DRC was dealt with head-on.

RPF Secretariat

At the secretariat, I had a small team of dedicated RPF cadres; we worked hard and for long hours. I was still single, and working was like a hobby for me. There were a few senior cadres like Major Alphonse Furuma, the Inspector General for RPF, and Captain Tega, the Commissioner for Youth, whom I worked with to look for other cadres to work full-time at the Secretariat. I had a very dedicated and able personal assistant, Methode Ruzindana, and an equally loyal and able secretary, Marie. Grace, my other very dedicated, loyal and able secretary had gone to work for Vice President Kagame. Because the state in Africa is a very tempting place, it took us time to assemble the team. Finally we had people to handle finance and administration, diplomacy, social affairs, logistics and other matters.

My plan was to organize a retreat, do basic military training for newcomers, who had to imbibe the politico-military culture of the RPF, and then prepare to launch RPF nationwide even as we prevented other political parties from doing the same. Before the retreat, I had contemplated a diplomatic trip to find friends for the new RPF government. I had personally dealt with President Museveni and several NRM cadres, like Amanya Mushega, Eriya Kategaya, Kahinda Otafiire, Henry Tumukunde, Chefe Ali, and many others. Kale Kayihura and I had worked closely together, always seeking ways to bring our bosses and governments to mutual understanding and common interests. During the crisis days of April and May, 1994, I had been able to meet President Daniel Arap Moi of Kenya through the efforts of my brother's friend, Moses Wetangula. In a brief meeting, I had hoped to obtain some humanitarian aid from him but was not successful.

Tanzania was always skeptical toward RPF, mainly because of its ethnic composition and secondly, because we were close to President Museveni. Some in the Tanzanian governing circles felt Museveni was militaristic and extending his influence regionally. Some had not forgotten that he had taken up arms against the regime of President Milton Obote, which they had supported. The question of Tutsi and Hutu was very much known in Tanzania since they had hosted Tutsi refugees from Rwanda since 1959, Hutu refugees from Burundi and, lately, Hutu refugees from Rwanda.

In the aftermath of the signing of the Arusha Peace Agreement, as the process lost momentum, I had one time accompanied General Kagame to meet President Mwinyi of Tanzania to explain RPF's concerns. We were not officially treated as Tanzania's guests. We checked into a modest hotel in Dar-es-salaam. General Kagame had just sat on the bed when a big rat sped across the room. We had to look for an alternative hotel that night. Our meeting with President Mwinyi was rather cold, as he seemed to think we were the main cause of the little progress in the implementation of the Arusha accords.

Through Kale Kayihura of Uganda, I had been introduced to a Tanzanian by the name of Adam Marwa. Through Adam Marwa, I was able to secure a meeting with the late Mwalimu Julius Kambarage Nyerere, the first President of independent Tanzania. To me, meeting Mwalimu Nyerere was like a dream of a lifetime come true. Mwalimu Nyerere is an African legend. He had fought for the independence of Tanganyika from the British colonial rule, and for its union with the island of Zanzibar, to form the new Republic of Tanzania. With other prominent African leaders of his day, they had formed the Organization of

African Unity. Convinced of the egalitarian principles in African culture, he had moved his country toward collectivization, or *ujamaa,* in the famous *Arusha Declaration of 1967* on socialism and self-reliance.

Though his social and economic policies ultimately did not work and Tanzania finally abandoned the socialist path, Mwalimu Nyerere voluntarily relinquished power and remained a very respected statesman in Tanzania, Africa, and internationally. He promoted the unity of Tanzania through a common language, Kiswahili. He supported decolonization and fought against apartheid, especially through the Frontline States arrangement. He was controversial internationally when he supported Biafra in the Nigeria-Biafra secessionist war of 1967-1970, and when Tanzania attacked and removed Dictator Idi Amin from power. He was a man of robust intellectual powers, eloquent, and elevated Kiswahili to great heights (he translated Shakespeare's *Julius Caesar* into Kiswahili).

When Adam Marwa and I drove to the retired President's home in Msasani, in Dar es Salaam, I did not know what to expect. He had been President of Tanzania in the 1960s when my mother had briefly been a refugee in Tanzania and we were little children. On arrival, I was struck by his very modest residence. There were no cars packed in the compound. There was no special security at the gate and it seemed Marwa knew his way around. We sat on wooden stools on the veranda, and soon Mwalimu Nyerere arrived, dressed casually in sandals. He made us feel at ease, and after a brief introduction, he said he was sad about what had happened in Rwanda. He said he was angry that Tanzanian authorities had failed to condemn the killings in Rwanda. He also mentioned that there was a time he felt Rwanda and Burundi would have been better off if they had become part of the East African community at the time of independence. He said he admired Prince Rwagasore of Burundi, and thought he was a Pan Africanist. He also mentioned how he had tried to work with President Kayibanda of Rwanda to ease population pressures in Rwanda by allowing settlement in Tanzania but it had not worked. He finally said he hoped the younger generation of African leaders would carry the torch of uniting African people within countries, and among African countries. Mwalimu Nyerere's humility and wisdom was touching. He would later visit Rwanda during the year.

Elsewhere on the diplomatic front in Kigali, I cultivated relations with the U.S Ambassador, David Rawson and U.K. special liason to Rwanda, Lillian Wong. Ambassador Rawson had an uneasy relationship with the RPF from the Arusha days. He had replaced Ambassador Robert Flaten whom General Kagame hated with passion. We thought he was too close to the regime of President Habyarimana. We understood that David Rawson had lived in Burundi, had a realistic and pragmatic outlook on the challenges of ethnicity in Rwanda and Burundi, but was considered by RPF as more sympathetic to Hutu. RPF's public posture was that it had overcome the problem of Hutu and Tutsi. RPF did not trust Ambassador Rawson. I did not find any problem dealing with him.

The United Kingdom had never had a full-fledged representation in Rwanda before. Ms. Lilian Wong was an advance party to prepare for the eventual opening of a British embassy in Kigali. France's and Belgium's influence in Rwanda was virtually at its lowest, while the U.S and British interests in Rwanda were on the rise. Through my brother's friend in London, I had also had an opportunity to be introduced to Baroness Lynda Chalker, then U.K. State Minister for Overseas Development. From Lynda Chalker to Clare Short, and subsequent British officials, Rwanda has had unquestioning friends in London. Baroness Lynda Chalker later become a very good family friend.

I considered China and India of strategic value to Rwanda in the future. In 1995, I made a trip to India and China, to explore, on behalf of the RPF, the possibilities for strong partnerships with the Chinese Communist Party, and to learn firsthand, from India, the prospects of developing small scale industries in Rwanda. It was an extended trip on which I was accompanied by Major Alphonse Furuma, an officer from RPA's engineering department, and Mr. and Mrs. Mbundu. I did not make the choice for the latter couple. Vice President Kagame did. In India we met the Deputy Minister of foreign affairs, and had a very busy schedule to see how India has progressed from being a hungry nation to a self-sufficientt one, and a net exporter of food in a matter of three decades. We also learned how India's small scale industries contribute a large fraction to its gross national income, and a big percentage of its exports.

In China, we arrived in Nanjing, and drove by road all the way to Shanghai, through Wuxi and Suzhou. My fascination with China, through Chairman Mao's collected works, had ceased to be just an intellectual exercise. Now I could get a glimpse of the China that Mao had created, and which Chairman Deng had started reforming since 1976. Along the way we could see that China was like a huge construction site. There was heavy air pollution too, making one feel like choking at times. After Shanghai we travelled to Beijing, where we were hosted by the ruling Chinese Communist Party.

During this period, the RPF Secretariat had initiated the start of a party newspaper, *The New Times*. RPF would need its own mouthpiece to inform the public, mobilize membership, deepen the ideological understanding of the RPF cadres, seek accountability of the RPF cadres who were now swamped in government bureaucracy, and be the voice of the survivors of the genocide. Major Furuma and I had a big role in helping our enthusiastic cadres who were involved in the setup of the newspaper.

Another initiative I undertook was to establish an RPF company to do business. In my residence, I thought of a name, *Tri-Star Investments*. I also thought of *Mutara Enterprises* as the other company. The idea of three stars was related to the three ethnic groups in Rwanda. The idea of Mutara in my mind stood for the name of King Mutara Rudahigwa, who died in Burundi in 1959 under mysterious circumstances. For somebody with ideological outlook, the idea of doing business was like a dramatic U-turn. It was a pragmatic compromise, given the realities of governing a country like Rwanda. During the RPF rise to power it had relied on three sources of financial and material support. Weapons were mainly supplied by Uganda, and once in a while supplemented by purchases from worldwide black markets. Financial contributions came from RPF members who supported the war effort.

Some other governments occasionally made modest but regular contributions. Now that RPF was in power, its members would not only cease to make contributions, but instead expected RPF to help them. RPF needed to support orphans, widows, and demobilized and wounded former RPA combatants. There were genocide survivors whom RPF needed to support. RPF cadres needed support as they grappled with the new realities of living with families. Many of our members who had been refugees in other countries had now returned and needed help. RPF could create a small fund to support small business development for our members, and to entice the hostile Hutu into the RPF. Soon, RPF would need to compete with other political parties and we needed to think ahead and act strategically to make RPF financially sound.

Many senior RPF cadres, especially Tito Rutaremara and Aloysea Inyumba, were hostile to the idea of setting up the companies. Vice President Kagame saw the strategic value of the effort. Senior military officers like Sam Kaka, Kayumba Nyamwasa, and Joseph Karemera supported the idea. My brother, Gerald Gahima, helped in the process of incorporating the RPF companies. Dr. Ben Rugangazi, chosen by Vice-President Kagame, would oversee the operations of the companies for many years to come.

CHAPTER NINETEEN

Unexpected Luck

RPF's military triumph of 1994 expanded the market for many eligible bachelors in Kigali. I was one of them. Many of the cadres of RPF/RPA were young people at the start of the civil war. They still were. The civil war was over, but the impact of genocide was felt by each one of us. Like so many other Tutsi at this time, the question of numbers and collective survival was very much a troubling one. Tutsi had always been a minority, even with the return of the 1959 refugees; the genocide had dealt a devastating blow to us. We had to get married and produce more children. In addition, in most African cultures, a man is a man to the extent that he is married and has children. I felt a lot of pressure from my mother and relatives to get married. Since I was a senior official, and had self-imposed limits in terms of socializing and networking, I relied heavily on friends and relatives to be on the lookout for me.

In those days we travelled in looted vehicles that had no ignition keys. Starting a car required the ingenuity of our drivers who somehow would initiate contact between live wires, provoking sparks. Often starting the car required manpower since a car had to be pushed first. One late morning I was heading home for lunch when my car broke down in Kigali's neighborhood called Kirov.

The prevailing mood of siege and insecurity among us caused us to be armed with pistols and go around with military escorts.

As my driver and escorts scrambled to get the car re-started, I saw a friend of mine, Sam Nkusi, pass by. He stopped, and asked if he could help and give me a ride home. I had known Nkusi during the days of the civil war. He was instrumental in boosting RPA's communication capabilities. Living in Canada at that time, he had procured Motorola two-way radios and equipment that improved RPA's performance. Earlier during my North American visits at the United Nations and in Washington, D.C. Nkusi had given me my first computer, a grey Macintosh laptop. I had travelled by bus from Washington DC to the USA/Canadian border to meet Nkusi for the delivery of the laptop. Before then, I had never handled a computer. Nkusi had briefly shown me how to start it and shut it down. That was it. I learned how to use it through trial and error, and occasionally would call his home. If I could not get him, his wife, Debra, would help with troubleshooting. Later, I bought a portable printer and became self-reliant in my mobile secretarial duties. Once in power, RPF had entrusted Nkusi to run the national telephone company, Rwandatel.

Once in Nkusi's car, I sat near a beautiful young woman, whom Nkusi introduced as Dorothy Rwetsiba from Uganda. I gathered from Nkusi that Dorothy had recently come from Canada, and was now working with Vice President Kagame.

She was a young sister to Nkusi's wife, Debra. I tried to provoke Dorothy to speak Kinyarwanda, but she wasn't forthcoming. I detected a calm demeanor about her. I presumed she didn't know much Kinyarwanda, but even her Kinyankole (the language spoken in Ankole, Uganda), which I spoke well, was not much. She spoke perfect English. You would have thought you were speaking to a British woman. We shared lunch and then parted.

As I headed back to my office, I knew I had met my future wife. In subsequent days and weeks, Dorothy came to dominate my new life. I would find every pretext to visit her at Nkusi's house, almost every evening after work. One time I used the pre-text of picking a printer from her house, and conveniently left it there repeatedly, so that I could have reason to go back. Nkusi's two daughters, Samantha and Teta, then in elementary school. became my friends as I slowly became an evening fixture at the Nkusi's. The little girls would kindly serve *vitalo* (a Rwandan bev-erage), *mandazi* (a homemade pastry) and hot tea. I probably wasn't the only man eyeing Dorothy at this time. Occasionally I would turn up at the Nkusi's and find other young men, prob-ably there to present their credentials as well. As soon as I would arrive, one by one they would melt away. I guess my seniority in the pecking order was an asset to my advantage.

Within few weeks I suggested to her that I would like us to marry her. Dorothy was shocked. How could we get married when we have just met? She said we had just started dating and it would take years before we could get married. She came from North America and that is how things are done. I told her I am an African, of age, and was not interested in the dating business. I told her that in her, I was convinced I had found a perfect partner for life. What else would I be waiting for? I wondered whether she thought I was either a careless adventurer or an outrageous risk taker. Either way, my proposal was overwhelming. She kept her cards close to her chest. She neither said yes nor no. That kept my chase and adrenaline going and I loved that. I had fallen in love with her on first sight. She had then fallen in love with me too. She was cautious, and wanted time to consult her family.

I later learned that her father, the late Ambassador William Rwetsiba, was from Ankole, Uganda. Rwetsiba had been one of the very first Ugandans to study in England when Uganda was a British colony. He had become a teacher at the secondary schools of Budo in Buganda and Ntare School in Ankole, before being active in Uganda's struggle for independence. He had been one of the leaders of Uganda's People's Congress, and could easily have been the first Prime Minister of Uganda at independence in 1963, had he not been out-maneuvered by the late President Milton Obote of Uganda. He later served in various capacities as permanent secretary, and as Cabinet Minister at the East African Community before fleeing for his life during Idi Amin's regime. He would later become Uganda's Ambassador to Canada, and to China. He was married to Mrs. Joyce Rwetsiba, a Rwandan , daughter of Mr. and Mrs. Karasanyi, from Shyira, Ruhengeri.

When Dorothy suggested to me that we take a trip to Kampala to meet her parents, I had done sufficient homework on Ambassador Rwetsiba, his interest in international relations and politics. I was intrigued though, how he had gone all the way to Rwanda to get a Rwandan woman for a wife. It seemed to me that Dorothy's own father had been a risk taker. Now, decades later I was venturing into Uganda to get a Ugandan woman for a wife. We took the road trip from Kigali to Kampala, and I occasionally remembered how many times I had taken that trip during the civil war. Now I was embarking on a different mission, a very important one.

We were warmly received by Mr. and Mrs. Rwetsiba in their home. The couple had a very dignified air to them, and I presume I charmed Mr. Rwetsiba through a conversation on history and current events. We were served a meal, with wine. I could see that the boy from refugee camps was on unfamiliar terrain, but doing the best I could to appear civilized. Mrs. Joyce Rwetsiba is a warm, caring and perfect hostess. I wanted to impress her and show that her daughter was not getting married to a rich man, but to a humble freedom fighter whose manners could gradually be polished by her daughter. By the time Dorothy and I returned to Rwanda I knew I had won over Mr. and Mrs. Rwetsiba. Dorothy would be mine, and I would be hers.

On December 16, 1995, Dorothy and I got married. Every who is who in Rwanda was gathered to witness the event. Dorothy's immediate and extended family was there. So was mine.

That evening, Dorothy and I took to the floor to open the dance on Kenny G and Aaron Neville's *Even If My heart Would Break:*

> ....So let the mountains tumble
> Tumble to the sea
> Let the rivers overflow
> It won't bother me
> Let the stars go out tonight
> Cuz I can see them in your eyes
> And I wanna love you
> even if my heart would break .

As we danced through the night to Koffi Olomide's *Noblesse Oblige*, I felt good. Finally, I thought and believed, life was going to be better and stable despite decades marked by exile, war, and genocide.

CHAPTER TWENTY

Becoming a Diplomat

Dorothy must have been surprised at the nature of life at the Rudasingwa household. Our home looked like a military detachment with soldiers always hovering around. I still had a peasant soldier's habits like eating *katogo* (mixed plantains and beans) in the morning. Perhaps soldiers live in the here and now not knowing what tomorrow will bring. Dorothy slowly weaned me off these habits and introduced me to formal meals. There was cereal I had never eaten in my life. Food had to be served with vegetables and salad. Wine was served at dinner time. My military escorts reluctantly surrendered to Dorothy a few of the prerogatives they had had over me.

Having lived as a refugee all my life, I looked forward to discovering Rwanda, socializing with old and new acquaintances, finding a piece of land upcountry to farm, building our own home, and making RPF a mainstream, competitive and powerful political party. I had sought to be a pediatrician, but life had taken me in a different direction. I had wanted to be a soldier like Che Guevara but soldiering was no longer on the horizon. I had done guerilla diplomacy, but now the new thing was politics. I thought I would serve in politics for some time, and figure out how to retire early and hopefully reconnect with the medical profession.

Before 1995 ended, Vice-President Kagame called me to his office, and told me he wanted me to become Rwanda's Ambassador to the United States. He told me RPF's relationship with the United States was vital and that I had worked on it more than anybody else within the RPF, so far. I was surprised, especially that coming shortly after my marriage. But, as RPF cadres, we had been taught that the revolution chooses where to deploy you. Accepting the new responsibility, I only mentioned that I needed to do one more thing at the RPF secretariat. I had to do a politico-military training of the new staff we had recruited. I could see his face tighten and I wondered why he wasn't so enthusiastic about it? Having worked with General Kagame over the years, I had become an expert in reading his face. Often his face and silence tell you more than what he says.

We parted and I broke the news to Dorothy, who, like me, was surprised, but accepted it as a done deal. Dorothy's family's life had also been on the go. Her father, Ambassador William Rwetsiba had briefly served in Idi Amin's regime as a Minister in the East African Community. Like many of his peers, his relationship with the brutal dictator turned sour and he had to flee the country. Dorothy's family then became refugees in Kenya, Swaziland, and Canada.

She would later tell me that she had hoped she would never get married to a doctor, soldier, and politician. In me, she had everything she had hoped to avoid.

I quickly organized the training in Nasho, Kibungo, in eastern Rwanda. The place is in the middle of a game reserve. I had chosen the location because of its symbolism. As mentioned earlier in this book, Nasho was the place where Tutsi from Uganda had been banished, and a good number perished, in 1982. Expelled by the government of Milton Obote, hounded by his Ministers Rwakasisi and Rurangaranga from Ankole, they were disowned by the Government of President Habyarimana. I invited Vice President Paul Kagame to officiate at the passing out of the RPF cadres who would work as permanent staff at the RPF Secretariat. Earlier I had invited a friend of mine, Chefe Ali, then a Brigadier in the Ugandan army to give a lecture to the students. We slept in the same tent and reminisced about world revolutions, their struggle in Uganda and ours. I gathered later that Kagame was not happy about that. This training was the last function I performed as RPF Secretary General. I then entered the world of formal diplomacy.

I was later intrigued by a meeting that President Pasteur Bizimungu held at his residence in Kanombe. Vice President Kagame and Chairman Alexis Kanyarengwe and most RPF executive members were there. President Bizimungu introduced the subject of my new deployment as Ambassador to the United States. It put me in a very uncomfortable position because never before had I witnessed something like that happen to any RPF cadre. We were all used to taking responsibilities as RPF deemed fit. President Bizimungu asked what people thought about it. The opinion was divided. Some said the pressing priority for RPF was to get established in the country, and that is where I needed to be. In my mind, I was of this opinion for personal as well as political reasons. Others said RPF's, and now Rwanda's, relationship with the United States was very important, and, a strategic challenge that needed a senior cadre like me who had worked on that front. Dr. Charles Murigande, then President Bizimungu's diplomatic advisor, even joked that I was needed in both places and could not be divided. I could only be in one place at a time. I did not speak. This is the pattern of Vice-President Kagame's way of working. He takes a unilateral decision, and later brings the matter to the attention of others to give a semblance of democratic decision-making.

In early 1996, as I waited to be accepted by the United States as Rwanda's nomination for ambassador, I took a trip to Ethiopia and Eritrea. I decided to take Dorothy with me, to have a honeymoon on the side. I was accompanied by Pascal Ngoga, who was the diplomatic director in the RPF Secretariat. Our intention was to cultivate relations between RPF and the ruling parties in Ethiopia and Eritrea. Eritrean colleagues had been in the trenches for almost three decades, and had recently won their independence. Ethiopia had similarly gone through a civil war during which it had become a Cold War battlefield. In Addis Ababa, we had good discussions with senior party officials, who also organized for us to see the historical sites from where their political and military campaigns had been waged. I had pity on Dorothy, who instead of having a proper honeymoon, was being subjected to mountain-climbing on rugged terrain. She survived it, and we then travelled and visited the historic area of Axum. It is amazing to witness what a rich and long history Ethiopia has.

In Eritrea, we met President Isaias Afewerki. The Eritrean people had heroically fought long battles with Ethiopia, first when it was leaning towards the west, and then under the brutal pro-soviet communist rule of President Mengistu. When Mengistu was overthrown in 1990, Eritrea formally seceded and became the new State of Eritrea. President Afewerki then had a very modest demeanor. When we visited the port of Massawa the following day, we were surprised, one evening, when we met President Afewerki in one of the shops, without military escorts. The Ethiopia-Eritrea trip was the best honeymoon a freedom fighter could afford for Dorothy. For now, it was time for the next diplomatic business.

Through Nairobi, Kenya, Dorothy and I travelled with British Airways, first class, through London Heathrow, bound for Washington, D.C., United States. I had always read that capture of the state accorded the ruling elite both power and access to resources. I realized how true this was. Travelling first class on British Airways is amazingly comfortable, and strikingly expensive. It is as if you have your own bedroom in the air. You are pampered by cabin crew with champagne, wine, and exotic food embellished with what looked like flowers to me but which Dorothy explained was called "garnishings". You are provided with pyjamas to change into and sleep if you so wish. Cabin Crew addressed Dorothy and me as Ambassador and Mrs. Rudasingwa. As we got closer to Washington,D.C. Dulles International Airport, the pilot announced that passengers should remain seated as Ambassador and Mrs. Rudasingwa disembark first. As we got off the plane, we were met by a U.S. protocol officer.

For moments during the journey my mind would wander, reflecting on my own personal journey, and how fortunate I was. From refugee camp to rebel days, now I was returning to Washington D.C., this time with a wife, and representing the Rwandan state. I had previously come to Washington D.C. to fight the Rwandan state. Now that I was part of the Rwandan state, my new assignment was to win friends for it, and fight its enemies. In the process, the state would look after me. So far, so good.

When RPF captured state power in July, 1994, Joseph Mutaboba became the Charge d'Affaires in the Rwanda Embassy, located on 1714 New Hampshire Avenue, in Washington D.C., replacing the previous government's diplomat, Ambassador Uwimana. There was another diplomat, Marianne Baziruwiha, who worked with Joseph Mutaboba. When I visited the embassy for the first time, I was shocked by what I saw. Otherwise a beautiful small building close to Dupont Circle, the embassy looked dilapidated from the outside. The interior was dirty and crumbling, with old furniture arranged in disorganized fashion. There was an old computer and some typewriter. The basement was disgraceful. There were old newspapers, saucepans, and all sorts of rubbish. One embassy official, Marianne Baziruwiha, lived with her family in a small apartment on the top floor. Mutaboba and Baziruwiha had been in the embassy for more than a year. They explained to me that it was how they found it. I did not buy the justification for living and working in a dirty environment.

Since childhood, my mother had always insisted that one has to clean up, and live in a clean environment. In the small hut

I grew up in the Rwekubo refugee camp, this was Mama's rule number one, and she enforced it with rigor. This was state property, belonging to Rwandan citizens, and those who are privileged to be its custodians had to clean up. I told Dorothy the situation at the embassy. She volunteered to assist me try to do some cleaning. Assisted by the few staff we had, we spent a week removing the trash, cleaning, and reorganizing the old furniture. The place was infested with cockroaches (inyenzi!). One day the Congolese (Brazzaville) Ambassador came to pay a courtesy call on me. We were talking when a few cockroaches started climbing on one of his legs. I was praying that he would not see them and quickly intervened to take them off before he realized the menace.

Within the embassy, you would have thought you were in an African home. On the top floor Marianne would be cooking beans, and the pervasive smell would greet you as you entered the building. Rwanda also owns the residence building on Sycamore Street Washington D.C. just at the borderline with Silver Spring in Maryland. The house was in a similar condition while Joseph Mutaboba lived there. Dorothy and I lived in a small two-bedroom apartment in Washington D.C., and later rented a three-bedroom house on Davis Street, near the U.S. Vice-President's official residence, as we renovated the residence. I left Kigali with four of my trusted staff at the RPF Secretariat: Methode Ruzindana, Eugene Kayihura, Marie my secretary and John Mugabo my driver. Naturally they were all Tutsi, since I could not trust any Hutu at that time. They were all diligent and loyal. Of the four, I soon discovered that Eugene Kayihura was the sneaky one, with direct contact to Vice President Kagame. I found it strange that they would talk regularly, but soon realized that Vice President Kagame worked in that fashion, deploying people to spy and tell on you. I also learned how to ignore that.

I presented my credentials to President Bill Clinton in April 1996. The ceremony began with a U.S. government limo picking Dorothy and I up from the small apartment where we lived. Adorning the American and Rwandan flags, we were driven to the White House, where over ten other ambassadors were waiting for a similar event. I had earlier been asked by the State Department to forward the remarks I wanted to make before President Clinton. I had written no more than two paragraphs, essentially telling the President and the U.S government that Rwanda had suffered immensely, and had to reconcile and rebuild. Rwanda needed U.S support. I was inwardly angry with President Clinton, but the task of a diplomat, I had gathered, was to conceal his or her emotions. President Clinton had presided over international inaction during the genocide of 1994. When my name and Dorothy's were read out, right after the Sudanese Ambassador, we stepped forward and greeted him. He appeared charming and friendly, and then to our surprise, said, "Oh, I hear you two guys were recently married". Somehow it broke the tense feelings I had, and I responded in the affirmative. He said he sympathized with Rwanda and pledged support for our reconciliation and reconstruction efforts.

Ideologically, I had, since college days, been conditioned to think of America in adversarial terms. Ever since I came to the United States for the first time in 1991, somehow my mind had begun to soften a little by opening up to the new realities of what was at least seen in terms of American accomplishments. It had vast territory, a short but rich and tumultuous history as a republic, a diverse population of over 300 million people who are proud to be Americans despite their backgrounds and beliefs, first class academic institutions, foundations that give out billions of dollars every year, think tanks that influence policy, a robust and innovative economy, a mighty army and an educated citizenry. American people had fought for their independence like us, and like Rwandans, had then fought a civil war among themselves. Unlike Rwanda, however, by and large they have been internally peaceful and secure.

There was plenty to learn in Washington, D.C. Before coming to take up my diplomatic post, I had been given a general briefing without specifics. There was no Rwandan policy to champion as such, except that which I knew and championed in the RPF rebel days when one had to understand a general line, and like an entrepreneur, improvise the rest.

Many people across the world would consider being ambassador to Washington, D.C. as a dream. But, the U.S. capital is complex. Everyone who comes to this city has to scramble to get the attention of whoever you are trying to do business with. With a small and poor mission like the Rwandan Embassy you have got to prioritize what you do. You may not have pinstripes, nor have money to throw lavish cocktails that are the hallmark of doing business in diplomacy.

Diplomacy is a centuries old tradition that developed in the days when Popes and emperors had to seek to influence each other. Later, from the 8th century onwards, this further developed in the city states of northern Italy, France and Spain. Originally diplomats came from the nobility and aristocracy in feudal Europe. The French revolution of 1789, the Congress of Vienna, the two world wars, the cold war, the decolonization and emergence of independent countries in Africa, and the end of the cold war have all shaped what we know of diplomacy today. In Washington, D.C. the separation of powers and the checks and balances condition you to become "street-wise", since you may never obtain one and definitive answer from any one of the institutions that check and balance each other.

When I came to Washington, D.C. Rwanda was already infamous for the civil war and genocide. U.S. top political leaders were already guilty for what they had not been able to do for Rwanda. President Clinton and Secretary Albright must have had uneasy consciences. People like Assistant Secretary Susan Rice; President's assistants, like Gayle Smith and John Prendergast, and Great Lakes Special Envoy, Howard Wolpe, knew intimately the failings that had characterized the administration they served. Each one of them could not claim to be an innocent bystander. This culpability of the international community in failing to prevent, stop or mitigate the Rwandan genocide was a great asset in the hands of RPF. Like every RPF leader, I put it to good use to get access in this great city of lobbyists, pen pushers and myriads of smart people who live by their wits. My target list included State Department, Congress, White House, Pentagon, Think Tanks and NGOs, the African American communities, Universities, the World Bank and the International Monetary Fund (IMF), and individuals who may have an interest in Africa and Rwanda in particular. With time, Susan Rice, Gayle Smith, Howard Wolpe, John Prendergast, Ted Dagne of the Congressional Research Office, and Roger Winter of the U.S Committee for Refugees became good friends of mine. We met regularly for lunch and we talked about the Great Lakes, the Sudan, and the new breed of African leaders

The idea of the new breed of African leaders was coined by President Bill Clinton during his trip to Africa in 1998. This new breed was supposed to include Yoweri Museveni of Uganda, Paul Kagame of Rwanda, Meles Zenawi of Ethiopia, and Isaias Afewerki of Eritrea. The four were supposed to represent Africa's renaissance. As a diplomat, this was a godsend, and I used every occasion to promote it. Other skeptical African diplomats never believed or warmed up to it. Initially Dorothy and I attended as many receptions as possible but later we became a little more selective as to which ones were relevant to our work.

In diplomacy the last three feet, as one American journalist put it, are what matters since one on one interaction carries a premium in building useful relationships.

Earlier in my diplomatic tour I made a conscious effort to look for anything that would help Rwanda's ordinary people who were suffering. I knew the humanitarian needs I had left behind, the orphans, widows, the handicapped and many other needy people. I had come across a U.S. military officer, Colonel Bob Morris, then living in Alaska, who interested me in military excess stuff.

I took a trip with him across a number of military bases that were closing down, and ended up in one in Alaska. During my early years in school we would hear of such places like Alaska and Greenland, and the Eskimos and think they were not on the same planet as us. On my return to Washington, D.C. I travelled on a military C-5 Galaxy, an amazing U.S military transport plane. On the trip I also had a chance to be on a stationary sea carrier, the *USS Lincoln*. Those were in the pre-9/11 days, and I was considered a friend of America.

Still with an appetite for books, I visited libraries and bookstores in Washington, D.C. I always wondered when Rwanda woul have such libraries and bookstores. I set out on a book mobilization campaign, but ended up with people sending old magazines and books of no interest. When I spent a whole day with my embassy staff trying to sort out the good from the useless, I called off the campaign. Times had changed in terms of my reading habits. I was now very much interested in reading topics on economics, business, globalization and international development. In Marxist literature I had read that economic relations are the basis of political relations, and nowhere was this supposed to be evident than in the mother of capitalism, the United States. During the 1990s the information revolution was gathering momentum. Information technology, entrepreneurship, innovation and business development dominated my reading.

During my days in Washington, I wrote over three hundred letters to universities and colleges, including all the Ivy League ones, looking for scholarships for Rwandan boys and girls. Most answered, telling me that Rwandan children had to compete like all the others for the scholarships. In Washington I had a sense of urgency to portray Rwanda as a special case. Then luck came my way one day. Dorothy and I had been invited to a U.S Supreme Court dinner, in honor of Judge Richard Goldstone, the South African who was the first Prosecutor of the International Criminal Tribunal for Rwanda. Dorothy and I sat near a priest. She had a conversation with him first, and later I was brought in. His name was Monsignor William Kerr, then President of La Roche College, a small college in Pittsburgh, Pennsylvania. In his conversation with Dorothy he had mentioned how he had been praying for a while to meet somebody from Rwanda one day. He felt he had a calling to help some Rwandans. Dorothy told him we were from Rwanda and that her husband was Rwanda's Ambassador to the United States. We spoke briefly Dorothy and I invited him for breakfast the following morning.

Within two weeks he came back and we talked at length. I talked to him about Rwanda and my personal and family story. We parted. Two weeks later he called to inform me that he had discussed Rwanda with his Board of Trustees. The board had decided to grant full scholarships to twenty Rwandan youth. That was my happiest day in Washington D.C. I broke the news to Dorothy, who after all had spoken first to Monsignor Kerr. She too was very excited. I relayed the information to Vice President Kagame and to the Minister of Education, Dr. Joseph Karemera.

Two weeks later, Monsignor Kerr called me with unexpected good news. The Board of Trustees of La Roche College had also decided to award an Honorary Doctorate to my mother, Coletta Bamususire. I was touched and humbled by the news. Excited, I called my mother to break the good news, and she somehow poured cold water on it. First of all, she said, it is fake. How could they give the highest degree to someone who has never been to a formal classroom? Second, it is the business of women to look after their children, and they need not receive degrees for that. I sweet talked her into coming to the United States to receive the degree. She came with my brother and we drove together to Pittsburgh on graduation day. When her name was read out, and her citation followed, she got a standing ovation. She was now Dr. Coletta Bamususire, the first La Roche College alumni from Rwanda. In the following years, La Roche College granted scholarships to more than 100 African girls and boys from Rwanda,

Uganda, Ethiopia and other places. Monsignor William Kerr passed away two years ago but La Roche College and his efforts will live forever, due to the hope they gave to young people.

Following my first child, Archadius, a boy, who was born in Kampala, Uganda on October 22 1993, our second child, Mwiza, a girl, was born on January 16, 1997, in Johns Hopkins Hospital in Baltimore, Maryland. My mother-in-law, Mrs. Joyce Rwetsiba,came to help Dorothy. During my medical school days, my professor of Obstetrics used to tell us that you can always tell how developed a society is by simply looking at how mothers are treated during childbirth, and how babies are treated after that. What a difference it was compared to Mulago hospital, where I had worked as an intern. With our family expanding, I also realized how our kids would have a different upbringing from mine. Dorothy had been born and raised in a middle-class family, the elite of post-colonial Uganda. There are many things she is able to relate to with regard to our children. She can sing with them lullabies that her own mother used to sing to her. She could sing with them *London Bridge is Falling Down* and relate to characters, like Mary Poppins, in movies. She has relived her life as a kid with our children. For me, it has been a steep learning curve. Since I did not have a father when growing up, there is limited copying and emulating I can relate to. As I have watched our children grow I have often wondered what I would have done with my father had he lived.

CHAPTER TWENTY ONE

Congo War I

My diplomatic work in Washington, D.C. was marred by Rwanda's two military interventions in the Democratic Republic of Congo. The country now known as the Democratic Republic of Congo has had a very traumatic history and different names. With a population of about 73, 599, 190, it is a vast territory with an area of 2,344,858 sq. km. Established in 1908 as a Belgian colony, the Republic of Congo gained independence in 1960, in conditions of political and civil strife. With over 200 tribes and ethnic groups, it was ruled together with Rwanda and Burundi, by Belgium. The Democratic Republic of Congo is enormously endowed with natural resources, partly explaining why Belgium found it a lucrative possession, the west made it a favorable staging ground during the cold war, neighbors have meddled in its internal affairs thus fueling unending violent conflict. It natural resources include cobalt, copper, niobium, tantalum, petroleum, industrial and gem diamonds, gold, silver, zinc, manganese, tin, uranium, coal, hydropower, and timber. Its coltan is used in our cell phones. Its uranium was used in the atomic bomb that was dropped by the United States on Japan in 1945.

Foreigners have always looked at Africa as a source of raw materials, and Congo typifies this scramble. The treachery, violence, conspiracies and manipulations that characterized this period in the Congo led to the assassination of Congo's most famous nationalist, Patrice Lumumba, at the hands of what many believe was a western conspiracy. Lumumba is well known as a martyr in Africa's and international socialist and communist circles.

A favorite of the west during the Cold War, Colonel Joseph Mobutu took over power in 1965, and became president for 32 years, having the country renamed Zaire, and himself Mobutu Sese Seko. When the civil broke out in Rwanda in 1990, President Mobutu supported President Habyarimana by sending Congolese troops. His public international role later changed to be one of a mediator, though he was never trusted by the RPF. As a member of the Arusha peace negotiations, I had an opportunity during the civil war days, to visit his castle at Gbadolite, somewhere in the jungles of DRC. He had sent one of his private jets to pick the RPF delegation from Entebbe, Uganda. The private jet landed on a first-class runway in the middle of nowhere, and we were driven to President Mobutu's castle, and accommodated in villas.

When we met the Government of Rwanda's delegation, he was there to briefly officiate at the ceremony. He spoke very nice French, wore his characteristic cap and Zairean "authentic" shirt and pants, and carried himself elegantly, probably emulating European kings and emperors he had read about. President Mobutu's regime was a perfect fit for Frantz Fanon's description of Africa's post-colonial elite, with its vast appetite for consuming western products, and less ingenuity in producing what they consume. President Mobutu and his entourage drank western wines, western water, imported western fruits and vegetables, had mansions in Europe, and kept their money in Swiss banks.

By the 1990s, the Zairean state was bankrupt, fragmented, and opposition to Mobutu's rule on the rise. He ruled from Gbadolite and his yacht in N'sele. Across the country, there was little presence of the central or local government. There were no public services, and his soldiers were left on their own to levy whatever they could get from the poor population. Zaire was a failing state. As long as there was a cold war, Mobutu had a role and function to perform. With the demise of the Soviet Union, Mobutu's role as an indispensable tool against communism in Africa was becoming less and less attractive. After all, hadn't human civilization witnessed the end of history, as Francis Fukuyama had written in *The End of History*? If all of Africa was now struggling to be like the west, what was Mobutu's appeal?

When RPF assumed power in July, 1994, the relocation of the previous government's military and interahamwe militia to eastern Congo, alongside millions of Hutu refugees, was a timely godsend to President Mobutu, struggling to remain relevant to the regional and international power game. It would turn out to be his Achilles heel. RPF knew very well that it had a grave and persistent danger along the border it shared with Congo. The old regime had almost fully reconstituted itself in the refugee camps in eastern Congo. Salaries were paid. Training of soldiers and militia was going on. Plans were always underway to attack Rwanda. While appearing to be firmly in control, the whole RPF regime behaved and acted as if under siege. The international community hardly ever responds to such grave developments in an efficient and effective manner. When it does, it acts late, slowly, and in a tentative manner. The so-called international community is steeped in inertia, unable to change course in time to prevent the next tragedy. The refugees in eastern Congo had become hostages to the old regime's military and militia. International humanitarian relief agencies had knowingly or unknowingly become captive to the old regime's machinations in the refugee camps

The whole international community had adapted the usual "wait and see" approach, hoping that one way or another the situation would go on like that. President Mobutu must have found solace in the fact that the situation provided him with an opportunity to act as a broker in the evolving situation. France must have had its own calculation too. It had lost influence in Rwanda and the entire elite allied to it over the years were now exiled. Could this elite stage a comeback, with the help of President Mobutu. The United States and Britain, especially their militaries and intelligence communities, were now overtly or covertly on the side of RPF, the new winners in Rwanda.

As I settled in the ambassadorial role in Washington, D.C. Vice-President Paul Kagame visited the United States in 1996. I accompanied him the meetings he had with the Secretary of Defense, William Perry, and with Timothy Wirth, the Undersecretary for Global Affairs during the Clinton Administration. In all the meetings, Vice President Kagame raised the issue of an untenable and dangerous situation in the refugee camps. The international community had to do something about it; otherwise Rwanda would have to take the matter into her own hands. I had the impression that the U.S. government officials, not promising to deal with the situation, were giving a green light to Rwanda to deal with the situation. Later that year Rwanda decided to invade Congo, dismantled the refugee camps, scattered the military and militia, and began what would later be described as the First Congo war, with far reaching human rights and humanitarian consequences that reverberate almost two decades since.

The Hutu refugees had been coerced into Congo by the defeated regime. The new regime in Kigali coerced them back into Rwanda. Suddenly, the world woke up to a massive exodus of refugees heading back to Rwanda, just as they had poured into Congo in 1994.

Paul Kagame and his military advisers had to quickly decide what to do next, to sustain the momentum of their first action in Congo. To RPF, the first natural allies of the Rwandan Tutsi were the Banyamulenge in eastern Congo, whose citizenship credentials successive Congolese governments were yet to resolve. Their grievances were a mobilization opportunity for Rwanda. The next opportunity that was exploited by Vice-President Kagame and his military was Laurent Desire Kabila, an old rebel who had fought against Mobutu's regime in the 1960s. Rwanda needed to "Congolise" Rwanda's operation in Congo. The Banyamulenge were a minority and Kabila, hailing from Katanga, would be a useful factor. Kabila was known to the Tanzanians, with whom he had lived, and to Ugandans as well. Overnight, Rwanda helped create the rebel group, Alliance of Democratic Forces for the Liberation of Congo (AFDL), and made Laurent Kabila its head. In an effort to "Africanize" Rwanda's operation, Vice-President Paul Kagame invited President Museveni to get involved in the Congo. Other countries, notably Angola and Burundi, were also involved.

Rwanda's formal and official position was that it was not involved in the Congo rebellion. As Rwanda's Ambassador in Washington, D.C. my job was to justify the violent closure of the refugee camps, by pointing out that the international community had failed to prevent and stop the 1994 genocide, and had failed to resolve the refugee problem. I always pointed out that the international community had been forewarned but, as usual, had not taken heed. The most difficult job, however, was to lie that Rwanda was not involved in the Congo rebellion. There was a kind of unspoken and unwritten understanding among the people I dealt with, like Susan Rice, Gayle Smith, John Prendergast, and Ted Dagne that we all knew what the truth was. Not surprisingly, the United States government did not pressure us in any way. President Mobutu's regime could not survive the rebellion. It quickly crumbled like a stack of cards, as President Mobutu, old and sick, sought refuge from country to country, finally dying of prostate cancer in Morocco. Vice-President Paul Kagame and his RPA had triumphed again, as he installed Laurent Kabila as the new President of Rwanda's large and dysfunctional neighbor, which assumed a new name, from Zaire to the Democratic Republic of Congo (DRC).

One morning, in 1997, I opened the pages of the *Washington Post* and the headline was "Rwanda Admits being in the Congo".

For the first time, Vice-President Kagame was formally telling the world that the Congo war had been planned in Rwanda and executed by Rwanda's "mid-level officers". Its first objective, he said, was to close the refugee camps. The second was to kill or scatter the old regime's military and militia. The third was to remove President Mobutu. This revelation created a credibility problem for RPF, and for me in my diplomatic work. How could we be believed next time? Rwanda's venture into DRC continued to consume a disproportionate fraction of my time and effort in Washington, D.C. Even as Paul Kagame was being hailed by President Clinton and his advisers as one of the new breed of African leaders, Rwanda was preparing for the second venture in DRC.

CHAPTER TWENTY TWO

Congo War II

It has been said that generals always prepare to fight the last war. The end of the civil war and genocide in Rwanda had created the conditions for the first Congo war. The First Congo War created the conditions for the Second Congo War. Once again Rwanda's military was at the forefront of a big regional war that would soon be described as Africa's World War. President Kabila had come to power in a failing state, without his people's mandate, and without an army of his own. He had come to power with a ragtag rebel army, under the wings of a more disciplined and experienced army, Rwanda's RPA. He had to rely on a foreign army, from small Rwanda, and predominantly from a minority Tutsi, to rule. Nothing symbolized this uncomfortable reality than that James Kabarebe, a Rwandan RPA Tutsi officer (Paul Kagame's head of personal security during Rwanda's civil war), was now DRC's Army Chief of Staff. President Kabila's Foreign Minister was Dr. Karaha, another Tutsi from eastern Congo, as Rwanda had wished. The Tutsi officers of the RPA, whom Kagame had revealed were responsible for toppling Mobutu and installing Kabila, were running the show in a manner that must have irked many Congolese and President Kabila himself.

Though the RPA had been the leading factor in the fall of Mobutu, many countries, especially Uganda and Angola, had given their full support and had quickly been sidelined as Kagame took all the credit in the First Congo War. Kagame was now demanding more than his fair share of Congo's power, economic resources and mineral concessions. Kagame's personal overbearing attitude, manifesting itself in his officers' way of micro-managing President Kabila, slowly created unease and later conditions for open conflict. Once again, Vice-President Kagame and his advisers in DRC conceived another plan, for a swift operation to remove President Kabila and install another president favorable to Vice-President Kagame's political and economic interests.

As the second war unfolded in1998, Rwanda had to find a way of explaining it. At first we denied Rwanda's presence, but with overwhelming evidence, we quickly had to say President Kabila had allied himself with the former Rwanda government military, Forces Armées Rwandaises (ex-FAR). This time, however, our arguments were weak. A military operation in DRC's capital, Kinshasa, was far away from Rwanda, and hence less plausible than one in refugee camps at the border as an explanation for responding to Rwanda's security needs. Sure of his power in the DRC game, and having marginalized his former allies in the First Congo War, Vice-President Kagame had not even bothered to solicit the support of President Museveni of Uganda or the Angolans. He scrambled to do so at the last moment. President Museveni was willing to go into the Congo, but this time with ample room for his own independent course of action. The Angolans decided to join President Kabila's side, alongside Zimbabwe and Namibia. Diplomatically and militarily this was President Kabila's major success against Vice-President Kagame, whose only lukewarm ally was President Museveni of Uganda. There was widespread international condemnation and pressure for Rwanda to withdraw from Congo.

The events of the next few days of the Second Congo War were the most challenging nightmare in my service as a diplomat in Washington, D.C. Rwanda's RPA was now moving to a third war in less than ten years. It had fought and won the Rwandan civil war, albeit at a very high price. The First Congo War had been a quick one, but neither Rwanda nor DRC had counted the cost as yet. Now, there was a third war that RPA was fighting in a foreign land. There had been little, if any, preparation of the international community. And, unlike the previous Congo war, it had all the characteristics of an unjust war that Rwanda would lose no matter how long it took. Was General Paul Kagame now over-reaching? What capacity did small and poor Rwanda have to fight two successive foreign wars in such a vast territory? The Second Congo War had come as a surprise to me as it was for many leaders in Rwanda, ordinary Rwandans, and the international community. However, I had a duty as a Rwandan diplomat to defend my government, RPF, and Vice President Kagame. Since our men and women were involved, risking their lives even when they least understood why they were fighting this time, I felt I had a call beyond duty to represent them with the same passion, zeal and energy.

As the battle lines were drawn in Kinshasa, it turned out that James Kabarebe, Vice President Kagame's chief military advisor on Congo, and until then President Kabila's Army Chief of Staff, had made a fatal miscalculation by underestimating how quickly DRC would mobilize on an anti-Rwanda, anti-Tutsi platform. Overnight, being Rwandan, Tutsi or a Munyamulenge became synonymous with being the enemy that had to be targeted and killed. With a small force far away from Rwanda, the RPA had hoped to use surprise, speed and sheer resolve to achieve what it had achieved before as soon as possible. Many Tutsi were hoping for another victory irrespective of how ill-conceived, ill-planned, and ill-executed the latest RPA war was.

At some point we had a full blown crisis. In Kitona, close to the DRC-Angola border, thousands of our troops were trapped, with Angolan troops behind them, and President Kabila's in front of them. The stakes were extremely high, and our boys could be annihilated any time. Vice-President Kagame had to swallow his pride and ask for the United States to help. Through Dr. Emmanuel Ndahiro, Vice-President Kagame conveyed to me the urgency of the situation. Our troops would be entirely destroyed by the Angolan troops behind them. Could the United States use its influence to convince Angola to desist from attacking our troops as we try to evacuate them? I quickly looked for the Assistant Secretary of State for African Affairs, Susan Rice, to convey the message. She promised to talk to the Angolan Ambassador in Washington, D.C.

Events were moving very fast and hour by hour the situation was becoming more dangerous. Vice-President would relay anxious messages to me through Dr. Ndahiro. I would urgently seek Dr. Susan Rice to convey the messages. She would in turn promise that the U.S. was doing the best they could to influence Angola. Sometimes I would have to drive myself to her private residence in Washington, D.C. to talk to her about the grave danger our boys were in. She was understanding and willing to help. Ultimately, I was told one day, all our boys had been airlifted to Rwanda, and that Jonas Savimbi, the Angolan government's arch enemy, had been contacted to allow use of an airstrip in his area of control. I still believe if Angola had wanted to use its full force to destroy our troops in Kitona, it would have been able to do it. Diplomacy probably did contribute to the prevention of a bloodbath of RPA boys in a foreign land.

CHAPTER TWENTY THREE

President Bill Clinton in Kigali

In 1998, both Secretary Madeline Albright and President Bill Clinton visited Rwanda. Both had every reason to do so. President Clinton and his Ambassador to the United Nations presided over the international system while over 800,000 Rwandans were butchered, day by day, for a hundred days, and hundreds of thousands after. Madeleine Albright was at the United Nations when the U.N. Security Council voted to withdraw the U.N peacekeeping force in Rwanda as the genocide and massacres gathered momentum. Secretary Albright supported the U.N. Security Council resolution that gave a mandate to France to launch the controversial Operation Turquoise in Rwanda in the final days before the RPF took over power. With recent declassified information, it is clear that President Clinton and his administration had enough information on the horrors that engulfed Rwanda in 1994. They simply chose not to act. The U.S military had burned its fingers in Somalia. Rwanda was a small African country, and race was an issue. Rwanda was a small country without vast natural resources like oil, gas, gold, uranium or diamonds. At the bargaining table, the U.S listened more to France's skewed vision on Rwanda, rather than considered the plight and legitimate interests of Rwandans.

When Secretary Albright visited Rwanda I attended the meeting she had with President Pasteur Bizimungu, Vice President Kagame and other Rwandan officials. Secretary Albright announced the so called Great Lakes Justice Initiative, and pledged support to Rwanda's reconciliation and reconstruction efforts. Later in the year, we were informed that President Clinton would visit Uganda and hoped to see both President Bizimungu and Vice President Kagame in Entebbe, Uganda. Other African Presidents (Arap Moi of Kenya, Yoweri Museveni of Uganda, Meles Zenawi of Ethiopia, Laurent Kabila of DRC, Benjamin Mkapa of Tanzania) and Salim Ahmed Salim, Secretary General of the African Union had been invited to a summit in Uganda. We were not at all happy with the proposal. Rwanda had suffered while President Clinton watched, and now he did not even have the courtesy to come to Rwanda to apologize.

At first, they said Air Force One, the U.S. Presidential plane, a Boeing 747, could not land at Kigali International Airport. But the airport had accommodated even the C-5 Galaxy during Operation Support Hope in 1994. Then they cited security concerns in a country that had emerged from civil war, genocide, and was at war with another country. When they finally agreed that President and Mrs. Clinton would come, it was decided they would not move beyond the airport. The ceremony would take place there. Everyone, including President Bizimungu and Vice President Kagame would have to go through metal detectors manned by stern U.S. Secret Service security. The meetings included a scripted encounter with Rwandan survivors of genocide, and a short meeting with President Bizimungu, Vice President Kagame and I. President Clinton was with his National Security Advisor, Sandy Berger. President Clinton pledged support to national reconstruction and reconciliation efforts. He also re-pledged support to the Great Lakes Justice Initiative. The main event was the speech he gave before an attentive and mixed audience comprising of government officials, diplomats and civil society.

President Clinton was careful enough in his speech not to directly mention the United States as the sole and indispensable superpower that had influenced the rest of the international community to do nothing in preventing and stopping genocide. He spread the blame, rightly so, to the whole international community, including the Africans themselves. He was careful not to highlight his own culpability as the most powerful and influential leader in the whole world during the 100 days in which the genocide and the most horrendous war crimes and crimes against humanity were carried out. He promised: 1) support to the genocide fund; 2) support Rwanda in establishing the rule of law; 3) hold accountable those who commit such crimes; 4) identify and spotlight nations in danger of genocide; and 5) mobilize the international community to act when genocide threatens. Almost all the above promises have not been met, and Rwanda is more vulnerable than it was in 1994. President Clinton and Ambassador Rice are among the staunchest advocates that President Kagame has abroad.

That afternoon President Bizimungu joined President Clinton on Air Force One, bound for Entebbe, Uganda, for the summit with other African leaders. There, President Clinton announced another initiative, the International Coalition Against Genocide (ICAG). There was a follow-up meeting in Washington, D.C. at the White House, in which officials from both sides attended. ICAG finally died a natural death after President Clinton left office. President Clinton and many of his advisors and top administration officials will live with wounded consciences forever.

CHAPTER TWENTY FOUR

Encountering Bretton Woods

My diplomatic work in Washington, D.C. included dealing with two global institutions, namely, the World
Bank and the International Monetary Fund (IMF).
After World War II, in July, 1944, in the city of Bretton Woods
in New Hampshire, United States, the victors championed by the
United States met to establish the International Bank for Reconstruction, now known as the World Bank, and the International
Monetary Fund (IMF). The main ideas that were being promoted
by the conference included open markets, lowering the barriers
to trade, facilitating the movement of capital, fostering post-war
reconstruction, political stability and peace. The two institutions
have come to dominate the life of developing countries, especially
least developed countries, the majority of which are in Africa.

Poor countries like Rwanda are like companies that have
gone bankrupt and are in receivership. The International Monetary Fund is like the cop who assesses the financial situation and
informs the World Bank and the rest of the donor community
whether they can safely do business with you. The IMF looks at
you revenues and expenditures, and recommends how you should
improve your revenues, and reign on your expenditures so that

over time your books are balanced. The World Bank does its own assessments, and ideally, develops a Country Assistance Strategy, with the participation of the host country.

My strong ideological inclinations from the days in college, and my subsequent revolutionary outlook, had taught me that the World Bank and the IMF were the tools of western capitalism. Their objective, we were taught, was to keep poor countries poor through conditionalities out of which there was no possible exit. These conditionalities came to be baptized the *Washington Concensus*. Coined by John Williamson in 1990, the Washington Consensus referred to a set of policies, including fiscal discipline, a redirection of public expenditure priorities toward fields offering both high economic returns and the potential to improve income distribution, such as primary health care, primary education, and infrastructure, tax reform (to lower marginal rates and broaden the tax base), interest rate liberalization, a competitive exchange rate, trade liberalization, liberalization of inflows of foreign direct investment, privatization, deregulation (to abolish barriers to entry and exit) and secure property rights.

However, the moment you come to run a country, you adopt a pragmatic approach, given the realities on the ground. Emerging from civil war and genocide, Rwanda was a special case that depended largely on aid from donors. You had to deal with the IMF and World Bank to access concessionary loans. During my days in Washington, D.C., James Wolfenshon was the World Bank President, and he had come to the Bank with an air of reform that emphasized country ownership and leadership. Working with bank officials, I had input into the first post-genocide Country Assistance Strategy, especially its emphasis on human resource development. Callisto Madavo, a Zimbabwean, was the Vice-President in whose mandate fell Rwanda.

I wrote a letter to the World Bank President, reminding him of Rwanda's special status, and calling for a "mini Marshall Plan" for Rwanda. During my tenure, I signed on behalf of Rwanda a credit line of 50 million U.S. dollars as an Emergency Recovery Credit. I found dealing with the World Bank much easier than the IMF, which was then still enveloped in mystery and secrecy. When I looked for documents on the Rwanda programme I was told I had to get special authorization from Rwanda's Minister of Finance or Governor of the Central Bank. IMF has become more open these days, with most of its country information available online.

CHAPTER TWENTY FIVE

Attacked from Within

Icame to Washington, D.C. with a desire to make the Embassy of Rwanda a people's embassy. RPF's supporters in the United States were few Tutsi who had supported the RPF during the civil war. As I assumed office in 1996, I had my very first meeting with some of them who lived around the Washington, D.C.area. I showed them the status of the embassy and thought I could mobilize them in a self-help process of rehabilitating the embassy building. In retrospect, that was asking too much from them. The RPF supporters, most of them Tutsi, had supported RPF to military victory, and most of them had lost their beloved ones during the genocide. It was their time to be supported now that RPF was running the government. I did not know any Hutu who I could reach out to, and I was not interested in that at the time. I invited other Rwandans to the embassy to discuss what we could do together.

During a visit to California, Dorothy and I spent a night at the home of a Rwandan Professor, Alexander Kimenyi (deceased), who taught at Sacramento State University. Kimenyi was a leader in the Rwandan Diaspora community in the United States. He had been instrumental in the founding of *Impuruza*, (clarion call in Kinyarwanda), a journal that spoke to the dire conditions of Rwanda and Rwandese refugees, and the need to mobilize for change. He was also instrumental in the 1988 Washington, D.C. meeting of the Rwandan Diaspora, which the newly reconstituted RPF at that time had found every reason to sabotage.

I was conscious about the fact that I represented Rwanda and all Rwandans. With time, I realized that there was a gradual hostility towards me from some elements in the Rwandan Tutsi community in the United States. Some may have been frustrated that with RPF's victory, having expected payback, they had not received anything in return. Some wanted to have a say in how the embassy was run. I determined the embassy had to keep a distance, and avoid being held hostage to any group. We run a small but effective operation at the embassy. We were few, and had no time to get involved in the intrigues that are common in all Diaspora communities.

As I kept a distance, I started reading false local media reports about me from Rwanda, complaining how I lived expensively, drove expensive cars, gambled, and lived in an expensive house near Vice President Al Gore's official residence, and was arrogant and detached from the Rwandan community. One headline was, *Rudasingwa Yigize I Kigirwamana I Washington, D.C.* (Rudasingwa has made himself an Idol in Washington DC). My monthly salary was 1600 US $. When I reported for duty in the embassy had one old minivan, and I purchased an official car for the ambassador for 26,000 U.S. to be paid in installments. I temporarily lived in a small apartment, and then a rented a three-bedroom house for a year for around 3,000 US $ plus per month while the Rwandan official residence was being renovated. In my entire life I have never gambled.

The negative vibes from Kigali were relentless. Soon, I was accused of having thrown out a Rwandan diplomat from the embassy, and for having detained another in a shipping container. The first story involved Ms. Marianne Baziruwiha, a diplomat at the embassy. She lived with her children in the small apartment in the embassy building. I was concerned that whenever we left the embassy at the end of a working day, we left the building to Ms. Baziruwiha and her teenage boys. Who knew who else would have access to the building? I proposed to Ms. Baziruwiha that we would help her in finding a small apartment for her to rent. She was resistant to the idea. One day I surprised her by locking her out of the building, having alerted the U.S. Secret Service. She was allowed to get her things under supervision.

The second false story involved Methode Ruzindana, a very diligent and close confidant of mine since the early days of RPF's coming to power. During one winter I remember him repeatedly coming to work late for some time. I took disciplinary action of suspending him from work for a week. In retrospect, I was disproportionately harsh both to Baziruwiha and Ruzindana, and I have had time in recent years to meet with them, talk about those events, and told them I was sorry to the extent my harsh decisions hurt them. They have, in turn, explained to me how they were being manipulated, and how the false stories from Kigali originated from RPF itself, not with them.

One day, I received a call from Emmanuel Gasana (deceased), who then worked as a diplomatic adviser to Vice-President Paul Kagame. I was to report to Kigali for urgent consultation within 48 hours. I did report as instructed. I was summoned to a meeting at the President's Office, Village Urugwiro. There I found President Bizimungu, Vice President Kagame, Tito Rutaremara, Denis Polisi and many other RPF senior cadres. I could feel a tense atmosphere, and I knew this was a disciplinary tribunal. I was the accused. President Bizimungu broke the ice, and asked me why I had been disrespectful to the Rwandan Foreign Minister, Anastase Gasana. I was also asked why I had mistreated one of my staff.

I had written a letter to then Minister of Foreign Affairs, Anastase Gasana, highlighting the plight of the embassy building and lack of resources to pay staff. The embassy building was literally collapsing. I came one morning to discover a heap of rubble on my desk, the ceiling in my office having collapsed. Repeated stress calls to Kigali had been fruitless. The Minister of Foreign Affairs, finally wrote to me through his assistant, asking me to account for the money they had previously sent. I was angry and frustrated. I replied by asking who this assistant who gives instructions to ambassadors was. My letter did reflect anger, but was not insulting. Vice-President Kagame had prepared the RPF leaders and they each took time to chide me. I explained the circumstances of my response to the Foreign Minister. Vice-President Kagame said as a senior RPF cadre I should know how to handle people in our broad based government (how to handle Hutu) even if I may be right. I would later learn that he had instructed that the meeting raise the issue of alleged financial mismanagement at the RPF Secretariat while I was Secretary-General. The matter was not raised, and I think he realized what a dangerous subject it would have been for him.

After this meeting, I slowly realized that my relationship with Vice President Kagame was in a period of gradual, subtle and yet sure decline. Ever since I had left for my diplomatic posting in Washington, D.C. there had been a subtle yet persistent smear campaign by him against me. In choreographed meetings, RPF cadres would seek my head, protesting that I was a failure, had destroyed RPF, and instead of being fired I was always rewarded with high posts. Vice-President Kagame would pretend he was protecting me, saying he knows there are things I am able to do. I always searched myself and wondered how I could have destroyed such a powerful organization within such a short period of time. I was the Secretary-General for about two years during which time the Arusha Peace Agreement was derailed, genocide occurred, RPF won the civil war, and we set up an administration in exceptionally difficult circumstances. Like all RPF cadres and those we worked with, I worked very hard to the best of my abilities.

I was even more confused during President Clinton's visit to Rwanda when Vice- President Kagame consistently argued that there was no need for me to come to Kigali to be present in the meetings. In one of the meetings chaired by President Bizimungu, I wondered aloud why there had been that resistance to allow me to be present during such high a profile visit, probably the highest in one's diplomatic service. I read it from President Bizimungu's face, and the arguments that Vice-President Kagame made that it had been the latter's work. In recent years I have learned that Vice-President Kagame always mentioned to senior RPF and RPA officers how I was being "used" by the Americans. It was also repeatedly mentioned in RPF circles how I was ambitious. This is a coded worded that Kagame uses for anyone who takes a principled stand and is confident. Interpreted, it means that you are a competitor for the job of President. I return to this issue in concluding chapters.

Aware of this trend, I realized I could not be in government for a long time. I asked to see Vice-President Kagame to discuss an important matter. He received me in his home in Urugwiro Village. Over lunch and in a cordial manner, I told him that I was tired of being attacked everyday for reasons I did not understand. I told him I had joined the RPF as a volunteer, and I did not want to become his burden. I suggested that it would be appropriate for me to leave government and seek some other vocation. He responded by saying that being attacked is part and parcel of public service, which every revolutionary should expect. He himself is always being attacked, he said. The revolution was still in its infancy, and we could not abandon it. He encouraged me to stay on, but I was not convinced that he was being genuine, because I also knew that he was behind the smear campaign. I could not read exactly what could motivate him to do that.

On March 27, 1999, Dorothy and I had a baby boy, Aaron Ngenzi. He was born at Columbia Hospital for Women, in Washington, D.C. Joyce Rwetsiba, was again there to witness the arrival of the baby and to help Dorothy. We were now a big family of five and in transition again. By then, I had been informed that my diplomatic tour had come to an end, and I had to report back to Rwanda. We had been endowed with a baby at the very beginning of my diplomatic tour in 1997, and now we were graced with another baby at the end of our tour.

My diplomatic tour in the United States as a representative of a small, poor, but sovereign country had taught me a few lessons in international relations. I had, on behalf of the RPF, staged a campaign of playing on the guilt of a superpower's failures in 1994. I had used deception with regard to Rwanda's two Congo wars, and, though not believing my narrative, various government and non-government audiences respected what I was saying and listened to me. The President of the United States and his Secretary of State had visited Rwanda during my tenure, spoken about the failures of the international community and pledged support to Rwanda's recovery. I had obtained full scholarships for Rwandan children in an American college. With limited means, I had rehabilitated the physical premises that belonged to the Government of Rwanda. The US-Rwanda relations were now stronger than they had ever been.

I had stopped hating the United States, discovered its people and institutions, and developed an interest in the country as a living school in which there was a lot to emulate and a lot to avoid. As my family headed home, I was glad I had made a contribution to the evolving and growing relationship between a superpower and a small country emerging from the ravages of civil war and genocide. Because Rwanda happens to be in a very dangerous neighborhood, it mattered that it has a privileged relationship with a superpower.

CHAPTER TWENTY SIX

Going Back Home

I returned to Rwanda in 1999, with a big family and without a job or a home. The whole family was now camped at my brother-in-law's house. My sister, Doreen Kayitesi, and her husband, General Martin Nzaramba, were kind enough to host my family. Like most civil servants in Rwanda, I had no savings since, even as a diplomat, we lived from hand to mouth. I realized, for the first time, that the person who had the key to help me resolve my immediate accommodation problem was Vice-President Kagame. Ever since I had arrived in Kigali, I had sought to debrief President Bizimungu as well as the Foreign Minister, Amri Sued, but had not found much enthusiasm from both. I made a point of informing Vice-President Kagame that I was in town.

About three weeks later, I was told he was to meet me at the Officer's Mess. When I met him briefly, he said I should report to his office. I took the opportunity to ask for help in getting means of transport and accommodation. He allowed me to stay in one of the houses in a small estate called Belgian Village, and gave instructions that one of the cars parked behind his office be given to me. No longer a diplomat or politician, I started receiving a salary of a Major in the Rwandese Patriotic Army. I really did not have much work to do, and I tried to improvise day by day to make myself busy.

One of the very first official missions I was sent on during this period was a trip to Ethiopia and Eritrea. In 1998, Eritrea and Ethiopia had gone to war. Since Vice- President Kagame was friends with both Prime Minister Meles Zenawi of Ethiopia and President Isaias Afewerki of Eritrea, the Americans had tried to use the relationships to encourage dialogue between them and bring the conflict to a peaceful resolution. Vice- President Kagame's wars in Congo, and the war between former friends and allies created a big problem for President Clinton's pitch for the new breed of African leaders. President Museveni of Uganda and Vice-President Kagame decided to send a joint delegation to meet Prime Minister Zenawi and President Afewerki to promote the peace effort.

I joined Uganda's Deputy Prime Minister and Minister of Foreign Affairs, Eriya Kategaya (deceased), on Museveni's Presidential jet to Ethiopia and Eritrea. Eriya Kategaya had been one of the young Ugandan politicians who, together with Yoweri Museveni, had inspired me to revolutionary thought and practice. In Addis Ababa we met Prime Minister Zenawi, who made it clear that the ball was in Eritrea's court. President Afewerki had stabbed him in the back by occupying Ethiopian territory. He said we should convince him that he should withdraw from Ethiopian territory. In Asmara we met President Afewerki, who asserted Eritrea's right to territory that belongs to it.

As we concluded our mission, it was clear that the two African nations were on a path to war. Shortly after our visit, Ethiopia and Eritrea, both among the poorest of nations, fought a vicious war in which each side wasted many millions of dollars, and lost tens of thousands of young men. By the end of the war, Ethiopia had pushed Eritrea from the contested territory, and both called for international arbitration to decide on the border issue.

The second mission I got involved in was of my own initiative. Since 1990, and especially from 1994, RPF's relationship with France had been acrimonious. As a diplomat, I had studied history and found that, occasionally, former enemies could find common ground and build new relationships. France was a powerful nation. It could be a spoiler and deploy its vast political, diplomatic, military and economic resources to tire us out. I thought that we could go through France's allies in Africa to intercede on our behalf. During my diplomatic service in the United States I had met an American by the name of Sean McCormick. McCormick then worked in the Clinton White House, and had since left Government to work for a private company. He too had an African friend, a Muslim cleric from West Africa who had contacts with a good number of African Heads of State. I asked McCormick if we could have access to Omar Bongo, President of Gabon. I regularly briefed Vice-President Kagame on the progress of the initiative.

A meeting was organized for me to go and meet President Omar Bongo. Vice President Kagame let me use one of his private jets. Two other government officers, Edith Gasana and Damascene Rudasingwa, travelled with me to Libreville, Gabon. Both spoke perfect French. When it was time to meet President Bongo, I was amazed to witness the degree of luxury in his office. It reminded me of President Mobutu's castle in Gbadolite. President Bongo had been in power since 1968 and preferred to refer to himself as the Dean of African Presidents. Gabon produces oil, and has a small population of about 1.5 million. He did not fully trust his own people, entrusting his personal security to hired Moroccans and French. He received us in an office that exuded luxury everywhere. He was a rather short man and appeared friendly.

After a short greeting, I went ahead and talked to him, through my colleague from Rwanda as an interpreter. I explained our complicated relationship with France. I was in the middle of explaining when I realized his eyes were closed. I changed to my native language and told my colleagues, Edith and Damascene "turekeraho ndabona nyakubahwa yisinziriye" (let us stop here, his Excellency has fallen asleep). I was surprised when President Bongo opened his eyes and said, "Go ahead, I am listening". I told him that Vice President Kagame would like to visit. He responded that he would try to help us with the French, and he would be happy to receive Vice-President Kagame. On our back to Rwanda we briefed the President of Congo(Brazzaville), Denis Sassou Nguesso.

When it was time for Vice-President Kagame to visit Gabon we were concerned about his safety. When the security in Gabon told us he would inspect a brief guard of honour we were reluctant. A soldier could shoot or stab him. A scheduled state dinner was cancelled when we insisted that Kagame's Chef be present when the food was being prepared and served. President Bongo met Vice-President Kagame and we kept hoping that Rwanda and France would patch up gradually. As Vice-President Kagame's private jet took off from the runway, a French mirage fighter was just behind us, leaving us to wonder whether this was a military salute, VIP protocol, or a reminder that mighty France could be dangerous, even far away from Rwanda.

When I returned to Rwanda in mid-1999, Vice-President Kagame had already become a more powerful man. He was not only the ultimate boss of all security institutions (army, police and intelligence), but had also become the Chairman of the RPF in 1998. While I was away a lot had transpired in the RPF, and I did not immediately realize the full grasp of all the dynamics, since politics is local. In 1999, Prime Minister Celestin Rwigyema was replaced by Rwanda's Ambassador to Germany, Bernard Makuza. The Speaker of Parliament, Joseph Sebarenzi, a Tutsi, was forced to resign. During my diplomatic tour in the United States, an RPF Minister (Seth Sendashonga) had been assassinated in Nairobi, Kenya, in 1998. Theoneste Lizinde, then RPA Colonel, had escaped into exile, and later on assassinated in Nairobi, Kenya. Rwanda had been to war twice in DRC, and new power brokers had merged in the military and the civilian technocrats who served Kagame.

Vice-President Kagame was on bad terms with President Bizimungu and with the Speaker of Parliament, Joseph Sebarenzi. In a period of weeks, he asked me to call various western ambassadors for meetings with him. The German, US, and British Ambassadors were considered to be the most influential among the others. I took notes during these meetings Vice-President Kagame. He would explain how government reforms had stalled because of President Bizimungu. He would tell them that Bizimungu was corrupt, citing some issues with a commercial building, trucks, and taking land that belonged to peasants somewhere in Masaka, in Kigali's suburbs. As for the Speaker, Sebarenzi, he would explain that he was ambitious and trying to use the parliament to create his own constituency.

Soon, the matter of President Bizimungu escalated to another level. In one of the RPF meetings, Vice-President Kagame and other RPF cadres attacked President Bizimungu directly. When, in a proposed cabinet reshuffle, President Bizimungu retained Patrick Mazimpaka, his close friend and Minister in the Office of the President, Kagame stuck to his guns and insisted Mazimpaka had to go. It became a battle of wills, but really a tip of the iceberg. Kagame sent me to various senior RPF cadres to explain and lobby for his position. I did so, but realized that opinion was divided, most urging caution and an amicable solution to the crisis.

Vice-President Kagame then dispatched me to Kampala to explain to President Museveni. In a meeting I had with him, President Museveni also urged caution. He advised that RPF still needed a Hutu at the top. If RPF was removing Bizimungu, he asked me, who was the other Hutu of choice? I argued that Paul Kagame had enough credentials to become the President this time. President Museveni later tried to lobby President Mkapa of Tanzania to advise us the same way, but the Tanzanians kept a

distance from Rwanda's dangerous politics. I also had an opportunity to talk to Susan Rice, then U.S. Assistant Secretary of State
for African affairs. Like President Museveni, she voiced U.S. concerns, and urged caution and restraint.

In 2000, President Bizimungu had to resign, and Vice-
President Kagame became the President of the Republic. For
the first time since 1990, Paul Kagame was the Chairman of
the ruling RPF, the head of all the security institutions, and
now the President of the Republic. Previously, he had ruled
from behind-the-scenes but now he had formally assumed
all the powers. Any pretense of power-sharing was now gone.
By then all the other political parties (MDR, PL, PSD, PDC,
UDPR, and PI) that had been co-opted by the RPF had been
degraded to the extent that RPF had only to choose individuals
who would not pose any problems to Kagame and the RPF. It
was now clear that RPF was no longer interested in promoting
politics in which Hutu and Tutsi could work together as equal
partners.

Earlier before this drama started unfolding, I had approached
Vice-President Paul Kagame to tell him I felt under-utilized and
I should probably leave government and find something else to do.
Within days, Cabinet appointed me to be his Director of Cabi-
net. When he became President I retained the post. I was now
the most senior civil servant in the country, running the high-
est office in Rwanda, and serving the most powerful man in the
whole country. When I discussed this new role with my siblings,
I would joke, in the words of Colonel Theoneste Lizinde, citing
President Habyarimana, " ngo ni ntahavana kapurali nzahavana
majoro" (if I am not demoted to corporal I will be promoted to
Major). I was already aware that my relationship with President
Kagame had changed. He was eager to use me against President
Bizimungu, but there was a look on him that showed he was not
fully comfortable with me either. The new job was strategic and
powerful. I was from RPF, a Tutsi, one of the inner small core of

military officers that run Rwanda, and now a gatekeeper to the most powerful man in the country.

On September 21st 2000, Dorothy and I had a new baby girl, Tina Tona. She was born in Morningside Hospital, Sandton, South Africa. Mrs. Joyce Rwetsiba was again present to witness the baby's arrival and to help Dorothy, since I was not even present this time to witness Tina's great arrival. My new service in Rwanda had been graced with another child. We were now a family of six.

CHAPTER TWENTY SEVEN

Hugging Fidel Castro

Shortly before General Paul Kagame was sworn in as President, I had the pleasure and privilege of travelling to Havana, Cuba, for the summit of the Group of 77, a United Nations caucus which was established in 1964 by 77 member countries. It is the largest intergovernmental organization of developing countries in the United Nations, "which provides the means for the countries of the South to articulate and promote their collective economic interests and enhance their joint negotiating capacity on all major international economic issues within the United Nations system, and promote South-South cooperation for development." For me, it was like a pilgrimage to Mecca. The Cuban revolution, Fidel Castro and Che Guevara had been a source of my inspiration during the period preceding the Rwandan civil war.

During the late 1980s, I used to frequent the Cuban Ambassador's residence in Kampala to read the Cuban Communist Party's paper, the *Granma*. Granma was the name of the yacht that Fidel Castro and his band of revolutionaries used to travel from Mexico to Cuba to launch the revolutionary war. The *Granma* had long articles, and sometimes equally long speeches of Castro. With some colleagues from Uganda" s military, we would hang out at the embassy, just to highlight our revolutionary credentials.

I was shocked to see the state of Havana city. Its beautiful buildings looked dilapidated. Its public and private transportation comprised of very old vehicles, probably of the 1950s and 1960s. I remembered that Communist Cuba had been subjected to an embargo by the United States for decades. I wanted to believe that it was the only explanation for the state of decay of the otherwise very beautiful city. We were all thrilled as we waited for Fidel Castro to come and speak before the gathering. In his usual green fatigues, he was evidently old and frail, but he still spoke for a long time. It had been arranged that President Castro would meet our delegation. Our delegation was of interest to Castro because at the time Rwanda was then a member of the Human Rights Council in Geneva. Cuba wanted Rwanda's vote.

Standing in the conference lobby, Fidel Castro hugged me and Rwanda's Minister of Finance, Donald Kaberuka. He asked for Rwanda's help. Fidel's warm embrace was like a leap into history. That night, I faxed an appeal to President Kagame to consider our delegation supporting Cuba. I knew it was unlikely that Rwanda would dare side with Cuba, as that would attract the wrath of the United States. I never got any response from President Kagame. When the vote came, if I can remember, Rwanda abstained. Looking at Fidel Castro, I realized that his Presidency was as old as I, and I was inwardly questioning why a true revolutionary would be in power for that long. Nevertheless Fidel's hug was like a dream come true. In my heart I was thinking that RPF's revolution must not come to that. It was clear to me that Fidel Castro and his colleagues, as well as the communist ideology itself, had had a hand in Cuba's current problems. Before I headed home my delegation had discussions with Cuban officials on Cuba-Rwanda cooperation in healthcare. There was no follow up from Rwanda's Ministry of Foreign Affairs, and I believe that initiative died a natural death.

CHAPTER TWENTY EIGHT

Gatekeeping @ Kagame's Court

When President Bizimungu was forced to resign from the Presidency, RPF staged a sham process to look like General Kagame had been elected through the right constitutional process. Dr. Charles Murigande stood "against" General Kagame in Parliament. As expected, Kagame won a "landslide victory". As Kagame's Director of Cabinet, my responsibility was to run the Office of the President. High on the agenda was to create an effective and efficient Presidency, rehabilitate the premises, establish a structure for the Office of the President, recruit personnel, build systems and motivate the workforce to support the new President in his work. Evidently, President Bizimungu's Presidency had been starved of resources. You would have thought that we were in the immediate aftermath of the civil war and genocide of 1994. The premises were unkempt. The offices were still unpainted. There was a meager skeleton of advisers and technical staff. President Kagame made it clear to me that he did not want most of President Bizimungu's advisers and staff. He was so impatient, that one time I had to fire President Bizimungu's

Chief of Protocol and his financial and administrative officer while I was on a trip abroad.

Building the Foundation

With David Himbara, President Kagame's new Principal Private Secretary, we created three tier structure of: 1) Advisors; 2) technical staff; and 3) councils that comprised of citizens from civil society and business. The structure was intended to improve efficiency while making the Presidency accessible to the general public, to influence and be influenced by it. From the very start President Kagame gave it a blessing, but he did not seem very enthusiastic about it. Almost the whole workforce at the Presidency was Tutsi, something that I was felt uncomfortable about. Within two years, the whole campus had been rehabilitated, with a campus wide computer network. The President's executive office got a facelift, with extensions, and his Cabinet Office was computerized with modern audio-visual capabilities. He had a task of making his Ministers utilize the high-tech features of the Cabinet Office, including powerpoint presentations. At the insistence of the President, the workforce at the President's office was the first to receive private cars under the new government scheme to motivate employees, while reducing the cost and waste of using government cars. While the rationale was understandable, and it had to be done because President Kagame demanded it, it was a high tax burden that was not sustainable.

Conversation on National Prosperity

The next challenge to address was the cabinet process and the content of cabinet deliberations. The Cabinet is the highest executive decision making body. The President was supposed to chair the cabinet once a week. Most often he did not, leaving the matter to Prime Minister Makuza. Cabinet sessions were often bogged down in little details that should have been dealt with by junior staff. Through the offices of the President and Prime Minister, we organized a joint delegation to Mauritius to learn how the small island in the Indian Ocean was successful in running an efficient and effective cabinet process. Beyond process, especially on matters of social and economic development, the cabinet was plagued by discussions based on aid.

Since Rwanda is a poor country, heavily dependent on foreign aid, each ministry scrambles to get its piece of the aid pie. The tax base is narrow, and national revenues are not sufficient to fund both the recurrent and development budgets. Ministries daily court diplomats and other international aid personnel to give some money, at least for seminars and workshops. The nature of the conversation in cabinet had to be different. I approached President Kagame about the need to change the conversation, and possibly to get some foreigners to facilitate it.

I contacted the World Bank Country Director for Rwanda, Emmanuel Mbi, and inquired about such facilitation and whether the Bank would be willing to help with that. Mbi gave me the contacts of an American lady whose organization had worked with the Bank. Her name was Kaia Miller, and she lived in Boston, Massachusetts. I called her and mentioned that Rwanda's cabinet would like to hold a retreat to discuss issues of economic development. She told me she worked with someone by the name of Michael Fairbanks, and that they would be happy to facilitate the Cabinet retreat. In 2000, the whole cabinet, and most senior leaders in Rwanda sat for a whole week, cell phones turned off, as Michael Fairbanks, Kaia Miller, Malik Fal, and cabinet Ministers from South Africa facilitated a lively conversation on how nations prosper.

The takeaways from the retreat, mainly borrowed from Harvard's Professor Michael Porter's *The Competitive Advantage of Nations*, were that prosperity in Rwanda is Rwanda's choice; that nations cannot compete on the basis of cheap labor and low prices; that Rwanda would get higher prices for its coffee, tea and tourism by adding value; that competitiveness is the productivity with which a country uses all its resources (human, capital and natural resources); that the business of business is to create wealth; that private and public sectors play different but interrelated roles in creating productivity; that nations compete by offering the most conducive environment for business; that you can achieve both economic growth and social equity; and, that natural endowments are important, so are policies, institutions, and quality of firms. Michael Fairbanks introduced to the participants the notion of the seven forms of capital, namely, natural endowments such as location, minerals, and climate; financial; humanly made capital, like roads, bridges, buildings; institutions; knowledge resources; human capital like skills, insights; and culture. For a nation to prosper, we were told, all these forms of capital have to increase and interact with each other.

The retreat discussed elements in a successful change process. Using a model from a seminal Harvard Business Review article by Professor John Kotter, *Why Great Transformation Efforts Fail*, Michael Fairbanks and his colleagues discussed how to create a climate for change through building a sense of urgency, building guiding teams, and getting the vision right; engaging and enabling the organization through communication for buy-in, enabling broad-based action and creating short term wins; and through implementing and sustaining the change by being relentless and making it part of the organizational culture.

Introducing Pete Senge's *Fifth Discipline*, the retreat facilitators also articulated the importance of "mental models" or "mindsets" in shaping the process of creating prosperity. They are, they said, basically personal maps of how the world works. These sets of beliefs can be pro-or anti-development, and they can change. In short, change had to begin with our beliefs and attitudes, our mental models on how we were going to create equitable prosperity for all Rwandans. The facilitators also told us that the process of building a new order requires organizations that are capable of adapting and changing. Since organizations are social in nature, the people within them have to master themselves, build learning teams around a shared vision, and learn to "think system". It was evident that thinking system, working as a team and collaborating were not strengths that we had in government or in society as a whole. It was refreshing to listen to these ideas. A good student of historical and dialectical materialism would not have found them new. It remained to be seen how we would translate all this into real change and gains for all Rwandans.

President Kagame was very happy with the cabinet retreat, and asked me to engage Kaia Miller and Michael Fairbanks to work with us to promote value-adding for coffee, tea and tourism. He also asked me to pursue help from the World Bank. When I asked Emmanuel Mbi, the World Bank Country Director for Rwanda who had recommended the two consultants, he said the Bank does not support that kind of work. I was disappointed. When I reported back to President Kagame he was equally disappointed, and decided that we would fund the work from Rwanda's own resources. I relayed the instructions to the Minister of Finance, Donald Kaberuka. I detected a hesitancy on the part of Kaberuka, but he would finally give his full support of to the effort because President Kagame wanted it. Kaberuka, an economist himself and now the President of the African Development Bank, most likely found the consultant's views not rocket science. I did not find the ideas rocket science either. But, sometimes, though paradoxical, you may be able to change an internal conversation by using external facilitators. Rwanda's internal conversation was too focused on aid, the World Bank, IMF, routine workshops and seminars. Once President Kagame gave it full support, everyone had to come along whether they wanted it or not. Subsequently, through the work of Michael Fairbank's *Onthe-Frontier Group*, it would lead to some degree of value adding in coffee, tea, tourism and, overall, an improved image of Rwanda as a place ready to do business and compete.

It had been a long journey as far as my ideological inclination was concerned. From being the harsh critic of capitalism, I was now courting the disciples of capitalism to teach Rwandans the way to personal and national prosperity. Their views did not entirely displace a few of the Marxist tenets that still underpin modern economic analysis. I still wondered how the models we were discussing could be translated into real gains of the rural peasant, or the increasingly large numbers of the urban unemployed. Still, I thought contact with capitalism's disciples could help Rwanda access knowledge and skills in management, science, technology, innovation, entrepreneurship, trade and investment. Though the price of the consulting has not been proportional to the value Rwanda has obtained, it has been, in my estimate, worth the effort.

Conversation on Security

Another conversation, this time on a sensitive subject of security, did not go far. After the civil war and genocide, post 1994 RPF was understandably obsessed with security, albeit in narrow sense. There was, as I mentioned earlier in the book, a sense of siege within RPF and the Tutsi. Our outlook was conditioned by our perspectives on security. Yet, there was an air of triumphalism and invincibility within the RPF/RPA. RPA had won the civil war in 1994. It had pursued the defeated ex-FAR and militia, closed the refugee camps in DRC, launched a military campaign that ended with the fall of Africa's longest serving pro-western dictator, President Mobutu, and installed a pro-Kagame President Laurent Kabila in Kinshasa. A second foray into Congo in 1998 had been abortive, but still Rwanda's army was considered, regionally and internationally, a strong, efficient and effective machinery. President Kagame was seen as a visionary and strategic General. In Washington and London, the key western backers seemed to adore him. Still, the decisions to go to war in DRC had, as usual, been solely taken outside constitutional powers. Rwanda's parliament had not been consulted. President Bizimungu, as well as other senior leaders in RPF, had been informed after the fact.

Clare Short, the British Secretary for the Department International Development (DFID) at that time was President Kagame's adoring friend. She had suggested that DFID would support a national conversation on Rwanda's security, geared towards security sector reform. King's College, of the University of London, could help us organize such a conversation along the lines of the dialogue on national prosperity. Just as we had Harvard's people on the economic front, we could have King's College on the security front. President Kagame tasked me to organize that. As I contacted the professors at King's College, I could already sense that the conversation was bound to be difficult.

RPF had a limited conception of security that suited its politics. The 1994 Human Development Report defines human security as people's "safety from chronic threats and protection from sudden hurtful disruptions in the patterns of daily life." Seven types of security are listed as components of human security: economic security; food security; health security; environmental security; personal (physical) security; community security; and political security. Human security addresses such issues as organized crime and violence, human rights and governance, armed conflict and intervention, genocide and mass crimes, health and development, and resources and environment.

RPF looks at human rights and governance, armed conflict and intervention, and post-war and post-genocide reconstruction with a lot of sensitivity. Matters of security sector reform were even more sensitive than anything else. RPF had a narrative that was followed by every RPF and government official. According to this narrative, RPF had stopped the genocide when the whole international community abandoned Rwandans. RPF had fought and won the war in Rwanda and in the DRC. Only RPF knew how to stop and prevent genocide. RPF needed no lectures from foreigners about managing the security of Rwanda. The subject of security sector reform in post-conflict, post-genocide societies was ambitious.

> The Organization for Economic Cooperation and Development (OECD) Development Assistance Committee (DAC) Guidelines on Security System Reform and Governance agreed by ministers in 2004 define the security system as including: core security actors (e.g. armed forces, police, gendarmerie, border guards, customs and immigration, and intelligence and security services); security management and oversight bodies (e.g. ministries of defense and internal affairs, financial management bodies and public complaints commissions); justice and law enforcement institutions (e.g. the judiciary, prisons, prosecution services, traditional justice systems); and non-statutory security forces (e.g. private security companies, guerrilla armies and private militia).

Subjecting Rwanda's military to civilian oversight, bringing a measure of transparency to its otherwise secretive operations, and relating the issue of security sector reform to the rule of law were matters that President Kagame and his RPF advisors were not yet ready for. In the end a general draft position paper was written by the King's College Professors, and the one-day event took place, and any hint by the professors to broaden the debate beyond RPF's narrative were treated with suspicion and stonewalling. Clare Short had not been forthcoming with her promise for DFID's financial support to the process, and President Kagame was not motivated either to support it. It was shelved and allowed to die a natural death.

Nurturing the Workforce

From the early days when RPF captured state power, the whole machinery of the state had run simply on the passion, enthusiasm, and energy of the RPF cadres and Rwandans who cared to contribute to raising Rwanda from the ruins of 1994. Many did not have the necessary qualifications to work in a modern bureaucracy. Those that had academic qualifications had not worked in a state bureaucracy before. Finding the right people to be in the right place, with clear job descriptions and performance criteria remained big challenges in the whole of government. From the time we landed at the office of the President, we had to create the structure, define roles and recruit personnel. We had rehabilitated the work place, provided the tools (a campus-wide computer network), and created a costly scheme for private car ownership. It was a privilege for me to work with motivated men and women, who worked long hours even without compensation. Nevertheless, I could see we all had to get down to learning how to be better managers and leaders every day.

During my last year in Washington, D.C., I had attended a time management seminar organized by Franklin Covey. Based on Steven Covey's bestselling book, *Seven Habits of Highly Effective People*, the workshop was of great help in planning ahead, on a weekly basis, what one considered to be one's priorities. The basic premise of Covey's work is that we have to gradually move from dependence, independence and finally to interdependence, from private victory to public victory. The starting point of victory is to begin with the end in mind (even imagining the eulogy at your own burial); being proactive to seize the opportunities in your life, setting your priorities right by putting first things first, thinking win-win instead of win-lose, synergizing (linking your efforts with those of others to have maximum impact), horning your listening skills by seeking to understand others before they can understand you, and finally, sharpening your saw (physical, mental, emotional, and spiritual energy).

I also found Covey's work on time management very useful. Good time management, he argues, would require you to spend more time in quadrant II in the matrix. That is where preparation, planning, prevention, relationship building and personal development take place. At the Office of the President, I personally found it extremely difficult to strike a balance between quadrant I and II. Most of my days were in quadrant I. My day was always filled with fire-fighting activities. I thought I should engage the workforce at the Presidency in this kind of training, which I had found useful. I tried to look for Franklin Covey's presence in Africa and found out they had an office in Johannesburg, South Africa. I called the office and spoke to somebody by the name of Jay Owens. I told him what I was looking for and soon we organized to have two workshops, one on time management and a second one on leadership

	Urgent	Not Urgent
Important	**I** - Crisis - Pressing Issues - Deadlines - Meetings	**II** - Preparation - Planning - Prevention - Relationship building - Personal Development
Not Important	**III** - Interruptions - Some mail - Many popular activities	**IV** - Trivia - Some phone calls - Excessive TV/Games - Time wasters

Franklin Covey's four roles of leadership sounded like the kind of leadership I would have liked to promote at the Presidency: to be good role models for the rest of government and society, to be pathfinders, to empower others, and to align thinking and actions in the whole government and society to achieve transformation.

I invited all personnel at the Office of the President, and others from various government departments and civil society to attend. Jay Owens was animating and I thought we had great time learning from him. I was surprised a few days later after the second workshop when President Kagame called a meeting with my junior staff, and criticized me for having organized the workshop and even hinted that I may have shared money with Jay Owens. It hurt me, because I hadn't sought or received money from Jay Owens, a very decent man. I kept on wondering why a Head of State would think in those terms. I assured him nothing improper had taken place, that the effort was geared towards developing ourselves, as his team, to deliver on the promises RPF and himself had made. From then on, I realized that my relationship with him was unravelling towards some end game which I could not fully grasp.

In the early days after I returned from Washington, D.C., I visited President Kagame's chief of security detail, Tom Byabagamba, in King Faisal Hospital, in Kigali. On his bedside was a copy of the book, *48 Laws of Power* by Robert Greene. I picked the copy and read Law No.1:

Law 1
Never Outshine the Master

Always make those above you feel comfortably superior. In your desire to please or impress them, do not go too far in displaying your talents or you might accomplish the opposite – inspire fear and insecurity. Make your masters appear more brilliant than they are and you will attain the heights of power.

I was surprised that there were copies around a number of offices. Was that a message on how to deal with President Kagame?

Dealing with President Kagame himself proved to be a challenge that I had never imagined. One of the challenges I faced, I realized, was that my immediate boss happened to be the President of Rwanda. We had worked together, but my responsibilities then had taken me away from the theatre of war most of the time. Even as RPF Secretary-General I did not work with him directly every day. Now, for the first time, I would work directly for him, and report to him. There was a need to understand his strengths, weaknesses, pressures, goals, work styles and needs. I needed to understand our mutual expectations, and especially his goals and objectives. I needed to understand myself better so that we could build a profitable working relationship.

In their seminal 1980 Harvard Business Review article, *Managing Your Boss*, John Gabarro and John Kotter warned:

> At a minimum, you need to appreciate your boss's goals and pressures. Without this information, you are flying blind, and problems are inevitable. Bosses, like everyone else, are imperfect and fallible. They don't have unlimited time, encyclopedic knowledge, or extrasensory perception; nor are they evil enemies

I was determined to make the relationship a fruitful one for him, the Presidency, myself, the government and Rwandan society in general. Most of the time, I would see that he was under intense pressure. I would, in general, appreciate the overall and specific goals. I also tried to just read his mind, using my intuition and overall knowledge I had about RPF, and went ahead and did what I needed to do.

Constitution-making and Elections

The period 2000-2004 was a busy one for Rwanda. It was necessary to end the political transition that began in 1994 after RPF came to power. RPF wanted a constitution, and new national symbols to replace the old ones. I was already stressed by what I saw as missing ingredients of a successful transition. RPF had failed to work with other political parties. Within RPF and outside it, the Hutu had been marginalized. I personally was not enthusiastic about changing the national symbols. I wondered whether symbols had to change every time there is change. I also thought a whole Rwandan generation, both Hutu and Tutsi, identified itself with the old symbols of the 1959 revolution. I had also learned that flags and national anthems, important as they were, had not matched the aspirations of the African people, whose hopes had been destroyed by dictatorial regimes across the continent. There were more important priorities for Rwanda. There was some minimal debate as to whether there should be Presidential and parliamentary elections. Some people in RPF thought it was premature to go for elections, since the Hutu would elect one of their own in any free and fair election. I was among the few but influential voices around President Kagame who cautioned that we could not postpone elections forever. Better we manage them smartly, even allowing cheating, but to levels like 75% of the vote, which would be much easier to explain.

The first to be accomplished was the change of the national symbols. In 2001, Rwanda adopted a new national anthem, flag and court of arms:

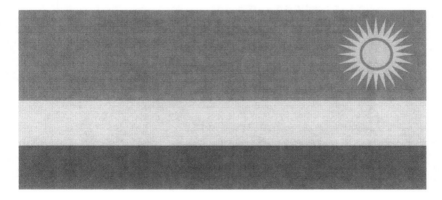

The green symbolizes prosperity; the yellow, potential and real economic development; the blue, happiness; and the sun, symbolizing enlightenment. The court of arms has unity, work and patriotism as the pillars of the new dispensation under RPF and President Kagame.

The new Rwandan National Anthem was *Rwanda Nziza*.

-Kinyarwanda lyrics

> Rwanda nziza Gihugu cyacu
> Wuje imisozi, ibiyaga n'ibirunga
> Ngobyi iduhetse gahorane ishya.
> Reka tukurate tukuvuge ibigwi
> Wowe utubumbiye hamwe twese
> Abanyarwanda uko watubyaye
> Berwa, sugira, singizwa iteka.
>
> Horana Imana, murage mwiza
> Ibyo tugukesha ntibishyikirwa;
> Umuco dusangiye uraturanga
> Ururimi rwacu rukaduhuza

Ubwenge, umutima,amaboko yacu
Nibigukungahaze bikwiye
Nuko utere imbere ubutitsa.

Abakurambere b'intwari
Bitanze batizigama
Baraguhanga uvamo ubukombe
Utsinda ubukoroni na mpatsibihugu
Byayogoje Afurika yose
None uraganje mu bwigenge
Tubukomeyeho uko turi twese.
Komeza imihigo Rwanda dukunda
Duhagurukiye kukwitangira
Ngo amahoro asabe mu bagutuye
Wishyire wizane muri byose
Urangwe n'ishyaka, utere imbere
Uhamye umubano n'amahanga yose
Maze ijabo ryawe riguhe ijambo

English Translation

Motherland, would be always filled of happiness
Us all your children: Abanyarwanda
Let us sing your glare and proclaim your high facts
You, maternal bosom of us all
Would be admired forever, prosperous and cover of praises.

Invaluable heritage, that God protects to you
You filled us priceless goods
Our common culture identifies us
Our single language unifies us
That our intelligence, our conscience and our forces
Fill you with varied riches
For an unceasingly renewed development.

Our valorous ancestors
Gave themselves bodies and souls
As far as making you a big nation
You overcame the colonial-imperialistic yoke
That has devastated Africa entirely
And has your joy of your sovereign independence
Acquired that constantly we will defend.

Maintain this cape, beloved Rwanda,
Standing, we commit for you
So that peace reigns countrywide
That you are free of all hindrance
That your determination hires progress

Source: http://www.nationalanthems.me/rwanda-rwanda-nziza/

With a new flag, court of arms, and national anthem, RPF sought to reinvent Rwanda. The symbols of the Hutu Revolution of 1959 were discarded. New symbols representing RPF, or "Tutsi" power, were now in place. People who grew up in Rwanda since the 1959 revolution, especially Hutu, do not identify themselves with these symbols. Their attitude is "Those are *their* symbols, not *ours*".

The next item on the agenda was a new constitution. On May 26, 2003, President Paul Kagame promulgated the new Rwanda Constitution. Apart from reference to genocide, the preamble was similar to the Arusha Peace Agreement of 1993. Democracy, rule of law, fundamental freedoms, unity, equal rights, power sharing and dialogue were all mentioned. So was reference to international legal instruments in human rights and humanitarian law. Like the Arusha Peace Agreement, the constitution provides for separation of the powers of the executive, the legislature and the judiciary. It even clearly stipulates that the judiciary is independent. Throughout what should have been consultations with other political forces and other stakeholders before the national referendum on the constitution, it was clear that RPF wanted to make a constitution that was tailored to President Paul Kagame. Seven year terms, excessive presidential powers to hire and fire most of the senior leaders in all branches of government, and curtailing political freedoms in practice were entrenched in the constitution

Finally, the general elections ending the transition were held on 25 August, 2003. Everything had been done to make sure RPF comes out with a maximum vote. Other political parties had either been fully co-opted (PL and PSD) or intimidated using the law and flimsy charges (MDR). Faustin Twagiramungu and Jean-Nepomuscene Nayinzira, the competitors in the election, had to stand as independents. The RPF and RPA security network made sure these two could not campaign freely. People were barred from attending their election rallies. On the polling day, RPF cadres, and soldiers manning the polling stations had even marked ballot papers to check how Hutu leaders in government, like Prime Minister Bernard Makuza, would vote. The Chairman of the National Electoral Commission, Professor Chrysologue Karangwa, an overzealous Tutsi wanted to give RPF maximum victory by any means necessary.

On election day, I followed the election results through General James Kabarebe and James Musoni, who at that time was the Executive Director of Rwanda Revenue Authority. When the results came, RPF cadres had gone beyond what would have been reasonable rigging. RPF had all the votes. There was an internal crisis as President Kagame and his other top RPF cadres scrambled to climb down from over 100% to 95.1%, giving former Prime Minister Twagiramungu 3.6% of the vote, and, Nayinzira, 1.6% of the vote. Later, when President Kagame and I met, lamented saying, " You see, your cadres are fools; how could they mismanage the whole thing?" I had nothing to say. In my mind I had already confirmed that RPF had taken a wrong turn, and was heading in the wrong direction.

Kisangani Wars

During my term at the office of the President, from 2000-
2004, other issues dominated President Kagame's agenda. In
August, 1999, Rwandan and Ugandan troops fought in DRC's
third large city, Kisangani. The former allies and comrades-in-
arms from the days of Uganda's resistance to RPF's struggle and
military victory in Rwanda were now enemies. The fighting in
Kisangani tested the limits of the relationship between Presidents Museveni and Kagame. Both armies were in a foreign land
for reasons that could no longer be justified. Questions of ego
and adventurism amongst Rwanda's and Uganda's military commanders on the field were a big factor. Excessive ego and desire to
control places, people and events on the part of President Museveni and President Kagame had ultimately led to the Kisangani
debacle. It takes time and effort to build a relationship. It takes a
short time to destroy one.

At the height of the political and military crisis between
Uganda and Rwanda, Tanzania's President Ben Mkapa tried
to reconcile the former friends turned enemies. In a meeting
in Mwanza, President Mkapa listened to President Museveni's
explanation of the Kisangani events, adding that it had created
enzigo (a need for revenge), between him and Kagame. President
Mkapa shook his head and saying he did not understand this
"mambo ya enzigo" (this whole thing about enzigo). He advised
that they better find a way of resolving it.

Later, as tension was building up between Uganda and
Rwanda, President Kagame sent Dr. Charles Murigande,
Dr. Emmanuel Ndahiro and I to see President Museveni
in Kampala. We had a long meeting in the night, in which
we discussed the deteriorating relationship between the two
countries. President Museveni was irked by a statement made
by Dr. Ndahiro. There were deployments by the two sides in
the DRC areas in north Kivu. Dr. Ndahiro suggested that

Uganda should desist from deploying there since it was likely to lead to clashes with Rwanda's troops. To President Museveni, this might have sounded like a threat and he fired at us a long lecture, warning that should we try mischief again, we would learn a lesson we would never forget. As if that was not enough, I made matters worse a few moments later by hinting that some people say that his own brother, Salim Saleh, and General Kazini who commanded Uganda's forces in Congo, were partly to blame for the escalation. He lectured us gain that he knows his soldiers well, he knows that some of his relatively uneducated soldiers were his best fighters, and that it was not Rwanda's business to interfere in Uganda's choices.

Dr. Murigande created a calmer atmosphere when he narrated to President Museveni the Biblical story of the ancient Jewish prophet, Jonah, who resisted a mission from God to go to Nineveh to tell people to repent, only to end up in the belly of a fish. I do not remember what the moral of the story was, but I do remember President Museveni, himself a Christian well versed in the Holy Bible, relaxing and smiling. Dr. Ndahiro and I were sent for another mission later to meet President Museveni. After meeting President Museveni, Kale Kayihura, his military advisor, Dr. Ndahiro, and I, were trying write a short paragraph on how Uganda and Rwanda could work together in DRC, when I got a call from President Kagame, instructing us to come back home immediately.

Though I had worked with President Museveni a number of occasions before, I could sense that President Kagame no longer trusted me to deal with Uganda any more. Strangely, the last thing he ever asked me again to do on the Uganda front was to head, jointly with General James Kabarebe, a committee to devise a military response to Uganda's possible future attack on Rwanda, or a preemptive one if necessary. I did not show much interest in the matter, and General Kabarebe met me only once in my office to discuss it. We never met again on the matter. I presumed it was now being handled by others, and President Kagame never asked me about it.

During that period, we also had to deal with the fall out of a letter President Museveni wrote to British Secretary for International Development, Clare Short. Both President Museveni and President Kagame were close to Clare Short. Uganda and Rwanda are the closest allies to U.K in the region. Ugandans were shocked to find the letter in our hands.

The letter was quite revealing for two reasons. First, we who had been inspired by Yoweri Museveni found it unfriendly and insulting that he would describe all of us as ideologically bankrupt. Second, from somebody who had created a reputation for preaching African self-reliance, it was disheartening that he would be begging from the British to build his army. On anything that touched President Kagame, his inner kitchen staff had to rise in one voice to denounce President Museveni. The principle mobiliser at this time was Dr. Emmanuel Ndahiro, with Joseph Bideri playing the trigger-happy sharp-shooter, always eager to write caustic missives, occasionally using the Daily Monitor whose editors we had motivated to be pro-Rwanda. I wrote twice, once in the New Vision, and another time in the Daily Monitor, responding to Amama Mbabazi's piece regarding the sour relations between the two countries.

President Kagame and I had to go through the letter I had drafted for the Daily Monitor, paragraph by paragraph. I had concluded the letter saying that there was a time for war and a time for peace; and that it was the time for peace.

Hotel Builder

The last project I did for the RPF government was the construction of a five star hotel, Hotel Intercontinental, which later became Serena Hotel. The Government of Rwanda had contracted a South African firm of Architects, and a Uganda based international construction company, ROKO, to build the hotel. Work had begun, but then stalled. President Kagame called a couple of Ministers, including Minister Kaberuka of Finance, and Minister Sam Nkusi of the Ministry of Infrastructure, to ask why the project was stalling. At the end of the meeting, President Kagame asked me to lead the team of the ministers and other technical staff with a task of completing the project by the end of 2003. It was a signal that the project was dear to him, and he wanted to use the power of the office to make sure the project had funding, and the contractors understood this was a high stakes project.

In the course of time, I had to stop the day to day work at the Office of the President, and set up shop at the project site. I worked with an extremely dedicated group of Rwanda government technical staff. At one point over 2000 people worked at the site, working in shifts, and most of them foreigners from Uganda and South Africa. I discovered that most Rwandans did not seek work at the project site because it involved working long hours. The final phase of the work also required skills that Rwandans possess.

As President Kagame put pressure on me, I in turn put pressure on the South African consultants, the contractor, my staff at the project site, and the government's financial institutions. The contractor was demanding payment, and government was finding it difficult to keep up with the fast pace of work. President Kagame instructed me to convene a meeting with the Central Bank President, Francois Kanimba, his Vice- President, Conso Rusagara, as well as representatives of Banque Populaire and Caisse Sociale to make sure funds were available from these institutions. Working from a narrow capital base, the leaders of these latter two institutions told me their precarious situation but I made sure they understood that my boss wanted it done, immediately. They had to make the funds available. I came to learn about the elaborate system of letters of credit, the role of Alfred Kalisa who helped a lot with the transactions that involved the bank, *Bank* of Commerce Development and Industry (BCDI), which he co-owned with RPF, and the Eastern and Southern African Trade and Development Bank (PTA Bank).

As the year slowly drew to a close, the pressure was intense. My staff and I would leave the project site to go home at midnight, and we would be early to be around the project site at 4 am to pressurize the contractor to begin the morning shift. One time, standing on top of a Caterpillar, an earth-moving machinery, I addressed all the workers at the site, promising them a bonus if they worked longer hours. I was under pressure from Dr. Ndahiro to move the business of airlifting building materials from South Africa to Silverback Cargo, RPF's company. I also had to manage the special and bizarre relationship between President Kagame and Bosco Rusagara, the businessman whose clearing and forwarding company had the contract to clear all materials that were destined for the hotel.

We had already poured over 30 million US dollars into the project, and the chain that was supposed to run the hotel, Intercontinental Hotels, insisted the finishing had to meet their standards. Southern Sun of South Africa was supposed to be the intermediary. Hence, all the workers who were doing the finishing work had to be from South Africa. There were several subcontractors at the site. I was very much focused on construction work, and not on various tendering work that went on. The Secretary of the National Tender Board, David Musemakweri, was responsible for this matter. I then learnt that Jack Nziza was involved in the tendering decisions.

One night, at around 3 am, I got a call from a furious President Kagame asking me why I had given gift shops to people like Alfred Kalisa, and Joy, late General Rwigyema's sister. He also asked me why I had given tenders for landscaping to Mrs. Rosette Kayumba (General Kayumba Nyamwasa's wife), and Alfred Kalisa's wife, Mrs. Isabelle Kalisa. As it always happened during the four years I worked closely with Kagame, I noted that he worked mainly at night, and I am a day person. He would make his calls late at night, and I had developed a habit to give Dorothy breathing space (and protecting my conversation with a Head of State) by either going to the sitting room, or relocating to the bathroom to take his calls. When he asked me about this I did not have a clue. It was not my duty. When I told him I did not know and that I would ask, he said, "So what are you doing at the project?"

I told him there was a lot of work to do there. He asked me why we should reward people who hate us, like Mrs. Isabelle Kalisa. Then he asked me to find Alfred Kalisa of BCDI and tell him to make a choice between us and his wife. I was silent on the phone. He probably realized that I was not fully supportive of the idea, and would not do it. Then he said he would tell Jack Nziza to handle that. I was relieved. How could I approach any man to ask him to abandon his wife so as to be friends with President Kagame? Alfred and Isabelle Kalisa had been kind and supportive to RPF during and after the civil war. One time Chairman Kanyarengwe and I were accompanied by Kalisa to meet President Babangida of Nigeria. Isabelle Kalisa helped me draft a memo we delivered to President Babangida. Whenever I visited Nigeria, I stayed with the family. President Kagame made it clear to me that all decisions concerning the three small gift shops at the hotel, and the landscaping, had to be reversed. In turn, I instructed David Musemakweri of the National Tenderboard, and Sam Nkusi, State Minisiter for Infrastructure, to formally reverse the decisions. In my mind, I was wondering where the President gets time to worry about three small gift shops and planting grass on a small compound, when he has millions of people and a whole country to deal with.

When it came to recruiting hotel staff as we got close to hotel operations, Jack Nziza was everywhere. He was supposedly doing security checks, but he made sure most of the staff was hired well knowing they would be his informants. Merit was not a major consideration at that time. Loyalty to the security organs of the state was. The Rwandan recruits were almost all Tutsi. In early 2004, Hotel Intercontinental started operations. I had decided not to deal with the Southern Sun hotel on Lake Kivu in Gisenyi, northern Rwanda. I agreed with the contactors that we could only handle one project at a time. The Gisenyi hotel work had to wait till the main project in Kigali was done. By the time hotel operations began, Rwanda had spent almost 40 million US dollars.

Jacuzzi Wars

While I struggled to finish the hotel project, I had another incomplete one at the Presidency, one that would cause me much anguish and a trigger for my departure. As part of the overall rehabilitation of the Office of the President at Urugwiro Village, there was a small complex in front of the executive office that was under renovation. It was planned to be a place where the President would host small receptions. It was close to completion, when we discovered that some very few and minor kitchen items, from a Kenyan supplier, were rusty and of poor quality. I instructed the Director of General Administration to get in touch with the suppliers and make sure they supply as per agreement.

One day, I was at Kanombe Airport, seeing off President Kagame, to an international trip, when then Commissioner of General Police, Frank Mugambage, took me aside, and told me that the President had asked him to investigate me on the matter of rusty saucepans and sinks. I said they should go ahead. Soon one of his bright officers, Bayingana (we called him boy because of his youthful looks), would find me at the hotel project site to begin the investigations. It hurt me that the President would not raise the matter with me, and would prefer to work through law enforcement without first hearing my version of the story.

While on a brief visit to the United States, one night I received a call from one of my secretaries who told me that President Kagame had been in a very angry mood that day. This was not particularly surprising since President Kagame exudes negative energy at the office on a daily basis. She told me one of the civilians who worked on the project had been detained. I was used to his emotional outbursts. His arrival at the office was occasionally greeted with fear from the main gate to his executive office. Soldiers at the gate, secretaries, and staff in general would always be in panic mode as he arrived. Sometimes, his wife, Jeannette, would alert staff that he was coming and that he was angry. Since I run his office I would on such occasions go to his office and find a pretext to brief him on some matter. I would read his face carefully, and if I found him not interested, I would find reason to quickly extricate myself and allow him to nurse his anger alone. Most of the time, he would conceal his anger and deal with me as if nothing was bothering him. I had never been physically abused by him, but I was aware that he did occasionally beat his military officers.

When I came back from my trip to the United States, I tried to piece together what had happened. Soon after, my brother, Gerald Gahima, came to my house to tell me that he had met President Kagame on other matters, and that he had complained that I was arrogant, had disobeyed him, and that if I had been around he would have beaten me. It so happens that the matter, once again, was a very trivial one that I am even embarrassed to narrate it. Someone reading this may conclude that we Africans, irrespective of rank, are pitifully petty. Since it has been subject to much speculation, it is better I explain as it shades some light into President Kagame's inherent insecurity and character flaws.

As part of the renovation of the President's Club (as we called it), we had imported bathtubs. Unfortunately, the contractor was not wise enough to leave room for getting the bathtubs inside once the narrow doors had been fixed. Earlier, I had given a tour of the premises to President Kagame and his wife Jeannette. When he saw the two bathtubs lying outside the building, he asked me why and I explained that it had been an oversight on the part of the contractor, who now had to figure out other options of getting them inside, The contractor had explained to me that they would either have to remove the doors, expand the entrance, and re-fix the doors, or, they would remove part of the wall, put the bathtubs into place, and re-fix the wall. I recounted the options to President Kagame, and he was against removing the doors, or removing part of the wall.

On the day I was leaving for the United States, Serge, the civilian who worked on the project as a consultant, told me they had found a solution for the bathtubs that did not involve removing the door or the wall. He explained the option briefly. They would remove a couple of iron sheets from the roofing, lift the bathtubs, lower them into place, and then re-fix the narrow gap in the roof. I told him to go ahead and do as proposed. When the President came to know about this, he was furious. I had disobeyed him, he told people, including my brother. The bathtub or Jacuzzi war, as Dorothy and I call the silly episode, would prove to be a fatal mistake, one that would subsequently be the basis of a treason charge against me.

When I sought for an appointment with him, it took two weeks. This was very unusual. Normally we would sometimes speak on the phone a number of times a day. I was always a priority if and when I wanted to see him. He normally returned my calls promptly.

When he finally met me, his anger had subsided, but he asked me, "Theogene, if you were in my shoes what would you think if you give instructions to a subordinate, and he disobeys you?" He said he did not know what he would have done to me had I been present the day he discovered what I had done. I explained to him the circumstances, and reassured him I was not being disrespectful. I could see he was not convinced and I thought the matter was over.

CHAPTER TWENTY NINE

Daddy, I Hate Government

My routine and exhausting work at the Presidency took so much of my time, that there would be little left for my family. I was on call twenty four hours, seven days a week. I left home for duty at 7 am, and often returned after midnight. Sometime my kids would not see me for days. One day, my wife made a telling and serious request: could we make an appointment to see each other? The hotel project had even exerted more demands on my time. I had a special secure cell phone on which the President called me. I carried a second cell phone that virtually rang all the time. Senior government officials, diplomats, office staff, business people, and generally other members of society called me seeking the attention of the office or the President himself. As a gatekeeper, you protect the President while making sure the public and his government officials have access to him. Occasionally, he would refuse to meet people, and I would have to step in to deal with the matter. Sometimes, he would meet people in public functions and they would tell him how they have tried to reach him without success. He would say his people (especially me) did not tell him.

Some time in mid-2003, I ventured to take my family out for lunch on a Saturday. Many days of absence from my family's daily routine had begun to take its toll on me and my family. An occasional treat of this kind served as a palliative for me to cool down my guilt-laden conscience. As the kids excitedly climbed into the car, and Dorothy was getting ready in the passenger seat, my hotline rang. It was President Kagame and he wanted me immediately for a meeting. It had happened many times before when I was with Dorothy, and I guess she was used to it. Some time the hotline would ring when we were in the middle of having dinner, and I would windup quickly to respond to "Afande's" call. When I told the kids that we could not go, and we had to wait until I was done with some work, there was profound disbelief on their faces. As I hurriedly ushered them into the house, my six-year old daughter, Mwiza, asked me, "Who was that on the phone?" I told her it was President Kagame. Then she said, "Can I talk to him?" I told her next time I would allow her to talk to him. Then she asked again, "Daddy, who do you work for? I told her, "I work for Government." She paused for a moment, and then said, "Daddy, I hate government". I asked her why she hates government. She said, "government always wants to be king and queen, wanting to be boss all the time." I told her government is good because it keeps bad people away from us. She said, "there are no bad people in our house." I told her government provides schools and hospitals. She said she already has a school, Green Hills Academy. I told her we would continue the conversation later when I returned. I could see her main concern was why President Kagame and something called government would take away the attention and time of her father.

As I drove to the meeting with President Kagame I kept on thinking about Mwiza's question. Had President Kagame and government service pushed me to the extremes of self-and family neglect? On the surface I looked accomplished and powerful. I had access to a highly sought after Head of State. I had several people working under me, and others from various institutions of government who wanted my attention as they solicited the attention of the President. Dorothy and I hosted diplomats and visiting dignitaries at our house, courting them to become Rwanda's friends. Occasionally, visiting friends would be given VIP treatment as I used the President's special helicopter to take them to see mountain gorillas in the Virunga mountains in the north of the country. Sometimes, I would use RPA's motorized boats to give the VIPs a tour of Lake Kivu. I had on a number of occasions used the President's executive jets on missions wthin Africa, and once in a while travelled with him on his first-class jet with a first-class service on board.

By the end of 2002, Dorothy and I had completed building a beautiful mansion we had started constructing from the days when we were in Washington, D.C. I used to call it the *Titanic* because we had borrowed heavily to build it and I felt we could lose it any moment I left government. My monthly earning from government about the equivalent of U.S. $1,200, but the majority of government workers earned less than U.S.$ 100 , in a country where the majority are poor, earning less than a dollar per day. At my household there was an army of workers: a chef, two maids, security, a driver and a gardener. I was driven in a government-owned Toyota Land Cruiser, and my wife had her own Mercedes Benz.

Despite all the above trappings of power and privilege, I was facing a deep personal crisis. My mind was at war with itself, and I was physically exhausted. Back in 1998, I had suggested to then Vice-President Kagame that I should leave government. The reasons then had more to do with attacks that were coming indirectly from him. He had convinced me that the revolution was still young and required all of our efforts. Working closely with him since my return from Washington, D.C. in 1999, I was able to learn a lot about the state of RPF, the government, and the President himself.

Since 1994 I had witnessed the capture of state power by RPF. At the time, I loved asserting RPF's power over other political parties but still felt there was need to coexist. I had spent little time in Rwanda to influence the evolution of RPF's relationship with other political parties. I had seen the fallout of Seth Sendashonga, Faustin Twagiramungu, and others who had joined the RPF coalition on the basis of the Arusha Agreement. I was uncomfortable about the fading away of the Arusha spirit, but I did not mind at the time, since RPF and Tutsi survival were my primary consideration. I had seen how Vice President Kagame ruled from behind the scenes, making President Bizimungu increasingly look like a figurehead. That was not new. That is how then Vice Chairman Kagame controlled RPF, even when Chairman Alexis Kanyarengwe was the formal boss of the organization. I saw the potential danger, but, like everyone else, I kept the matter to myself. It was in all our interest, we used to say. The Tutsi had to rally behind Kagame. His habits would gradually decline as the institutions grew stronger and their rule gradually replaced the rule of one strongman.

I had seen how Kagame orchestrated his capture of the top political post of RPF chairmanship in 1998 and of the Presidency in 2000. As I run his office I realized how he controlled the legislature, the executive, the judiciary, all security institutions, and the party, RPF. I saw the degradation, co-option, and/or destruction of other political parties. Privately, in my mind, I was beginning to question the wisdom and sustainability of Kagame's and RPF's quest for absolute dominance. I would not have minded a prominent and vanguard role of the RPF, but, ten years after war and genocide, some degree of healthy competition was necessary to keep the organization on its toes, and prevent the possibility of losing it all in the future.

A more sinister realization was, however, the extent to which President Kagame and a few in the security establishment were involved in targeted assassinations and human rights abuses in Rwanda and the DRC. During the civil war I had worked mainly on the external front, and my interaction with the military was minimal. Now, at the Presidency I was working directly with officers who run the elite Presidential Republican Guard that protects the President. I facilitated them in various ways, allowing them privileged access to resources necessary for their work. Sometimes I travelled with them in the advance party to prepare for the President's visits abroad. I talked to a number of senior military officers who assumed that I was very close to President Kagame and, therefore, I knew all he knew. I picked a lot of information from conversations.

There were details on how the Habyarimana plane was shot down; how the operation to kill the Bishops and priests of Kabgayi was carried out; how the massacre of Kibeho was carried out; how our military had killed Hutu in Congo until they simply got tired; how they would ferry dead bodies by helicopter from the insurgency operations in northern Rwanda and bury them in mass graves in Akagera National Park; how Jack Nziza managed the assassinations of Seth Sendashonga and Col. Theoneste Lizinde in Nairobi; how General James Kabarebe had organized the assassination of President Laurent Kabila; how several Hutu soldiers in President Bizimungu's security detail had been killed and buried in secret locations after he was removed from power; etc. It saddened me that young officers and men of what was supposed to be a revolutionary army would talk about killing so easily and with laughter and smiles on their faces. President Kagame had transformed elements of what was supposed to be a revolutionary people's army into fascist, reactionary killing machines.

After being removed from the Chairmanship of RPF in 1998, Colonel Alexis Kanyarengwe gradually disappeared into obscurity. He decided to attend to his private matters, beekeeping here and real estate there. As for former President Bizimungu, he was not lucky. After being deposed by Kagame he kept a low profile for a while but soon decided to start a political party, Ubuyanja. President Kagame was so annoyed that one time he instructed me to go and meet the President of the Supreme Court, Rwagasore, the Prosecutor General, Gerald Gahima and the Commissioner General of Police, Frank

Mugambage, to see how to arrest and prosecute Bizimungu. I met the three in my brother's office. I conveyed the message but read fear, discomfort and skepticism on their faces. I was later told that they had not yet found sufficient reason to proceed with what President Kagame wanted. Eventually, President Kagame ordered the police to arrest Bizimungu. Together with former minister Charles Ntakiru-tinka, he was tried on flimsy charges of corruption and divisionism and sentenced to 15 years in jail. If RPF could not work with Hutu like Seth Sendashonga, Faustin Twagiramungu, Pasteur Bizimungu, Charles Ntakirutinka, Alexis Kanyarengwe, Biseruka and many others who shared a common vision of a Rwanda in which all Rwandans are equal before the law, and have equal opportunity in building a shared Rwanda together, who would RPF work with? These were troubling questions to me.

By the time I returned to Rwanda in 1999, RPF had effectively become a rubber stamp. The RPF meetings were like a routine chore in which the Chairman's word was final, and matters were decided beforehand. The RPF meetings in the Secretariat to decide on cabinet matters in advance were sterile. After a while, I made a decision not to attend any one of them. When the new symbols (flag, anthem and court of arms) were inaugurated I made sure I was not in the country. I paid very little attention to the general elections of 2003, except once in a while where I attended the choreographed rallies that made me sad as I remember Frantz Fanon's assessment, in his *The Wretched of the Earth*, of the hollow nature of the party after winning national independence:

> This brings us to consider the role of the political party in an under-developed country. We have seen in the preceding pages that very often simple souls, who moreover belong to the newly born bourgeoisie, never stop repeating that in an under-developed country the direction of affairs by a strong authority, in other words a dictatorship, is a necessity. With this in view the party is given

the task of supervising the masses. The party plays understudy to the administration and the police, and controls the masses, not in order to make sure that they really participate in the business of governing the nation, but in order to remind them constantly that the government expects from them obedience and discipline. That famous dictatorship, whose supporters believe that it is called for by the historical process and consider it an indispensable prelude to the dawn of independence, in fact symbolizes the decision of the bourgeois caste to govern the underdeveloped country first with the help of the people, but soon against them. The progressive transformation of the party into an information service is the indication that the government holds itself more and more on the defensive. The incoherent mass of the people is seen as a blind force that must be continually held in check either by mystification or by the fear inspired by the police force. The party acts as a barometer and as an information service. The militant is turned into an informer. He is entrusted with punitive expeditions against the villages. The embryo opposition parties are liquidated by beatings and stonings. The opposition candidates see their houses set on fire. The police increase their provocations. In these conditions, you may be sure, the party is unchallenged and 99.99 per cent of the votes are cast for the governmental candidate. We should add that in Africa a certain number of governments actually behave in this way. All the opposition parties, which moreover are usually progressive and would therefore tend to work for the greater influence of the masses in the conduct of public matters, and who desire that the proud, money-making bourgeoisie should be brought to heel, have been by dint of baton charges and prisons condemned first to silence and then to a clandestine existence.

I then turned the the microscope on myself and I did not like what I saw. I had become my own enemy. Like the character Boxer in George Orwell's *Animal Farm*, my motto seemed to have been, "I will always work hard." If I doubted RPF's purpose and its new direction what was mine? First, I was silent in the face of RPF's straying into a dangerous direction, and silent in the face of the evil that was being committed. In the case of deposing Bizimungu, I had allowed myself to be manipulated by Kagame to become an advocate for his conspiratorial move to seize the Presidency.

My service to President Kagame had reached a level that one could easily describe as idolatry or a slave-master relationship at worst. My work at the Presidency had gradually evolved to become a duty to make the President and his family happy. One time I spent nights supervising a company of rural peasants planting grass at the President's new multi-million dollar residence in Kiyovu to meet a deadline for him to enter his new presidential palace. President Kagame wanted to celebrate Christmas and the New Year in his new and luxurious residence. We worked round-the-clock and even airlifted furniture from Italy to meet his deadline. I had to organize his frequent trips abroad, including to holidays in Mauritius, South Africa and the United States on government resources. I had now become a project manager to build a hotel and meet a deadline so that President Kagame could host a regional meeting, the Common Market for Eastern and Southern Africa (COMESA).

My work at the Presidency had become routine and uninteresting. I could no longer see clearly how what I did at the presidency translated into the real gains of the ordinary people. Most of what I did, I felt, many other people could do: meetings; preparing "ordre de mission" (permissions to travel abroad) which the President would finally decide on; preparing his trips abroad; preparing the dossiers for the president to take to cabinet meetings many of which he did not attend; and attending some of his meetings which mostly took place during the night. Beyond the strategic conversation on economic development, and the abortive conversation on security, I did not see what other role I could play; and I did not want to live a life of a bureaucrat, tied to a desk and paper-shuffling.

Though President Kagame commanded lots of resources from public and private sources (the RPF companies), I was beginning to feel personal shame that we had betrayed Rwandans in general, and, in particular, RPF/RPA fallen comrades, RPF/RPA rank and file, genocide survivors, widows and orphans. Though Rwanda's poor live on less than a dollar per day, we were spending on private jets, presidential and private residences, five star hotels, and Defense headquarters to a tune of approximately a quarter of a billion U.S dollars in less than five years.

DRC had become Rwanda's seemingly incurable disease, and there was no opportunity whatsoever to have a discussion on lessons learned, and how to deliver Rwanda's soldiers from their permanent state of war. Many soldiers would come to me with all sorts of requests for help (weddings, funerals, assisting siblings to go back to school, etc.), but DRC always loomed large over their horizons with a lot of uncertainty.

It was evident the Hutu in Rwanda live a very subdued existence, sort of second-class citizen status. They know where to go and where not to go. In government and non-governmental institutions across the country, Hutu know they are being watched. They prefer to be silent, and sometimes a few of them become louder than Tutsi to buy acceptability. National justice, through gacaca, and international justice through the ICTR, are, rightly so, seen as victor's justice, since only crimes committed by Hutu are investigated, prosecuted, and punished. A sense of defeat and collective guilt largely imposed by RPF hangs over them. The Tutsi may look confident that their sons have absolute control of the security institutions and the country, but they too live fearful, uncertain lives, not knowing for how long the promise by a small group of Tutsi's hold on power will last.

A spiritual flicker of hope was beginning to convict me, beckoning me to another path that would simultaneously reconnect me to both God and the ordinary people. Shortly before leaving Washington, D.C. in 1999, I had reconnected with a colleague who had served as RPF's representative in Brussels. James Butare was his name, and he worked for a new Christian mission to spread the Gospel. I invited him to our residence and he talked to me about Christ. By then, I had softened and was no longer the rabid atheist that I used to be. I had married in the Catholic Church in 1995, to an Anglican wife whose grandfather, Canon Buningwire had been one of the earliest converts to Christianity in the then Kingdom of Ankole, in southwest Uganda. My atheistic predisposition was still evident in the days before our wedding ceremony when I resisted doing penance and taking the Eucharist.

Witnessing death on the battlefield and the genocide had created serious emotional, psychological and intellectual turmoil in me. I was questioning God's purpose in unleashing such human suffering, yet I did not believe in God. I overwhelmed myself by being busy all the time, but any moment of quiet led my mind to come back to the whole issue of the meaning and purpose in my life. As James and I talked, I could sense my ground was beginning to shift, and I was now open to allowing a conversation on matters of God.

Back in Kigali, my sister, Doreen Kayitesi, a born again Christian, kept on interesting me on matters of Jesus Christ. She attended church, Zion Temple, where Pastor Gitwaza preached. Young and charismatic, Pastor Gitwaza was attracting an increasing number of converts, including some from Rwanda's military. I had slowly started reading the Bible, and soon I was attending church once in a while. Twice, I attended service at Zion Temple and heard Pastor Gitwaza preach and I liked it. I knew that President Kagame was discouraging military officers from attending Gitwaza's church, but I attended anyway. One day in his office he questioned me as to why I would attend Gitwaza's church. Before I could answer, he changed the subject. The second time, while with him on a trip in Denver, Colorado, USA, he again raised the matter in the presence of some members of the delegation. He wondered why an educated person like me could go to Gitwaza's church. I listened to him and made no comment.

By 2003, there was a relentless voice in me, partly calling me to evaluate myself and take a totally new stand on matters of the revolution, and partly beckoning me to a new spiritual path altogether. I reflected on the words of Jesus Christ, "What good is it for someone to gain the whole world, yet forfeit their soul?" (Mark 8:36). I did not hate government like my daughter, Mwiza, but my interest in working for the RPF government was now at its lowest. Before the general elections of 2003, I had decided I would leave government. How and when, and to what new path, remained a challenge. I did not consult my wife, or my siblings, as I considered my options.

My mother, Coletta Bamususire (Mama).

My father-in-law, the late Ambassador William Rwetsiba, and my mother-in-law, Mrs. Joyce Rwetsiba.

December 16, 1995, I and Dorothy's wedding ceremony.

My wife, Dorothy Rudasingwa, and I.

My son, Aaron Ngenzi Rudasingwa, and my daughter,
Tina Tona Rudasingwa, in front of our former house
(Titanic) in Kigali.

My eldest daughter, Lissa Mwiza Rudasingwa.

My eldest son, Archadius Ndatinda Rudasingwa.

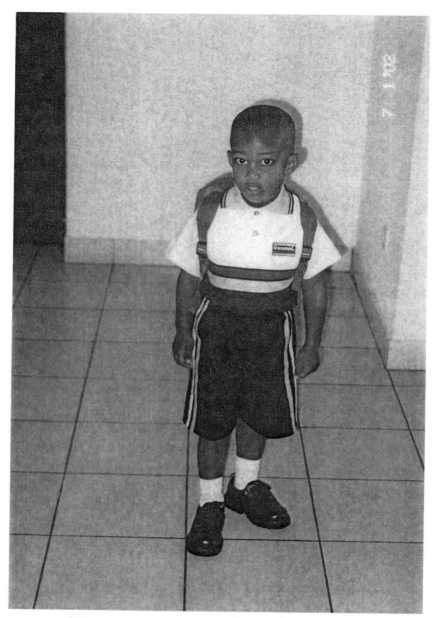

My youngest son, Aaron Ngenzi Rudasingwa.

My last born, Tina Tona Rudasingwa.

Aaron, Tina, and Mwiza with me.

Tina, Aaron, and Mwiza with Dorothy Rudasingwa.

Tina, Mwiza, Aaron, and Archadius.

My younger sister, Doreen Kayitesi.

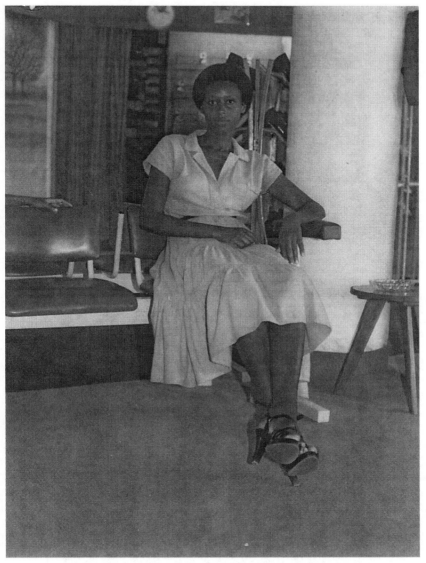

My late elder sister, Edith Abatesi (Toto).

My elder brother, Gerald Gahima.

1996, with then Vice President Kagame and U.S. Secretary of
Defense, William Perry.

1996, with then U.S. Congress House Speaker Newt Gingrich.

1996, presenting a Letter of Credence to then President of the
United States, William Jefferson Clinton.

Signing a U.S. $ 50 million credit to Rwanda with World Bank
Vice-President, Callisto Madavo.

CHAPTER THIRTY

Opportunity

At the end of 2003, during an annual government retreat in the Akagera Hotel situated in the Akagera National Park, President Kagame attacked Gerald Gahima, who was then Vice-President of the Supreme Court. He falsely accused Gahima of conflict of interest in his handling of private loans. Gahima was not in the meeting to defend himself. I had deliberately decided not to attend the meeting either, as I had enough work at the Hotel project. I was made to understand that President Kagame also alluded to something that was not going right at the Office of the President. Gahima knew Kagame before me. Both attended the prestigious Ntare School in Mbarara in the seventies. Though bright, Kagame was not readmitted to Ntare School after his O'Levels due to his indiscipline. He had then attended a high school in Kampala, and, subsequently drifted into petty crimes so as to survive. The appearance of Fred Rwigyema in the ranks of Yoweri Museveni's FRONASA in 1979 seems to have been young Kagame's saving grace, discovering purpose in an otherwise stale and dangerous life on the streets of Kampala. He accompanied Fred Rwigyema and became one of the historic 27 men who started Yoweri Museveni's insurgency in 1981.

Having grown together in a close-knit family, we assembled at Gahima's home one evening in January, 2004 to consider his options. A Judge who is attacked by a Head of State in public loses the ability to function because the public has no confidence in him. If the deploying authority loses confidence in you, there is no way you can function either. President Kagame was no longer interested in him, but wanted to first spark a public outcry against him. I believe Gahima had stepped on the toes of so many interests, simply because the country was crying for justice and accountability in the post-civil war, and post-genocide period. There were Tutsi who were not happy with Gahima about the execution of the program to return some properties to the original Hutu owners. Every time there was an attempt to hold some Tutsi elements to countability, often on the orders of the President, there would be an outcry from the Tutsi lobby in RPF, and Gahima was the scapegoat. There were many Hutu who were not happy with Gahima because he was the visible symbol of the Tutsi victor's justice, and of seeking accountability for genocide.

Then there was the usual human jealousy. There were people in RPF who felt two that influential brothers around Kagame, RPF and government was too much. That evening, as our families assembled at the Gahima's, he told us he was resigning, and he had written a letter of resignation to President Kagame. We were unanimously in agreement that it was the right course of action.

In my heart, without telling my wife and siblings, I felt Gahima's departure from government was a perfect opportunity for me to leave government as well. I knew President Kagame's psychology. He had been building momentum to strike both of us, but at different times. The departure of Gahima meant that he would become even more suspicious of me. I knew his vindictiveness. My method of departure meant life or death, judging from what had happened to other RPF leaders and Rwandans. With the few diplomatic skills I had gathered over the years I plotted my own exit.

For a long time I had been asking President Kagame to allow me to take a leave of absence. A few days after Gahima's resignation I wrote a short internal memo asking the President for a one year leave of absence to go to the United States to study and write a book. He promptly accepted. I was now left with the task of explaining the move, first to Dorothy, and then to my siblings. Dorothy knew that I had been asking for this for a while. I explained that now President Kagame had given me permission to go and study and write. She would remain in Rwanda with the kids. I wasn't sure how the family would survive during my absence, but I was taking a leap of faith. When I told my siblings, they were not happy at all. They felt President Kagame was punishing our family. They were right, but the timing of my departure was my own choice.

I quickly followed up on my memo and the President's acceptance. I asked to meet him and he received me at the Presidential residence in Kiyovu. He was in a relaxed mood and it was two just two of us. I told him the Hotel InterContinental project was more or less done, operational, but not yet fully finished. I told him I was leaving matters in the hands of William Nkurunziza (of Rwanda Investment Agency) and Ms.Chantal Rugamba (of the National Tourism Agency) who had been my hardworking teammates on the project. He asked me about my plans, and I told him I wanted to leave as soon as possible. I tactfully also asked him to help me with a return ticket to the United States. He accepted and told me he would instruct his social secretary and other gatekeeper, Ms. Patricia Kanyiginya to help me with a return air ticket.

Then, surprisingly, he raised the issue of a hostile report in *Umuseso* newspaper. The private newspaper had run a headline saying, "The President Builds, Rudasingwa Destroys". He asked me if I knew who could be behind such a story. I told him I had no idea, but suspected whoever it was had some internal informants at the Office of the President. He said he had information implicating Valens Kajeguhakwa, a businessman who had fallen out with him, as the backer of *Umuseso*. In my heart I knew that directly or indirectly, through his security people, he had been the source of such a campaign. *Umuseso* newspaper had a love-hate relationship with President Kagame and his security agents. It would take a stand and report on the injustice and corruption in the RPF system, triggering harsh measures against it (it was finally banned, and its editors fled to exile). Occasionally it would pick on some people that were falling out of favor with the President, and they would slander and lie about them. My brother Gahima was one of such victims of *Umuseso*. Issues of Umuseso that had Gahima as one of the front page stories would sell like a hot cake. Dr. Emmanuel Ndahiro , Jack Nziza and probably others were behind the malicious propaganda that was being channeled through *Umuseso*. I did not mind being falsely attacked, but I was particularly disheartened how they would attack Gahima and his family. Knowing that all this came from the RPF circles with President Kagame's blessings made me feel that it was time to go. The revolution had come full circle and had come to devour its own children.

Within a week I bid farewell to Mama, Dorothy and the kids, my siblings, and my office. I formally wrote to the office administration that I was going on a one year sabbatical. It was a day for the weekly cabinet meeting and my friend Donald Kaberuka, Minister of Finance, came to my office and found me packing my few documents. I told him I was leaving for a sabbatical. Minister Kaberuka himself had had a difficult time with RPF cadres. An economics PhD, Kaberuka was smart and sure of himself, qualities that endeared him to the donor community which constitutes the blood line to a poor country like Rwanda. The same qualities that made him an asset to Rwanda tended to make President Kagame very insecure. Twice President Kagame had wanted to drop him from cabinet because, he said, he was tired of foreigners telling him how smart Kaberuka was.

When I set off on the journey to the United States, I fully understood what I was running away from but did not know what

I was running into. Studying and writing a book were pretexts. What was I really going to do with my life, and with my family of six? The choice of the United States was conditioned by my general knowledge about the country, and some relationships that would be helpful as I figured out my next steps. I had hoped to do some postgraduate studies, and then slowly get back into the medical profession. I would also find time to write a book about my life and the RPF struggle. I still considered myself an RPF cadre who had become disillusioned with the practice of a revolution that had gone astray. I felt that life was short and I had no energy and stamina left to undertake another national project to bring the RPF revolution back on course. The risk of such a second national project in life was extremely high. I now had a family of six to tend to. I would be a private citizen and contribute in some other modest way to Rwanda's national and community life. I had given enough of my youthful energy, and I now needed to be a little more selfish, and leave others to make their contributions as well.

I arrived in the United States without money. I relied on the hospitality of my friends and relatives. I did apply to the Fletcher School of Law and Diplomacy at Tufts University in Medford, Massachusetts; and I was admitted. I was a practitioner going back to school to back my diplomacy with the theories underpinning it. In the interim period I started this book project.

During my years at the presidency, I was able to meet a good number of interesting people. One relationship would lead to another. I had met Kaia Miller through a contact at the World Bank. Kaia Miller, Michael Fairbanks and Malik Fal facilitated the cabinet retreat on national prosperity. Their company, Onthe-Frontier, had an ongoing multi-million dollar consulting project supposedly to upgrade Rwanda's competitiveness in the coffee, tea and tourism sectors. Through them I had come to meet Professor Michael Porter of Harvard Business School. When I was invited to Kaia Miller's wedding ceremony in Boston, I sat near a young looking American man by the name of Greg Wyler. I was told he had invented something in the technology world but I did not know what. As I usually did, I sold to him the idea of a Rwanda that had suffered in 1994, and now now experiencing a miracle of rebirth. At the center of the miraculous rebirth was the hero, President Kagame. Americans quickly grasp the idea of heroes, good guys and bad guys, and celebrities. I invited him to Rwanda and introduced him to President Kagame. Soon Greg Wyler introduced us to another friend and business associate of his, John Dick. Listed as one of the 15 richest people on the small British Island of Jersey, John Dick also introduced us to Joe Ritchie, a Chicago businessman, who in turn introduced us to the evangelist and author of the best seller, *The Purpose Driven Life*, Pastor Rick Warren.

When I sought a quiet place to begin writing my book, John Dick and his wife, Mickey, offered to host me at their residence, St. John's Manor, on the Island of Jersey. His official title there is the Seigneur of St. John's Manor. When I arrived at St. John's Manor, I could not believe what I saw. The residence has a beauty, elegance and character to it that I can hardly describe. There, on St. John's Manor I stayed for one month, during which I started to write this book. During the stay I was also able to read Henry Kissinger's *Diplomacy*, and Michael Porter's *The Competitive Advantage of Nations*.

St. John's Manor has extensive grounds, beautiful lawns, with flowers, trees, springs and statues around it. I walked around the grounds every morning and evening. Despite the comfort and hospitality at the manor, I was experiencing intense turmoil, and I was failing to discover a voice and story to tell in the book. I knew I had an important story to tell. But the problem was that at that point, the story was still clothed in lies and deception. I remember Dick coming to me one day with an international newspaper, talking about the role of President Kagame in the shooting down of President Habyarimana's plane in 1994. I quickly told him it was a lie, concocted by the French and the Hutu extremists to hide their own role in the crime. He also asked me about the rigging of elections in 2003, and I told him President Kagame is simply very popular and foreigners do not get it.

Here I was, running away from President Kagame and a revolution that had gone sour, with crimes on its hands, and yet still protecting it from foreigners. What then was I going to write about? On the one hand, my old revolutionary sentiments were kind of being resurrected. I frequently came back to my favorite song, *Fernando,* by Abba and would listen to it over and over again as I walked around the manor. I would remember the nights of October, 1990, and the sacrifice that Rwanda had had to give, the fallen comrades, the genocide, and the continuing deaths. But now I was older. Though there were things that I was ashamed of that RPF had done, and was continuing to do, I felt I had no regrets to have been part of the hope and dream of national transformation and reconciliation that the RPF once stood for and inspired. Could I do it again? What was the "it" in this question? My stay at the manor was memorable, but my mental turmoil could not allow me the peace to discover a voice that was authentic, as yet.

After a stay at St.John's Manor, my restlessness would take me to Jordan to attend the World Economic Forum Middle East, then back to the United States where, in New Hampshire, as I checked in a motel, I saw the book *The Purpose Driven Life* being talked about. The following day I bought a copy. Though the author recommends that you read it over a course of 40 days, I decided to read it in two days. I was not yet convinced about a return to God, but the book rekindled a desire to be open to a new life, one that would be disruptive, but anchored on something new. What was my new purpose, I asked myself.

I was in New York on the way to my brother-in-law, Derrick, and Irene Rwetsiba's home in Maryland, when I got an international call from Rwanda. The person on the line was Christopher

Bizimungu. He introduced himself as a captain who is the Director of Military Prosecutions in the Rwanda Defence Forces. He said there were a few questions they wanted to ask me, and I should return to Rwanda. They had also contacted my wife to ask for my contacts in the United States. A few days before Captain Bizimungu's call, my brother had called to tell me that he had had a meeting with President Kagame in the presence of his intelligence chief, Dr. Emmanuel Ndahiro. The President was not happy that I was promoting myself as a hero in the United States. Apparently, this had been reported by Dr. Zac Nsenga, who was then Rwanda's ambassador to the United States. This was in reference to a talk I had given at Tufts University, on Rwanda's post-genocide reconstruction.

If anything, I had spoken like a government official, and a transcript was available if the President was interested in reading it. In introducing me, Michael Fairbanks, had, as most Americans do, spoken of me generously as one of the heroes of the Rwandan story. Those were his words, not mine. As I headed back to Rwanda, I was anxious, and for the first time, fearful.

I was scheduled to arrive in Kigali on the 10th June, but I decided to arrive a day earlier. That same evening I was called by President Kagame's social secretary, Patricia Kanyiginya, telling me they were expecting me the following day. On 10th June, at 3 pm I was summoned to the Department of Military Prosecutions. My brother, Gerald Gahima, accompanied me to the offices, but he was barred from attending my interrogation. It was ironical that a former Prosecutor General and Vice-President of the Supreme Court would be found unqualified to attend the interrogation. During the interrogation, it turned out that the bathtub matter would be raised to the charge of disrespect to the Commander in Chief. After three hours of an uneasy interrogation by Captain Bizimungu and his colleagues (he had to regularly excuse himself to go out as if to receive instructions from someone), he announced to me that the charge was serious and I had to be detained. I did not argue with him, and simply mentioned that I was innocent and that the decision would come back to haunt whoever was making it.

Outside, there was heavy security. I said farewell to a distressed Gahima, as a pickup truck waited to take me to detention in a military barracks in Kanombe. I could not even call my wife and kids. At the barracks, I found there two other officers, including an old schoolmate of mine at Makobore High School, Col Kamili. He was shocked to see me, and I was surprised to see him too. Apparently, he was jailed because after taking a few drinks he had casually said that the regime is pushing most Rwandans against the wall. He was overheard by an informant who relayed the information to President Kagame, who promptly ordered his detention. That evening, my wife Dorothy, my sister Doreen, my sister-in-law Debra, and Gahima came to visit me, and brought food, clothes and a mattress. I was tired after a long trip from the United States. The events of that day had been exhausting and confusing. However, for the first time I felt an intense feeling of relief. I was sure that night that I had totally and irrevocably divorced President Kagame and RPF. The days of innocence, pretense and denial were over.

I had deep sleep that night and woke up to a day in which my past seemed like a movie. I shared katogo (plantains and beans) with my fellow officers and later that morning went back to sleep. In the early afternoon, one security officer came to our room and told me I was needed at the Department of Military Prosecutions again. In my mind I was wondering whether this was going to be another disappearance as is common in Rwanda. I woke up, and was driven to the office where Captain Bizimungu told me he was releasing me, but I had to remain within Kigali and could only travel with permission. When I was initially detained, the charge was 'disrespect to Commander in Chief". As I was being released from custody, there was an additional charge, corruption. The matter of the rusty sinks at the Presidential club was the basis of the charge. As I was being driven back to my house, I realized how the world I was returning to was very different indeed. I was truly glad to be home, to see Dorothy and the children, my mother, my siblings and their families, and a few friends. I felt like Lazarus, the Biblical man that was brought back to life by Jesus Christ. Not so many people detained on President Kagame's orders are able to come out that quick, or alive. It had been a miracle.

There followed about two agonizing months of waiting and uncertainty. When was I going to be prosecuted or to appear in court? How was my family going to survive? For a while I was on welfare from my sister and brother. My wife had no job. I came to witness firsthand the risk of being on a collision course with a totalitarian state. After several weeks, President Kagame asked me to come and see him. Evidently times had changed. His security guards now looked at me like I was an enemy. His Principal Private Secretary, Brigadier Kazura, was there to attend the meeting. As he entered the room I could see he had a tense face. After greeting us, he said he was surprised to hear that I had been detained. He said he had first heard it from his wife Jeannette. I was quiet, showing disbelief on my face. Then he said, "Theogene, do you know that foreigners who are asking me about you can complicate matters for you?" He mentioned Lynda Chalker, Britain's former Minister for International Development, and Kaia Miller, my friend from Boston. I told him I had not asked anybody to intervene on my behalf, and that if I am to defend myself I will do it better than anybody else. He asked me how the case was progressing. I told him I had no problem defending myself in the case of corruption, because I knew I was innocent, but I had a problem with the charge of disrespect to him. I told him I had never been disrespectful to him, and wondered how it would be settled in court. He was thoughtful for a moment, and then instructed Brigadier Kazura to tell the military prosecutors to drop the charge of disrespect to Commander in Chief. I thanked him and further asked if he could allow me to travel to the US to start my graduate studies at the Fletcher School. He gave me permission.

During this period of waiting, my brother Gahima decided to flee into exile in the United States. I quickly prepared to leave for the United States. Before I came back to Rwanda in June, 2004, I had been fortunate to get a Visiting Scholar position at the Haas School of Business, University of California, Berkeley. The Dean of the Business School, Tom Campbell, had been a Congressman from California during the time I was Rwanda's Ambassador to the United States. He had been interested in African matters and I had helped his congressional delegation's visit to the Great Lakes region. It happened that my new acquaintance, Joe Ritchie, was also friends with Tom Campbell. My old friend, Ted Dagne, also knew Campbell. Campbell was kind enough to invite me to the Haas School of Business where he introduced me to Professors Drew Isaacs and Kristi Raube. When I returned to the United States, I was accommodated at International House, a dormitory with shared bathroom areas. It was like a return to my high school days. My work at Haas Business School as a visiting scholar centered on entrepreneurship and business development in Africa. Joe Ritchie, a Chicago Businessman, provided a small monthly stipend to support my work.

On the first Sunday after arriving in Berkeley, I felt an urge to explore where I could attend church. I took a stroll around and entered a couple of church buildings and finally came to one where, around 9 am, I saw a big congregation outside. It was First Presbyterian Church of Berkeley. It was the end of the first morning service. I felt an urge to go for the next service that was beginning shortly. I sat in the pew right at the back.

The senior pastor who preached that morning was Mark Labberton. That day he preached on silence. I related to the sermon. It was as if he was talking about my situation. There was now silence in my life. I was, again, in a strange land, having left behind my relationships in Rwanda. I could not hear my children, my wife, relatives or friends. From a busy life of politics, there was now silence. Then there was a spiritual silence, some kind of void that old ideology and other beliefs could no longer fill. There is the silence of death. And, for those who believe in God, there is silence, when, even, with devoted prayer, there is silence as a response. I had already known that exile, like a vast sea or desert, can be a place of silence. I liked the sermon and started attending the First Presbyterian Church regularly, the first time since my childhood days.

I returned to Rwanda as my permission expired, then waited; and there was no word from military prosecutions about court proceedings or further investigations. In November, 2004 I asked again if I could go back to continue with my graduate studies and my Visiting Scholar work at the University of California, Berkeley. I was granted permission again. I spent that Christmas and New Year away from my family. Early in 2005 attended the Fletcher School residency in Singapore. Over the years, I had been intrigued by the economic rise of what was then called the Asian Tigers (Malaysia, Singapore, Taiwan and South Korea). I had been interesting President Kagame in the region, and had even participated in the Malaysian networking event, the Smart Partnership. I had organized for President Kagame to meet the Malaysian and Singapore Prime Ministers. During the visit our delegation spent a few days on a learning tour. It was a pleasure for me to be in Singapore again, this time as a student of international affairs.

On my return from Singapore I met Gahima, my brother, whom I had not seen for months. Gahima was then working as a Judge in Sarajevo, Bosnia and Herzegovina. We were in a Washington, D.C. hotel room at night when I received a call from Dorothy, my wife. She told me I was urgently needed in Kigali. A conversation followed between me and my brother. I told him I had to go back to Rwanda. He was against the idea. He argued that if there was anything to prove, I had been back to Rwanda twice and nothing had come of it. He said I know it very well that President Kagame was behind the persecution using legal means, and would not give me justice. This time, he feared he might even kill me. I fully understood what he was saying, and the risk I would be taking this time. However, I told Gahima that I was not willing to give President Kagame a reason to call me a fugitive running away from justice. In addition, my wife and children were still in Rwanda. Gahima argued that it would be much easier and safer to organize the family to find me in the United States. I was of the opinion that a man does not run away, leaving a family hostage to a totalitarian regime. My brother seeing that I was determined to go, reminded me of a Kenyan writer, Ngugi wa Thiongo, saying that the so-called brave die in battle, while cowards live longer. It was a sad moment when we parted, never knowing when we would meet again. I was leaping into a dangerous unknown.

When I arrived in Kigali in early February, 2005, I realized the stakes were indeed high. The night I arrived in Kigali I met my wife and my sister and told them this was my final attempt to appease President Kagame. If I survived, I made it clear to them, I was going into exile again. I told Dorothy to keep it at the back of her mind, and to be light in terms of material possessions. I have always seen Dorothy's attachment to her multiple photo albums, the *ebihingirwa* (stuff that were given to her by her family and the extended family, friends, and relatives before we got married), our kids' stuffed animals and, yes, even her clothes. On my part, I have been a nomad all my life. I have no childhood pictures, and I do not recall any picture of anyone in our family except one, mama's adorning the traditional *amasunzu* pattern in her hair, and little boy Gahima wearing a dress. Because I did not see my father, and there is no picture of him, I have always tried to imagine what he looked like. Was he tall or short? Was he big or skinny? Was he light skinned or dark skinned? I grew up in poverty and have learnt to be less attached to stuff. I told Dorothy God would give us more things if they were necessary.

When I arrived in Kigali I was informed that I should prepare to appear in the military tribunal. I was given a big file from the prosecution regarding my corruption case. I did not even bother to read it. I knew the details of the whole matter. I asked two lawyers, Maître Haguma and Maître Munyemana to represent me. I did send a few pages to Gahima to advise on the way forward. To conceal the political nature of the case, this time my former Director General of Administration, James Gatera, and the civilian consultant, Serge, were the co-accused.

Before I appeared in the military tribunal in Nyamirambo, on the fringes of Kigali, something strange happened. When I returned to Rwanda, I found Dorothy had become a regular Churchgoer. She and the children now regularly attended St. Etienne, an Anglican church. I joined them the first Sunday after my arrival in Kigali. My family was seated in one pew, while my sister- in- law Debra was seated in a pew behind us. Close to communion time, a young looking man came and whispered into my ear that I was needed outside. I asked him who he was, and he declined to tell me. I refused to go out. He came back the second time, but I ignored him. By then, the congregation was alert, especially the people who were seated with us. I then asked Dorothy, after the service, to go out and check what was going on. She stepped outside, when the service was over, and found the man standing at the entrance of the church. She asked him what he wanted from me. He said we knew each other and that there are friends of mine who wanted to ask me something. By the time Dorothy came back into the church, I could see Silas Udahemuka, then Chief Intelligence Officer for President Kagame's Republican Guard, on my far left, close to the wall. He looked anxious. I asked Dorothy if he regularly came to the church.

She said she had never seen him there. As soon as the church service was over and I stepped out, Silas Udahemuka was there to greet me. I could see around the church compound an unusual concealed security presence. I asked my sister-in-law, Debra, to drive close behind us until we reached home. I have always wondered what was behind the strange events of that morning. Did they want me to disappear and then claim I had run away from justice? Only President Kagame, Tom Byabagamba and Silas Udahemuka would have the answer to that question.

In the following weeks the military tribunal began the sham proceedings. On the morning of March 18, 2005, the court presided over by Col. Ibambasi read the verdict. I was, together with all the co-accused, acquitted of all the charges. Outside the courtroom, a small group of well-wishers and family spontaneously gathered in an adjacent room to sing, pray and thank God. We were quickly chased away and we found another nearby location in Nyamirambo. There we sang Burundian singer Apollinaire's song:

> Nta kintu mfise, cyo kwirata,
> Nta ni kintu nzigera mbona
> Atar'urukundo wangiriye
> Nirwo nshima, nirwo nirata
> -mbega ubuntu butangaje....

In short, nothing to boast of except God's love. For days before the court acquittal, I had experienced intense spiritual energy, despite multiple challenges in the family situation. Over the previous months, the family's survival had become ever more precarious. I could not work. Together with her sister and another friend of theirs, Dorothy had found some small business to provide meals at Green Hills Academy, a school owned by Mrs. Jeannette Kagame and her friends. As soon as my problems intensified, the business was terminated. I would sit on the veranda with my wife, not knowing what to do next, and where our next meal would come from. Our kids were used to a particular lifestyle and I felt sad when I found myself helpless in providing for them.

My brother and sister provided for us in those dark days. As it happens in Rwanda, once you fall from favor, you become like a leper. People you assumed were your friends run away and hide from you. The phones fall silent. Nobody visits you and you can't visit anybody.

During that period my sister, Doreen, younger than me in age but older in terms of Christian faith, had been insisting that a friend of hers, a peasant woman of great faith, should come and pray for me. Though I had been attending First Presbyterian Church in Berkeley, and temporarily St. Etienne in Kigali before the security incident, there was the intellectual and scientist in me that found succumbing to the whims of a peasant woman not very attractive. Doreen would gently tell me that in matters of faith, one needs to suspend reason and intellectual debate, and just believe. Finally, one day the peasant woman came and put her hands on me and prayed as we sang Psalm 121 in Kinyarwanda:

> I lift up my eyes to the mountains—
> where does my help come from?
> My help comes from the LORD,
> the Maker of heaven and earth.
>
> He will not let your foot slip—
> he who watches over you will not slumber;
> indeed, he who watches over Israel
> will neither slumber nor sleep.
>
> The LORD watches over you—
> the LORD is your shade at your right hand;
> the sun will not harm you by day,
> nor the moon by night.
>
> The LORD will keep you from all harm—
> he will watch over your life;

the LORD will watch over your coming and going
both now and forevermore.

I instantly felt a peace that surpassed all my understanding.
One evening, on March 17, 2005, I called my sister and her husband, a cousin of mine, and Dorothy and declared to them that
I had been born again. From then on, I told them, I was on a
mission to serve God, and serve His people, the hungry and sick.
By that act, the intellectual in me was also hedging. I knew that
the following day God was going to decide on my case in the
military tribunal. Wouldn't it be wise on my part, I thought, to be
decisive and tell God that I was now fully behind Him instead of
giving a lukewarm and hesitant signal? In any case, God decided
in my favor, and I had every reason to be thankful. This was my
second conversion, the first having been my conversion to Marxism. From Marx to Christ it had been a long journey. Each of the
conversions had taken place during a period of brokenness and
exile from the state. The second conversion was also a response to
alienation and exile from God.

Once I had been acquitted by the military tribunal I wanted
to get away as soon as possible. My plan was to leave for the
United States and then organize for Dorothy and the kids to join
me later. I requested for a meeting with President Kagame and
he promptly agreed to meet me. As I walked on the compound,
it was like a strange land to me. I had helped shape its outside
appearance, and tried to shape its inner content as well, but it was
now a beast that was waiting to pounce to destroy me, as it had
destroyed many others before me. Dr. Ephraim Kabaija was now
his Director of Cabinet, and we spoke briefly before we went in
to see the President.

President Kagame appeared calm. After a brief greeting, there
was some silence, and I was the one who broke the silence by asking him how the economy was doing. He said it was doing fine. I
told him I had been acquitted of all the charges, pretending that

he was learning about it for the first time. Then he asked me how Singapore was. I was surprised, but it did confirm that he was following my movements with interest. I told him I was there as part of my graduate studies at the Fletcher School of Law and Diplomacy. He asked me if I still had contacts in Singapore, and if I could help reestablish the links for Rwanda. I told him I would try. He then asked me about my brother, saying that he had heard he had been in South Africa, at Miko Rwayitare's.

The late Miko Rwayitare had been among RPF's supporters during the civil war. He was a successful businessman who had made a fortune out of telecommunications. President Kagame never warmed up to him after RPF came into power. Rwayitare had sought a stake in Rwanda's cell phone business but that had to go to RPF's Tri-Star, in partnership with MTN from South Africa. Rwayitare had established relationships with Uganda and bought a big stake in Uganda's telecommunications. When my friend, Greg Wyler from Boston, appeared on the scene looking for a local partner, and suggested Rwayitare, I was subsequently instructed by President Kagame to tell Wyler to talk to Tribert Rujugiro instead. Rujugiro is another successful Rwandan businessman who made a fortune out of the tobacco business. Rujugiro was the leading financier to RPF during the civil war. Apparently, it was true Gahima and his wife had been at Rwayitare's home in South Africa, together with Rwanda's then ambassador to South Africa, Dr. Joseph Karemera. The President did not elaborate and I did not understand what the problem was. I believe that like me, Gahima's movements were being closely watched. Towards the end of the meeting I told the President that my plan was to leave for the United States and continue with my interrupted responsibilities at Fletcher and Berkeley. He did not say yes or no and we parted.

As I drove home, I decided to leave that very afternoon for Entebbe, Uganda, and then get connections through Europe to the United States. I told Dorothy I was leaving, and we headed to Kanombe airport. I went through all the formalities, and then waited for departure in the waiting lounge. From where I was seated, I could see policemen and immigration officials relentlessly on phones and looking at me. A few minutes before boarding, an immigration officer then came and told me to follow him to his office. There he told me that I could not travel without permission from the President. I told him that I had seen the President and that he knew that I was travelling. The officer told me I needed his clearance.

I immediately called President Kagame's Director of Cabinet, Dr. Kabaija, who had been in the meeting. I asked him to check with the President if he has any problem with my leaving the country. He told me the President had left for home and that I should try to talk to Patricia, the President's Secretary. I called Patricia, and told her to ask the President for me if he had any problem with my departure. A few moments later I got a call from Captain Willy, President Kagame's powerful bodyguard. He relayed the president's message to me as follows: 1) we did not discuss my plans in the meeting; 2) he was not aware that I was leaving that day; and 3) he is not the one who gives permission to travel. Surprised, I said, "Oh, its ok", and then hung up. With my sister Doreen, we descended the steps, and headed home.

I had to start planning my next moves, now that this had hit a dead end. Towards the end of March, 2005 I started hinting to Dorothy that she should probably take the children to visit their grandmother in Kampala, Uganda. Dorothy was not enthusiastic, but I insisted. I surprised the children when I told them that they would travel to Uganda the following day, the 1st of April. They thought I was joking, since it was April Fools' Day. On the 1st of April, Dorothy and the kids took a flight to Entebbe, Uganda. They were not aware that I was orchestrating their escape. My plan was to move to my sister's house once Dorothy and the kids were safe in Uganda. I would then take my time and plan an escape from Rwanda. I felt so angry that any man, even President

Kagame, would have such an overwhelming control over my life and my family's. I was going to escape, but before that President Kagame needed to hear from me directly that I was quitting government for good, and that I wanted to be a free man, freed from any obligations. I would make it known to him indirectly that God was now my new and only boss, not him. I did not want him ever to say that I run away and then wrote to him. I knew I was taking a big and deadly risk, but I made that decision.

On 4 April, in the course of the night, I penned a personal letter to President Kagame:

Kigali, 4th April 2005

His Excellency the President
The Republic of Rwanda
Village Urugwiro
P.O Box 15
Kigali
Rwanda

Your Excellency,

Fourteen years ago, when our country was at dangerous crossroads, I made a voluntary and deliberate choice to join the ranks of young men and women who dedicated their lives to create a new Rwanda. A just cause was adequate to make one stake one's life, at a time when the future looked uncertain and yet the hope of victory prevailed.

The birth of a new nation has come at a big price: of dead heroes and living patriots, and over a million innocent lives who perished in the last days of an evil regime. Through

God's will and their sacrifice, not our bravery and wisdom, we were spared to serve the struggling nation. Healing and building a nation is an endless and noble task, an undertaking in which every generation is called upon to offer its contribution. Indeed, as the saying goes, every generation must discover and execute its mission. Hopefully, one day history will be kind enough and look upon us as nation builders.

Sir, I should take this opportunity to thank you for the opportunity that you have given me to serve this country. It was an honor and privilege to work with you in various capacities. The challenge was enriching, for every morning I thought about Rwanda and its citizens, and how best I could help Your Excellency fulfill our promise to the people.

My lifetime pledge is that never through me would this country come to harm. My commitment to the Rwandan people is total, to the very last moment of my life.

Mr. President, I have no doubt, that in more ways than one, I might have fallen short of your expectations. Wholeheartedly, I would like to apologize if I have unknowingly offended you in any way. Yet, I would urge that were such moments to exist, and they must in a long working relationship, they should not cloud the otherwise good work we have done together. Error is the nature of every born and living human being; from creation to the very end. In a way, the marathon of the last fourteen years has been such that we have had to learn as we run, and to master the daily intricacies of survival and statecraft under fire. Occasionally, therefore, even with the best of intentions, errors are made.

Your Excellency, I have come to personal crossroads again, when I have to redefine the content and form of my contribution to Rwanda and the world. My new found calling and passion is in serving God, academic pursuits, and playing an advocacy role on global concerns of peace and prosperity. Once again, voluntarily, deliberately and for the above personal reasons, this is what I have chosen to do from now on. Besides, I would like to pay more attention to the needs of my young family.

In this regard, I do not intend to undertake, now or in the future, any political or government responsibilities. Furthermore I would like to request Your Excellency to discharge me from military obligations as a Major in the Rwanda Defense Forces.

I could not possibly ask for something that is not in your powers to give; nor seek a right that is over and above what citizens of Rwanda are entitled to. To be a free private citizen of Rwanda is all I humbly ask for, as I wait for Your Excellency's favorable response.

I wish you and your family all the best in the years ahead.

May the Almighty God bless you.

Dr. THEOGENE RUDASINGWA

Early in the morning I gave a sealed envelope containing the letter to my former secretary, Maggie, to deliver to the President's executive office. That same night I sent a text message to Dorothy in Uganda, quoting a verse in the Bible's Old Testament story of Sodom and Gomorrah where Lot's wife looked back and was turned into a lump of salt. I was telling her not to look back, not to come back. She was confused. We went back and forth, texting, till five am in the morning. She decided to come and check on me, against my strong advice.

I had sent her and Gahima a copy of the letter, and shown it to my sister as well. They were all not happy with me. They thought I had taken a very unnecessary and risky step. Nobody had ever spoken to President Kagame in those terms and survived. We were in a complicated situation and I had made it even worse. After Dorothy arrived from Kampala we gave away all our household property. I tried to get Dorothy into the picture that it was going to be a long waiting game, whose end result we could not predict. She had to be strong and prepare to look after the children, alone if necessary. I convinced her to leave immediately and go back to Uganda. I transferred my few personal belongings to my sister's home. We had already given away all our household belongings.

We were on our way back from a visit to Mama in Nyagatare, northeast of Rwanda, when Gahima called me from Sarajevo. He wanted me to go to the airport and catch a flight to Entebbe, Uganda. I told him I couldn't since nothing had changed from the last time I was humiliated at the airport. He told me President Kagame was on a trip to the United States, and that Joe Ritchie (the businessman from Chicago) was in touch with him and Dr. Emmanuel Ndahiro. Gahima had kept Joe Ritchie informed about my predicament. Gahima told me that Ndahiro had said that as far as the President was concerned I did not have any problem. Gahima suggested I travel to the airport to test the validity of Ndahiro's statement.

I was reluctant, but I gave my brother the benefit of the doubt. We hurriedly drove to Kigali, and then Dorothy and I were escorted to the airport by my sister-in-law, Anne Gahima, and my sister Doreen. Unfortunately, there was a repeat of the past. We went through security and immigration, and waited for departure. Suddenly I saw an officer by the name of Hodari racing on the tarmac, coming towards the terminal building. He entered the waiting area, talked to an immigration officer, and then came to greet me. I remembered the young officer when he attended a course at Fort Benning, in the United States. Hodari is now the commanding officer of the elite Republican Guard. The immigration officer told me I could not leave without permission from the Ministry of Defense. I told him I had never travelled on permission from the Ministry of Defense. From whom was I supposed to ask for permission, I asked. The immigration officer could not answer. I told him that the actions they were taking would come back to haunt them, and I left for home, truly angry and frustrated. I even left my passport behind, since I now treated it like a useless piece of paper. Gahima called me and I told him what had transpired at the airport.

On the evening of April 18, 2005, Dorothy, my sister Doreen and I were seated on the bare floor of our empty house when I received a call from Patricia, the President's Social Secretary. She said the President wanted to talk to me. Soon he came on the line, calling from the United States. He asked me, in a friendly tone, where I was. I told him that I was in Rwanda, waiting for his permission to travel. I recounted how I had been barred from travelling twice. The first time I had been told by immigration that I needed permission from the President himself. The second time I had been told I needed permission from the Ministry of Defense. He then castigated "those fools" who are confused because he is not the one who gives permission to people who have court cases. I explained to him that I no longer had a court case. He told me the second incident was due to a confused immigration officer, Kalibata, who had detected that I was going through Uganda, a country that we had problems with. Then he hurled insults at my brother. Who did he think he was? Why didn't he raise the issues with Dr. Ndahiro or our ambassador in Washington DC, Dr. Nsenga. "He is a fool like Kalibata himself", he said.

Finally, he asked me if I still wanted to leave, and I responded in the affirmative. Could I wait till Friday, he asked. I told him if he did not mind, I would leave immediately. He said I could leave any time I wanted. Would the immigration people allow me to depart, I asked. He said they would. I then briefly told him that I was disappointed that I would be treated by RPF as a common criminal. Then he said, with the usual cynical laughter, "Those are your cadres!" When I appeared at the airport on April 19, bound for Entebbe, the immigration officers and security were over-friendly, even offering to hold my bags. It was too late, I told them, to be flattered in that manner. As Dorothy and I boarded the short flight from Kigali to Entebbe, I felt a deep anguish, wondering if or when we would return to Rwanda. Knowing President Kagame, I was not even sure the flight would reach the destination. When we arrived in Entebbe, Dorothy and I were greatly relieved that we were now safe. The kids were happy to see me as Dorothy and I planned our next move.

On the 21st of April, 2005, the Rudasingwa family boarded an Emirates flight to Dubai, bound for JFK, New York in the United States. We waited to tell the children where we were headed until we were airborne. They were so happy we were going to America. We arrived in New York on April 22, 2005. I had first come to the United States in the early 1990s representing the rebel movement, RPF. I had then come back to the United States as Rwanda's ambassador, after RPF's military victory of 1994. Now, I was returning to the United States as a refugee, with a big family, running away from the very system I had helped create.

CHAPTER THIRTY ONE

Coming to America

I arrived in New York city with "precious cargo" of five, since we left behind Archadius, my oldest son, with my sister. We landed penniless in America's bubbling city of New York. I recalled a favorite song of mine by Neil Diamond's, *Coming to America*, and the opening lyrics:

> Far,
> We've been traveling far
> Without a home
> But not without a star
>
> Free,
> Only want to be free
> We huddle close
> Hang on to a dream

We were coming from far, without a home, running away from persecution, hoping to be free and hang on to some dream. But what was the dream? As a young boy I had lamented the death of some American man who was killed by bad people. In college, America had become the embodiment of what I hated most, capitalism. I had, as a rebel Marxist RPF freedom fighter come to convince America to isolate the regime I was fighting. I thought that at some time the world would rise to fight to the finish the evil empire. We had nothing to lose but our chains, we had been taught. Later, serving as Rwanda's ambassador, I gradually became open minded to what the American proposition really was. I had been persuaded that there was plenty to learn in America, plenty to emulate, and plenty to avoid. I was coming to America at the height of my brokenness, alienation from RPF and Rwanda, and at a time of second conversion, to Christianity. I had been a refugee since childhood, in Burundi, Tanzania, Kenya and Uganda. Now a middle-aged man, the United States was my latest place of refuge. I had lived in Rwanda for a total of only about five years in my entire life. I was a refugee again, now with small children condemned, like me, to live outside their homeland at a tender age. For Dorothy, like me, exile was not new. I felt sad that I was leaving behind my mother and my sister. Dorothy was leaving behind her own mother who lived in Uganda.

Just one week after our arrival in the United States I received a call from Patricia, the President's Social Secretary. She told me the President wanted to talk to me. When he came on the line, he greeted me and asked where I was. I told him I was in Berkeley, California. He then asked me where Dorothy was. I told him I had left her in Washington, D.C. at her brother's place as I prepared for them to join me. He paused for a moment and then said, "I am not happy with Dorothy. She told a close relative of hers that she was glad to leave that backward country called Rwanda". I told him I was not aware of that, but I highly doubted it. I told him my wife is a very discreet person, and reminded him he himself had worked with her and knew this was the case. I promised him I would find out from Dorothy.

In my mind I found it a very uncomfortable conversation. Here was a Head of State on an international call, talking to his former Chief of Staff about what his spouse was rumoured to have said. Wasn't this very fact proof of backwardness, I thought.

He then raised the second issue. He had recently received my letter of resignation, and discussed its contents with General James Kabarebe and General Charles Kayonga. There were things and insinuations in the letter that they did not understand. I asked him whether there were clarifications he wanted me to make. He said, "When you come back we shall talk about it".

I took the opportunity to tell him I was looking for a new vocation, but that I did not have to leave in humiliation. I told him I had given the best of my youthful energy to what I thought was a good cause. I did not expect to be treated like a common criminal by RPF. I wasn't getting any younger, and had to settle down to something that interested me. He laughed and said I was still young and yet sounded as if I was the oldest in the RPF group. He also said my problems were not the worst. As we concluded the conversation, he told me Jakaya Kikwete of Tanzania had been nominated to become the new Chairman of the ruling party, Chama Cha Mapinduzi (CCM), and hence poised to become the next President to succeed President Benjamin Mkapa. That was my last conversation with President Kagame. The last communication I had from him was an email that was written on his behalf by Davinah Milenge, his Principal Private Secretary at the time, reminding me that I am soldier. We have not spoken since.

For two weeks, my family was accommodated in a small apartment that belonged to my very good friend and supervisor, Professor Drew Isaacs of Haas School of Business. To the north of the city of Berkeley is another small city of Albany, a community of about nineteen thousand people. This is where we settled and where our children attended elementary, middle and high school. The Berkeley-Albany area with its public libraries and supportive community, provided a good environment for the kids' learning. The population was mixed and friendly, and you did not feel a sense of being a foreigner. The kids made friends and loved being in California.

I introduced my family to First Presbyterian Church of Berkeley, First Pres as it is called. We all became active members of the church. The congregation is predominantly white, and our big family, normally preferring a particular back pew, was always visible. We all felt at home in the church community. Having converted to Christianity shortly before we left Rwanda, I was like a baby in the development of my faith. Pastor Mark Labberton and his colleagues were skilled in preaching to a sophisticated, and sometimes skeptical, university community. I was one such member of the church. One's mind is never an empty shelf that has to accommodate a new idea. Mine was rife with science, ideology, effects of war and genocide, personal loss and alienation. How would this whole baggage accommodate my new found Christian faith? How would my new Christian faith accommodate, or perhaps overcome, this baggage? First Pres did contribute to my early spiritual growth during this period. The church's program of bringing voices from the margins of the developing world, and providing learning opportunities to members of the congregation through visits to the hurting world were a unique approach of this church.

Founded in 1869, the University of California, Berkeley is located in the small city of Berkeley on the eastern shore of the Bay Area. The university is reputed to be the most politically liberal university in the United States, and is part of the University of California system. The seat of political activism in the 1960s, it was the birthplace of the Free Speech Movement in 1964. It is also famed for the opposition to the Vietnam War, and the People's Park protest that turned violent after the National Guard was called in. The University has a distinguished place in the world of learning as evidenced by the following accomplishments:

> Berkeley faculty, alumni, and researchers have won 70 Nobel Prizes, 9 Wolf Prizes, 7 Fields Medals, 15 Turing Awards, 45 MacArthur Fellowships,[8] 20 Academy Awards, and 11 Pulitzer Prizes. To date, UC Berkeley and

its researchers are associated with 6 chemical elements of the periodic table (Californium, Seaborgium, Berkelium, Einsteinium, Fermium, Lawrencium) and Berkeley Lab has discovered 16 chemical elements in total – more than any other university in the world. Berkeley is a founding member of the Association of American Universities and continues to have very high research activity with $652.4 million in research and development expenditures in 2009. Berkeley physicist J. Robert Oppenheimer was the scientific director of the Manhattan Project that developed the first atomic bomb in the world, which he personally headquartered at Los Alamos, New Mexico, during World War II.

Source: http://en.wikipedia.org/wiki/University_of_California,_Berkeley

Every morning as I walked past Boalt Hall, UC Berkeley's Law School, I paused to read the words inscribed on its wall:

> You will study the wisdom of the past, for in a wilderness of conflicting counsels, a trail has there been blazed. You will study the life of mankind, for this is the life you must order, and, to order with wisdom, must know. You will study the precepts of justice, for these are the truths that through you shall come to their hour of triumph. Here is the high emprise, the fine endeavor, the splendid possibility of achievement, to which I summon you and bid you welcome. ~ Cardozo

Here, in a renowned public university, I embarked on becoming a practitioner-academic, following trails that others have blazed, so that I could study the life of mankind in order to order it with wisdom. Justice in Rwanda had eluded me, but I felt there was another life to live.

At Haas Business School Management of Technology program under Professor Drew Isaacs, I found a refuge. With another friend of mine and supervisor, Professor Kristi Raube, Isaacs had founded a popular international program called *Bridging the Divide*, providing an opportunity for students to participate in research in developing countries to bridge the digital technology divide. My research interest was entrepreneurship, innovation and business development and how these could be pathways for overcoming Africa's poverty. Drew and Kristi were indeed helpful in many ways in helping me and my family settle in the San Francisco Bay Area, and provided guidance in my new transition to the world of academia.

Before I left Rwanda, it had been part of my new dream to facilitate learning trips from Rwanda and Africa to Silicon Valley. Silicon Valley is also called the Santa Clara Valley, extending between the Santa Cruz Mountains and the San Francisco Bay, from Palo Alto, Sunnyvale, and Mountainview and all the way to San Jose. The "silicon" part in the Silicon Valley name comes from the development of the computer chips in this area. Although California is famous for the movie industry in Hollywood and its wines, it is the computer technology, and high tech development in Silicon Valley that was of interest to many in the world who wanted to copy this model. I learned that various factors contributed to the development of Silicon Valley: 1) Leading Universities that provided a large pool of skilled engineers and scientists in one area; 2) the development of military radio and radar technologies that had an assured market from the US Department of Defense; 3) Law firms that provided the required infrastructure for formation, funding and expansion of high tech companies; 4) the availability of venture capital; 5) the role of diaspora communities, especially of Indian and Chinese origin; and 6) The University of Stanford's leadership role. Silicon Valley is almost synonymous with entrepreneurship and innovation. I always wondered what it took to combine such elements in combating poverty in the developing world.

With the help of Haas Business School Professors Isaacs and Raube, I developed and briefly taught a course, *Business and Technology for the Developing World*. It was a steep learning curve for me. The last time I had tried to teach was in the poverty stricken quarters of Nairobi where high school students comprised of unruly kids from the slums. My value added was now my knowledge of the developing world. My students, some of them doing PhDs, engineering and most doing their MBAs knew a lot more about innovation, entrepreneurship, technology and business development. My role was to integrate this knowledge and apply it to developing country situations.

The course was introductory in nature, providing an opportunity for students to understand the key business and development challenges facing the developing regions in the 21st Century; an appreciation of the link between sustainable business and sustainable development; an analysis, from theory and practice, of the link between technological innovation, entrepreneurship and sustainable business in the developing world; a spectrum of sectorial opportunities for sustainable business in developing countries; insights into the policy and reform environment that shape business and technology development in the developing regions; an introduction to aid, trade and foreign direct investment as tools for developing the capacity to do business for sustainable development; knowledge about best practices in public sector-private sector partnerships for sustainable development; and insights into leadership and managerial challenges in developing sustainable business in the developing world.

Two seminal works, Clayton Christensen's *Innovators Dilemma*, and the late CK Prahalad's *The Fortune at the Base of the Pyramid*, together with the United Nations Development Program's (UNDP) *Human Development Reports* since 1990, provided a good source for framing the poverty challenge. Hernando de Soto's *Mystery of Capital*, World Bank's *Annual World Development Reports* since 1987, Amartya Sen's *Development as a Freedom*, the World Health Organization's (WHO) *Alma Ata Declaration* on Primary Health Care, and the UN's *Millennium Development Goals* were additional resources that helped me develop an outlook on development that encompassed the roles of business, government, civil society and international multilateral and bilateral finance institutions and foundations.

The basic premise of the *Innovator's Dilemma*, applied to the developing world was that where there are un-met, and under-met, or over-met needs, there are opportunities for a newcomer to come up with a disruptive technology which is simple to use, convenient and cheap. The mobile phone in Africa is a good example. Prahalad's work speaks to the opportunities for alleviating poverty through business at the bottom of the population pyramid.

In *The Fortune at the Base of the Pyramid*, Prahalad argues that there is great potential among the world's poor in terms of aggregate purchasing power, if the required commercial infrastructure can be developed at the bottom of the pyramid to create buying power, shape aspirations, improve access and generate local solutions to local problems. The bottom of the pyramid framework incorporates cooperation among and between the stakeholders. Prahalad makes a very strong point in highlighting what he calls the "power of the dominant logic":

> All of us are prisoners of our own socialization. The lenses through which we perceive the world are colored by our own ideology, experiences, and established management practices. Each one of the groups that is focusing on poverty alleviation—the World Bank, rich countries providing aid, charitable organizations, national governments, and the private sector—is conditioned by its own dominant logic

Hence, he says, why, after so many decades, with trillions of US dollars spent on aid, poverty and inequality remain a global menace in our time. Part of the development challenge is to challenge, and even disrupt, this dominant logic.

Hernando de Soto, in his *The Mystery of Capital* makes a case for lack of a representation process in the Third World, which in the west has translated assets into capital:

> In the West, by contrast, every parcel of land, every building, every piece of equipment, or store of inventories is represented in a property document that is the visible sign of a vast hidden process that connects all these assets to the rest of the economy. Thanks to this representational process, assets can lead an invisible, parallel life alongside their material existence. They can be used as collateral for credit. The single most important source of funds for new businesses in the United States is a mortgage on the entrepreneur's house. These assets can also provide a link to the owner's credit history, an accountable address for the collection of debts and taxes, the basis for the creation of reliable and universal public utilities, and a foundation for the creation of securities (like mortgage-backed bonds) that can then be rediscounted and sold in secondary markets. By this process the West injects life into assets and makes them generate capital.

He goes on:

> Third World and former communist nations do not have this representational process. As a result, most of them are undercapitalized, in the same way that a firm is undercapitalized when it issues fewer securities than its income and assets would justify. The enterprises of the poor are very much like corporations that cannot issue shares or bonds to obtain new investment and finance. Without representations, their assets are dead capital.

The poor inhabitants of these nations—five-sixths of humanity—do have things, but they lack the process to represent their property and create capital. They have houses but not titles; crops but not deeds; businesses but not statutes of incorporation. It is the unavailability of these essential representations that explains why people who have adapted every other Western invention, from the paper clip to the nuclear reactor, have not been able to produce sufficient capital to make their domestic capitalism work.

In this debate enters William Easterly in his *Whiteman's Burden*, arguing that foreign aid has not worked because governmental bureaucracies with their elaborate plans are not the best vehicle for growing economies; Jeffrey Sachs who argues in *Ending Poverty* that the developing nations need more foreign aid to end poverty; Amartya Sen's *Development as Freedom* arguing for human interlinked capabilities in the political, economic, social, and security domains as well as transparency guarantees, all working together as means and ends; the *UN Millennium Development Goals*, in addition to the annual well written *Human Development Reports* from the UNDP, and the *World Development Reports* from the World Bank. My practice in government had introduced me to the works of Michael Porter on competition, and Michael Fairbank's group around the seven forms of capital in creating national prosperity.

I had absorbed much of the language of communism and socialism in my revolutionary years. Now I was a student and teacher of the fundamental tenets of capitalism. Things get more complicated in academic and revolutionary circles, and I was struggling to find a simpler way to engage students while refining my own outlook on what it takes to develop a nation, with communities, women , children, households and small businesses as a starting point.

CHAPTER THIRTY TWO

Tina's Equation

2005 was an exceptionally long and difficult year for our families. My brother and his family were also now in exile, in the United States. We had left behind our aging mother and our sister, Doreen. On the eve of the New Year, 2006, I gathered my whole family for prayer. Before prayer I asked the children what we should be thankful for. Dorothy and I are used to our dinner table conversations being like a mini General Assembly at the United Nations. Most of the time the children talk a lot and we listen. We take turns to lead prayer, and sometimes we burst into laughter, amidst prayer, after hearing what the minds of kids can imagine. Sometimes it would be candy, or French fries, or a complaint about one of their siblings, some imaginary tale, or solicitation of gifts from parents.

That night we were all in a somber mood. I insisted that they each tell us what we should be grateful for. One said we should be grateful that we are in America. Another said we should thank God we have seen the dollar bill. Another answered in general terms that we were together and safe. Our youngest child, Tina, was then five, turning six the following year. Normally talkative, she seemed to be in a pensive mood. She put her hand up and said we should thank God for love. I asked the children again, like a probing teacher, "what else?" Everyone was silent, except Tina, who put up her hand again. She said, "We should thank God for forgiveness." Dorothy and I looked at each other, wondering whether Tina understood what forgiveness meant. She had just started kindergarten. By then the whole household had become attentive.

I posed the question again, "what else?", and Tina put up her hand, and said, "We should thank God for freedom". Dorothy and I were shocked. These could not be the words of a five year old. What did little Tina know about freedom? As parents we had made sure our children were not told about my incarceration, trial and problems with President Kagame. For a while we saw Tina scribbling words on a piece of paper. Then she asked, "Daddy, if you have love, forgiveness and freedom what do you have?" I was astonished by Tina's question. It was the first time ever in my entire life for anyone to pose a question of that nature. Like a teacher or parent asked a difficult question by a student or child, I said, "Tina, let us pray, go to sleep and I will tell you the answer tomorrow."

The truth was that I did not immediately have an answer to Tina's question. Tina told us she had an answer to her own question. Then she handed me the piece of paper, and then said, "You see daddy, when you have love, forgiveness and freedom, you have life."

Her very words, misspelled but eligible, were expressed in an equation form:

$$(LOVE + FORGIVENESS + FREEDOM = LIFE)$$

Dorothy and I had no words. I knew I had heard something unique and special. That five-year old Tina would have found love, forgiveness and freedom as profound things was surprising enough. For her to have imagined a relationship among them, and their relationship to life, I found absolutely touching and life-changing. Her equation was very simple and elegant. I immediately called it Tina's Equation.

The equation fully resonated with the African idea of *Ubuntu*, and my conversion to Christianity, whose foundation is love of God and love of neighbor. Paul of Tarsus (also known as Saul), who began his career persecuting Christians until his conversion, took serious the teachings of Jesus Christ when he said:

> If I speak in the tongues of men or of angels, but do not have love, I am only a resounding gong or a clanging cymbal. If I have the gift of prophecy and can fathom all mysteries and all knowledge, and if I have a faith that can move mountains,but do not have love, I am nothing. If I give all I possess to the poor and give over my body to hardship that I may boast but do not have love, I gain nothing.

> Love is patient, love is kind. It does not envy, it does not boast, it is not proud. It does not dishonor others, it is not self-seeking, it is not easily angered, it keeps no record of wrongs. Love does not delight in evil but rejoices with the truth. It always protects, always trusts, always hopes, always perseveres.

> Love never fails. But where there are prophecies, they will cease; where there are tongues, they will be stilled; where there is knowledge, it will pass away. For we know in part and we prophesy in part, but when completeness comes, what is in part disappears. When I was a child, I talked like a child, I thought like a child, I reasoned like a child. When I became a man, I put the ways of childhood behind me. For now we see only a reflection as in a mirror; then we shall see face to face. Now I know in part; then I shall know fully, even as I am fully known.

And now these three remain: faith, hope and love. But the greatest of these is love.

1 Corinthians 13: 1-13 (NIV)

My conversion had opened doors to listen out for life-changing words, even from babies. Was Jesus Christ now inviting me to relate to my fellow Rwandans through the lens of love.

CHAPTER THIRTY THREE

Insights from Fletcher School

W hen I returned to the United States in April 2005, I had lost hope of being readmitted to the Fletcher School of Law and Diplomacy for my graduate studies in international relations. I had missed almost a whole year, and I did not think it was possible to study, teach, and find means of looking after my family. At UC Berkeley, I had obtained a small grant from *Intel*, the US chip-manufacturer to continue with my work on technologies to promote health in Africa. Fletcher School surprised me one day when I was told I had a full scholarship to resume my graduate studies. It was not easy to balance family, teaching at UC Berkeley and studying at Fletcher. Since my graduate studies were mainly online, it made it a lot easier for me to study at home, frequently with kids all over me.

My graduate studies at Fletcher School were partly an experience in comparing notes between my practice since 1990 on the one hand, and the theory of international relations on the other. The GMAP (Global Master of Arts Program), as it is popularly called, touches on various themes, namely, international politics, international security, negotiations, international finance, international economics, transnational organizations, strategic leadership and management in foreign policy and business.

MY TAKEAWAYS FROM FLETCHER SCHOOL

On Negotiations: I was keen to learn what happened with the Northern Ireland peace process, the Israel-Palestinian Oslo peace process, the negotiated settlement to end of the South African apartheid regime, and what was going on with the Six Party talks regarding the intractable problem of North Korea and the nuclear program. We negotiate every day. We negotiate with spouses and children. We negotiate prices. In conflict situations, conversations are very difficult, and, like every such conversation they involve taking positions on what happened, who is to blame, and identity. It is necessary to take into account the other side's interests, and invent options so that in the final outcome the parties are all winners instead of one side feeling it is a loser. The idea of taking into account the other side's interests, and inventing options for a win-win solution, seemed to me very appealing. In retrospect, I realized how Rwanda's Arusha peace negotiations was positional bargaining, with the RPF and the government side taking little trouble in understanding the other side's interest, and each side seeking to take the maximum from the table. I would recommend to every Rwandan to read *Getting to Yes: Negotiating Agreement Without Giving In* by William Ury, Roger Fisher, and Bruce Patton; and *Difficult Conversations: How To Discuss What Matters Most* by Bruce Patton, Douglas Stone, Sheila Heen and Roger Fisher.

On Just Wars and International Security: The idea of a *just war* is rooted in Greek (Plato), Roman (Cicero), and Christian philosophers and theologians (Augustine and Thomas Aquinas). The starting point of the just war theory is that war is bad, but may be necessary under certain conditions and must be fought in an ethical way. It makes a distinction between **Jus ad bellum** (the conditions under which the use of military force is justified), and **Jus in bello** (how to conduct a war in an ethical manner).

According to the Just War theory, six conditions must be satisfied for a war to be considered just:

- The war must be for a just cause.
- The war must be lawfully declared by a lawful authority.
- The intention behind the war must be good.
- All other ways of resolving the problem should have been tried first.
- There must be a reasonable chance of success.
- The means used must be in proportion to the end that the war seeks to achieve.

In 2006, the United States was in the middle of the wars in Afghanistan and Iraq, both conditioned by the events of September 11, 2001. In both countries the USA and its international coalition forces were engaged in counterinsurgency. Asymmetric wars, the Professors taught, were becoming the pattern of warfare in the 21st Century. They were called asymmetric wars because they involved non-state actors who were eager to deny a powerful enemy an opportunity to deploy the full arsenal of its warmaking machine. The Rwandan civil war in the 1990s was such an asymmetric war, with RPF, a non-state actor, pitted against the Rwandan state.

In 2001, a non-state actor, Al Qaeda under Bin Laden had struck at the heart of the United States by the terrorist acts directed at the Twin Towers and the Pentagon. The shock, awe, and fear changed the world as we know it, we were taught. As a student of revolutionary warfare from Marx, Lenin, Mao, Che Guevara, Frantz Fanon and Fidel Castro to recent wars of national liberation in Angola, Mozambique, Uganda, Ethiopia, Eritrea, and Sudan, this was not new to me. What was new was the global context in which the United States was a leading player in the asymmetric wars.

Insurgency and counterinsurgency are subsets of war. Though globalization and technological advancement have influenced contemporary conflict, the nature of war in the 21st century is the same as it has been since ancient times, "...a violent clash of interests between or among organized groups characterized by the use of military force." Success in war still depends on a group's ability to mobilize support for its political interests and generate sufficient violence to achieve political consequences. Means to achieve these goals are not limited to regular armies employed by a nation-state. At its core, war is a violent struggle between hostile, independent, and irreconcilable wills attempting to impose their desires on another. It is a complex interaction between human beings and is played out in a continuous process of action, reaction, and adaptation. As an extension of both policy and politics with the addition of military force, war can take different forms across the spectrum of conflict. It may range from large-scale forces engaged in conventional warfare to subtler forms of conflict that barely reach the threshold of violence. It is within this spectrum that insurgency and counterinsurgency exist.

Insurgency and its tactics are as old as warfare itself. Joint doctrine defines an *insurgency* as an organized movement aimed at the overthrow of a constituted government through the use of subversion and armed conflict. *Counterinsurgency* is those political, economic, military, paramilitary, psychological, and civic actions taken by a government to defeat an insurgency.

Source: *U.S. Army/Marine Corps Counter-Insurgency Field Manual* by Sarah Sewall, David Petraus, John Nagl and James Amos.

The online student discussions with professors were indeed spirited. Some argued that to prevent such wars, the United States would have to have a window into the hearts and minds of the peoples and cultures of the world, because that is where needs and perceptions have to be addressed to deny terrorists breeding ground. In the words of Joseph Nye, the US needed to deploy more of its *soft power*, and act with others, in a preventive way, rather that acting unilaterally with hard power once insurrections have begun. Nation building, complex emergencies, forceful diplomacy and escalation in war were interesting themes we discussed.

It was during this period that I found out more about reasons why the United States decided not to respond to the crisis of civil war and genocide in Rwanda. The debacle in Somalia led to Presidential Policy Directive (PDD 56) of May 1997. Note that before the US intervenes in any situation, its national interests are a key consideration. Why for instance, should President Bill Clinton have intervened in Rwanda? Rwanda is a small country, without natural resources, inhabited by Africans, in a volatile region, and of minimal geostrategic interests at that time.

Annex A: Illustrative Components of a Political-Military Plan for a Complex Contingency Operation

- *Situation Assessment.* A comprehensive assessment of the situation to clarify essential information that, in the aggregate, provides a multi-dimensional picture of the crisis.
- *U.S. Interests.* A statement of U.S. interests at stake in the crisis and the requirement to secure those interests.
- *Mission Statement.* A clear statement of the USG's strategic purpose for the operation and the pol-mil mission.
- *Objectives.* The key civil-military objectives to be accomplished during the operation.

- *Desired Pol-Mil End State.* The conditions the operation is intended to create before the operation transitions to a follow-on operation and/or terminates.
- *Concept of the Operation.* A conceptual description of how the various instruments of USG policy will be integrated to get the job done throughout all phases of the operation.
- *Lead Agency Responsibilities.* An assignment of responsibilities for participating agencies.
- *Transition/Exit Strategy.* A strategy that is linked to the realization of the end state described above, requiring the integrated efforts of diplomats, military leaders, and relief officials of the USG and the international community.
- *Organizational Concept.* A schematic of the various organizational structures of the operation, in Washington and in theater, including a description of the chain of authority and associated reporting channels.
- *Preparatory Tasks.* A layout of specific tasks to be undertaken before the operation begins (congressional consultations, diplomatic efforts, troop recruitment, legal authorities, funding requirements and sources, media coordination, etc.).
- *Functional or Mission Area Tasks / Agency Plans.* Key operational and support plans written by USG agencies that pertain to critical parts of the operation (e.g., political mediation/reconciliation, military support, demobilization, humanitarian assistance, police reform, basic public services, economic restoration, human rights monitoring, social reconciliation, public information, etc.).

Source: http://www.fas.org/irp/offdocs/pdd56.htm

On Responsibility to Protect: The principle of Responsibility to Protect under international law, clearly stipulates that:

Sovereignty no longer exclusively protects States from foreign interference; it is a charge of responsibility that holds States accountable for the welfare of their people.

The Responsibility to Protect principle stands on three core ideas:

The State carries the primary responsibility for protecting populations from genocide, war crimes, crimes against humanity and ethnic cleansing, and their incitement;

The international community has a responsibility to encourage and assist States in fulfilling this responsibility;

The international community has a responsibility to use appropriate diplomatic, humanitarian and other means to protect populations from these crimes. If a State is manifestly failing to protect its populations, the international community must be prepared to take collective action to protect populations, in accordance with the Charter of the United Nations

Source: *The Responsibility to Protect: Ending Mass Atrocity Crimes Once and for All* by Gareth Evans

The principle emerged from a report by the U.N. High Level Panel on Threats, Challenges and Change, *A More Secure World: Our Shared Responsibility* which identified six global threats and challenges: namely, Economic and social threats, including poverty, infectious disease and environmental degradation; Inter-State conflict; Internal conflict, including civil war, genocide and other large-scale atrocities; Nuclear, radiological, chemical and biological weapons; terrorism; and transnational organized crime.

Translated into ordinary language, the Responsibility to protect idea simply means if any government commits war crimes, crimes against humanity, or genocide, or is unable to stop the crimes on its territory, the international community has an obligation and duty to intervene and protect the people.

On Coercive Diplomacy: Forceful persuasion, as Alexander George describes in his insightful book, *Forceful Persuasion: Coercive Diplomacy as An Alternative to War,* seeks to achieve three objectives, namely to force an adversary to change his goals, reverse an action already taken, or to make fundamental changes in his government. The coercer must think about, in advance, how to create a sense of urgency, what punishment will be imposed if the adversary fails or refuses to comply, or whether in fact there are other positive inducements to encourage compliance.

Alexander George developed a framework with four variants to achieve the above objectives:

1. Ultimatum: with three elements, "a demand on the opponent; a time limit or sense of urgency for compliance with the demand; and a threat of punishment for noncompliance that is both credible to the opponent and sufficiently potent to impress upon him that compliance is preferable"
2. Tacit Ultimatum: No time limit is set
3. Try-and-See: just a demand on the opponent
4. Gradual Turning of the Screw: relies on gradual and incremental use of coercive pressure rather than threat of decisive military action

In retrospect, coercive diplomacy would have been the appropriate framework during the period preceding the 1994 genocide in Rwanda. It is a tool to deploy in the current situation in Rwanda, and the volatile region in the Great Lakes region.

On International Finance, Trade and Economics: Beyond acquiring improved literacy in the world of global finance, trade and economics, the discussions enabled me to understand the dynamics of what has been called the Washington Consensus, a term coined by John Williamson to describe a set of policies by the Washington-based institutions

These policies were:
- Fiscal discipline
- A redirection of public expenditure priorities toward fields offering both high economic returns and the potential to improve income distribution, such as primary health care, primary education, and infrastructure
- Tax reform (to lower marginal rates and broaden the tax base)
- Interest rate liberalization
- A competitive exchange rate
- Trade liberalization
- Liberalization of inflows of foreign direct investment
- Privatization
- Deregulation (to abolish barriers to entry and exit)
- Secure property rights

Source: http://www.who.int/trade/glossary/story094/en/index.html

The list has been extended to include what Dani Rodrik calls the "Augmented" Washington Consensus:

- Corporate governance
- Anti-corruption
- Flexible labor markets
- WTO agreements
- Financial codes and standards
- "Prudent" capital-account opening

- Non-intermediate exchange rate regimes
- Independent central banks/inflation targeting
- Social safety nets
- Targeted poverty reduction

Source: http://neweconomist.blogs.com/new_economist/2006/01/rodrik_on_the_a.html

Can the Washington Consensus really be the cure to the global poverty crisis? Many have argued that these policies have impoverished the recipient countries to which they are directed. Others have asserted that the poor countries have limited options and little room for maneuver. The countries of Western Europe and Japan did not rise to economic prominence due to the Marshall Plan, important as it was. The much celebrated Asian Tigers of Singapore, Hong Kong, Malaysia, Taiwan and South Korea did not transition from Third World status to developed nation status due to aid from the World Bank, IMF and aid in general. Recent success stories of the BRIC countries (Brazil, Russia, India, and China), I would add South Africa, have not achieved that due to help from Washington, D.C. They have employed the policies selectively, but this has been more home-grown rather than dictated by the World Bank, IMF and western donors. Successful countries invest in their people (education and health), infrastructure, right policies that enable private sector development, foreign trade and investment, the right macro-economic conditions and political stability.

Spirited debates reminded me of my days in government, both in Washington, D.C. as Rwanda's ambassador and in Rwanda as the President's Chief of Staff. The major preoccupation was to negotiate with the World Bank and IMF. Rwanda's Minister of Finance, Donald Kaberuka did a good job on that front, although I found him too much of a product of the Washington Consensus. They all loved him, because he knew them and spoke their language. He was pragmatic, since he knew Rwanda's dire needs and limited choice for sources of revenue. Minister Kaberuka had two IMF officials, Fred and Jacob, deployed in his office to make sure the Central Bank and Ministry of Finance books were in order (often doctored) to attract the next tranche of funding from donors. Rwanda's foreign exchange reserves always had to be the equivalent of six months of imports. The IMF always insisted the government had to reign on its expenditure and improve its revenues through taxation. Most of the conditions in the Washington Consensus should be generated from within. Part of the motivation for Rwanda to get involved in the conversation on prosperity was to gradually move away from the straightjacket of the Washington Consensus.

On Strategic Leadership and Management: In his *The Practice of Management*, Peter Drucker, the Austrian journalist turned Economist who became, what many believe, the father of modern management, wrote that a manager had five important tasks: 1) Setting objectives; 2) Organizing; 3) Motivating people and communicating; 4) Measuring; and 5) Developing people. Though leaders and managers work hand in hand, some argue that they are different. In *Primal Leadership*, Goleman et al. suggest that the effective leaders must continually develop two types of competences, namely, personal competence and social competence:

This is what Daniel Goleman calls *emotional intelligence*, in his bestseller, *Emotional Intelligence*. In short, emotions matter. You have to be aware of yourself and manage yourself. Then you have to be aware of your social environment and then manage the social relationships. If you can do that with a high degree of professionalism and exceptional humility, you are a level five leader, according to Jim Collins, the author of *Good to Great* and *Built to Last*. I could already see that many of us in the Rwandan leadership had problems in the area of emotional intelligence. It does not matter whether you are a leader in government, business, and civil society or in a community; emotional intelligence is necessary for you to manage and lead well.

In *Primal Leadership*, Daniel Goleman argues that different leaders have different leadership styles, and may have the capacity to use different styles in one situation, or deploy different styles in different situations. There are visionaries and those who coach. There are those who are affiliative and others who are democratic. There are those who are pace-setters and others who are commanding. In all types of organizations, the character, judgment and decision by one leader have led to success or collapse of empires, nations, and corporations big and small. Leaders have made decisions that have led to war or ended it. Consider the decision by President Truman to use the nuclear bomb in Japan that ended the Second World War, and Adolf Hitler's decisions that started it. In 1979, Idi Amin of Uganda annexed a little known strip of territory in Tanzania called the Kagera salient and within months a combined force of Tanzanian troops and Ugandan exiles toppled him. A fateful decision by President Kagame to shoot down the plane carrying two Heads of State (Habyarimana of Rwanda and Ntaryamira of Burundi) triggered the 1994 genocide in Rwanda. Ethiopia and Eritrea have fought and lost so many lives and lots of resources over a barren territory that is called Badme. Having a healthy body and mind, the right advisors, the right domestic agenda, a correct assessment of your internal strengths and external conditions, as well as tenacity, are particularly crucial, if not indispensable, in foreign policy leadership.

In *Victims of Groupthink*, an influential book published in 1972, later published as *Groupthink: Psychological Studies of Policy Decisions and Fiascoes*, Irving Janis described what he called Groupthink, a psychological group condition characterized by the following symptoms:

- Illusion of invulnerability –Creates excessive optimism that encourages taking extreme risks.

- Collective rationalization – Members discount warnings and do not reconsider their assumptions.
- Beliefs in inherent morality – Members believe in the rightness of their cause and therefore ignore the ethical or moral consequences of their decisions.
- Stereotyped views of out-groups – Negative views of "enemy" make effective responses to conflict seem unnecessary.
- Direct pressure on dissenters – Members are under pressure not to express arguments against any of the group's views.
- Self-censorship – Doubts and deviations from the perceived group consensus are not expressed.
- Illusion of unanimity – The majority view and judgments are assumed to be unanimous.
- Self-appointed 'mind guards' – Members protect the group and the leader from information that is problematic or contradictory to the group's cohesiveness, view, and/or decisions.

Janis was of the view that where groupthink exists, members are not likely to consider alternative views, and the group will take irrational and faulty decisions. Groupthink is likely to take place where groups have a high degree of cohesiveness, where members have a similar background, and where such members are insulated from outside views. Janis gave examples of groupthink in US foreign policy: The Japanese attack on Pearl Harbor, the Bay of Pigs crisis and the escalation of the Vietnam War.

When applied to Rwanda, it is evident that the Monarchist regime before the 1959 revolution suffered from groupthink, and so have all the regimes since then (MDR-PARMEHUTU under President Gregoire Kayibanda, MRND under President Juvenal Habyarimana, and now RPF under President Paul Kagame). Because groupthink divides people into us and them, and the other is the enemy, it may account for the cycle of deadly conflict, war crimes, crimes against humanity, and even genocide.

Most importantly, leaders should beware of success as well as failure. When we succeed we tend to believe it is because we are talented and our strategies are smart; we also tend to be over-confident, and do not ask why we are succeeding. We take it for granted. In a recent Harvard Business Review article, *Strategies for Learning from Failure*, HBR Professor Amy Edmondson makes a case for making organizations psychologically safe for failure:

- Frame the work accurately so that expectations are known before hand;
- Don't shoot the messenger, the bearer of bad news, so that you can encourage them to come forward;
- Acknowledge your own limits by being open about your own failures;
- Invite participation;
- Set boundaries and hold people accountable.

In *Think Again: Why Good Leaders Make Bad Decisions*, Sydney Finkelstein et al. attribute good leaders' bad decisions from past experiences and judgments that mislead, as well as self-interests and attachment that biases them. The antidote to such, Finkelstein says, is to provide fresh experience, new data and analysis; to build processes that challenge biased thinking and action; to put in place a governance team that will stand in the way of flawed judgment of one leader; and, put in place continuous monitoring and reporting throughout the whole decision-making process.

On the Language of International Law, International Human Rights, and International Humanitarian Law: Besides learning the mechanisms and content of the World Trade Organization (WTO), and how Letters of Credit work, I was keen to absorb precise definitions of what these laws were since they had become part of the language in Rwanda. I had previously used many of the above terms, without caring to learn about their origins, and in what situations they are applicable. Rwanda's civil war and genocide, and their consequences in the Great Lakes region of central Africa implies that leaders and enlightened citizens have to learn the content and language of these human treaties, covenants and human rights instruments.

International Law is the law:

> International law is the set of rules generally regarded and accepted as binding in relations between states and nations. It serves as the indispensable framework for the practice of stable and organized international relations

International Humanitarian Law:

> International humanitarian law is a set of rules which seek, for humanitarian reasons, *to limit the effects of armed conflict*. It protects persons who are not or are no longer participating in the hostilities and restricts the means and methods of warfare. International humanitarian law is also known as the law of war or the law of armed conflict.

International Human Rights Law

> International human rights law refers to the body of international law designed to promote and protect human rights at the international, regional and domestic levels. As a form of international law, international human rights law is primarily made up of treaties, agreements between

states intended to have binding legal effect between the parties that have agreed to them; and customary international law, rules of law derived from the consistent conduct of states acting out of the belief that the law required them to act that way. Other international human rights instruments while not legally binding contribute to the implementation, understanding and development of international human rights law and have been recognized as a source of *political* obligation.

The Universal Declaration of Human Rights, the African Charter on Human and Peoples Rights, as well as the following human rights instruments, are part of international human rights law.

Besides the adoption of the two wide-covering Covenants (International Covenant on Civil and Political Rights and International Covenant on Economic, Social and Cultural Rights) in 1966, a number of other treaties (pieces of legislation) have been adopted at the international level.

They are generally known as *human rights instruments*. Some of the most significant include (Source: http://www.unfpa.org/rights/instruments.htm)

- Convention on the Prevention and Punishment of the Crime of Genocide (CPCG) (adopted 1948, entry into force: 1951)
- Convention Relating to the Status of Refugees (CSR) (adopted 1951, entry into force: 1954)
- Convention on the Elimination of All Forms of Racial Discrimination (CERD) (adopted 1965, entry into force: 1969)
- Convention on the Elimination of All Forms of Discrimination Against Women (CEDAW) (entry into force: 1981)
- United Nations Convention Against Torture (CAT) (adopted 1984, entry into force: 1987)

- Convention on the Rights of the Child (CRC) (adopted 1989, entry into force: 1990)
- International Convention on the Protection of the Rights of All Migrant Workers and Members of their Families (ICRMW) (adopted 1990, entry into force: 2003)
- Convention on the Rights of Persons with Disabilities(CRPD) (entry into force: 3 May 2008)
- International Convention for the Protection of All Persons from Enforced Disappearance (adopted 2006, entry into force: 2010)

The 1949 Convention on Genocide:

In the present Convention, genocide means any of the following acts committed with intent to destroy, in whole or in part, a national, ethnical, racial or religious group, as such:

(a) Killing members of the group;
(b) Causing serious bodily or mental harm to members of the group;
(c) Deliberately inflicting on the group conditions of life calculated to bring about its physical destruction in whole or in part;
(d) Imposing measures intended to prevent births within the group;
(e) Forcibly transferring children of the group to another group.

War Crimes:

Article 147 of the Fourth Geneva Convention defines war crimes as: "Willful killing, torture or inhuman treatment, including... willfully causing great suffering or serious injury to body or health, unlawful deportation or transfer or unlawful confinement of a protected person, compelling a protected person to serve in the forces of a hostile power, or willfully depriving a protected person of the rights of fair and regular trial, ...taking of hostages and extensive destruction and appropriation of property, not justified by military necessity and carried out unlawfully and wantonly."

Crimes Against Humanity:

The International Tribunal at The Hague defines crime against humanity as crimes committed in armed conflict but directed against a civilian population. Again a list of examples is given in article 5:

- Murder
- Extermination
- Enslavement
- Deportation
- Imprisonment
- Torture
- Rape
- Persecutions on political, racial and religious grounds.

On Democracy, Tyranny and Genocide: Societies that have experienced genocide, war crimes, crimes against humanity and other serious human rights abuses have also been societies under dictatorial (or tyrannical) regimes, and in conditions of war. Examples to date include: the Armenian genocide, in the last days of the Ottoman Empire during the First World War and after; the Jewish Holocaust, Germany under Adolf Hitler, during the

Second World War; Cambodia under the Khmer Rouge regime of Pol Pot after the civil war that brought the communist regime to power in 1975; in Bosnia-Herzegovina, where , after declaring independence from the former Republic of Yugoslavia, Bosnian Serbs supported by the Serb-dominated Yugoslav army targeted Bosnian Muslims and Croatian civilians; Darfur, Sudan, under the Islamic regime of President Omar Al Bashir; Rwanda, in conditions of civil war under the regime of President Habyarimana, and after his death in 1994, the so-called Provisional Government; in the Democratic Republic of Congo (DRC) during two wars imposed by Rwanda's RPF regime under President Paul Kagame.

The common denominator in all these examples is a society experiencing violent conflict, transitioning to or from war, and the presence of a dictatorial regime. In his book, *Modern Tyrants: The Power and Prevalence of Evil in Our Age*, Daniel Chirot's eight propositions shed some light on corelated factors associated with the rise of tyrannies, which in turn create a permissive environment in which genocide, war crimes, crimes against humanity and other gross human rights abuses take place. In *The Future of Freedom: Illiberal Democracy at Home and Abroad* by Fareed Zakaria, an attempt is made to explain that there is tension and marriage between liberty and democracy. Quoting Samuel Huntington in *The Third Wave*:

> Elections, open, free and fair, are the essence of democracy, the inescapable sine qua non. Governments produced by elections may be inefficient, corrupt, shortsighted, irresponsible, dominated by special interests, and incapable of adopting policies demanded by the public good. These qualities make such governments undesirable but they do not make them undemocratic. Democracy is one public virtue, not the only one, and the relation of democracy to other public virtues and vices can only be understood if democracy is clearly distinguished from the other characteristics of political systems.

On the other hand, Zakaria argues;

> Constitutional liberalism, on the other hand, is not about the procedures for selecting government, but rather government's goals. It refers to the tradition, deep in Western history, that seeks to protect an individual's autonomy and dignity against coercion, whatever the source–state, church, or society. The term marries two closely connected ideas. It is liberal because it draws on the philosophical strain, beginning with the Greeks, that emphasizes individual liberty. It is constitutional because it rests on the tradition, beginning with the Romans, of the rule of law. Constitutional liberalism developed in Western Europe and the United States as a defense of the individual's right to life and property, and freedom of religion and speech. To secure these rights, it emphasized checks on the power of each branch of government, equality under the law, impartial courts and tribunals, and separation of church and state.

Rule of majorities can easily become tyrannical, hence the tension with liberty. According to Zakaria, most democracies in the world today are *illiberal*.

In *Democracy*, Charles Tilly highlights the chronology of the development of democracy over time and across various societies. He clearly shows how it is never a linear process, and how it takes different forms. However, he argues, for comparative purposes one could look at the development of political rights and civil liberties that give content to the practice of democracy.

Freedom House has a checklist of questions related to the development of liberal democracy (Exercise for Rwandans: answer Yes or No to each of the questions below, with regard to President Kagame's RPF regime, and on a scale of 10, give a grade):

POLITICAL RIGHTS

A. ELECTORAL PROCESS

1. Is the head of government or other chief national authority elected through free and fair elections?
2. Are the national legislative representatives elected through free and fair elections?
3. Are the electoral laws and framework fair?

B. AND PARTICIPATION

1. Do the people have the right to organize in different political parties or other competitive political groupings of their choice, and is the system open to the rise and fall of these competing parties or groupings?
2. Is there a significant opposition vote and a realistic possibility for the opposition to increase its support or gain power through elections?
3. Are the people's political choices free from domination by the military, foreign powers, totalitarian parties, religious hierarchies, economic oligarchies, or any other powerful group?
4. Do cultural, ethnic, religious, or other minority groups have full political rights and electoral opportunities?

C. FUNCTIONING OF GOVERNMENT

1. Do the freely elected head of government and national legislative representatives determine the policies of the government?
2. Is the government free from pervasive corruption?
3. Is the government accountable to the electorate between elections, and does it operate with openness and transparency?

ADDITIONAL DISCRETIONARY POLITICAL RIGHTS QUESTIONS

1. For traditional monarchies that have no parties or electoral process, does the system provide for genuine, meaningful consultation with the people, encourage public discussion of policy choices, and allow the right to petition the ruler?
2. Is the government or occupying power deliberately changing the ethnic composition of a country or territory so as to destroy a culture or tip the political balance in favor of another group?

CIVIL LIBERTIES

D. FREEDOM OF EXPRESSION AND BELIEF

1. Are there free and independent media and other forms of cultural expression? (Note: In cases where the media are state-controlled but offer pluralistic points of view, the survey gives the system credit.)
2. Are religious institutions and communities free to practice their faith and express themselves in public and private?
3. Is there academic freedom, and is the educational system free of extensive political indoctrination?
4. Is there open and free private discussion?

E. ASSOCIATIONAL AND ORGANIZATIONAL RIGHTS

1. Is there freedom of assembly, demonstration, and open public discussion?

2. Is there freedom for nongovernmental organizations? (Note: This includes civic organizations, interest groups, foundations, etc.)
3. Are there free trade unions and peasant organizations or equivalents, and is there effective collective bargaining? Are there free professional and other private organizations?

F. RULE OF LAW

1. Is there an independent judiciary?
2. Does the rule of law prevail in civil and criminal matters? Are police under direct civilian control?
3. Is there protection from political terror, unjustified imprisonment, exile, or torture, whether by groups that support or oppose the system? Is there freedom from war and insurgencies?
4. Do laws, policies, and practices guarantee equal treatment of various segments of the population?

G. PERSONAL AUTONOMY AND INDIVIDUAL RIGHTS

1. Do citizens enjoy freedom of travel or choice of residence, employment, or institution of higher education?
2. Do citizens have the right to own property and establish private businesses? Is private business activity unduly influenced by government officials, the security forces, political parties/organizations, or organized crime?
3. Are there personal social freedoms, including gender equality, choice of marriage partners, and size of family?

4. Is there equality of opportunity and the absence of economic exploitation?

Source:http://www.freedomhouse.org/report/freedom-world-2012/checklist-questions

Another consideration is the relationship between democracy and economic development. While there is no obvious cause and effect relationship between economic development and democracy, there is a strong correlation. Higher and increasing levels of prosperity create enabling conditions for democracy to develop. On the other hand, entrenching the rule of law, freedom of space, institutional chacks and balances, popular sovereignty, public space for debate, tolerance as well as individual political and economic rights creates enabling conditions for social and economic development.

On Environmental Stewardship. I benefited a lot from Garrett Hardin's *Tragedy of the Commons*, and the Documentary, *An Inconvenient Truth* (Directed by Davis Guggenheim, about former Vice-President Al Gore's campaign to educate citizens about global warming). Never before had I attained a level of consciousness regarding the importance of the collective will and action to protect planet earth that we share, including air, water, farmland, fish, wildlife, biodiversity, etc. Using common grazing land as an example, Hardin argued that each farmer obtains individual benefit by adding one more cow to the land, while collectively the increase of the total herd leads to overgrazing. The main message of *An Inconvenient Truth* is that global warming is real, and that it takes individual and collective response to stop and reverse a planetary tragedy that is unfolding.

CHAPTER THIRTY FOUR

Return to the Health Profession

D ue to funding problems at UC Berkeley, I ended up working with a San Francisco- based international consulting non-governmental organization, called Pangaea Global AIDS Foundation. In its early days, HIV/AIDS struck the gay community in San Francisco. Slowly mobilized, the gay community took the lead in responding to the pandemic, by establishing the San Francisco AIDS Foundation to deal with the challenge locally and later, Pangaea Global AIDS Foundation to contribute to global efforts to stem the tide of HIV/AIDS in the developing world. I met Pangaea's CEO, Dr. Eric Goosby, during my days in Washington DC. I worked with him again in Rwanda the Office of the President. Ambassador Eric Goosby currently heads the U.S. Office of the Global AIDS Coordinator, whose mission is to implement U.S. President's Emergency Plan for AIDS Relief (PEPFAR).

One of my earliest experiences at Pangaea was to interest Dr. Goosby in what I described to him as the small and medium enterprises (SMEs) in Africa. At a lunch with the Chief Financial Officer of the organization, I told him these small businesses employed most people in Africa, and were a big contributor to the national income of African countries. Unfortunately, they had been hit hard by the HIV/AIDS pandemic, leading to serious economic and social consequences. I remember Dr. Goosby saying whatever I was saying made a lot of sense. Pangaea immediately put SMEs as one of the projects we could pursue, but, unfortunately, since it all depended on funding, we had little luck.

The second idea I consistently brought to the attention of all my colleagues at Pangaea was that the current resource mobilization and consulting model from the west to African countries was not sustainable, and would soon hit a dead end if there were no efforts to innovate. Most African countries that received money for HIV treatment, prevention, care and support had come to expect it, and were not making enough effort to make sure they would be on their own at some point in the future. Probably this was not the best forum to raise the matter, although I did raise the issue during the International AIDS conference. The third related matter I persistently raised with Dr. Goosby was the relationship between single disease programs like HIV/AIDS and the overall healthcare system, but most importantly, with the wealth-creating capabilities (development of a country). Unless there is an effort by a donor country like the United States to deploy its resource envelope in a synergistic manner, encompassing both overall health and development, it may save lives for a time being but in the long run its impact will be minimal. One has to build health systems, as well as wealth systems, in an interrelated fashion to make maximum and sustainable impact.

Finally, I brought to the attention of Pangaea that the best way to design and implement a good HIV/AIDS program in resource-limited settings of Africa, Asia and Latin America, is to adopt a community approach and have a women and children focus. This would have a powerful multiplier effect across the whole society. In pushing for the community approach, I was also highlighting the Alma Ata declaration on primary healthcare, and how it is the best approach to realize the Millennium Development Goals. The International Conference on Primary Health Care took place in

Alma-Ata (then in the Soviet Union, now in Kazakhstan) in 1978. The Alma Ata Declaration defines health as:

> a state of complete physical, mental and social wellbeing, and not merely the absence of disease or infirmity, is a fundamental human right and that the attainment of the highest possible level of health is a most important world-wide social goal whose realization requires the action of many other social and economic sectors in addition to the health sector

The Alma-Ata Declaration defined primary health care.

> Primary health care is essential health care based on practical, scientifically sound and socially acceptable methods and technology made universally accessible to individuals and families in the community through their full participation and at a cost that the community and country can afford to maintain at every stage of their development in the spirit of self-reliance and self-determination. It forms an integral part both of the country's health system, of which it is the central function and main focus, and of the overall social and economic development of the community. It is the first level of contact of individuals, the family and community with the national health system bringing health care as close as possible to where people live and work, and constitutes the first element of a continuing health care process

The declaration further stated that primary health care:

1. reflects and evolves from the economic conditions and sociocultural and political characteristics of the country and its communities and is based on the application of the relevant results of social, biomedical and health services research and public health experience;

2. addresses the main health problems in the community, providing promotive, preventive, curative and rehabilitative services accordingly;

3. includes at least: education concerning prevailing health problems and the methods of preventing and controlling them; promotion of food supply and proper nutrition; an adequate supply of safe water and basic sanitation; maternal and child health care, including family planning; immunization against the major infectious diseases; prevention and control of locally endemic diseases; appropriate treatment of common diseases and injuries; and provision of essential drugs;

4. involves, in addition to the health sector, all related sectors and aspects of national and community development, in particular agriculture, animal husbandry, food, industry, education, housing, public works, communications and other sectors; and demands the coordinated efforts of all those sectors;

5. requires and promotes maximum community and individual self-reliance and participation in the planning, organization, operation and control of primary health care, making fullest use of local, national and other available resources; and to this end develops through appropriate education the ability of communities to participate;

6. should be sustained by integrated, functional and mutually supportive referral systems, leading to the progressive improvement of comprehensive health care for all, and giving priority to those most in need;

7. relies, at local and referral levels, on health workers, including physicians, nurses, midwives, auxiliaries and community workers as applicable, as well as traditional practitioners as needed, suitably trained socially and technically to work as a health.

At the United Nations General Assembly meeting of 2000, eight international development goals were put forward:

1. Eradicating extreme poverty and hunger,
2. Achieving universal primary education,
3. Promoting gender equality and empowering women,
4. Reducing child mortality rates,
5. Improving maternal health,
6. Combating HIV/AIDS, malaria, and other diseases,
7. Ensuring environmental sustainability, and
8. Developing a global partnership for development.

At Pangaea, I used to argue that the best pathway to combat HIV/AIDS, and achieve the Millennium Development Goals and other goals, was primarily through primary health care.

African countries, through the African Union, put forward their own goal through the Abuja Declaration (Abuja, Nigeria) of 2001 in which they pledged to spend 15% of their national budget on health. Since then, only one country (Tanzania) has reached this goal.

A number of factors can partly explain this mixed and generally low performance with regard to reaching the international targets in health:

- *A narrow resource base*

Most of the Sub-Saharan countries fall in the category of least developed countries, characterized by high poverty levels (where households live on less than a dollar per day), limited tax revenues, and a general dependency on external aid flows for recurrent and development budgets. In these resource-limited settings, with many competing and urgent needs, governments find it difficult, or unwilling, to prioritize health let, alone HIV/AIDS.

- *Aid dependency and high expectations*

Over the past 30 years of the HIV pandemic, there has been tremendous progress in mobilizing resources to respond to this health and development crisis. Progress across sub-Saharan Africa is a spectrum, with some countries doing better than others. As more resources have flowed to respond to the HIV/AIDS crisis, most governments and other stakeholders have come to expect this aid money, not national resources, to cover prevention, treatment, care and support activities. The emergence of PEPFAR and Global Fund, have, undoubtedly, contributed to driving down the epidemic and saving lives. On the other hand, these resource flows have created high expectations and a dependency that they will will always be there, and cover everyone ultimately and permanently.

- *Lack of political will and leadership*

Within the national development plans, and national vision 2020s, prioritization of any item is a highly political matter. The budgeting, policy, and strategy process is not always inclusive, participatory, transparent, or efficient in allocation of resources. Often budgets are routine matters that are handled by the Minister of Finance, officials from the World Bank, and the International Monetary Fund. At the country level, where institutions and governance are weak, the powerful President or Prime Minister will often have his way on items that he or she considers important. The Minister of Health, until resources for HIV/AIDS from outside became a major source of revenue, did not have much clout in cabinet. The degree of progress in prioritizing HIV in national, regional, or continental organizations highly depends on leadership and mobilizing political will.

- *Limited engagement and mobilization of communities, civil society and private sector*

For HIV/AIDS to be prioritized in policies, strategies, planning and budget processes should normally be a process of vertical and horizontal consultation and engagement with various stakeholders. Community based organizations, faith-based organizations, NGOs, people living with HIV/AIDS, and other civil society organizations can exert pressure on governments, regional and continental organizations to make HIV a budgetary priority. Often these stakeholders have little or no say in the budget process. The further you go from country to regional and continental organizations, the less these stakeholders are involved in the budget or policy process.

- *Too many players and policies, and little harmony and co-ordination*

Although Sub-Saharan countries and development partners committed to the Paris Principles on aid effectiveness, and African countries are organized at the level of continental and regional organizations, there seems to be a challenge of policy coordination or harmonization on HIV/AIDS or any other development issues. This leads to duplication and inefficiency.

- *Continental and regional organizations have varying and generally limited footprint in the member countries*

The African Union, the United Nations Economic Commission for Africa, the regional organizations, and the African Development Bank have different footprints in the member countries to influence the policy debate on HIV/AIDS . Other than the African Union, which is largely political, the rest of the organizations are oriented more towards economic and trade matters, and until recently did not envisage having health matters as their priority, let alone HIV/AIDS.

- *Not all donor resources reach governments*

The World Health Organization (WHO) estimates that as much as 50% of donor resources do not flow through government, and donors are frequently reluctant to account for these resources. In addition, a large proportion of these resources may be spent even before they reach the recipient country, through use of external contractors with very high transaction costs. The

International Monetary Fund has also estimated that external resource flows are often used to build a country's foreign currency reserves and debt obligations, rather than social obligations like health (for every dollar, only U.S.$ 0.27 may be available in in the recipient country).

- *Limited utilization of in-country and south-south expertise to drive down costs without endangering quality*

As mentioned above, the use of external contractors and consultants consumes a huge portion of resources in global health. Supporting in-country capacity building is a cost-effective and sustainable way of responding to scaling up HIV combination prevention in particular, achieving high impact outcomes in the health sector. While most African policy statements highlight this as well as the importance of south-south cooperation this has yet to be translated into implementable strategies and actions.

- *Limited innovation in mobilizing financial resources at community, national, regional, continental and at global level*

Regular revenue collection at country level and Official Development Assistance has to be improved to respond to HIV/AIDS and health needs. To date, the need to be innovative in raising resources over and above Official Development Assistance (ODA) has been a global challenge. There has been limited progress in African countries and organizations on this challenge of innovative financing.

- *More money is spent on curative services rather than prevention, with a lot of inefficiency*

The WHO has indicated that current health spending in developing countries is more biased towards curative services, impoverishes because of direct out-of pocket spending for health, and tends to reach those who are able and better off than the majority of the people in districts and communities, wasteful, and compromises on quality. It is estimated that 20-40% of resources are wasted in this way.

- *Limited linkage between HIV/AIDS programs and overall health systems, and limited linkage between health and other sectors as envisaged in primary healthcare*
- *Beautiful strategies, policies and budgets on paper but not implemented due to operational bottlenecks between the first and last miles*
- *Limited investments in science and technology*

CHAPTER THIRTY FIVE

Going Back to My Roots

By 2008, I was already thinking about how to apply all the knowledge, skills and experience in a setting I knew best, Africa. I had a well-paying job at Pangaea, but I felt I wasn't adding any value to the organization seated in San Francisco. The organization asked me where it could best deploy its expertise in Africa. Rwanda was out since I could not go back. I immediately thought about Ghana, Ethiopia and Zimbabwe. They were far enough from Rwanda's ever active security operatives. Except for Ghana, I was familiar with the others. I had frequented both countries during the civil war and I knew a few friends there. The three countries were English speaking, and Pangaea staff would not have a problem with communications.

As I contemplated returning to Africa, I had the burden of trying to distill all the lessons I had gathered so far into a few insights to help me with my new role. I now looked at myself not only as a "development evangelist" but also as a "spiritual evangelist" who would speak to the condition for Africa's spiritual renaissance. My philosophy on development had not yet fully crystallized, and I was yet to link my spiritual development to the overall mission.

In 2008, I took a brief trip to Zimbabwe, on Pangaea Global AIDS Foundation's mission to explore opportunities for collaboration with a private Methodist Church institution, Africa University. This was my second visit ever to Zimbabwe. I had visited Zimbabwe during the Rwandan civil war, Harare, its capital city, which then looked more like a European city than it did to most African cities. Zimbabwe struggled and got her independence in 1980 from a local colonizing white settler regime under Ian Smith. Before then, it was called Rhodesia, named after a British settler, Cecil Rhodes. As school children, we used to recite these European names. We were told they had "discovered" Africa. Zimbabwe inherited a relatively decent economy, was self-sufficient in food and was generally considered a breadbasket for southern Africa. It had good public infrastructure, and a sizeable educated class. By 2008, Zimbabwe was in political turmoil, running one of the highest inflation rates in human history. A third of its population was living abroad, and its public infrastructure in ruins. The remaining population was starving, and amidst this chaos, cholera struck the city of Harare, claiming over five thousand lives.

Once I arrived in Harare I was driven to the city of Mutare, in the province of Manicaland, There, I toured the provincial hospital of Mutare. I was shocked by what I saw. The hospital run without water. The operating theatres were mostly closed. I went to one small room that had about a dozen newborn babies, without anything to cover them. I saw the resilience of demoralized staff doing everything possible to get the hospital running. Later, I visited Africa University, which stood in Zimbabwe like an oasis in a desert of poverty and disease.

As we drove into Africa University, I spotted two young shabbily dressed boys seated by the gates. I asked the driver who the boys were and he said they were a common sight there, looking for help. Instantly, I recalled one of Pastor Mark Labberton's sermons in First Pres, on *interruptible compassion*. We should always be ready to interrupt ourselves to show works of compassion, just as our Lord Jesus Christ did. That afternoon, in a Church service,

I listened to the choir sing "Africa Shall Rise" and I was touched by the song's message. I thought about the hopelessness I had seen since arriving in Zimbabwe, the boys at the gate, and the hope I was witnessing at Africa University. When I was asked to speak to the audience, in what I now call my first sermon, my theme was "The Boys at The Gate".

The "boys at the gate" somehow spoke to Africa's condition, I preached. We know how to do politics and we have great cultures. We know how to make money, and we have millions of schooled people. We have built ourselves impressive structures and monuments. We have had defining moments where our leaders and African people spoke and did great things. In material terms, we have the capacity to banish hunger and disease. Yet, in the current conditions, we have not yet become the best we could be.

We were all like the boys at some gate, with anticipation day by day that something better will come up. Occasionally, the boys at the gate get a handout, but they come again. What the boys and their families needed was not only compassion, but also the means to be self-reliant. The experts on political, social and economic development have ignored the spiritual dimension. Compassion is a rare commodity in the rough and tumble of Africa's, and the world's, business and politics. All that I had read and experienced before, during and after service in government, all the way to leading American universities, now only made sense if a spiritual dimension was added.

The spiritual core, I concluded in my sermon at Africa University, was Tina's Equation: Love+ Forgiveness + Freedom = LIFE. Zimbabwe, like most of Africa, was running low on love, forgiveness and freedom. No wonder the quality of life in Zimbabwe and in Africa is poor. For Africa to rise, we all have to replenish our common and individual pools of love, forgiveness and freedom. As I flew back to San Francisco at the end of a hectic week I kept on thinking about the boys at the gate. Hadn't my life so far been one of a boy at some gate? Aren't most African governments like boys at the gates of the World Bank, IMF, and at the doors of rich countries, and rich foundations? Moved by the story of the Zimbabwean boys at the gate, I once suggested to my children to come with me and we spend a day in San Francisco incognito as beggars. My wife instantly shot down the idea, since, as she rightly argued, it was an unnecessary risk and that our children should never consider begging as an option. I backed down.

CHAPTER THIRTY SIX

Building a New Outlook

In 2009, I was beginning to be very restless, eager to go back to Zimbabwe. I had two challenges before I could venture back. First, I had to convince Pangaea Global AIDS Foundation to establish itself in Zimbabwe. Second, I had to convince Pangaea to modify their traditional approach to prevention and treatment of HIV/AIDS, by incorporation of a women-and children bias, grounded at the community level, and through primary health care. It was always a hard sell, and I perfectly understood why. The Western consultants, normally chasing western money, following western medicines, are disciplined about what they do and what they do not do. They do not have the social and emotional baggage that an African like me has when you find yourself amidst crushing needs of Africans, and little or no resources. "We do HIV/AIDS, we do not do development, we do not do primary health care" is what you hear from many in the international arena. Pangaea finally agreed they would send me to Zimbabwe, and support me for only one year, after which I would have to come up with my own funding. I had hoped I would go back with my family, so that my children could rediscover their African roots. Under such stringent conditions and uncertainty, Dorothy and I decided I would go alone, and hopefully re-unite later, God willing.

However, the most important challenge for me was to come up with a simple development philosophy that integrated ideas and experiences that I had gathered in my life thus far.

The Ubuntu-Health-Wealth-Wellness Cycle: Overall well-being is the goal of every individual, family, community, nation and the society as a whole. To achieve this we have to be healthy, and we have to work to create and share wealth. At the core of this endeavor towards wellness are the love, forgiveness and freedom that give meaning to every individual, family and community. The core of the continuum is the African concept of *Ubuntu*. Ubuntu is a Bantu language word that stands for humanness, which translates into hospitality, kindness, mercy and love. It is the idea that our humanity is a shared one. Tina's Equation is an expression of this idea of Ubuntu.

The Knowledge-Skills-Capital Triangle: Every society requires investing its capital into creating curative, preventive, rehabilitative and promotional health, as well as wealth (both private and public) for individuals, families, communities and nations. Remember that capital has many forms, and in this case includes political capital as well as social capital. Knowledge, both indigenous and acquired, is a key element. Know-how, or skills, is necessary to produce, manage and lead.

This is where the west has an edge on Africa. Africa needs to develop the knowledge and skills to create wealth. With more wealth, you can reinvest in developing more knowledge and skills.

The Good Life in Seven Metaphors: My upcoming work, *The Good Life in Seven Metaphors*, came as a product of several dinner table conversations with my family. I was probing my children back and forth, and trying to figure out how to keep ourselves sane in a very fast moving America. In our very first days in America, I was surprised by son. My third born, Aaron Ngenzi, pushed back when I told him he could not watch TV on a school night. He said, "Daddy, this is America, we do what we want." We had come to America, the place of abundance, freedom to indulge, amazing technologies, and pop culture. During our first week in California, our youngest kids tried to help themselves to candy, and I told them we had to buy it. They had never seen so much candy and different brands of cereal in their lives.

To live a good life, we agreed, one had to live: 1) like a child, who is always curious to learn and try new things; 2) like a farmer, who is patient to wait for a season, plant a seed and wait for harvest; 3) like a teacher, who is also a student, who learns and shares his/her knowledge; 4) like a good and responsible businessman/woman, who endeavors to buy and sell without discriminating; 5) like a soldier, who is disciplined to keep himself and others safe so that he/she can win a war, through sacrifice if necessary; 6) like a monk, to find moments of quietness to contemplate and reflect in a world that is choking under noise; and yes, 7) like a privileged prince, who is humble and grateful that he or she has been given much, and therefore much is expected from him/her.

The Haradali Woman: Coined by my daughter Mwiza, and a drawing by her of an African woman carrying her baby on her back. I had spent time thinking about the name of a not-for-profit organization that would be the vehicle for my international and community work. I thought of a mustard seed in Kiswahili, Haradali. I was inspired by Jesus Christ's parable of the mustard seed, "Though it is the smallest of all seeds, yet when it grows, it is the largest of garden plants and becomes a tree, so that the birds come and perch in its branches" (Matthew 13:32, NIV). I thought women and children should be Haradali's focus. First, because women and children are the majority in any African community. Second, because women are the engines for child survival and development in particular, and national development in general. Third, they are often the most marginalized, and most vulnerable. Every year it is estimated that throughout the world about 9 million children die before their fifth anniversary. Half of them are in Africa. Over 500 million mothers die every year during delivery. Half of them are in Africa.

Through a community approach, and women-and children-focus, the Haradali woman simplifies my *Seven Pillars One Bridge Model* with the following inter-related components:

1. The Head: Empowering women, children and the community with knowledge is in itself transformative. The mindset that embraces new knowledge, new ways of doing things, and looking to the future with hope is equally important;
2. The Hands: for skills, and hard smart work;
3. The Legs: the community and its members have to move forward on two legs, one representing material well-being, and the other, spiritual well-being;
4. The Bridge (belt at the waist): The seven pillars include a)Talent, b) SITE (Science, Innovation, Technology and Entrepreneurship), c) community supply chain for production and consumption; d) innovative and sustainable financing, e) building community systems, f) building community partnerships, and g) developing a community's managerial and leadership capacity.
5. The Heart: All the above work together when individuals and families in the community exhibit a heart that embraces Ubuntu or Tina's Equation (Love + Forgiveness + Freedom = LIFE)

When it was time to leave for Zimbabwe in 2009, I had already summarized talking points that would guide me in the work that I was embarking on as a "development evangelist". When I returned to Zimbabwe in 2009, I was thinking that I would ultimately settle there. I had even decided that I would settle in Mutare, in Manicaland. The boys at the gate were still on my mind. I worked with the community and the church at Africa University to build a modest home for the whole family. I had also met a group of women suffering from HIV/AIDS, whose plight and resilience had touched me. I visited a group of clinics in Marondera district where brave nurses were holding the fort in clinics without water, electricity, equipment and medicines.

Dealing with the bureaucracy in a broken system can be exhausting and frustrating. In such moments I used to feel like missing the efficiency with which the Rwandan state moved things. Now that I had enough time to move around, I realized the extent of political, economic, and social devastation in Zimbabwe and in all sectors. I remember climbing the stairs in the Ministry of Health and being greeted by garbage at the entrance and a stench of urine. Here was a public institution, in charge of public health, unable to dispose of its waste, thereby endangering public health. By 2009, Zimbabwe had had to swallow its pride in order to deal with inflation, and had now allowed use of the U.S. and South African currencies. Life was extremely difficult for ordinary Zimbabweans. The political and business elite were engaged in a cutthroat competition for power and dwindling economic resources.

Having lived in Rwanda, Uganda and now Zimbabwe, I now realized how true Frantz Fanon's vitriolic attack on the national elite in his *The Wretched of the Earth* was:

> The national middle class who takes over power at the end of the colonial regime is an under-developed middle class. It has practically no economic power, and in any case it is in no way commensurate with the bourgeoisie of the mother country which it hopes to replace. In its willful narcissism, the national middle class is easily convinced that it can advantageously replace the middle class of the mother country. But that same independence which literally drives it into a comer will give rise within its ranks to catastrophic reactions, and will oblige it to send out frenzied appeals for help to the former mother country. The university and merchant classes which make up

the most enlightened section of the new state are in fact characterized by the smallness of their number and their being concentrated in the capital, and the type of activities in which they are engaged: business, agriculture and the liberal professions. Neither financiers nor industrial magnates are to be found within this national middle class. The national bourgeoisie of under-developed countries is not engaged in production, nor in invention, nor building, nor labor; is it completely canalized into activities of the intermediary type. Its innermost vocation seems to be to keep in the running and to be part of the racket

Zimbabwe had a chance to create a sizeable middle class, with financiers and industrial magnates among them. With a two-way hostility between Zimbabwe's President Mugabe and the West, and the donor funds largely cut off, the country was in much pain. In this vacuum it was common to find Chinese businessmen frequenting hotel lobbies, where, I imagined, they were cutting deals with a host of local Zimbabweans. I also witnessed how the expatriate community, with a small coterie of Zimbabweans, lived like kings and queens, dining and wining in this sea of poverty. Most of the expatriate community in Zimbabwe was "doing HIV". I realized how most of them did not even know the actual conditions upcountry (although it was not entirely their fault since the government imposed restrictions and surveillance on their movements). Zimbabwe reminded me of Rwanda after 1994. Donors love seminars and workshops. Consultants fly in business class to assess, monitor, and evaluate. I was beginning to feel ashamed that I would be considered to be one such a consultant. Government officials and civil society scramble to write proposals, and donors solicit them. Unable to help even one clinic with water to improve the chances of survival for women and newborn babies, I could see my expansive agenda would soon collide with Pangaea's. Pangaea was a small organization with limited means and a narrowly focused agenda. I decided to end my contract with the organization prematurely, so that I could concentrate on building Haradali.

CHAPTER THIRTY SEVEN

Sweet Reunion
with Comrades

I was in Zimbabwe in February, 2010 when I read the news that a Rwandan officer, Lieutenant General Kayumba Nyamwasa had fled from Rwanda and was now in South Africa. General Nyamwasa had served as RPA's Director of Military Intelligence during the civil war, a Deputy Chief of the National Gendarmerie, Chief of Staff of the Army, Head of the National Security Service, and Rwanda's Ambassador to India. He had joined another Rwandan officer, Colonel Patrick Karegeya, who fled Rwanda after jail sentences on trumped up charges. Col. Karegeya had served as Rwanda's Head of External Intelligence and Deputy Head of the National Security Service. It was a very significant development. Among senior leaders of RPF, Gahima had fled in 2004, myself in 2005, followed by Col. Karegeya and now General Nyamwasa. Gahima had served as Deputy Minister in the Ministries of Public Service, Justice and later as Rwanda's Prosecutor General, and Vice-President of the Supreme Court.

None among the four has previously shown resilience and patience in dealing with President Kagame as General Nyamwasa. On hearing the news, I called Col. Karegeya and he confirmed that the general was safe in South Africa. I remembered how, way back in 2003, President Kagame had shown me an internal memo from Jack Nziza, alleging that General Nyamwasa was working on behalf of Ugandans to overthrow him. He also told me that General Nyamwasa had, without his knowledge, "connived" with former British overseas development Minister, Baroness Lynda Chalker, to go to study in England. In my mind I wondered how a whole Chief of Staff of Rwanda's military would simply disappear without the Commander in Chief's knowledge. In any case it is not possible in Rwanda because President Kagame micromanages all foreign travel.

I had also heard several times from President Kagame's confidant, National Security Chief, and former personal doctor, Dr. Emmanuel Ndahiro, saying Nyamwasa was ambitious, building an army within the army so as to eventually overthrow President Kagame. Dr. Ndahiro had made it almost a personal mission to approach many officers to recruit them into the anti-Nyamwasa camp, including my own former brother-in-law, General Martin Nzaramba. That is how President Kagame works.

Since I knew I was, like my colleagues, behind-the-scenes a victim of the same kind of malicious campaigns by President Kagame, using Dr. Ndahiro and others, I would listen and say little. Part of the problem is that while we were in the Kagame system, we could not talk to each other or compare notes. Even among brothers like me and Gahima we rarely talked about Kagame's rising dictatorship.

President Kagame would complain about me to Gahima in my absence, and would similarly talk to me about Gahima in negative terms. General Nyamwasa weathered all that. He had been posted to India as Ambassador, but the campaign against him had intensified during his absence. Now it had come to his narrow and dramatic escape.

My brother and I had spent five years without doing any politics. We had decided we would not go back to politics. That however, did not prevent President Kagame from being relentless in attacking us when we had long left Rwanda. He also made sure he tried everything he could to frustrate our livelihoods by intimidating our employers, or potential ones.

When I heard about Nyamwasa's escape, I thought it was important to appraise the United States, President Kagame's closest ally, on the situation in Rwanda. Immediately after leaving Zimbabwe, I headed for Washington DC. When Gahima and I met Ambassador Jonnie Carson, the Assistant Secretary of State for African Affairs in early 2010, we brought to his attention that Rwanda was again drifting into dangerous waters, and civil war and bloodshed were a possibility if there were no concerted efforts to prevent that.

In May 2010, I took another trip to Zimbabwe, this time putting on a Haradali hat. While in Zimbabwe, I felt an urge to check on Nyamwasa and Karegeya in South Africa. It was such an emotional reunion with Karegeya and his wife Leah, and Nyamwasa and his wife Rosette. The whole experience had an eerie feeling to it. Here were colleagues who had gone through the thick and thin of a revolution, only to see it turn against many before it turned against them. I listened to the dramatic escapes of both Karegeya and Nyamwasa, and the plight of their families, especially Nyamwasa's, as they dealt with the fall out. We reminisced about times gone by, and compared notes on how President Kagame usurped power while we watched. I kept on wondering how possible it was for Rwanda to get violence out of Rwanda's politics, and how exile could be banished forever. Unfortunately, we all concurred, violence and exile are weapons of dictatorships, and you could not overcome them without dealing with the dictatorship itself. At the end of my visit we agreed that we should do everything possible to expose dictatorship in Rwanda. A few days later, General Nyamwasa fired the first shots in a Ugandan newspaper, the *Daily Monitor*, comparing President Kagame to Uganda's ruthless dictator, Idi Amin.

I returned to San Francisco on 12th June, 2010. I had promised my family that we would visit the east coast, to catch up with family, relatives and friends. I was dealing with a difficult transition of being on my own, with a new social enterprise, Haradali, without means of sustenance for my family and for the new organization. Dorothy and the children were scheduled to leave on 19th June, 2010.

Early in the morning before we got up, Dorothy received a call from her sister, Debra, who lives in Canada. She urgently wanted to talk to me. On the line she told me that Nyamwasa had been assassinated in South Africa. Was he dead, I asked, Debra. She did not know. I broke the bad news to Dorothy, got out of bed and moved around the room without knowing what to think about or do.

Instantly, I decided I was going to fight President Kagame's dictatorship to the very end. It was not Nyamwasa's near death experience that *caused* me to take that decision. It was simply a powerful *trigger* that shocked me out of my complacency and selfish indifference. It was another case of interruptible compassion, inviting me to a different kind of thinking and action. Previously, I had been insensitive to the suffering of Hutu, and Tutsi who were victims of the RPF regime. Now President Kagame was demonstrating that his enemies have no ethnic distinction. Tutsi were equally expendable targets of his brutal rule. I had had a similar snap decision on October 1st, 1990, on the gates of Mulago Hospital in Kampala, Uganda. I had then decided to join the RPF. Now there was nothing to join. I knew that a revolutionary moment was in the making. I found myself humming Bob Dylan's song, *Blowin' in the Wind*:

> ..Yes, how many years can some people exist
> before they're allowed to be free?
> Yes, how many times can a man turn his head
> pretending he just doesn't see?
>
> ..Yes, how many ears must one man have

before he can hear people cry?
Yes, how many deaths will it take till he knows
that too many people have died?

The answer my friend is blowing' in the wind
the answer is blowing' in the wind

General Nyamwasa and his wife Rosette survived the assassination attempt, but the Rwandan security agents and their hired assassins tried a number of times to kill the couple and Karegeya in the hospital. In taped conversations that we shared with the British and US governments, General Jack Nziza negotiates the price with would-be assassins to kill Nyamwasa, Karegeya, all their families and hospital staff. Dan Munyuza, who until recently was the head of President Kagame's external intelligence explains in detail how poisons are being used against President Kagame's enemies. The court case continues in South Africa.

CHAPTER THIRTY EIGHT

Rwanda Briefing

General Kayumba Nyamwasa, Colonel Patrick Karegeya, Dr. Gerald Gahima and I decided to jointly write a document, exposing President Kagame's dictatorship. In August 2010, the day President Kagame was inaugurated for his second rigged seven year term, our pamphlet, *Rwanda Briefing*, came out, spreading like a virus on the internet overnight.

In its introduction, *Rwanda Briefing* sounded the trumpet:

> Rwanda's recovery from the ravages of war and genocide is generally regarded as a rare success story in post-conflict reconstruction. Visitors to the country are impressed by its economic growth, security situation and cleanliness, as well as the orderliness of its people and the efficiency with which its institutions conduct business. To its passionate friends, Rwanda is a shining example of democratization, reformation, and an effective and efficient government. Supporters of the Rwandan government largely attribute Rwanda's success in post-war reconstruction to President Paul Kagame. The rebel general-turned-civilian politician cultivates a cult-image as the sole hero of the country's achievements. President Kagame is perceived by most

outsiders as both invincible and indispensable to national and regional stability.

There is, however, more to Rwanda and Paul Kagame than new buildings, clean streets, and efficient government than President Kagame's famous friends in high places in Europe and America care to admit. Rwanda is essentially a hard-line, one-party, secretive police state with a façade of democracy. The ruling party, the Rwandese Patriotic Front (RPF), has closed space for political participation. The RPF does not tolerate political opposition or open competition for power. The government ensures its monopoly of power by means of draconian restrictions on the exercise of the fundamental human rights of citizens. The press, civil society and opposition parties are deprived of freedom to operate freely. President Kagame and the ruling party that he leads depend on repression to stay in power.

State institutions, especially law enforcement agencies, the judiciary and security services, serve to protect the RPF's, and ultimately Kagame's power monopoly instead of protecting the fundamental human rights of citizens. Repression has again become particularly acute in recent months. There have been assassination attempts, killings and enforced disappearances of members of the press and political opposition within and outside Rwanda. Purges of political enemies, real and imagined, within the ruling party government continue unabated. These purges have now been extended to the military. A climate of fear and terror has enveloped the nation.

Rwanda is in crisis. The situation that prevails raises serious questions about the country's future. Are the country's development achievements sustainable? Can Rwanda continue to be peaceful while the government continues to be repressive and the majority of the people consider the government illegitimate? How do we balance individual freedoms and the requirement for a stable community? How should citizens respond when rulers mistake the state to be their personal estate and deprive their subjects of their inalienable rights? Should they resist peacefully or take up arms? If armed conflict is ill-advised, given its potential to cause human suffering, how else then can citizens reclaim their rights to hold the government accountable? What strategies would help Rwanda avoid violent conflict that appears inevitable and to set it on the path towards peaceful resolution of the problems that drive conflict in Rwandan society?

In its conclusion, *Rwanda Briefing* warned:

A minority government as repressive and unaccountable as Rwanda's current regime cannot remain in office forever. Neither brute force nor the financial and material support of external backers can sustain a government that the people overwhelmingly consider to be illegitimate in power indefinitely.

Change of government in Rwanda is as necessary as it is inevitable. The people of Rwanda have a legitimate right to demand and expect such change. The best hope for enabling Rwanda to avoid inevitable conflict of catastrophic proportions is to promote a peaceful settlement that will recognize the right of the majority to determine their own destiny and to enjoy their fundamental rights, while addressing the concerns (especially for security and the risk of political and economic marginalization) of minorities.

The people of Rwanda, together with rest of the international community, have a moral duty to work to end this repressive system of government. Rwanda is literally again on the brink of an abyss. The consequences of failing to act to reverse the drift toward violent conflict and bloodshed could be as tragic as the events of 1994. In the aftermath of the 1994 genocide, most of the international community made pledges to never again allow atrocious conflict on the scale of what happened in Rwanda then to take place on their watch. The complicity of collusion and silence that contributed to making the 1994 genocide possible ought not to be repeated. The manner in which the international community has engaged the government of Rwanda to date clearly indicates that the lessons that ought to have been drawn from the 1994 genocide have not been learnt.

The reaction of Rwandans to *Rwanda Briefing* was instant and strong. It could not be ignored because all its authors had been at the core of the RPF enterprise, and were all particularly close to President Kagame himself. The regime in Kigali denounced all of us as impostors, thieves, terrorists, revisionists, frustrated elements who were bent on dividing Rwandan people, collaborators with FDLR, and Hutu apologists. All four authors of *Rwanda Briefing* were tried in absentia, convicted and sentenced to 20 years in jail (Gahima and Karegeya) and 24 years in jail and stripped of military ranks (Kayumba and Rudasingwa).

Not surprisingly though, we were not condemned by mainstream RPF leaders whom you would have expected to rise in RPF's defense. Most of these RPF leaders have been silenced and marginalized. We were denounced by some family members who saw us a group of Tutsi who had betrayed a group (ethnic cause). Some have since then kept a distance, while others, though in agreement with what we say, sometimes ask us, "did you have to do it, and now?" I always respond to such, "if not us, then who? If not now, then when?" Overwhelmingly, the reaction from the Hutu in exile was positive. They had not expected the four of us, long known to be the pillars of President Kagame's RPF regime to be speaking out against him. *Rwanda Briefing* was a timely and bold statement. It opened doors for a long, exciting, though difficult, conversation amongst us Rwandans.

Rwanda Briefing created expectations overnight. The appearance of General Nyamwasa with Colonel Patrick Karegeya on the list of President Kagame's opponents in exile was assumed by many as an indicator that a quick military solution to remove President Kagame from power was in the making and possible. The fact that four of us had linked up was assumed to be an indication that some political military organization was in the making. Many in Rwanda's military were sending messages to us, saying they were behind us, should a spark be ignited. We were under pressure to do "something". Amongst the four of us we slowly began to warming up to the idea forming "something". But what form would that something take? With whom would we work with? What would be the vision and core values of such an entity?

We started the process of consulting all the opposition groups in exile, mainly in Europe. The four of us were unanimous that if we had to be involved in anything, it had to include all ethnic groups. It was an uphill task since the majority of the Hutu in exile could not yet trust us. Some of the prominent names in exile were: the former King of Rwanda, Kigeli Ndahindurwa; former Prime Minister, Faustin Twagiramungu; former Prime Minister, Celestin Rwigyema; former Speaker of Parliament, Joseph Sebarenzi; former Defense Minister, General Emmanuel Habyarimana; Paul Rusesabagina, of Hotel Rwanda Foundation, and many other prominent Rwandans representing a variety of political and civil society groups. Notable among the bigger political entities was FDU-Inkingi, the party of the political prisoner, Ms. Victoire Ingabire.

We extended the consultation far and wide among Tutsi in exile, and many other people who had served in the RPF government at different times. A meeting was scheduled to convene on December 10th, 2010. Up to the last moment, we did not know who would turn up. Since our colleagues in South Africa could not attend, it was left to me and my brother Gerald Gahima to convene the meeting and host it in the United States. In the run up to the event we went back and forth preparing the founding documents. There were some suggestions of names for the political entity.

Two developments threatened to derail the process as we moved closer to the date. One idea among some few Tutsi we were collaborating with strongly suggested that we should first secure an understanding among us the Tutsi, before we negotiate with the Hutu. To them we responded that this is not just a matter among Tutsi. After all, haven't we Tutsi run away from a regime that is supposedly Tutsi? Another strand of thought came from prominent Hutu leaders who seemed not to trust other Hutu, each one of them insisting that we do not collaborate with other Hutu. One even said we were scrambling for the worst elements among the Hutu. To him we cautioned that all of us had some baggage from our past. We could only succeed if we humbled ourselves and accepted others as they are, as long as they also accepted us as we are, to create something new and better. We refused to accept both the "Hutu" and "Tutsi" conditions, since they were different versions of the same problem we were trying to solve: divisive politics based on ethnicity and region.

CHAPTER THIRTY NINE

The Rwanda National Congress (RNC) is Born

On December 12, 2010, in Bethesda, Maryland, United States, in a small Jewish community center, a group of Rwandans gathered to deliberate on creating a new political organization. Present at the creation of the new organization, the Rwanda National Congress (RNC) were Jerome Nayigiziki; Jean Paul Turayishimye; Patrick Karegeya; Gerald Gahima; Gervais Condo; Kayumba Nyamwasa; Emmanuel Hakizimana; Jonathan Musonera; Joseph Ngarambe; and Theogene Rudasingwa. Also Present were four other Rwandans who preferred to remain anonymous. Dorothy Rudasingwa and Anne Gahima witnessed the birth of the organization, and made sure food and refreshments were available to us. A friend of mine, Ralph Grunewald and his wife Marilyn not only housed one of the founders, but offered help in providing every kind of help we needed. Grunewald read through the founding documents and provided his input at a critical stage in the birth of this organization.

In its *Founding Proclamation*, RNC asserted:

> Rwanda is an ancient nation. No doubt, every government
> that has exercised control over the Rwandan state during
> the course of our country's long history can rightfully be
> credited for developments that have been of benefit to its
> citizens. On balance, however, virtually every Rwandan
> government has historically preyed on the citizenry and
> has suppressed the realization and enjoyment of the inher-
> ent and universal rights of those whom it governed. Auto-
> cratic government (in the form of a government controlled
> by an absolute monarch or an all-powerful president) has
> generally been the norm during our history. While Rwanda
> is a diverse society, the diversity of its national character
> (based on class, ethnic identity, religion or region of ori-
> gin) has often been manipulated by elite political leaders
> to satisfy their selfish and egoistic interests and to acquire
> or monopolize power and access to resources. Our people
> have never had the opportunity to fully realize their aspira-
> tions for freedom, security and prosperity.

It further enunciated its vision;

> We envision a new Rwanda that will be a united, demo-
> cratic, and prosperous nation inhabited by free citizens
> with harmonious and safe communities who will live
> together in peace, dignity and mutual respect, regardless
> of class, ethnicity, language, region, origin or other differ-
> ences, within a democracy governed according to univer-
> sal principles of human rights and the rule of law.

And its core values;

> The political-and societal- transformation we seek to bring
> about in Rwanda can only be achieved if it is rooted in

values that are both relevant to our people's cultural heritage and reflect the aspirations of the majority of Rwandans at this time in history. These values, which shall be the foundation of our nation-rebuilding process, include human dignity and respect for human rights, equality and non-discrimination, mutual respect, democracy and the rule of law, integrity, empathy, solidarity, patriotism, humility, forgiveness, the right and responsibility of citizens to hold leaders accountable, accountable leadership, truth, justice, fairness.

Its political programme;

1. Stop and prevent violent conflict, including genocide and grave human rights violations that Rwanda's people have periodically suffered and that have historically extended to citizens – men, women, and children – of neighboring states;

2. Eradicate a culture of impunity for human rights violations;

3. Create a conducive and progressive environment for inclusive social and economic development for all the people of Rwanda;

4. Establish, nurture and institutionalize democratic governance, particularly the rule of law in all its aspects;

5. Establish independent, non-partisan, professional civil service and security institutions;

6. Build a stable society that promotes and protects equality, embraces and celebrates diversity, and fosters inclusion in all aspects of national life;

7. Promote individual, community and national reconciliation and healing;

8. Promote harmonious relations, reconciliation and mutually- beneficial collaboration with the peoples and governments of neighboring states;

9. Resolve the chronic problem of Rwandan refugees;
10. Nurture a culture of tolerance to diverse ideas, freedom of discussion, and debate of critical issues.

And, in its *Interim Policy Document*, RNC listed its 13 strategies to achieve this societal transformation:

1. Mobilizing the People of Rwanda to United in the Struggle Against Dictatorship
2. The Need for a Transitional Government
3. The Imperative for National Dialogue
4. The Necessity of Reform of the State
5. Establishing a Constitutional and Legal Framework that Advances Freedom and Democracy
6. Reform of the Security Sector
7. Opening Space for Political Participation and Good Governance
8. Adoption of Consociationalism as Rwanda's Form of Organization of Political Governance
9. Economic Empowerment and Development
10. Truth-Telling, Justice and Memory
11. Repatriation and Re-integration of Refugees
12. Unity, Reconciliation and Collective Healing
13. A Progressive Foreign Policy Based on Common Values and Interests, Adherence to International Law and Mutual Respect Between States

Concluding, the interim policy document states:

> The Rwanda National Congress reminds all present and future generations of Rwandans that Rwanda is much more important than, and must transcend, any single person, any single dictator, any single ethnic group, any single region, or any single organization or political party.

Rwanda is an enduring and beautiful nation with a resilient people, each one of whom is endowed with inalienable rights as a human being and citizen of the nation. Rwanda is our only home, one in which we and posterity are entitled to live in peace and harmony. We can only survive and thrive as a nation if we work together to ensure prosperity, justice and peace for all its inhabitants.

Thus the Rwanda National Congress was born, and with it a new promise to the Rwandan people. Though its message was timely, it was not the first time the Rwandan people had been promised change; there was the promise of the 1959 Revolution, whose midwife was MDR-PARMEHUTU, assisted by the Belgian Colonial authorities. Within the revolution there had been another promise in 1973, whose midwife was the military under General Juvenal Habyarimana. The coup makers later mutated into MRND, which was assisted by a close ally, France. The 1990 RPF Revolution, assisted by Uganda, and later by the United States of America and the United Kingdom, came with yet another promise. Rwanda has become a nation of broken promises and missed opportunities. As the leaders of RNC set to take the message to the Rwandan people, they were aware that they would face a skeptical, cynical, fearful, and sometimes hostile audience.

We knew that it was bound to be a difficult conversation, one in which issues of trauma, guilt, identity, blame, and history would feature at every twist and turn.

CHAPTER FORTY

Voices Calling in
the Desert

The founders of the RNC were mixed, both Hutu and Tutsi. This balance, however important, was not the unifying factor as far as RNC was concerned. The overriding factor was the vision and values that RNC put forward. It is the first time in the history of Rwanda that Hutu and Tutsi voluntarily got together to create something new and build a new shared dispensation together. How we came to know each other is an interesting story that shows the ebb and flow of the Rwandan story.

Let me start with Gervais Condo, who is a Hutu. During the civil war of 1990-1994, as I have narrated in the earlier chapters, I used to travel to Addis Ababa, Ethiopia, where the African Union (then called OAU) has its headquarters. At that time, Gervais Condo was working at the Rwandan Embassy in Ethiopia. Through RPF supporters who lived in Ethiopia, I used to keep surveillance on Condo every time I was in town. On his part, Condo and his colleague, also a Hutu, Celestin Nsengiyumva, used to follow every detail of mine and RPF every time I landed in Addis Ababa. They would have the details of my Ugandan passport and my movements. Though we were opponents, I never thought they had plans of killing me.

Until November, 2010, I never knew Joseph Ngarambe, of mixed parentage (Hutu and Tutsi) who lives in France. He was introduced to me through another Rwandan. We talked over the phone a couple of times and he was fully on board.

The story with Jerome Nayigiziki is even more interesting. Introduced to me by a Rwandan by the name of Providence Rubingisa (whom I never knew before *Rwanda Briefing* was published), I first spoke to Nayigiziki over the phone. Nayigiziki and his colleague, Dr. Emmanuel Hakizimana belonged to another political organization, PDR-Ihumure. When we talked over the phone about founding RNC, at one point I suggested that I should go and meet him physically in Houston, Texas. I told him I had a return ticket, but due to limited resources I wondered if his family could accommodate me. He instantly accepted without hesitation. When it was time for me to go to Houston Dorothy asked me where I was going to stay. I told her I would stay with the Nayigiziki family. She asked me if I knew him and I said I didn't. She then asked me, "Is he an H or a T?" In Rwanda, H was the code word amongst us Tutsi for a Hutu, and T was our code word for Tutsi. She had a surprised look on her face and said, "Be careful." When I later learned from Nayigiziki and his wife Jackie how their families had suffered and died due to RPF's actions, I had tears in my eyes. Hakizimana, Nayigiziki and I met each other for the first time and we were on the same page.

Jonathan Musonera, a Tutsi like me, previously belonged to the same organization, RPF/RPA, and had grown up in Rwanda, learning to live a life of Tutsi discrimination that prevailed from 1959 to1994. Most of his family members were killed during the 1994 genocide. We did not know each other before.

Jean Paul Turayishimye, also a Tutsi, belonged to the RPF/RPA before he fled to the United Stated. We did not know each other before.

Since RNC was a startup organization, I knew that as its coordinator I had to devote all my attention and effort to its business. All startup organizations rise and fall in relationship to how much time and commitment founders invest in them. In short, my other newly founded organization, Haradali, had to wait. Like all people who found startup organizations, we were expected to do much with so little. My family had to leave behind our household items in California (with exception of my books!). My whole family of six was now camped at the Gahima's, a total of 12 people. In east Africa, it is common to see Indian families living together in one house or apartment. We called it living the Indian way. Gahima and I were now working for RNC full time.

As Gahima, Musonera and Ngarambe started RNC's mobilization campaign in Europe, and Nyamwasa and Karegeya started the work in South Africa, Condo, Nayigiziki, Turayishimye and I started our campaign in the United States.

The first encounters with Rwandans (mostly Hutu) were anything but simple. You would have thought the RNC was about the "gang of four" (how the regime in Kigali calls Nyamwasa, Karegeya, Gahima and Rudasingwa), all Tutsi, who worked with the RPF and were close to President Kagame. You would enter the room and find a grumpy, tight- faced and unfriendly audience of mostly Hutu. If there were any Tutsi, they would probably have been sent by the Rwanda embassy to report on us.

They would ask almost the same questions all the time. Here is a sample of some of them, and some of our responses:

- *How can we trust you?*

  We have to trust each other. Rwanda's history is a tale of wrongs that each side has exacted on the other side. From kings, colonial authorities, the 1959 revolution and MDR PARMEHUTU under Kayibanda, MRND under Habyarimana, and now to RPF under Kagame, Tutsi, Hutu and Twa have wronged and have been wronged. We are a country that has depleted its trust account. Since a good and stable life depends on trusting and being trusted, life has lost meaning in Rwanda. Whenever we want to draw on our trust account, we are told "Insufficient Funds". We must cultivate trust among us.

• *What is new, since there are other opposition political parties?*

First, some of the leaders in RNC know the system very well, since they contributed to building it. They know better how to fight it and bring it down. Second, for the first time Hutu and Tutsi have come together, informed by past and present successes and failures, to admit publicly that it is okay to be Hutu or Tutsi, and work together in a country governed by equality before the law, and equal opportunity. Third, our vision and values call on any Rwandan who is interested in truth telling to be part of the effort. We admit wrongs from all sides, and we preach forgiveness, true reconciliation and healing. Fourth, we have an open invitation for Rwandans (and non-Rwandans) to be part of our network. You can be a member, a sympathizer or just an interested person. You can join and leave the organization any time you want. Fifth, we work with other organizations, political or civil, since the task of change requires the efforts of as many Rwandans as possible. Last but not least, since some of the leaders of the RNC were already known in international circles, this could be an asset to the struggle for change.

• *Is RNC a political party?*

RNC is not a political party. Political parties are established under law to operate in a given country. RNC is not established by law. RNC is a movement for peaceful change. It is a networked political organization whose objectives and goals are clearly described in its political program and thirteen strategies. In future when political parties are allowed to function in Rwanda, and RNC establishes itself there, its members will decide if it is necessary to constitute itself into a political party. An example is RPF, which became a political party only after winning the civil war in 1994.

- *What are the guarantees that Hutu in RNC would not be treated like Colonel Alexis Kanyarengwe?*

The "Kanyarengwe syndrome" (in RPF) and the "Ruhashya syndrome" (in MDR and MRND) are the symptoms of the same disease: political organizations, in which one ethnic group dominates, in a deeply divided society. RPF was, and remains, an organization of Tutsi. Colonel Kanyarengwe, a Hutu, was there as a figurehead to help RPF project an image of being representative of all components of Rwandan society. On his part, however, he did serve a historic and noble role. MDR and MRND were organizations of the Hutu. Col. Ruhashya, Katabarwa, Kajeguhakwa and a few other Tutsi were there for the Hutu organizations to show that they were representative of the whole nation. Note that MDR PAR-MEHUTU and MRND lacked internal democracy, which has turned out to be the case with RPF as well. RNC genuinely advocates for internal democracy, and for being representative. RNCdoes not have, nor does it need, figureheads. People in RNC are considered for their worth and contribution and not for their ethnic or regional background. Members and leaders of RNC are equal partners.

- *Who shot down the Habyarimana plane?*

Until October, 2010, we used to avoid answering this question, but always gave hints as to who the culprit was. I return to this question in the next chapter.

- *What do you say about the 1959 revolution?*

The 1959 revolution is a historical fact. It happened and it had justification. It brought about social, political and economic changes that were inevitable and desirable. It delivered on some of its promises, but ultimately failed to grasp the fact that Rwanda belonged to all Rwandans: Hutu, Tutsi and Twa. Tutsi were persecuted, marginalized, and exiled. The revolution became, in word and deed, a Hutu revolution. MRND carried the torch of the Hutu revolution, until it was militarily defeated by RPF in 1994. If one accepts the 1959 revolution, its successes and failures, one also has to accept the just basis of the RPF revolution of the 1990s, its successes and failures todate. Tutsi had been exiled. Tutsi had been marginalized within Rwanda. There were human rights abuses, and lack of political and civic freedoms. Unfortunately, the RPF- led revolution has become a Tutsi revolution, notwithstanding the social, political and economic gains under the RPF dictatorship. Note that in both revolutions the majority of Rwandans, Hutu and Tutsi, suffer irrespective of, or despite, their ethnicity.

- *Which country supports you, and how will you fight Kagame without money?*

So far no country supports RNC financially, politically, or diplomatically. Such support is not the primary condition for a political organization to succeed. The primary factors for a political movement to succeed are: 1) Context. Do the objective conditions necessitate change? In current Rwanda they do. 2) Organization and mobilization. Are the people mobilized and organized to build superior strength in the medium to long term? Questions of good leadership, discipline and resources are key to sustained progress and success. The secondary factors can be found within Rwanda's external environment. Examples are what is going on in the Great Lakes region now (wars in DRC), and to what extent we can convince Kagame's allies that their investment in Kagame is misused, misplaced, counter-productive and dangerous.

• *Have you really separated yourselves from the RPF? If Kagame was to die or leave today wouldn't you go back to RPF?*

Our separation (Nyamwasa, Karegeya. Gahima, and Rudasingwa) from Kagame and RPF is total and complete. But remember, we do not hate Kagame as a person. Most RPF members are good, law abiding citizens, like former members of MDR-PARMEHUTU and MRND. Most of the officers and men of Rwanda Defense Forces are good soldiers. Most officers and men of the former Rwandan army, FAR, were good soldiers. RNC seeks to mobilize all Rwandans, including members of the RPF, officers and men of RDF and ex-FAR, former members of MDR-PARMEHUTU and MRND, as well as those of current political and armed organizations to work towards peaceful transformation of Rwanda.

• *Kagame only believes in violence, how do you expect to remove him from power through "just talking"? What is your Plan B?*

It is precisely because he believes in violent solutions that RNC and its partners believe the endless cycle of violence has to be broken by our generation. It has become a pattern in Rwanda's politics that you acquire power through violence, maintain it through violent means, and you only lose it when someone more violent than yourself defeats you. The winner takes it all, and the loser dies, is jailed, banished to exile, or learns to live the life of a secondary citizen. It was the case of the Hutu before the 1959 revolution. It was the case for the Tutsi after the 1959 revolution. It is now the case with the Hutu after 1994, and now increasingly with the Tutsi as well. Never before have Rwandans been united in demanding societal transformation through peaceful means. The Arusha Peace Agreement provided some hope but it was derailed by the actions of President Kagame and the RPF (shooting down the Habyarimana plane) and extremists within the MRND. Every war in Rwanda becomes more devastating than the previous one. War is costly in human and material terms. It sacrifices the young generation since it is fought by young people. It destroys social and economic infrastructure. It polarizes an already divided society. It has consequences that run through generations. It has deadly regional and international security implications. Innovation is not in building another army that will defeat and destroy Kagame's. The innovation is in reconfiguring power in Rwanda so that all citizens (Hutu, Twa, Tutsi) can feel comfortable that they are represented in a country governed on the basis of the rule of law, equality before the law, and equal opportunity. Achieving that by peaceful means is the central challenge that calls for ingenuity and innovation. Every time I ask: who is willing to go to the battlefield, or send one's son or daughter to the battlefield should RNC launch an armed struggle, I am always amazed to see how few are willing to do that. I always add: if you and your children do not want to go to the battlefield, who do you think will go there and die for you? We have not yet fully counted the cost of war, genocide, war crimes, and crimes against humanity from 1959 to 2013. Rwanda cannot afford another war.

- *How do you envisage working with other political groups, and with civil society?*

RNC's philosophy is to work with all sectors of Rwandan society. Before RNC was born, we began consultation with all political groups and civil society leaders. Subsequently, after RNC was born we have created a political platform with FDU-Inkingi. We have endeavored to work with other groups like CNR-Intwari, Amahoro, and PS Imberakuri. RNC is open to work with all interested Rwandans and organizations for peaceful change in Rwanda.

- *Kagame is very powerful. He has money. He has the government. He has powerful friends (Americans and the British). How do you expect to remove him from power?*

Power, money, state and friends cannot save dictatorships when their time has come. The American war of independence pitted a revolutionary army against the colonizing British Monarchy. The British Monarchy lost the war, despite the money and power. In the twentieth century there are many examples. Adolph Hitler finally committed suicide, having commanded power and money that was hitherto unparalleled in Germany and Europe. The Vietnam War against the powerful French, then a super power United States, ended in favor of the weak against the powerful. Back home in Africa, the apartheid regime was strong in terms of state power and money. In 1994, the African National Congress rose to power and apartheid became history. President Mobutu was once rich and powerful, and his regime collapsed like a house of cards. In Eritrea, Ethiopia and Uganda dictatorships fell despite their apparent power and money. But, peaceful movements have triumphed over the power of money and powerful friends. In India, Mahatma Ghandi's peace movement stood against the power and money of the British Empire and won. In the United States, Martin Luther King Jr's peaceful civil rights movement won the day against powerful and moneyed interests in the United States. By and large, Africa's decolonization was a peaceful process. In recent times, the Tunisian, Egyptian and Libyan examples of the collapse of powerful and moneyed dictatorships is another good example. After all, didn't Kagame and RPF start as underdogs in 1979 (RANU)? The greatest lesson in history is that the idea of freedom is a powerful one. Once it grips the hearts and minds of women, it becomes an irresistible force. Kagame will face the fate of all other dictators before him. As for the United States and the United Kingdom, they only have permanent interests in Rwanda and the DRC. As the case of Belgium and France before, assumed to be "friends of the Hutu", the Americans and the British are not "friends of the Tutsi." The American is friends with America. The British are friends with Britain. We have to convince the Americans and the British that their larger and long term interests are best protected in Rwanda and the Great Lakes region when most people are free and the region stable.

- *Gahima was responsible for unjustly putting people in jail on genocide charges while he was Rwanda's Prosecutor General*

More than one million Tutsi were butchered day and night in just 100 days. They did not commit suicide. They were killed by Hutu interahamwe militia, security agents, and ordinary people on Rwandan hills. Most of the people who did the killing were Hutu. Somebody has to account for these crimes. It is true that there has been injustice, and some innocent people got caught up in RPF' victor's justice, through the Gacaca and the International Criminal Tribunal (ICTR). Though a large number of Hutu have been killed at the hands of President Kagame's RPA before, during, and after 1994, in Rwanda and DRC, these crimes are yet to be acknowledged, fully investigated, prosecuted and perpetrators brought to justice. RNC seeks to bring justice to all Rwandans. The starting point is to tell the truth, to acknowledge all the crimes against both the Tutsi and Hutu, and use that as a basis for genuine reconciliation and healing.

• *General Kayumba Nyamwasa was responsible for human rights abuses in northern Rwanda during the insurgency, and also in DRC, while he was Rwanda's army Chief of Staff. He has also been indicted by a French Judge and a Spanish Court.*

It is true that human rights violations were committed in Rwanda during the period of insurgency after RPF came to power. Human rights violations were also committed before RPF came to power. Further, human rights abuses were committed by RPA in the DRC. General Nyamwasa has explained that he regrets the loss of life and human rights abuses that took place in Rwanda while he was the Chief of Staff of the army. He has also explained that on behalf of the Government, he had to deal with a strong insurgency that was growing in the north of the country. People have to acknowledge this fact as well. As for the war crimes, crimes against humanity and even possible acts of genocide (according to the UN Mapping Report of October 2010) President Kagame and General James Kabarebe should account for these crimes. Regarding the French and Spanish indictments, General Nyamwasa is ready to co-operate if and when the two are ready for him.

• *When will you take us back home?*

Nobody takes the other home. You will take yourself. RNC tells people to be mobilized and organized. There shouldn't be bystanders. You do not have to be in RNC to contribute to the liberation of your people and your country. "Whatever you do, do not do nothing", we tell people, You can contribute your talent, time, treasure (money) and your relationships. You can help in mobilizing Rwandan people to the great cause of self-liberation. You can help by explaining to foreigners in your community, work place, church, and social media what this peace movement is all about.

• *The four of you (Nyamwasa, Gahima, Karegeya, and Rudasingwa) have to tell the whole truth about RPF's crimes. Why did you take long before distancing yourselves from President Kagame and RPF?*

It is not only four of us, former members of the RPF who should tell the truth about RPF's crimes. There are many Hutu who were, and still are, members of the RPF. They too have to say what they know about RPF and their role in it. RPF and some Tutsi leaders are not the only ones to account for things that were done or not done in Rwanda. MDR PARMEHUTU, MRND, and some Hutu leaders should also account for things that were done or not done during the reign of these two organizations. Who is to account for the Tutsi who perished during the First Republic? Who will account for the deaths of President Kayibanda and politicians from the south during the Second Republic? Who will account for the massacres of Kibilira, Bugesera and Bigogwe in the early 1990s? Which Hutu politician has stepped forward to apologise for the crime of genocide against Tutsi? The point is that we all must face courageously our history, the good and the bad, without being held hostage to it because yesterday is gone. The purpose is not vengeance, but to acknowledge the hurt we have inflicted on each other, and thereby create room for individual, family, community, national, and regional healing. As for taking long to separate ourselves from the dictatorial regime of President Kagame, it is better late than never. We do not regret the good things we were able to do while RPF was able to say and do the right things. There are good things to say about the kings who ruled Rwanda for centuries. There are good things to talk about the colonial government. There are good things to say about the 1959 revolution, MDR PARMEHUTU and MRND. As for the bad things, they are widely shared, from the kings to the present rule of RPF. It takes time to recognize the pattern of evil. It is only 10-15 years from 1994 to the time that each one of the four members decided to part with Kagame. Even when you decide to part there are both personal and security considerations to take into account. Staying with Kagame is dangerous. Parting from him is even a more dangerous and risky journey.

CHAPTER FORTY ONE

A Confession

For most of the month of October in 2011, I was restless. During most meetings with Rwandans, we were almost always asked the question, "Who shot down the Habyarimana plane?" Everyone in the audience always assumed that we knew the answer to that question. Failure to open up and say what we knew about it was bound to cause problems in the difficult task of building confidence and trust. From the very beginning, RNC was determined to tell the truth as an indispensable way of building trust, reconciling the Rwandan people, and healing.

On the first of October, 2011, in a hotel room at Raleigh-Durham International Airport, North Carolina, in the United States, I wrote and publicized the following confession:

PAUL KAGAME KILLED PRESIDENT JUVENAL HABYARIMANA, PRESIDENTCYPRIEN NTARYAMIRA OF BURUNDI, DEOGRATIAS NSABIMANA, ELIE SAGATWA, THADDEE BAGARAGAZA, JUVENAL RENZAHO, EMMANUEL AKINGENEYE, BERNARD CIZA, CYRIAQUE SIMBIZI, JACKY HERAUD, JEAN PIERRE MINABERRY AND JEAN-MICHEL PERRINE

On August 4, 1993, in Arusha, Tanzania, the Government of Rwanda and the Rwandese Patriotic Front signed the Arusha Peace Agreement. The provisions of the agreement included a commitment to principles of the rule of law, democracy, national unity, pluralism, the respect of fundamental freedoms and the rights of the individual. The agreements further had provisions on power-sharing, formation of one and single National Army and a new National Gendarmerie from forces of the two warring parties; and a definitive solution to the problem of Rwandan refugees.

On April 6, 1994, at 8:25 p.m., the Falcon 50 jet of the President of the Republic of Rwanda, registration number "9XR-NN", on its return from a summit meeting in DAR-ESSALAAM, Tanzania, as it was on approach to Kanombe International Airport in KIGALI, Rwanda, was shot down. All on board, including President Juvenal Habyarimana, President Cyprien Ntaryamira of Burundi, their entire entourage and flight crew died.

The death of President Juvenal Habyarimana triggered the start of genocide that targeted Tutsi and Hutu moderates, and the resumption of civil war between RPF and the Government of Rwanda. The RPF's sad and false narrative from that time on has been that Hutu extremists within President Habyarimana's camp shot down the plane to derail the implementation of the Arusha Peace Agreement, and to find a pretext to start the genocide in which over 800,000 Rwandans died in just 100 days. This narrative has become a predominant one in some international circles, among scholars, and in some human rights organizations.

The truth must now be told. Paul Kagame, then overall commander of the Rwandese Patriotic Army, the armed wing of the Rwandese Patriotic Front, was personally responsible for the shooting down of the plane. In July, 1994, Paul Kagame himself, with characteristic callousness and much glee, told me that he was responsible for shooting down the plane. Despite public denials, the fact of Kagame's culpability in this crime is also a public "secret" within RPF and RDF circles. Like many others in the RPF leadership, I enthusiastically sold this deceptive story line, especially to foreigners who by and large came to believe it, even when I knew that Kagame was the culprit in this crime.

The political and social atmosphere during the period from the signing of the Arusha Accords in August 1993 was highly explosive, and the nation was on edge. By killing President Habyarimana, Paul Kagame introduced a wild card in an already fragile ceasefire and dangerous situation. This created a powerful trigger, escalating to a tipping point towards resumption of the civil war, genocide, and the region-wide destabilization that has devastated the Great Lakes region since then.

Paul Kagame has to be immediately brought to account for this crime and its consequences. First, there is absolutely nothing honorable or heroic in reaching an agreement for peace with a partner, and then stabbing him in the back. Kagame and Habyarimana did not meet on the battlefield on April 6, 1994. If they had, and one of them or both had died, it would have been tragic, but understandable, as a product of the logic of war. President Habyarimana was returning from a peace summit, and by killing him, Kagame demonstrated the highest form of treachery. Second, Kagame, a Tutsi himself, callously gambled away the lives of innocent Tutsi and moderate Hutu who perished

in the genocide. While the killing of President Habyarimana, a Hutu, was not a direct cause of the genocide, it
provided a powerful motivation and trigger to those who
organized, mobilized and executed the genocide against
Tutsi and Hutu moderates. Third, by killing President
Habyarimana, Kagame permanently derailed the already
fragile Arusha peace process in a dangerous pursuit of
absolute power in Rwanda. Kagame feared the letter and
spirit of the Arusha Peace Agreement. As the subsequent
turn of events has now shown, Kagame does not believe
in the unity of Rwandans, democracy, respect of human
rights and other fundamental freedoms, the rule of law,
power sharing, integrated and accountable security institutions with a national character, and resolving the problem of refugees once and for all. This is what the Arusha
Peace Agreement was all about. That is what is lacking in
Rwanda today. Last, but not least, Kagame's and RPF's
false narrative, denials, and deceptions have led to par-
tial justice in Rwanda and at the International Criminal
Tribunal for Rwanda, thereby undermining prospects for
justice for all Rwandan people, reconciliation and healing.
The international community has, knowingly or unknowingly, become an accomplice in Kagame's systematic and
shameful game of deception.

I was never party to the conspiracy to commit this heinous
crime. In fact, I first heard about it on BBC around 1:00
am on April 7, 1994, while I was in Kampala where I had
been attending the Pan African Movement conference. I
believe the majority of members of RPF and RPA civilians and combatants, like me, were not party to this mur-
derous conspiracy that was hatched and organized by Paul
Kagame and executed on his orders. Nevertheless, I was
a Secretary General of the RPF, and a Major in the rebel

army, RPA. It is in this regard, within the context of collective responsibility, and a spirit of truth-telling in search of forgiveness and healing, that I would like to say I am deeply sorry about this loss of life, and to ask for forgiveness from the families of Juvenal Habyarimana, Cyprien Ntaryamira, Deogratias Nsabimana, Elie Sagatwa, Thaddee Bagaragaza, Emmanuel Akingeneye, Bernard Ciza, Cyriaque Simbizi, Jacky Heraud, Jean-Pierre Minaberry, and Jean-Michel Perrine. I also ask for forgiveness from all Rwandan people, in the hope that we must unanimously and categorically reject murder, treachery, lies and conspiracy as political weapons, eradicate impunity once and for all, and work together to build a culture of truth-telling, forgiveness, healing, and the rule of law. I ask for forgiveness from the people of Burundi and France whose leaders and citizens were killed in this crime. Above all, I ask for forgiveness from God for having lied and concealed evil for too long.

In freely telling the truth before God and the Rwandan people, I fully understand the risk I have undertaken, given Paul Kagame's legendary vindictiveness and unquenchable thirst for spilling the blood of Rwandans. It is a shared risk that Rwandans bear daily in their quest for freedom and justice for all. Neither power and fame, nor gold and silver, are the motivation for me in these matters of death that have defined our nation for too long. Truth cannot wait for tomorrow, because the Rwandan nation is very sick and divided, and cannot rebuild and heal on lies. All Rwandans urgently need truth today. Our individual and collective search for truth will set us free. When we are free, we can freely forgive each other and begin to live fully and heal at last.

Dr. Theogene Rudasingwa
Former: RPF Secretary General, Ambassador of Rwanda
to the United States, and Chief of Staff for President Paul
Kagame.
E-mail: ngombwa@gmail.com; Washington, DC. October 1, 2011

Before going public with this confession, I had agonized over it for months. This was a highly sensitive and risky matter in which one had to take caution as to what one said about it. The stakes and implications are extremely high for President Kagame, RPF, the international community, and for the future of Rwanda. This particular issue had become a crushing and paralyzing burden on my conscience. In weeks before the confession, I felt that my second conversion to Christianity demanded that I come out with all the truth, not simply convenient ones for political expediency. Only when I had told the whole truth would I be freed from bondage to the past. The teaching of Jesus Christ in John 8:32, "Then you will know the truth and the truth shall set you free," became ever more urgent and persistent. I would listen to Chris Tomlin's song, "Amazing Grace, My Chains are Gone" over and over again. The British composer of Amazing Grace, John Henry Newton, had himself been a slave trader, enslaved himself, and later became an anti-slavery abolitionist.

I had planned to have a meeting with Rwandans in North Carolina in the United States on the 1st of October, 2011. I did travel to Raleigh- Durham Airport and checked into a hotel. For a week I had been drafting the statement, which I kept to myself. One voice would keep on telling me that I should release it; another would tell me to wait. One voice would tell me it is very risky, and that I might end up being killed by President Kagame, leaving behind orphans to live as I had lived for decades. Naturally on a matter like this one one listens to one's conscience. I did not consult anybody. Most would have urged caution.

Shortly after midnight, on 1st October, 2011, I decided to post my confession on my Facebook. Then I sent a copy to Dorothy, and then to the founding members of the RNC. I went to sleep, feeling greatly relieved. My chains were gone, and I could rely only on God as my shield and portion.

CHAPTER FORTY TWO

Palais de Justice, Paris

On April 20, 2012, in Paris, France, I appeared before the French judges Marc Trevidic and Nathalie Poux, to give testimony in the investigation concerning the shooting down of the Habyarimana plane. Accompanied by Ms. Winnie Musabeyezu and Dr. Paulin Murayi, we had driven from Brussels to Paris. Itself an irony, both colleagues in the RNC are Hutu, the former a daughter of Felicien Kabuga and the latter a former representative of MRND in Brussels. As we travelled on that rainy afternoon, I contemplated what a unique opportunity Rwandans had to overcome prejudice and work together for a common future. To an outsider, it would sound strange that I (Tutsi) was accompanied by Hutu to testify against President Kagame (a fellow Tutsi).

I have friends, some of them non-Rwandans, who have asked me whether it was necessary to tell this truth, knowing its dangerous implications. Others say, what is the point of raising the matter 18 years later, when Rwanda and Rwandans have "moved forward". Some Tutsi say, "so what if President Habyarimana was killed? Didn't Tutsi die while he was a President?" Even some Hutu, especially from the south of Rwanda, some of whom lost families during President Habyarimana's reign, say they celebrated when they heard the news that he had died. Many have asked or questioned the motive of my confession. To me, and for many Rwandans, however, I have discovered it is a very important issue that is very much related to the present and future efforts for ending the cycle of conflict, building bridges for reconciliation, and opening doors for long term healing. It is above all, a moral issue.

Eleven Facts and Questions:

1. Since the shooting down of the plane on April 6, 1994, it has almost been public knowledge within RPF circles that the shooting down of the plane was the work of "our boys", meaning the work of RPA. In fact, in Tutsi circles, Lt. Generals James Kabarebe and Charles Kayonga (who commanded the RPA battalion at the CND- Parliament building) are celebrated as the heroes who executed the operation to shoot down the plane.

2. I heard from President Kagame himself that he gave the orders to shoot down the plane. In July, 1994 he told me the killing of President Habyarimana, as he estimated and was proved right, would bring the war to an expeditious end, and to RPF's capture of state power. The deaths of many Tutsi were regrettable, he said, but at least now "we have the power."

3. President Kagame further said that the Tutsi who remained in Rwanda since 1959 were "unreliable in any case". He doubted the Arusha Peace Agreement would have worked anyway, and sooner or later RPF would have had to fight the Rwandan army again, or kill President Habyarimana. He thought it would have been impossible to remove President Habyarimana from power through elections. He was unpopular with the southern Hutu elite, but he had a firm following among the people, and in any

case he had his party MRND and security institutions behind him. President Kagame told me he had informed President Yoweri Museveni of Uganda about RPF's role in killing President Habyarimana. President Museveni had revealed the matter to Susan Rice when she was Assistant Secretary of State for African Affairs during the Clinton Administration. President Kagame also confirmed to Col. Alexis Kanyarengwe, as Chairman of RPF, and Pasteur Bizimungu (then Chief RPF Negotiator, Arusha Peace Process) that the Habyarimana plane had been shot down by the RPA force at the CND.

4. As Secretary-General of the RPF (1993-1996), and later as Chief of Staff for President Paul Kagame (2000-2004), I have heard from a good number of RPA officers and men a few more details about the operation to shoot down the plane: I) the operation was conceived by President Kagame himself. It was kept outside the formal command of the RPA at the time. Only Kagame, James Kabarebe and Tom Byabagamba in RPF's headquarters in Mulindi, Byumba, northern Rwanda, and Charles Kayonga at the CND building, in Kigali, had privileged communication on Motorola two way radios that were supplied by Sam Nkusi to RPA; ii) The Surface-to-Air Missiles that shot down the plane were requisitioned by RPA and supplied by Uganda's military. They were picked by Jack Nziza (now Brigadier General) from Mbuya Military Headquarters in Kampala, and transported to RPF's headquarters in Mulindi, Byumba, Rwanda. The supply was signed-off by a Ugandan Officer by the name of Dick Bugingo; iii) The missiles were concealed and transported from Mulindi to the CND building in trucks carrying firewood and other supplies; iv) The missiles were concealed and transported in pickups carrying garbage to the Masaka farm location

near Kanombe International Airport where RPA agents shot down the plane as it approached the airport; v) There were plans to shoot down the plane as it took off from Kanombe International Airport that day but bad weather prevented it; vi) President Kagame had hatched other plans before to assassinate President Habyarimana. Other planned locations included the road to his residence in Kanombe; at the CND building during the swearing ceremony; and in Kinihira, Byumba; vii) the operation to assassinate President Habyarimana was linked to the immediate resumption of war. To this effect, as soon as President Kagame heard from Charles Kayonga that the plane had been shot down, immediately he gave orders for all RPA military units to break the ceasefire and launch a three-pronged attacke to capture the capital city Kigali and take over the whole country.

5. At the time of the shooting down of the plane, the United Nations had a peacekeeping operation in Rwanda, UNAMIR. Effectively, this international presence, under the United Nations Security Council, was supposed to help the Government of Rwanda and the RPF implement the Arusha Peace Agreement. One of the signatories to the peace agreement was killed in a terrorist attack, and the Arusha Peace Agreement was derailed. The UN Security Council has never considered the matter of the terrorist attack and the United Nations has never conducted an investigation into this attack. Why?

6. On April 6, 1994, President Bill Clinton was not only President of the United States; he was also the most influential person in the international system. The U.S government did not make any effort at all to use its expertise and influence to call for an international investigation in the

terrorist attack that claimed the lives of two sitting Heads of State and all their entourage. I was once given instructions by Vice-President Kagame, through Dr. Emmanuel Ndahiro, to stop efforts in the U.S Congress to have a hearing on the role of the U.S before and during genocide. I was told by Dr. Ndahiro that this had been specifically requested by then Assistant Secretary of State for African Affairs, Dr. Susan Rice. Why?

7. The African Union, the continental African body of all African nations, conducted its investigation and compiled a report on the Rwandan genocide of 1994. Neither the African Union, nor even individual African leaders and countries, have ever called for an investigation into a terrorist attack that claimed the lives of sitting Heads of States. Why?

8. The United Nations carried out its own inquiry into the Rwandan genocide of 1994 and published its findings in its report. Considering the role of the terrorist attack in triggering the genocide, the United Nations has not carried out an investigation into the attack? Why?

9. The International Criminal Tribunal for Rwanda (ICTR) was supposed to investigate, prosecute, and punish not only those responsible for the Rwanda genocide of 1994 in which Tutsi were victims, but also RPA's role in war crimes and crimes against humanity in which Hutu were victims. Considering the gravity of the terrorist attack, and its role in triggering the genocide, the ICTR has deliberately refused to investigate this crime. Why?

10. The United States and the United Kingdom, President Kagame's principal allies, have discouraged, and even

stopped, successive Prosecutors at the International Criminal Tribunal for Rwanda from pursuing the matter of the terrorist attack, and bringing the perpetrators of this crime to account. Why?

11. Except for France, the European Union has never taken interest to investigate the terrorist attack that claimed the lives of two African Heads of State and three European citizens. Why?

CHAPTER FORTY THREE

The Real Paul Kagame

A RECAP

R wanda has had two violent revolutions so far, but dictatorship in Rwanda remains an enduring affliction that still haunts her people. Rwanda seems to be stuck in a situation reminiscent of pre-1959 or pre-1990 period. The pre-1959 saw the rise of a marginalized Hutu population led by elite that challenged the monarchist status quo. The birth of the Rwandan Republic, and the end of the Belgian colonialism, was a violent phenomenon. While bringing social, economic and political benefits to the previously marginalized Hutu community, the 1959 revolution ended up marginalizing the Tutsi community. Many Tutsi were massacred, and hundreds of thousands fled into exile. The revolution produced Tutsi refugees, followed by waves of insurgency (INYENZI) that ended in the 1960s. Within Rwanda, the short lived multiparty politics abruptly came to an end, as the political space was closed and the country became a one-party state, under MDR PARMEHUTU party. Power also became over-centralized in the hands of President Gregoire Kayibanda, who with time, relied more and more on people from his community in Gitarama, in southern Rwanda.

In 1973, there was a palace coup within the revolution, and General Juvenal Habyarimana, a Hutu from the north, came to power, subsequently forming his own party, MRND. Many politicians from the south died at the hands of the new regime. President Habyarimana injected new energy into what had become a moribund system under MDR-PARMEHUTU and was seen to be "soft" on Tutsi, but the regime remained a Hutu one, and increasingly biased in favor of the north. Rwanda was still a one-party state. Like the previous monarchy before 1959, and Kayibanda's regime till 1973, power became over-centralized in the hands of President Habyarimana. Tutsi remained in exile, and marginalized within the country. Towards the end of the 1980s and beginning with 1990, the MRND regime had lost momentum and was under attack internally from political parties (mainly of Hutu from the south) and from an invasion by Tutsi refugees (RPF) from Uganda. Under political, economic, military and diplomatic pressure, President Habyarimana reluctantly negotiated the Arusha Peace Agreement with RPF. The peace agreement provided a vision for democratization and the rule of law, power sharing among MRND, RPF and other opposition political parties, establishment of new security institutions (Army and Gendarmerie), and the return of the 1959 refugees. For a brief moment Rwandans were hopeful that peace, reconciliation, democracy and the rule of law were coming to Rwanda at last.

Then General Kagame struck, killing President Habyarimana, triggered genocide, and finally captured power, ending the Arusha Peace Agreement. In his ambition to get power by any means, General Kagame triggered a genocide in which 800, 000 Tutsi perished at the hands of the so called Provisional Government, its security institutions, and the interahamwe militia. Hundreds of thousands of Hutu have died in Rwanda, and the Democratic Republic of Congo, at the hands of President Kagame's RPA, in war crimes, crimes against humanity and even, possibly, acts of genocide, according to a UN Mapping report.

Rwanda's history seems to repeat itself more often than else-where in space and time. President Kagame's dictatorship far surpasses the previous ones. RPF's revolution of the 1990s has become frozen, and in its wake President Kagame has gradu-ally turned RPF and its sister, RPA (now RDF), into tools for his absolute dictatorship. What could have become a national revolution has become a"Tutsi revolution", a misnomer because like previous revolutions, the ordinary Hutu and Tutsi gradu-ally become tools of the ruling elite (Hutu or Tutsi) at the top. Rwanda has refugees. Political space is completely closed, and Rwanda, as before, has become a one-party highly militarized and secretive state. Political opponents, journalists, and human rights activists are harassed, imprisoned, killed, or forced to flee the country.

Even in exile, critics of the regime have no solace. The impris-onment of Victoire Ingabire of FDU-Inkingi, Bernard Ntaganda of PS Imberakuri, Deo Mushaidi of PDP-Imanzi and many oth-ers is testimony to the prevailing mood in Rwanda. The assas-sinations of Seth Sendashonga, Theoneste Lizinde, Rwisereka of the Green Party in 2010,.Rugambage, Charles Ingabire in Kam-pala, 2011, the assassination attempt of General Kayumba Nyam-wasa in 2010 in South Africa, the various assassination schemes that have been foiled in the United Kingdom, Sweden and other places, are some of the testimonies to the criminal nature of the regime. There is no independent media in Rwanda. The judiciary and legislature in Rwanda are not independent. Their powers have been usurped by President Kagame. Civil society and the private sector are controlled by President Kagame's small band of Tutsi military officers and a few RPF civilians allowed into the circle of the First family.

How have President Kagame and his family come to domi-nate Rwandan society to levels previously not seen in Rwanda's recent history? How does his system work? How has his charac-ter, shaped by being a refugee at a tender age, his involvement in violent wars in Uganda, Rwanda and DRC affected his outlook on life?

Since the 1980s, Paul Kagame has been at the center of violent conflicts spanning the territories of Uganda, Rwanda and the Democratic Republic of Congo. In these conflicts, there has been widespread destruction of life and other horrendous human rights abuses. Kagame bears personal as well as command responsibility for some of these crimes, including assassinations and other serious human rights abuses.

After a lifetime of unimaginable violence, Kagame is like a serial killer, a person with no regrets or remorse for the acts of violence that he or others acting on his instructions commit. He is not apologetic about this. On the contrary, he makes it a point in public and private conversations that indeed his opponents must die. Probably a result of his past crimes, President Kagame is very paranoid about plots to remove him from power and about his security in general. Since coming to power, Kagame has amassed a vast fortune. This fortune has been acquired by unethical and sometimes, criminal means.

Kagame's actions are influenced in large measure by a reckoning with his past. Kagame believes that a person's name or reputation is his or her most precious possession. He has established a false reputation of frugality, incorruptibility, accountability in government, and military hero who stopped the genocide. Preserving this false image is critical to the preservation of Kagame's monopoly of power in Rwanda.

Kagame's greatest concern is that of the people who have information (including corruption and responsibility for assassinations, war crimes and crimes against humanity, in Uganda, Rwanda and the DRC which may tarnish the public image that he has crafted. Kagame's criminal background, and the need to avoid being held accountable, explains why he is bent on staying in power at all costs, including the assassination of political opponents.

THE ANATOMY OF A DICTATORSHIP

First Family: President Kagame stands at the top of the social, economic, political and military pyramid in Rwanda. Second in command is his wife, Jeannette Kagame, who wields a lot of influence over her husband. She has influence on who falls or rises within the political system; appointments of Ambassadors, Cabinet Ministers, and other high level offices; places her own people in some strategic positions; and has influence on security services through General Jack Nziza. Mrs. Kagame has come to be the most influential in the HIV/AIDS/TB/Malaria health sector programs, where most aid money is. According to U.S. Government sources, from 2004-2009, Rwanda received over $ 540 million from U.S PEPFAR. In fiscal year 2011 alone, Rwanda received almost U.S. $ 132 million from U.S. PEPFAR. Since 2003, Rwanda has received a total disbursement of over U.S. $ 570 million from the Global Fund. With this in mind, the First Family has successively moved Dr. Agnes Binagwaho, the First Family Pediatrician, to manage these resources on their behalf. Prior to the Binagwaho's appointment as Minister of Health, the First Family appointed Caroline Kayonga, wife of Lt. General Charles Kayonga as Permanent Secretary of the same Ministry.

The Core: The third layer in Rwanda's power pyramid after the President and his wife, are a core of high ranking military officers who formerly worked as President Kagame's bodyguards during the civil war; intelligence and close protection personnel of the elite Republican Guard; and the entire Republican Guard itself. This inner circle includes Lt. General Kabarebe Minister of Defense; Lt. General Charles Kayonga, Chief of the Defense Forces; Col. Dr. Emmanuel Ndahiro, who was his personal doctor, and until recently, the head of the National Security Services; and Brigadier General Jack Nziza (not a former bodyguard, but has had a long relationship with President Kagame from the Uganda days, manages the informal security system, and is very close to Jeannette Kagame). This core group (directly or indirectly) run the elite and privileged Presidential Guard which protects the family, and exercise official and unofficial oversight over the Rwanda Defense Forces (RDF), the Reserve Force, and the Local Defense Units.

This core group of exclusively Tutsi officers also keeps an eye on other organs of the government, civilian (including the Legislature and Government Ministries) as well as military, to ensure that these organs and the people running them serve the interests of President Kagame and his regime. These senior officers also supervise the intelligence and close protection officers of the Republican Guard, who over the years have included Col. Tom Byabagamba, Col. Silas Udahemuka, Lt. Col Hodari (Commanding Officer, Republican Guard; and the powerful Lt. Col. Willy Rwagasana, President Kagame's Chief Escort. Kagame's former military escorts during the civil war, together with the current young military escorts, run the entire security apparatus. Although the fortunes of the individual members of this inner core rise and fall with time, the groups as a whole are the most stable of the various groups that constitute the leadership of Rwanda. They are indispensable to Paul Kagame. Kagame depends on them for his protection and for his political survival. As the most trusted assistants, some of them have access to information whose disclosure would be politically damaging to Paul Kagame. In turn this core group is hostage to him, since he has used them in criminal activities, and they cannot afford to be outside his sphere of influence.

Republican Guard: The elite 3,000 strong plus Republican Guard has the exclusive mission to protect the First Family. It is a privileged unit, with financial, material, training and equipment incentives that are over and above those of the rest of the armed forces. Members of this unit are groomed to take over command of battalions and divisions of the Regular Army. Kagame puts members of this Unit in control of Battalions and Division command positions.

The members of this Unit are almost all exclusively Tutsi.

Informal Security Networks: President Kagame has established informal security networks that work parallel to or in competition with security organs established by law. The primary objective of the informal networks is to identify and neutralize real and imagined enemies of the regime. The informal security networks are the President's enforcers. Many members of these informal networks are deployed in foreign countries, including embassies of Rwanda in countries where there are significant populations of Rwandan refugees. These informal networks are only accountable to the President, and in some cases, to his wife. The most prominent of these informal security networks are the ones operated by Brig General Jack Nziza. Kagame can always count on him to essentially constitute a powerful informal government that runs the formal government. In view of the unwavering determination and exceptional brutality that General Nziza has always demonstrated, and continues to demonstrate, in eliminating what he calls the enemies of the regime, he has acquired a special relationship with President Kagame and Jeannette Kagame that even other members of the inner core group no longer enjoy. General Jack Nziza is arguably now more influential with Paul Kagame than most of the members of the core group. General Jack Nziza meddles in the work of all institutions in Rwanda, including the legislature and the judiciary. He tries to impose his oversight over all institutions on the pretext of being after enemies or saboteurs of the regime. He usually gets his way, because of the ruthless reputation that he has acquired.

The Intelligence Services: The fifth layer of control is the Intelligence services, namely the National Security Service and the Directorate of Military Intelligence. Note that the intelligence services of the Republican Guard, and Kagame's informal networks, are superior, and ultimately control, these other intelligence services. The notable figure in these intelligence services is Lt. General Karenzi Karake (KK), brilliant, but passionately hated by President Kagame for long, and who was humiliated before he was given the task to head the National Security Service.

Rwanda Defense Forces: The sixth layer of control is the military. The military are the backbone of the Rwanda government. President Kagame discusses major policies and decisions with senior military commanders before discussing them with civilian assistants. The military commanders are the real government; the civilians in government are the technocratic servants of the military. The Rwanda Defense Forces are, in essence, not a national army. They owe allegiance not to the state, or its people, but to one political organization, the Rwandese Patriotic Front, and to its supreme leader, President Kagame. No wonder he calls RDF, "my army", and its officers, "my officers".

The RDF is spread throughout the country. They perform many political functions on behalf of the RPF. The military are responsible for mobilization for the party: convincing opinion leaders to join and serve the RPF. Military officers are responsible for the supervision of the local government officials that the RPF appoints, the RDF is responsible for the rigging of elections in favor of the RPF, and military officers are responsible for ensuring that opponents of the regime everywhere are identified and destroyed.

The Rwandese Patriotic Front: The seventh layer of control is RPF. The Rwandese Patriotic Front is unofficially the sole party that is allowed to practice politics in Rwanda. The party is President's Kagame's tool for controlling every aspect of life in Rwanda. The party controls the country through the officials that it appoints to public office at all levels. Its members constitute the overwhelming majority of all institutions. The party maintains strict control of all these officials by requiring them to take an oath and through disciplinary procedures that are a violation of the laws that require certain public officials to be independent.

The party secretariat functions as a parallel office of the Prime Minister. The RPF Secretariat is responsible for the appointment of all civilian public officials, including ministers, judges, and legislators; draws recommendations for Kagame to approve, if he has made his decision before hand; responsible for discussing and approving all policy development, including all policy proposals and major decisions to be discussed by Parliament; disciplining all civilian public officials who are members of the party, including ministers, judges, and legislators, who by law should be independent. Currently, RPF civilians like James Musoni and Aloysea Inyumba (before she passed away) wield a lot of influence due to the special relationship they have with President Kagame. The party is a vast network of informal government mechanisms that operate at all levels of the organization of state administration.

Financial Managers: The eighth layer of control are the people who run President Kagame's financial interests. President Kagame has a three-pronged strategy for sustaining his control of power in Rwanda:

(a) Establishing intelligence systems that are able to identify and neutralize all real or perceived threats
(b) Maintaining a strong military that is able both to protect the regime and to project his power abroad
(c) Securing the resources to finance the activities of the military and security institutions that keep him in power.

For these resources, President Kagame draws both on public resources and the business activities of the RPF. The men and women who are responsible for generating, managing and delivering these resources are very influential.

In government, the following people have been responsible for making sure that President Kagame can get access the government finances for personal and non-official purposes:

- Don Kaberuka, Former Minister of Finance, now President of the African Development Bank
- Manasseh Nshuti, Former Minister of Finance
- John Rwangombwa, and Governor of Central Bank
- Ms. Sayinzoga, Permanent Secretary, Ministry of Finance (Wife of Kagame's nephew).
- Jack Nziza, Permanent Secretary, Ministry of Defense.
- Claver Gatete, Minister of Finance

The business enterprises that President Kagame owns ostensibly belong to the RPF and the Defense Department, but are practically his personal businesses. He alone controls this business empire. The RPF has no treasurer or finance committee. The accounts of the businesses are secret and never audited independently. The managers of the businesses are answerable to Kagame alone. Kagame does not account to any organ of the RPF on these business and finance matters.

The holding company for the businesses run by civilians is Crystal Ventures Limited (CVL), a successor to former Tri-Star Investments, supposedly an RPF company. In fact this is a Paul Kagame's company. President Kagame's financial empire includes the following: Rwanda Investment Group (RIG), involved in a wide range of activities; Telecommunications (MTN Rwandacell and Altel); Banking; Construction and building products (NDP-COTRACO S.A.R.L); Real estate development ((Real Contractors, Bond Trading S.A.R.L); Catering (Bourbon Coffee), Security services (Intersec Security); Packaging (Design Packages); Beverage and food processing (Inyange Products); Communications (GPS Graphic Print Solutions); and Whole sale and Retail Trading, (Mutara Enterprises).

President Kagame also carries on business using institutions under the Ministry of Defense. The vehicle for this branch of his business empire is the Horizon Group, which was set up in 2008 by the Ministry of Defense. The subsidiaries of the Horizon Group include: a commercial bank (ZIGAMA-CSS); large infrastructure projects (Horizon Construction); agricultural products (Horizon SOPYRWA); and Horizon Logistics, providing logistical support to over 3,500 Rwandan troops under the United Nations Mission in Darfur (UNAMID) and the United Nations Mission in Khartoum, Sudan (UNAMIS). Horizon Logistics is also involved in export and import clearing and forwarding services. This suggests that economic and political interests of the holding do overlap as the earnings from one subsidiary company subsidize the operations of the other. By forming joint ventures with state owned enterprises, RPF and Military companies (directly under the control of President Kagame) receive free funding, and transfer any risks to the state should the ventures fail, which is often.

Formal Government: The ninth layer of influence and control is the formal Government institutions, situated very far down the ladder in the power structure of Rwanda. Hutu who are accommodated by the system are mainly found in the formal government. Members of the formal government are merely technocrats implementing the policies of others and are not influential unless they happen to have strong connections in the party or with the President. However, it should be noted that many of the people who will strong influence by virtue of their positions in informal structures also have official positions.

In fact, the RPF ensures that the most important government departments are entrusted to very trusted members. The institutions that are most critical to President Kagame's strategies for controlling the state are the following, and, like the security institutions, are all controlled by Tutsi (or presumed to be):

- – Central Bank: John Rwangombwa, Governor
- – Ministry of Finance: Minister, Claver Gatete
- – Ministry of Health: Minister, Dr. Agnes Binagwaho

- Rwanda Revenue Authority: Ben Kagarama
- Ministry of Justice: Tharcisse Karugarama
- Office of the Prosecutor General: Prosecutor General: Martin Ngoga

Kagame's Foreign Legion: The tenth layer of influence is exercised through an elaborate network of foreigners (and a few Rwandans) who have to sell President Kagame's image and narrative as the sole hero and savior of Rwanda. Because Rwanda is heavily dependent on aid, and his reputation as the western-celebrated leader of the "emerging Singapore of Africa" is crucial to the continuous flow of aid, this group of people is crucial in facilitating him. Through what he calls the Presidential Advisory Council (PAC), he is able to promote a soft and deceptive image abroad, especially where it matters most, in the United States and the United Kingdom. Through lobbying, public relations, and access to the media, these facilitators help President Kagame's self-promotion abroad, and shield him from accountability for the crimes he commits on Rwanda, DRC and abroad. The loudest mouthpiece in the whole group is Tony Blair. President Kagame's staunchest defender at the United Nations is U.S. Ambassador Susan Rice.

This foreign legion includes the following:

- Tony Blair, former Prime Minister of the United Kingdom
- Bill Clinton, former President of the United States
- Ambassador Susa Rice
- Rick Warren, Pastor and founder Saddleback Church, and author of bestseller, *Purpose Driven Life*
- Professor Michael Porter, Harvard Business School
- Larry Weber, Racepoint Group, a US public relations firm

- Mark Pursey, BTP Advisers, UK-based communications group
- Ambassador Andrew Young, Good Works International
- Scott Ford – President and CEO of Alltel
- Sir Tom Hunter – Scottish entrepreneur, philanthropist, co-founder Clinton-Hunter Development Initiative
- Dr. Donald Kaberuka – President of the African Development Bank Group, former Minister of Finance, Rwanda (Rwandan)
- Dr. Clet Niyikiza – GlaxoSmithKline (GSK) Vice President of Worldwide Research & Development
- Kaia Miller – founder of Aslan Global, Inc.
- Joe Ritchie – Rwanda's Honorary Consul in Chicago, founder Fox River Financial Resources, Inc and CEO of Rwanda Developement Board.
- Michael Roux – Rwanda's Honorary Consul General in Australia, Chairman, Asian Markets, KPMG; Roux International Pty Ltd; RI Group;
- Dr. Eliane Ubalijoro – Assistant Professor at McGill University, Canada (Rwandan)
- Bel Dowson
- Michael Fairbanks, Chairman Emeritus and founder of The OTF Group, a software and strategy consulting firm based in USA.
- Andrew Mwenda, *The Independent*, Kampala, Uganda
- John Dick, Independent Director, LGI, and Director, O3B

CHAPTER FORTY FOUR

Waging And Winning A Peaceful Revolution

"*Justice* is the first virtue of social institutions, as *truth* is of systems of thought. A theory however elegant and economical must be rejected or revised if it is untrue; likewise laws and institutions no matter how efficient and well-arranged must be reformed or abolished if they are unjust. Each person possesses an inviolability founded on justice that even the welfare of society as a whole cannot override. For this reason justice denies that the loss of freedom for some is made right by a greater good shared by others. It does not allow that the sacrifices imposed on a few are outweighed by the larger sum of advantages enjoyed by many. Therefore in a just society the liberties of equal citizenship are taken as settled; the rights secured by justice are not subject to political bargaining or to the calculus of social interests. The only thing that permits us to acquiesce in an erroneous theory is the lack of a better one; analogously, an injustice is tolerable only when it is necessary to avoid an even greater injustice. *Being first virtues of human activities, truth and justice are uncompromising.*"

John Rawl, *A Theory of Justice*

Rwanda is broken and hurting. It needs a deep revolution to unite and heal. This might sound like a contradiction because historically, that word evokes fear and trepidation. When Rwandans think of revolution they immediately think of war, death, exile, genocide, refugee camps and alienation. The events of 1959, 1973, and 1994, and their consequences, come to their minds. To Americans, revolution refers to their war of independence from Britain. To the French, it is the famous French revolution, Napoleon, and the wars he unleashed in Europe. In Algeria, Angola, Mozambique, Uganda, Ethiopia, Eritrea, Vietnam, China, Democratic Republic of Congo, Russia, and many other places, the word revolution brings memories of war, in which there are winners and losers.

The Oxford English Dictionary defines the word, revolution, as "a forcible overthrow of a government or social order in favor of a new system; a dramatic and wide-reaching change in the way something works or is organized or in people's ideas about it; an instance of revolving; or as the movement of an object in a circular or elliptical course around another or about an axis or center" Looking back in the history of human civilization over the millennia, the second part of the definition of revolution (*a dramatic and wide-reaching change in the way something works or is organized or in people's ideas about it*) becomes evident. Organization, how things work, or people's ideas. We call it the agricultural revolution when human stop climbing trees and hunting for survival, and they settle in communities, taming animals and cultivating crops. We call it the industrial revolution when humans start building factories to produce what they consume. We call it the information revolution when computers and the flow of information become central to the way we live, produce and consume. Some revolutions are dramatic, but others become evident over long periods of time.

The most potent and, sometimes, most profound of revolutions is in the field of ideas. Social and political revolutions often begin as an idea in someone's or some people's minds. The agricultural, industrial and information revolutions take place because of some new idea or an old idea framed in a new way. In Socrates, Plato, Aristotle, Cicero, Judaism, Christianity, Hinduism, Islam, Buddha, Confucius, philosophers, scientists, and theologians there is a powerful idea. In his seminal and influential book, *The Structure of Scientific Revolutions*, Thomas Kuhn introduced the idea of a *paradigm shift*, a term that has now become popular in all endeavors of life.

The Oxford English Dictionary defines a paradigm as a typical example or pattern of something; a model, a worldview underlying the theories and methodology of a particular scientific subject; and a paradigm shift as a fundamental change in approach or underlying assumptions. Through examples of Copernicus, Isaac Newton, Albert Einstein and many others, Kuhn explained that once in a while scientific progress cannot continue in the normal way within the existing framework or paradigm. A new paradigm comes into being and a paradigm 'shift' has taken place to give answers to old or new questions. Such was the case when, in the 16th Century, Nicolaus Copernicus shocked the world with the assertion that the sun, and not the earth, was the center of the solar system. Such was the case when the English mathematician and scientist, Isaac Newton, first described gravity and the three laws of motion. Such was the case with Albert Einstein's Theory of Relativity.

Precisely because the entire Rwandan society has been divided, broken and hurting for too long, we need a fundamental change in the way we approach the so many problems before us. We need to revisit many of the underlying assumptions that have underpinned our conduct and governance. We need a paradigm shift. We need a revolution in thinking, so that we can wage and win a peaceful revolution to stop self-destruction, unite the Rwandan people, and facilitate a process of healing.

The revolution has four broad tasks:

1) STOP THE TRAUMA
2) REPAIR AND RESTORE
3) UNITE AND HEAL
4) PREVENT FUTURE TRAUMA

For a long time, and especially during the last fifty years, Rwanda has been like a body whose cells cannot recognize self, and has been undergoing self-destruction. Rwanda has acquired an "auto-immune" disorder. This could be called *Rwanda Acquired Immuno Deficiency Syndrome* (**RAIDS**). Rwandan society is suffering from RAIDS. It is acquired, chronic and deadly. It weakens and destroys Rwanda. Once weak, Rwandan society suffers from all sorts of "opportunistic infections": refugees, conflict, poverty, disease, ignorance, dictatorship etc. The second source of trauma is **ADDICTION**. Rwanda's elite is *addicted to absolute power.* Rwanda's successive ruling elite have suffered from this addiction, preferring to die with the disease rather than accepting the problem, checking into rehab and seeking treatment. The first underlying assumption for Rwanda's sustained recovery is for all Rwandans (Hutu, Tutsi and Twa) to discover that each Rwandan is a building cell of the same body. We need to recognize and treat each other as *self.* The second assumption is that Rwanda's elite must stop its *self-inflicted harm,* which, if not stopped, harms the whole Rwandan society. The revolution must overcome and prevent RAIDS and ADDICTION simultaneously.

Rwanda is for all Rwandans. All Rwandans are created in a different way, since, like all humans, no two beings are ever exactly the same. We are Hutu, Tutsi and Twa, and and we are proud of who we are. Citizens of Rwanda should be equal before the law. We are both different and equal Rwandans.

The practice, however, has been that the Rwandan state, first and foremost, and members of our society, have inflicted, and still inflict, trauma to each other. Death, exile, imprisonment, fear, genocide, war crimes, crimes against humanity, marginalization, humiliation, torture, imposed silence, hunger, disease, and breakdown in families, are some of the examples of the endless cycle of trauma. In this vicious cycle, the winners of today become losers of tomorrow. Then the losers wait for their turn, and they become winners again, and a new cycle begins. This is the *win-lose paradigm*.

Another related cycle is one in which the perpetrator of trauma today becomes the victim of tomorrow. The victim of trauma today ends up being a perpetrator tomorrow. This seemingly endless state of "victimhood" and "perpetrator-hood" has desensitized us to human suffering, that we are beginning to take it as a given and unchangeable. This is the *victim-perpetrator paradigm*.

The monarch for centuries operated in a *king-subject(or monarchy) paradigm*, with its institutions and philosophy to support this order. The 1959 Revolution was hence profound, since it turned upside down all the underlying assumptions on which the monarchist system was built. A republic, founded on the principles of democracy, even if in words, was intended to be a *democracy paradigm*. Since 1959, however, the changes within the republic (under MDR, MRND and RPF) can hardly be called paradigm shifts. They are a mere change of guard, leaving the same paradigm intact, the *dictatorship paradigm*.

The central challenge in the revolution's task in ending repeated self –inflicted trauma is to break out of the win-lose, victim-perpetrator, dictatorship paradigms and shift to a paradigm of *"All Rwandans Are Winners"* or **ARAW**. The treatment for Rwanda's RAIDS and power ADDICTION can be found within the ARAW paradigm or framework. Within the ARAW paradigm/framework, all Rwandans can work to towards stopping and reversing trauma, repairing the damage and restoring their normalcy, genuine healing and reconciliation, and preventing any slide into anarchy, death and destruction.

There are seven dimensions on which we have to do the work of stopping trauma, repair and restoration, and healing and normalization:

- Individual
- Family
- Community
- Nation
- Region (Great Lakes region)
- Africa
- International community

There are seven pathways through which we can achieve a paradigm shift in which all Rwandans are winners:

- Truth telling
- Forgiveness
- Trust
- Justice
- Community
- Freedom-friendly State and its institution
- Servant Leadership

Trauma and brokenness in Rwanda is experienced at various levels: individual, family, community, nation, region, Africa and the international community. Consider my personal and family's narrative in this book. I was victim and a loser in the 1959 revolution. Before 1959, Hutu were the losers and victims. In 1994, I was a winner, and many Hutu were, this time, the losers. The MDR regime established after 1959 committed human rights abuses against Tutsi. My own father was one of the many who were killed during the massacres that followed the 1959 revolution. I was told he was crucified. After 1994, I was one of the architects of the RPF regime, under which many human rights abuses were committed and continue to be committed as I write. The victim of the 1959 revolution had, indirectly, turned into a perpetrator.

When the Gregoire Kayibanda regime was overthrown by General Habyarimana in 1973, subsequently many politicians from the south died at the hands of the state agents. The perpetrators of injustice after the 1959 revolution became victims.

In 1994, President Habyarimana himself, his family, and many Hutu turned into victims at the hands of former victim turned into perpetrator, General Kagame and RPF/RPA.

We have been a nation of victims and perpetrators for too long. It is not only individuals and families that have suffered as a consequence. Communities have broken down as we have been scattered into refugee camps, separated by long-term imprisonment, or simply into the "you" and "them" that has characterized Rwanda. At the level of the nation, complete rupture took place as an entire administration vanished, with all its institutions, and new ones created by RPF. Communities of practice disappeared when professionals turned into killers, were killed or run into exile. The Great Lakes region of east and central Africa has suffered as a consequence of the brokenness of Rwanda. Over 6 million Congolese and Rwandans have died from the effects of Congo's internal conflict, exacerbated by the endless wars Rwanda has imposed on its larger neighbor. Can we re-imagine and re- invent ourselves as a nation in which we are all winners?

To do so we must overcome ourselves first. At each level- individual, family, community, nation, Great lakes region, Africa, and the international community- we must take the journey in truth-telling, doing justice to others as we expect them to do justice to us, forgiving others as they forgive us, trusting others as we expect others to trust us, building communities of winners, rolling back the overbearing state and repossessing it from President Kagame's family rule as we build people-friendly institutions, and , nurturing the managerial and leadership potential in our government, private sector, civil society and communities.

Truth and Reconciliation

The power of truth telling has been evident in the work that RNC has been doing since its founding at the end of 2011. When *Rwanda Briefing* came out in August 2010, its effect was electric because here were senior members of the RPF telling on their very own creation. When, after the founding of the RNC, our leaders and members openly talked about the trauma we have caused to each other, the idea and approach attracted many to the organization. When I came out with the confession that President Kagame was responsible for the assassination of Seth Sendashonga, it opened doors for me to talk to Sendashonga's widowed wife, Cyrie. When I confessed that President Kagame was responsible for the shooting down of President Habyarimana's plane, it opened doors for me to talk to the Habyarimana family and the Ntaryamira family. When RNC acknowledges that the RPF regime is responsible for war crimes and crimes against humanity against the Hutu, we are invited into the crucial, and yet difficult, conversations as to what we can do together to end impunity and seek redress of these wrongs.

Truth is the basis for genuine reconciliation and healing. It is also the first step in ending trauma. Without acknowledging the wrongs, we are all trapped in anger, guilt, revenge and denial. However, while truth opens some doors it closes others. It is a risky proposal. Until we build a critical mass at community and national levels, the enemies of truth will always seek to subvert and distort it. At a personal level, truth telling has a powerful, cathartic, and healing effect. It is like you have burned bridges behind you, and there is no other way to go except forward. The truth telling has to go on at the community level, whether in Rwanda or outside. Ultimately, the decisive step will be when we are able to talk, at all levels, about the difficult subjects regarding how we have wronged each other and what to do with the truth that shall come out. This will be the true and genuine gacaca.

Forgiving and Remembering

Nothing is as difficult as asking a victim of serious crimes like genocide, war crimes and crimes against humanity to forgive and to remember at the same time. There is an inherent tension and unity in remembering and forgiving at the same time. I have read many academic papers on this subject, and I have always wondered whether the writers fully grasp the trauma in remembering, and even in forgiving. Forgiving is personal journey. No government's grand projects, like Rwanda's, can legislate forgiveness. Yes, governments and faith based institutions can put into place processes that encourage forgiving. True forgiveness is a personal choice, undertaken because of one's need for closure to an otherwise open wound that continues to hurt. If the other party can ask for forgiveness, and in earnest, it may motivate one to take the decisive step to for give.

From personal experience, I have found it much more difficult to ask for forgiveness than to forgive. When I made my confessions about Seth Sendashonga and President Habyarimana's assassinations, I was so anxious, and yet hesitant, to talk to their spouses and children. In my heart I felt so much dread. What would I tell them? Suppose they refused to talk to me? Suppose they rejected my request?

Seth Sendashonga was a colleague and comrade-in-arms who was killed for his beliefs. My relationship to the late President Habyarimana was indirect. I had seen him only once, in Arusha, Tanzania, during the signing ceremony of the

Arusha Peace Agreement. In my mind then, he was my opponent, because he presided over the regime that I was fighting. There was no personal enmity, though. When I picked the courage to place the calls, I already found that both Mrs.Cyrie Sendashonga and Mrs.Agathe Habyarimana were willing to forgive me.

When I talked to President Habyarimana's daughter, Ms. Marie Rose Habyarimana, we had a deep conversation that I reproduce here. After telling me that her family had forgiven me, she asked me, "What did you think about my father?" It was an unexpected question, and I did not want to answer it in a way that would hurt her. I told her that in all honesty, I did not know her father personally, except that he was the leader of the regime that had kept me in exile. Frustrated like every one of my contemporaries in refugee camps, we had taken the matter into our own hands to end the life of exile. I gave her an example of 1982, when Rwandans were expelled from Uganda, and then were refused to enter Rwanda, while others were banished to Nasho. The people who used to tell us stories about President Habyarimana were his former collaborators like Alexis Kanyarengwe, Theoneste Lizinde, Valens Kajeguhakwa, and Pasteur Bizimungu. She told me that she was young and did not know all that her father was doing, but she knew that he was a good man, trying to do everything possible to make Rwandans happy. She told me her parents never used to talk to them about Hutu and Tutsi. She was surprised about Valens Kajeguhakwa because she thought their families were very close. It was an emotional conversation, in which she concluded her words saying that she was more interested in the truth coming out than the retribution for the killers of her father. I have felt a calm and peace in my heart knowing that I have been forgiven. I had to take the first step by telling the truth, and then asking for forgiveness. We also have to remember together, so that we may not forget.

I often ask myself, however, when some Hutu leaders will emerge who ask for forgiveness for the crimes committed against Tutsi and Hutu by both the MDR and MRND regimes.

Trust

It is reported that Confucius, the great Chinese teacher and philosopher, once said that rulers have to depend on three things in order to rule: weapons; food; and trust. If all had to go, except one, under no circumstance should the ruler give away trust. You could rule without weapons, or rule a starving people, but you cannot survive for long without people trusting you. We take trust for granted, but it is the glue that holds together families, communities and nations. From early on we learn to expect that people will do as they say. They, in turn, expect that we shall do as we say. People trust you when you are trustworthy, and you trust them because they are trustworthy. Rules, laws, communities, networks and institutions simplify matters in the whole trust ecosystem and we may begin to take things for granted. When you buy an airline ticket, you trust that you will get a seat and reach your destination. When you buy food, you trust that it is not contaminated. Within communities, the networks of trust are called *social capital*.

In marriage as in the classroom, in government as in business, in churches as in non-governmental organizations, the question of trust is a fundamental one. Rwanda is a nation where society at large is almost empty on trust. The trust gauge is showing us red, and has been showing us red for a while, and we keep on driving until our vehicle, Rwanda, stops and burns. We were already running low on trust before the 1959 revolution, and then the revolution came, trust tumbled and the house burned. We were already running low on trust when the 1973 coup took place, and trust levels went down. Since 1994, whatever little remained in the trust account was depleted by war, genocide, war crimes, crimes against humanity and bad governance, and the house is in ruins.

The "winner-loser", "victim-perpetrator", and "dictatorship" paradigms are *trust-depleters*. Lack of openness, transparency and accountability in our leaders and institutions is a trust depleter. Lack of trust now permeates our society, in Rwanda and in exile. It is not only mistrust between Hutu and Tutsi; it now runs amongst Hutu and Tutsi. Hutu from the north and Hutu from the south. Tutsi from Uganda and others. In exile, the threat of assassination and spying by government agents using poisons or other unconventional methods that people cannot trust anybody. In meetings, sometimes you have to bear the thirst because you cannot drink water from anyone except a trusted source. You cannot sleep in people's homes because you cannot trust them, and they cannot be your guests either because they do not trust you.

Building trust can be compared to a savings account. You grow your account slowly by slowly. Among us Rwandans, we have not been saving on our trust account. It is very depleted. We have to start rebuilding trust. It is a challenge to each one of us. We start in our families, talking to our children and spouses about the importance of trust. We reach out to others in the community to build trust. In my personal experience, sometimes little acts can have big rewards; I have surprised some people in Hutu communities when I decide to spend a night with their family. Building on that, we have become trusted friends. We have to begin to use social events like wedding ceremonies, planned cultural events, funerals and other events to build trust within our communities. Within Rwanda and in exile, our communities are self-segregating, and we have to make every effort to normalize relations amongst us.

In the spiritual domain, love is the foundation of trust. Because God loves us, we are taught, we should love our neighbor as we love ourselves. We should do unto others what we expect others to do unto us. That is what we should teach our children, and that is what schools need to do. In the secular domain, building open, transparent, and accountable institutions, with checks and balances, within the rule of law, is a *trust enhancer*. When people know that we are all equal before the law, and that laws are fair, we begin to trust our government, our institutions and people who work for those institutions.

Justice

For a long time the state has been the source of injustice in Rwanda. Rather than being the promoter and defender of justice for everyone, the state is hostage to interests of a clique which it defends with passion. Playing a bad influence, the state, at critical periods, as in 1959 and 1994, has played on people's fears, even coercing or enticing people into being sources of injustice to others. Mass participation in the genocide and massacres of 1994, and after, is one such example. At the heart of the idea of justice is that there are certain inviolable rights of a person that no community or societal considerations should override. How does one balance these individual rights, against the requirements of a properly functioning community, state and society? For too long, first under the monarchy, then colonialism, and all the way to the post-colonial regimes, the idea of the centrality of individual freedom has not been given as much consideration as the community interests.

During the days of Rwandan kings, all people were subjects. Colonial authorities had the same frame of mind, since all the colonized were subjects. Elite who have ruled Rwanda since independence have, by and large, followed the same script, preferring to refer to people as *rubanda nyamwinshi* or *abaturage*, sometimes in a negative way to suggest they are ignorant and uncivilized. President Kagame and RPF often say, "Iyo abaturage biboneye ibyo kurya ibya demokarasi nuburengazire bwa kiremwa muntu ntacyo baba babyitayeho." (When citizens have enough food, they do not care about democracy and human rights). Some Hutu leaders from President Kayibanda's time to current ones, have tended to emphasize this "rubanda nyamwinshi" (popular, Hutu, majority) idea as a way of mobilizing Hutu solidarity. Individual identity is obliterated when we become statistics in the group identities of Hutu, Tutsi, Twa, etc. Every Rwandan must reclaim a territory, a niche so to speak, within which nobody, not even the state and the community, can violate as long as this individual does not infringe on other people's rights.

President Kagame and his RPF say we are all Rwandans, on one hand, while doing everything possible to justify why one-sided justice is good for the Tutsi and therefore good for the Hutu as well. Post-1994 justice in Rwanda (Gacaca and ICTR) has been a victor's justice, preferring to investigate, prosecute and punish Hutu who committed atrocities against Tutsi, while leaving out the Tutsi who are responsible for war crimes, crimes against humanity, and even possible acts of genocide (according to UN Mapping Report). This is a high degree of impunity that the international community, especially the governments of the United States and the United Kingdom, has supported and promoted. Every Rwandan citizen is an individual human being first and foremost; His or her rights must be guaranteed and protected by law. It is justice for every one of us or no justice at all.

Community

For many centuries that Rwanda has existed as a nation, the *hill (*umusozi) has been the micro-level, or basic level, through which the rulers of Rwanda have dispensed their rule. If all politics is local, then in Rwanda it plays out on the hills. For a long time, chiefs were deployed to rule a number of hills. The practice has continued up to now, with various changes and names, but the hill has remained the basic unit of control. Ethnic solidarities in response to oppression, or, as ways of forging political power and control, do play out on the hills. It is at the hill that the state has inflicted trauma. Individuals and community as a whole inflict damage on each other here. Hence, the hill is both a *polis* and a *community*. Unlike the polis of the Greek city state, the hill has been, till today, a controlled polis. The hill is also a center of culture, a production and consumption center, and a place where bonds of trust (social capital) mean much. It is on the hill that economic and social development should start from. It is on the hill that evidence of environmental degradation, deforestation, and demographic pressure are seen.

Unfortunately, it is on these very hills that a neighbor killed a neighbor. It is on these hills that Gacaca played out, seeking truth and justice in favor of Tutsi and against Hutu. It is at the hill that Hutu solidarity plays out when a community knowingly decides to conceal the truth about crimes that were committed on the hill. Currently, RPF and the security institutions are deployed up to the hill level (*nyumba kumi* and *secteur*). RPF has decreed that only it can deploy as far down as the hill. All other political parties are barred from going that far. There are other communities in Rwanda: at the work place, and among professional groups and school communities.

From 1959, when Rwanda started being a net exporter of refugees, many communities sprang up in countries where Rwandans sought asylum (Uganda, Kenya, Tanzania, Burundi, DRC and elsewhere). In refugee camps, Rwandans maintained their culture, especially language. It is in these communities that seeds of rebellion and longing for return ultimately crystallize. Now with internet and social media, new virtual communities are forming. RNC is actually a virtual community, relying on Skype, email and social media to keep together people who often have not seen each other physically.

In general, however, the hill and other Rwandan communities are suffering from low trust, and no wonder social capital as a product of trust in Rwanda has ebbed to its lowest. The victim-perpetrator, winner-loser paradigms have literally left the hill and Rwandan communities exhausted and vulnerable. The revolution has to have as its principal objective, the reconstruction of the hill, and other Rwandan communities, in the interest of the people who live and/or work in these communities. Dialogue and collaboration should be the pillars around which to promote the All Rwandans Are Winners (ARAW) paradigm.

Freedom-enhancing and People-friendly State, Society, and Institutions

Rwanda needs organizations and institutions to promote and defend the new mindset of "All Rwandans Are Winners." While the immediate task is to wrestle Rwandan society and the Rwandan state from the hands of President Kagame's family, and thereby immediately stop the trauma the family imposes on Rwandan people, in the medium to long term it is the new learning organizations and people-friendly institutions that will help Rwandans unite and heal. The new organizations and institutions, be they governmental, business, civil society and community should be like experimental labs, nurturing the values commensurate with truth telling, justice, forgiveness, trust, community, people-friendly institutions, and managers and leaders who walk the talk.

Six key *clusters* of organizations and institutions are key to the short term removal of trauma, and medium to long term repair and restoration prospects of uniting and healing Rwandan society (To be discussed in detail in my upcoming book: *Imagining Rwanda Inc. In 2030*)

1. Educational Institutions;
2. Security Institutions;
3. Justice Institutions;
4. Primary Health Care and Development organizations operating at the community level
5. Political and civil society organizations;
6. Private Sector and Media.

Educational Institutions are key to Rwanda's recovery from trauma. The educated class that has ruled Rwanda was formed in these institutions. It is the educated class that runs organizations and institutions in government, private sector and civil society. It is in educational institutions that our children spend most of their time, in the hands of teachers. This is where the ARAW values can be inculcated, for the benefit of the future citizens of Rwanda, families, communities and the nation at large. Children are the future of the nation. Yet our priorities do not reflect the importance of teachers in the development of our society. It is time for us to put our children and their teachers at the forefront of Rwanda's priorities. It should be a privilege and honor to teach. Teachers should be the most remunerated amongst workers, and they should have a workplace (the classroom), tools, and materials that allow them to be the best of teachers that bring out the best in our children.

Security Institutions in Rwanda have been instruments of dictatorship. In the hands of a narrow elite (Hutu or Tutsi), security institutions have been instruments identified with the ethnicity of the ruling clique. Under President Kayibanda and President Habyarimana, the security institutions were Hutu Institutions. Under President Kagame, the security institutions are Tutsi institutions. Ethnic or factional institutions have been at the heart of human rights abuses, genocide, war crimes and crimes against humanity against all ethnic groups. They have failed to guarantee equal rights and equal citizenship for all Rwandans. They have instead been loyal to the absolute ruler, and this has provoked civil war in the long run. The revolution has to end this dangerous trend, and as soon as possible.

The way to end it is through going back to a modified Arusha Peace Agreement and make a deliberate move to make sure that Hutu and Tutsi are fairly represented in all these security institutions at all levels of command. The security institutions should account to civilian authorities. President Kagame's informal security networks under Jack Nziza should be disbanded immediately. Most importantly, the security institutions should embrace the idea that they defend and protect all Rwandan people, and embrace ARAW as the new idea that underlies all national security strategies. It is within this framework that a resolution of the problem of armed groups based in DRC, and armed rebellion in general, can be found.

A fiercely independent and impartial justice system is vital to impress upon all Rwandan citizens that they are all equal before the law, that those who break the law will be brought to justice irrespective of who they are and what they do. Courts, Police, investigators, prisons, prosecutions and all those involved in the justice system must be champions and protectors of the rights of the individual. For now, Rwanda Government says Gacaca is over and justice has been done. The ICTR in Arusha is winding up its operations. We all know that justice has not been done for all those who still demand and deserve it. There are some challenges ahead. First, what do we do with President Kagame and officers and men of RDF who have committed war crimes, crimes against humanity, and even possible acts of genocide? What do we do with President Kagame, James Kabarebe, Charles Kayonga, Jack Nziza and others who were responsible for the killing of President Habyarimana and all those who died with him? What do we with the killers of the Byumba, Ruhengeri, Gisenyi, Kabgayi and Kibeho massacres? How about those behind the crimes described in the UN Mapping Report? How about those who committed genocide and are still at large in Rwanda and elsewhere? How about those who committed the massacres of Kibilira, Bigogwe and Bugesera? How about the killers of President Kayibanda and his colleagues? How about those who massacred Tutsi after 1959? With the burdens of accountability hanging on our necks, where is the innovation for motivation to embrace a common future?

How can we persuade Rwandans out of the madness that they will fight to the finish, even if all Rwandans perish? If such people could be persuaded to abandon the self-destructive winner-loser, victim-perpetrator mindset they are operating in, I believe Rwandans would accommodate them in the interest of peace and the future of our children. Second, what do we do with Rwandans in Arusha who have been either acquitted, sentenced by ICTR, have served their prison sentences, or are in other countries serving their sentences? What is in Arusha or in other places that we cannot have in Rwanda when President Kagame and RPF no longer hold the sway as they do now? These are our people too, and we have to bring them home. I believe many Rwandans, in the interest of peace and the future of our children and posterity, would welcome arrangements in which we all live under the same roof, Rwanda.

The needs of survivors of genocide, victims of war crimes, and crimes against humanity (both Tutsi and Hutu) are of such a magnitude that they cry out for new and innovative ways of responding to their needs. Society has to negotiate a grand pact for reparations, even if this means exceptional belt-tightening measures. We should not be the generation that created a problem, and left it to future generations to handle.

A comprehensive community-based health care and development compact is urgently needed to redress the pervasive and yet still hidden problem of mental, psychological and psychosocial illness in Rwanda. The full picture of this problem is not yet fully known, but is immense. Repeated trauma from violent conflict, dislocation, genocide, war crimes, crimes against humanity, prison life, over and above the crushing effects of poverty and disease has left a debilitating impact on literally every Rwandan. In the winner-loser and victim-perpetrator frameworks that have dominated Rwanda, all are sick. From President Kagame to the last peasant on the hill, every Rwandan needs to deal with individual brokenness. In each one of us there is a silent or open perpetrator and victim, either in thought or deed, or both. Excepting children, there are no innocent bystanders. The winner and the loser, victim and perpetrator are perpetually at war within us, creating turmoil that we try to conceal.

The problem is that in Rwanda stigma is attached to psychological problems. This has to be addressed urgently. One way of dealing with this silent pandemic is to re-orient the Rwanda healthcare system towards primary health care emphasis on mental health, maternal health and child health. Unfortunately, due to restrictions on speech, if people cannot talk about what they have gone through, healing becomes difficult, if not impossible. Stopping and reversing the climate of fear that prevails in Rwanda, coupled with free speech, and removing stigma on mental health would encourage the new breed of community health workers and community members to respond to the mental health pandemic.

Leading and Managing for ARAW

In all human history leaders have had a prominent role in human progress. Visions and decisions of leaders have led to great movements forward, or led to catastrophic losses that made their societies suffer serious setbacks. Rwanda's history has had leaders that made impact on Rwanda's progress over the centuries. These include kings and post-colonial presidents. Nevertheless, Rwanda's leaders are yet to genuinely show that they embrace the ARAW vision. The winner takes it all has been the central and organizing principle. It matters little that modern day rulers live in the high tech age, and have read the great works of science, philosophy and theology. The "winner takes it all" and the "loser suffers marginalization, death or exile" seem to have been particularly the case in the last fifty years.

Rwanda needs leaders and managers who can champion, promote and execute the ARAW Vision in all domains of society. There is need for ARAW leadership and management at the community level, in politics, private sector, in churches, in schools, state institutions, and civil society. Because trauma has been and remains a scourge on all sectors of our society, a new type of leader is required for Rwanda. .

In one of the Biblical passage that speaks to a kind of leader, Jesus Christ compares a good leader to a good shepherd, a servant, a multiplier of talents, and one who leads to win asymmetric contests. The passage that narrates the often repeated story of teenager David and giant Goliath also highlights the need for leaders with a different kind of mindset, especially in difficult times. As Jesus Christ taught (John 10:1-18), a good shepherd: 1) must gather his sheep and treat them as one flock; 2) must know each of them by name; 3) is recognized by his sheep; 4) goes ahead of his flock when he takes them out; 5) defends the sheep against attack by wolves; and 6) lays down his life for the sheep. Jesus Christ also taught the principle of serving others, instead of being served. During the last supper, Jesus Christ, to the consternation of his disciples, washed their feet. In his parable of the talents, Jesus Christ also recounted how to each one of us is given talents. We can decide to leave them unused, under-utilized, or we can multiply them by using them wisely and smartly. In the Bible's Old Testament, a recount of the oldest example of asymmetric warfare is recounted, starting with a confrontation between a teenager, David, and the giant Goliath. At the end of the context, Goliath is killed by little David, with no special weapon other than five stones and a sling.

For a country torn by genocide, war crimes and crimes against humanity, constant rebellion, exile, family breakdown, disunity and brokenness, what kind of leaders and managers do we need? We need ARAW leaders and managers.

Ten Maxims for ARAW Leaders and Managers:

1. Embrace the ARAW mindset and vision, to help Rwandans stop the trauma, repair and restore broken lives, normalize and heal Rwandans, and prevent future damage;

2. Learn and know common interests of all Rwandan people;
3. Defend and promote the common interests of all Rwandan people with fairness and justice;
4. Trust Rwandan people and be trustworthy;
5. Be humble enough to know that you are just one other Rwandan citizen, with rights and obligations;
6. Expect to serve the Rwandan people with integrity, rather than expecting to be served by them;
7. Know your own strengths and weaknesses, build functional and effective teams from diverse people whose capabilities are complementary, and promote a spirit of dialogue and collaboration;
8. Develop, coach and mentor other leaders and managers, and empower them to grow and multiply their own, and other people's talents;
9. Deploy limited resources in an innovative and entrepreneurial ways to achieve maximum results;
10. Look further, wider, and deeper to recognize opportunities when others might see threats, and be courageous enough to take the lead in transforming threats into victories.

CHAPTER FORTY FIVE

Seven Concluding Proposi-
tions and Predictions

Proposition One: *A revolution is haunting Rwanda. Anything short of a revolution in thinking will lead to a vicious
cycle of violence, war, winners and losers, victims and perpetrators.*

Rwanda has undergone two violent revolutions, each time
producing winners, losers, victims and perpetrators. Rwanda cannot develop, let alone have enduring peace and security, acting
within the same tried and tired frameworks. A new framework in
which we are all winners is a better alternative. The new mindset is
required at the level of the individual, family, community, nation,
Great lakes region, Africa and the international community. The
All Rwandans Are Winners (ARAW) paradigm/mindset/frame-
work has seven interrelated and mutually reinforcing pathways
of truth, trust, justice, forgiveness, community, institutions, and
managers and leaders as stewards of the new order.

Proposition Two: *The revolution's principal premise is to respond
to a revolutionary situation by stopping and reversing persistent
trauma on Rwandan people, and to create the conditions for uniting
and healing them.*

The Rwandan state is currently captive to President Kagame and his wife Jeannette, assisted by a couple of Tutsi military officers who behind-the-scenes run both the formal government and the informal security networks. Rwandan society is now hostage to the First Family. The immediate and urgent task of this revolution is to enable the Rwandan people to free themselves from this hostage crisis, and rescue the Rwandan state from the hands of the Kagame's family. The call is urgent, and the cry from the people is loud and clear. Refugees have to regain their right to go back home. Rebellion based in DRC must end. Political prisoners have to be liberated. Political parties have to function. Opposition leaders and journalists have been killed. Opposition leaders in exile have been killed or assassination attempts have been made on their lives. The United Nations reported in 2010 (UN Mapping Report) that President Kagame's regime was responsible for war crimes, crimes against humanity and even possible acts of genocide in DRC. As we go to press, the United Nations has already confirmed that Rwanda was involved in setting up the rebel group M23 and starting the latest rebellion in eastern DRC. Organizations opposed to President Kagame's dictatorship, though now mainly based outside, are increasingly collaborating to push the revolution to new levels.

Proposition Three: *The current revolution has to be not only peaceful; it has to be national, democratic and people-centered if it has to succeed.*

Throughout Rwanda's history, power has always been narrowly constructed. The ruler and a few people he chooses from his ethnic group run the society. Two revolutions and three regimes under three parties (MDR-PARMEHUTU, MRND and RPF) have left Rwanda deeply divided on ethnic and regional lines. This revolution seeks to genuinely reconstruct power so that the whole Rwandan society feels represented at all levels of government. The revolution embraces the diversity of being Hutu, Tutsi, and Twa and encourages cooperation and collaboration as Rwandans, building a nation in which we are all equal before the law, and where we have equal opportunities. Since our society has experienced deep trauma, we have to negotiate **a grand bargain**, in which democratic rights are balanced with guarantees so that democracy does not gravitate towards becoming the tyranny of the majority. Powersharing arrangements like those of the Arusha Peace Agreement, including security guarantees, are a good starting point.

Proposition Four: *To succeed in this age the revolution has to have i) a flat and non-hierarchical networked structure ii) cultivate disciplined minds and disciplined actions iii) collaborate and coordinate with allies and partners iv) generate resources v) constantly develop managerial and leadership capacity.*

The activities of this revolution are predominantly outside of Rwanda at this moment. Most opposition organizations are able to operate mainly virtually. Most people, especially the youth can be accessed through the internet and social media. Rigid hierarchies and complex reporting mechanism are increasingly becoming a thing of the past. In this fluid and fast pace, organizations have to create conditions in which members have to be disciplined in thought and action. Rwandan society is diverse, and it is dispersed and fragmented into various segments. Like a marketing challenge, the revolution has to seek to interface with various stakeholders in and outside Rwanda: civil servants, teachers, soldiers, members of political parties, churches, civil society, media, etc. Out of all these contacts, allies and partners will emerge. The revolution has to develop its own disciples, who fully understand the ARAW mindset, who teach it passionately and relentlessly, and live it by example. The leadership has to be unified to be effective, and withstand the daily onslaught of the Kigali regime to disorganize, buy, co-opt or intimidate opposition leaders. The Revolution also needs to generate resources in terms of money, time, expertise and relationships that are critical to the revolution's success.

Proposition Five: *The Rwandan opposition as a whole needs to overcome fragmentation, build a coherent framework and outlook, and develop unified leadership that strategizes, plans, coordinates, and executes flexibly toward an ARAW endgame.*

The RPF regime under President Kagame has enormous expertise in disorganizing, destroying, buying, and co-opting political parties and their leaders. This started as far back as the 1990s. With the rise of the RNC and its partners, the regime is trapped between a hard place and a rock. On the one hand, it would not like to give Hutu genuine participation within the regime. On the other, they fear that unless they make efforts, the Hutu will fall into the RNC-FDU orbit. Kigali's onslaught on the political organizations operating abroad has intensified. The late Aloysea Inyumba's charm offensives in Europe and North America, coupled with efforts to tempt Hutu opposition groups with dialogue, were designed to hoodwink weak Hutu leaders to submit to President Kagame's whims. It is my prediction that in the long run, as it happens in any revolution, some of these groups and their leaders will succumb to temptation and expose themselves. The remaining few (there are always few) will coalesce around a solid partnership and unified leadership that will steer the revolution to victory.

Proposition Six: *Eastern DRC may turn out to be President Kagame's Achilles heel. The current international and regional situation is changing, in favor of revolutionary forces.*

Long used to impunity, and his frequent interventions in DRC to plunder and kill, President Kagame has overextended himself and overreached. For the first time the United Nations has caught him red-handed and named Rwanda as having been the power behind the M23 rebel group and the recent rebellion in DRC. The Congolese people government have come out strongly and openly to expose the impunity and aggression of the Kigali regime. Even the United States and the United Kingdom, President Kagame's strongest allies, have voiced their concerns, and taken modest measures alongside the international community. President Kagame desperately needs endless wars in DRC, using Rwandan and Congolese Tutsi as cannon fodder. He always has to justify his ruthless domestic policies by claiming he is fighting FDLR in DRC. He desires DRC's natural resources. In the past he has sold himself as the policeman who guards the gates to the mineral rich DRC. He has deceived the world that he is a factor of stability in the Great Lakes. Now the edifice is crumbling. The consequences of these Congo wars to Tutsi in the region, in particular, are grave. The consequences for DRC are already grave with over six million dead from the effects of conflicts. The wars also have consequences within Rwanda. The next implosion within Rwanda may not be far away, and when it does happen, will have an eastern DRC dimension. We must not allow that to happen.

Proposition Seven: *The United States and United Kingdom governments are playing a bad influence in Rwanda, and it will come to haunt them in future, unless they change course.*

The question is often asked, "What did France want in Rwanda ?". Whatever France wanted in Rwanda, it came out of it bruised. I do not personally believe that France was an accomplice in the 1994 genocide in Rwanda. While I was in RPF, we used it as a card to silence France, especially when its Judges started the investigation in the shooting down of the plane in which President Habyarimana was killed. The French problem was that at a time they should have encouraged their ally to undertake badly needed reforms, they pretended the status quo would continue forever. By the time they woke, up it was too late. Now a superpower and its closest friend, the UK, have been in a strange dance with Rwanda, for a while mesmerized by Kagame's charm. Is it his charm or there is something else in the closet that Rwandans do not know?

What are the UK and USA interests in Rwanda? 1) Guilt. They failed to prevent genocide. They could not stop it. 2) DRC.

They have falsely assumed that President Kagame will always be their policeman at the gate, giving them influence to a region that is strategically rich in natural resources. 3) Stabilizing factor. President Kagame has sold himself as a stabilizing factor in a chaotic Great Lakes region. Now, the evidence is clear that President Kagame is a destabilizing factor in the region. His role increasingly looks like that of the West's staunchest ally during the Cold War; President Mobutu. 4) Rwanda's peacekeeping role in Darfur, Sudan. United States and the United Kingdom have security interests in the turbulent Horn of Africa 5) Possibly, 'a devil that we know'?

The United States and the United Kingdom have un-utilized and under-utilized leverage on President Kagame. Both are directly or indirectly the source of financial resources to Rwanda. Military and intelligence leaders in Rwanda have close relationships with the Defence and Intelligence communities in the United States and the United Kingdom. President Paul Kagame, Commader in Chief; Lt. Gen. Charles Kayonga , Chief of Defence Forces, RDF; Lt. Gen, Caeasar Kayizari, Major General Frank Mushyo Kamanzi, Chief of Staff, Army; and Lt Col. Hodari, Commander of the elite Republican Guard are all graduates of US military Schools (Fort Leavenworth, National Defense University, and Fort Benning). The U.S and UK military and intelligence establishments have lot of interest in President Kagame. The question is, to what ends and at what cost? Asked to choose, what would the US and UK choose? President Kagame who is on the way out, or the larger interests of the Rwandan people? If there are legitimate interests that the Americans and the British have in Rwanda, Rwandans can negotiate with them on a mutual benefit basis.

The US and the UK have persistently resisted, blocked or kept silent on: 1) an investigation by ICTR in the shooting down of the Habyarimana plane; 2) ICTR investigation into the human rights abuses of RPA; 3) the investigation into RPA human rights abuses in DRC, as per UN report 4) serious human rights abuses within Rwanda, including assassinations, disappearances, imprisonment and complete closure of political space. UK and USA are the largest financial backers of President Kagame's regime. Things are changing, though. Within the US and UK policy circles there is no longer unanimity on policy on Rwanda. President Kagame has become a burden to the US and UK. Will they abandon him in time to avoid the France-Rwanda syndrome?

The challenge of the peaceful revolution is to intensify diplomatic pressure to further isolate the Kigali regime, direct the energies of Africans and the international community, including the US and UK, towards the genuine interests of the Rwandan people.

CHAPTER FORTY SIX

Reunion with Mama

I t had been almost seven years since I last saw my mother. On the 17th of October, 2012, Dorothy and I waited anxiously at the Reagan National Airport in Washington, D.C. Mama was expected to arrive from Uganda where she had sought refuge for the past two years. As expected, *Rwanda Briefing*, the birth of Rwanda National Congress, and Mama's two sons'(Gahima and I) involvement put her and our sister Doreen Kayitesi in a difficult situation. Now at 85, she has become a refugee again. It is the third time in slightly more than a century that Mama's family has found itself in exile. Her late father, Ntunguranyi, was among the losers and survivors of the *Coup of Rucunshu* (1896), and was exiled in Karagwe (Tanzania) and returned to Rwanda at the end of the First World War. Ms. Kayitesi is now hostage to President Kagame's regime, under constant surveillance, and unable to leave the country, since her passport has been confiscated. She is not alone. The whole country is now hostage.

As Mama was wheeled into the arrivals waiting area, I could hardly believe that the small, shrunken old lady was Mama. I moved forward to greet her, but she greeted me like a stranger. I introduced myself as Theogene. Then she asked me who Theogene was. At this point I broke into tears, and pleaded with her to remember me, her son. After some time, she regained her memory and was able to remember me and my brother.

Though old and frail, Mama has not changed with matters of faith. A devout Catholic from the very beginning, she survives on her Rosary, prayer and the Holy Bible. Every time I visit her she inquires from me whether, finally, I have become a believer. Whenever I tell her that I converted to Christianity, she registers my response with a tinge of skepticism and disbelief. I guess she vividly recalls the days when I was an atheist.

Recently, I visited her with my children and she treated us to her favorite prayer, based on Psalm 71. Reading slowly in our native language, Kinyarwanda, she paused for a while as she said:

> Your righteousness, God, reaches to the heavens,
> you who have done great things.
> Who is like you, God?
> Though you have made me see troubles,
> many and bitter,
> you will restore my life again;
> from the depths of the earth
> you will again bring me up.
> You will increase my honor
> and comfort me once more.

Psalms 71: 19-21 (NIV)

We could see tears roll down her cheeks. That evening, as I reflected on her life, the condition of Rwandan women and children, and the African condition in general, I realized that Mama is truly a faithful and phenomenal African woman.

If Mama was to share survival lessons of her life they would go like this:

MAMA'S ELEVEN SURVIVAL LES-SONS

1. Whatever you do, do not give up, even as a refugee
2. Rely on humanitarian relief for the shortest possible time and be self-reliant
3. While in exile, settle down and stop being a nomad
4. Do everything you can to get your children immunized
5. Your children should always drink boiled water
6. Do all you can to get enough food for your children; if you have land, cultivate it
7. Get your children into school, any school as it will make a difference in their lives
8. Be a good neighbor, and share the little you have with others in the community
9. Whether poor or rich, clean up!
10. Never forget your country; there is no other like it
11. Have faith and trust in God. Pray. Pray. Pray

The story narrated in this book is partly the story of Mama's successes, trials and tribulations in exile, with her four children. Now she is in exile again, at 85. This is a typical Rwandan story. It is also an African story. It is, fortunately, a story that will, and must, change for the better.

EPILOGUE

What was really needed was a fundamental change in our attitude toward life. We had to learn ourselves and, furthermore, we had to teach the despairing men, that *it did not really matter what we expected from life, but rather what life expected from us.* We needed to stop asking about the meaning of life, and instead to think of ourselves as those who were being questioned by life—daily and hourly. Our answer must consist, not in talk and meditation, but in right action and in right conduct. Life ultimately means taking the responsibility to find the right answer to its problems and to fulfill the tasks which it constantly sets for each individual.

Victor Frankl, *Man's Search for Meaning*

Any reader who has been patient enough to read through this book until the epilogue will most likely ask if there is any meaning in a story like this one. Having read through these pages one may simply ask, "So what?" Can we find meaning in the death and destruction that has characterized Rwanda for too long? Can one find meaning in exile, alienation, suffering, and broken promises that seem to be the daily and hourly conditions of most Rwandans? How can we avoid the pessimism, hopelessness and cynicism that human suffering conditions? Victor Frankl, a survivor of the Holocaust, says we have to take the right action, right conduct, find right answers to life's problems, and fulfill tasks before us as individuals.

Surprisingly, the story of Rwanda repeatedly shows the resilience of Rwandans amidst the severest of trauma inflicted on Rwandan children, women, elderly, men, Hutu, Tutsi and Twa. We simply have a will to live. But what is the quality of our lives and how can we improve it? It seems we may begin by asking ourselves two questions: What do I believe in?; What can I do? Each one of us can endeavor to seek to answer each of these two questions. We cannot change our past, since it is gone for ever. We can, and must, build our common future together.

MY CREED

I believe in God and His Son Jesus Christ as
my personal savior

I believe my family is my anchor, fostering
the best in me and those under my care

I believe in the inalienable rights of the individual and the sanctity of human life

I believe in the cooperation and collaboration
in our communities

I believe in the unity and diversity of the
Rwandan people

I believe that love, forgiveness, freedom and
truth are foundational values that promote the
quality of life

I believe that human development progresses
in the material and spiritual domains; and that

poverty in either or both diminishes human
potential

I believe in Africa, self-reliance, co-operation,
interdependence, and human solidarity with the
rest of the world

In all I do I will serve God by serving the
poor, the hungry, and the sick in Rwanda, the
Great Lakes region, Africa and the rest of the
world

I will always serve the cause of liberty, justice,
peace and democracy in Rwanda and the Great
Lakes region

WHAT DO YOU BELIEVE IN?

WHAT WILL YOU DO?

Now what I am commanding you today is not too difficult for you or beyond your reach. It is not up in heaven, so that you have to ask, "Who will ascend into heaven to get it and proclaim it to us so we may obey it?" Nor is it beyond the sea,so that you have to ask, "Who will cross the sea to get it and proclaim it to us so we may obey it?" No, the word is very near you; it is in your mouth and in your heart so you may obey it.

Deuteronomy 30:11-14 (NIV)

ACKNOWLEDGEMENTS

The journey described in this book has been long, spanning a period of more than fifty years of my life. I have spent no less than eight years trying to discover a voice with which I could tell my story. Along the way, I have written and abandoned manuscripts whenever I discovered my authentic voice was lacking. However, this is still an unfinished manuscript, because my story continues. But there it is. There are people, places, and events that have affected me, my family, Rwanda, and the Great Lakes region.

Looking back, I have been able to make it this far simply by the Grace of God. It is indeed right and fitting to appreciate the countless blessings that I do not merit or deserve to Him who gives generously and mercifully. My life has been a miracle, as God has kept fulfilling His promise, against my transgressions.

There are so many people and organizations that have been so kind and generous to my family and to me, in one way or another. I could not possibly enumerate all of them on this page. Acknowledgement goes to: my teachers at Kahilimbi Primary School; Rwekubo Primary School; Makobore High School; Ntare School; Kigezi High School; Makerere University; and the Fletcher School of Law and Diplomacy. The people and Governments of Burundi; Tanzania; Kenya; the United States; and, especially Uganda , through whose hospitality my family was accepted to live as refugees. The late Gahondogo from Kahilimbi. The late Mzee Rwigamba from Rwekubo. Petronille and Alphonse

Kabutura. Enoch Nkunda. Professor Deborah Nutter. Professor Drew Isaacs. Professor Christie Raube. Professor Tom Campbell. Pastor Mark Labberton. First Presbyterian Church of Berkeley. Dr. Eric Goosby. Diana and Hannington Karuhanga. Irene and Derrick Rwetsiba. Debra and Sam Nkusi. Daphne and Alex Rugamba. Marilyn and Ralph Grunewald. Lindsay Musominari. Anne and Gerald Gahima. Jeff Weintraub. Professor Zofia Rybkowski. Bob Morris. Catherine Sepulchre (deceased). The Heart Open to the World. The Uganda Catholic Secretariat. Penelope Carlyle. Monsignor William Kerr (deceased). La Roche College. Rosette and Kayumba Nyamwasa. Leah and Patrick Karegeya. The late Dr. Sande Disi Paul. The late Nzirimo and all those who have died fighting for a just Rwanda.

My fellow members in the Rwanda National Congress (RNC) who have given me a new voice and opportunity to speak truthfully and work fearlessly towards a better Rwanda.

Ambassador William Rwetsiba (posthumously) and Mrs. Joyce Rwetsiba for their love, and for having considered me worthy to receive the most precious gift I have received in my life; their daughter and my wife, Dorothy Rudasingwa

Special acknowledgement and gratitude to my brother Gerald Gahima and my sister Doreen Kayitesi, partners in all we have done together as a family, and for always being there for me. Profound posthumous thanks to my late sister Edith Abatesi (Toto) with whom I shared the early adventures of life in a refugee camp.

My immediate family deserves more than I can say. My wife, Dorothy, more than anyone else, has encouraged me to tell this story, inspired me when I agonized over what to write, and accepted, with courage and a smile, the sacrifices that our family has had to endure due to my efforts to write. She proofread the manuscript. My children Archadius, Mwiza, Aaron and Tina have been truly a treasure to this book project. They have often been my inspiration, proving to be incubators for some of the ideas expressed in this book.

Above all, ultimately, this book is possible due to the efforts of my mother. Mama was my first teacher who introduced me to the world of knowledge. Mama was my first priest who introduced me to God. Mama was my protector and my cheerleader. It is to Mama that I dedicate this book.

BIBLIOGRAPHY

Africa-Union. N.p., n.d. Web. 18 Jan. 2013. <http://www.africa-union.org/official_documents/reports/report_rowanda_genocide.pdf>.

Chirot, Daniel. *Modern Tyrants.* N.p.: Free, 1994. Print.

Des Forges, Alison Liebhafsky. *Leave None to Tell the Story: Genocide in Rwanda.* N.p.: Human Rights Watch, 1999. Print.

De Soto, Hernando. *The Mystery of Capital: Why Capitalism Triumphs in the West and Fails Everywhere Else.* N.p.: Basic, 2003. Print.

Easterly, William. *The White Man's Burden: Why the West's Efforts to Aid the Rest Have Done So Much Ill and So Little Good.* N.p.: Penguin, 2007. Print.

Fanon, Frantz. *The Wretched of the Earth.* Trans. Richard Philcox. N.p.: Grove, 2005. Print.

Fisher, Roger, William L. Ury, and Bruce Patton. *Getting to Yes: Negotiating Agreement Without Giving In.* N.p.: Penguin, 2011. Print.

Frankl, Viktor. *Man's Search for Meaning.* N.p.: Beacon, 2006. Print.

Gahima, Gerald. *Transitional Justice in Rwanda: Accountability for Atrocity.* N.p.: Routledge, 2012. Print.

George, Alexander. *Forceful Persuasion: Coercive Diplomacy as an Alternative to War.* N.p.: United States Institute of Peace, 2009. Print.

"The Gersony Report." *Whale*. N.p., n.d. Web. 18 Jan. 2013. <http://www.whale.to/b/gersony_report.html>.

Guevara, Che. "A Farewell Letter to Fidel Castro." *History of Cuba*. N.p., 1965. Web. 18 Jan. 2013. <http://www.historyofcuba.com/history/cheltr.htm>.

Incore. N.p., n.d. Web. 18 Jan. 2013. <http://www.incore.ulst.ac.uk/services/cds/agreements/pdf/rwan1.pdf>.

Janis, Irving L. *Victims of Groupthink: A Psychological Study of Foreign-Policy Decisions and Fiascoes*. N.p.: Houghton, 1972. Print.

Lamb, David. *The Africans*. N.p.: Vintage, 1987. Print.

Lemarchand, Rene. *Rwanda and Burundi (Pall Mall Library of African Affairs)*. N.p.: Pall Mall P, 1970. Print.

Mamdani, Mahmood. *When Victims Become Killers: Colonialism, Nativism, and the Genocide in Rwanda*. N.p.: Princeton UP, 2002. Print.

Mazrui, Ali. *The Africans: A Triple Heritage*. N.p.: Little Brown, 1987. Print.

Office of the High Commissioner for Human Rights. N.p., 30 Sept. 2010. Web. 18 Jan. 2013. <http://www.ohchr.org/Documents/Countries/ZR/DRC_Report_Comments_Rwanda.pdf>.

Porter, Michael. *Competitive Advantage of Nations*. N.p.: Free, 1998. Print.

Pralahad, C. K. *The Fortune at the Bottom of the Pyramid: Eradicating Poverty Through Profits*. N.p.: Wharton School Publishing, 2009. Print.

Prunier, Gérard. *The Rwanda Crisis: History of a Genocide*. N.p.: Columbia UP, 1997. Print.

Rawls, John. *A Theory of Justice*. N.p.: Belknap, 2005. Print.

Rodney, Walter. *How Europe Underdeveloped Africa*. N.p.: Bogle-l'Ouverture, 1988. Print.

Rudasingwa, Theogene, et al. "Rwanda Briefing." *Africa Faith and Justice Networkl*. N.p., Aug. 2010. Web. 18 Jan. 2013.

<http://www.afjn.org/act-now/toolkits/doc.../175-rwanda-breifing.html>.

Rwanda Briefing. N.p., 13 Dec. 2010. Web. 18 Jan. 2013. <http://rwandabriefing.files.wordpress.com/2011/01/rawanda-national-congress-proclamation.pdf>.

Sachs, Jeffrey. *The End of Poverty: Economic Possibilities for Our Time*. N.p.: Penguin, 2006. Print.

Stone, Douglas, Bruce Patton, and Sheila Heen. *Difficult Conversations: How to Discuss What Matters Most*. N.p.: Penguin, 2010. Print.

Straus, Scott, and Lars Waldorf, eds. *Remaking Rwanda: State Building and Human Rights after Mass Violence (Critical Human Rights)*. N.p.: U of Wisconsin P, 2011. Print.

Tilly, Charles. *Democracy*. N.p.: Cambridge UP, 2007. Print.

United Nations. N.p., 16 Jan. 1999. Web. 18 Jan. 2013. <http://daccess-dds-ny.un.org/doc/UNDOC/GEN/N99/395/47/IMG/N9939547.pdf?OpenElement>.

United Nations. N.p., 15 Nov. 2012. Web. 18 Jan. 2013. <http://www.un.org/ga/search/view_doc.asp?symbol=S/2012/843>.

United Nations Development Programme. *Human Development Report 1990*. N.p.: Oxford UP, 1990. Print.

Zakaria, Fareed. *The Future of Freedom: Illiberal Democracy at Home and Abroad*. N.p.: W. W. Norton, 2007. Print.

CPSIA information can be obtained at www.ICGtesting.com
Printed in the USA
LVOW122136190513

334526LV00010B/153/P

9 781481 857659